P9-CEE-729

A LINE IN THE RIVER

A LINE IN THE RIVER

Khartoum, City of Memory

Jamal Mahjoub

B L O O M S B U R Y   P U B L I S H I N G
LONDON · OXFORD · NEW YORK · NEW DELHI · SYDNEY

Bloomsbury Publishing
An imprint of Bloomsbury Publishing Plc

50 Bedford Square
London
WC1B 3DP
UK

1385 Broadway
New York
NY 10018
USA

www.bloomsbury.com

BLOOMSBURY and the Diana logo are trademarks of Bloomsbury Publishing Plc

First published in Great Britain 2018

British Library Cataloguing-in-Publication Data
A catalogue record for this book is available from the British Library.

Library of Congress Cataloguing-in-Publication data has been applied for.

ISBN: HB: 978-1-4088-8546-8
TPB: 978-1-4088-8547-5
EPUB: 978-1-4088-8548-2

2 4 6 8 10 9 7 5 3 1

Typeset by Newgen KnowledgeWorks Pvt. Ltd., Chennai, India
Printed and bound in Great Britain by CPI Group (UK) Ltd, Croydon CRO 4YY

MIX
Paper from
responsible sources
FSC® C020471

To find out more about our authors and books visit www.bloomsbury.com.
Here you will find extracts, author interviews, details of forthcoming events and the option to sign up for our newsletters.

Contents

PROLOGUE

This is, without doubt, the most personal and ambitious book I have ever attempted to write. I say this not so much out of a sense of pride, but, rather, astonishment. Had I known, at the outset, what I was letting myself in for, in all likelihood the project would have been delayed, if not abandoned in despair.

Of course, life doesn't actually happen like that. This book emerged partly from a sense of anger and outrage at what was happening in Darfur. I couldn't quite believe that nothing had been learned from past mistakes. Khartoum seemed determined to continue along the same doomed path it had pursued throughout its recent history; denying the country's cultural and ethnic diversity in a stubborn display of delusion and arrogance.

The world at large, also, seemed not to have made much progress in the intervening years, and people with no prior knowledge were leaping into the fray, emotively declaring it a genocide. Darfur felt like a moment of déjà vu that took me back to the time I was writing my first novel. Then it had been famine that brought the world's gaze to rest briefly on Ethiopia and Sudan. It felt as if, for over twenty years, I had been trying to address the absence of context against which these tragedies took place, and had achieved nothing. Darfur felt, in a very personal way, like a declaration of failure on my part.

Now I begin to see this book as the culmination of everything I have ever written. It is also, somehow, organically related to all those other books that have absorbed me over the years, which I had to write in order to reach this point.

I began my first novel thinking I was going to write about a young man seeking to discover the part of his background that he doesn't know. He thinks this will complete him, resolve all his doubts, make him whole. That novel led me inwards and backwards in time over successive novels that sought to understand the nature of this vast and little-known country, and to come to terms with my own relationship to it. It was impossible to write about one thing without illustrating the context, filling in the blanks, sketching the landscape, and I seem to have been doing that ever since.

In a similar way, this project soon began to spiral out of hand. It felt like a book that was open-ended, limitless. It felt as if I could just go on writing and writing. I was trying to find an end point, and at the same time did not want to. I encountered another problem. Being primarily a writer of fiction, I came to this with the notion that to write reportage was to deal in cold, clear facts, but as soon as I put pen to paper, as it were, I found the account bending itself to fit my narrative, much as a work of fiction might. Writing is writing, and once the imagination engages with reality it finds its own course. So what is this book? Fiction, non-fiction? Personal memoir, political history, travelogue? I still find it hard to define. In an age when transgressing boundaries is in vogue, it seems to be neither one thing nor the other, although fashionable was the last thing I was trying to be. The form of the book reflects the time in which it was written, the age of uncertainty in which we live.

Over the years I had lost contact with friends and family in Khartoum. Going back was not only emotional, it also triggered an existential crisis of sorts. Who was I without this place that I had written about for so long? What would I become? How would I go on? What would I write about when this was over? It became apparent to me that I couldn't really go back, not permanently. Although I enjoyed visiting, too much had changed. I had changed. I had too many commitments elsewhere. This realisation lent the work a sense of finality, as if this would indeed be the last book I would ever write about

Sudan. Perhaps, subconsciously, this too was a reason for not finishing.

The conflict between trying to find a point of closure, and wanting it to go on indefinitely, stemmed also from the conviction that I could never write a book that would fully do justice to the matter in hand. At times it felt as though I was grappling with a subject so profound and so abstract as to evade all my attempts to capture it. In rare moments it felt as though I had reached a point of sublime beauty in which everything came together to transcend time and place.

The time frame I adopted coincided with the six years of the Comprehensive Peace Agreement (CPA) that had brought the civil war to an end, and closed, roughly, with secession. It ends before the South twisted its newly gained independence into its own internecine strife, a conflict that feels like an extension of the never-ending war that had gone before.

The notion of independence now seems hopelessly outdated. The intervening decades have largely witnessed a pattern of rising economic strength in the West matched by spiralling decay elsewhere. A pattern of dystopian proportions dominates the narrative of what used to be called the Third World. Almost daily we are faced with images of the desperate measures people are willing to take, risking their lives and those of their loved ones, in the hope of reaching the West. In their own homelands they see no future, only a lifetime of destitution and hopelessness. It is a damning indictment of any idea of progress.

This is not an academic thesis, it is a book of impressions. I was constantly struck, as I was writing, of the parallels between Sudan and the problems in the world today. Racial tension in the United States, the rise of the far right in Europe, the persecution of minorities all over. The West faces an existential crisis as social change challenges its understanding of its cultural and historical heritage. The key to social harmony and progress, in Sudan and elsewhere, lies in how we deal with diversity. This is not a problem that is about to go away, as the planet grows smaller and resources dwindle. Climate change aside, the greatest challenge facing the human race will be how to live together. In this sense,

Sudan's case offers a microstudy of the perils of not meeting that challenge with honesty and integrity.

I am acutely aware that a book like this will be seen by some as an endorsement of the view that Africa is a hopeless case. The head-in-the-sand school of cultural advancement. The well-meaning Marxists as well as the apologists for imperialism. I would insist that all is not doom and gloom. There has to be a place for constructive criticism. I don't believe in pretending that all is wonderful, but by the same token I do not believe we can give up. We must have hope. And much of what I have seen of Africa is encouraging, but the continent has suffered, since the era of independence in the 1960s, from trying to catch up with the West, rather than finding its own path. The West, eager to secure its own interests, has encouraged this idea. Africa needs imaginative solutions to its own unique problems. Some of that, I believe, is reflected here.

Now, even though the book is (more or less) concluded, I will still, in conversation, recall an incident or an anecdote and be seized by the conviction that it should have been included. There are countless people whose names do not appear here, but who were a source of inspiration to me growing up and whose spirit I have to some extent tried to capture. If this book is dedicated to anyone then it is to those people, my parents included, who inspired me in their selfless commitment to achieving the nation, to making the world a better place, not for the few, but for the many. Journalists, writers, academics, painters. People who were willing to suffer the consequences and who paid a price for their struggle. Today, such idealism has given way to the negative tropes of polarisation, religious sectarianism, cynicism and violence. All of which reject the idea of conversation in favour of closure, at a time when compromise and compassion are needed more than ever.

Jamal Mahjoub
Amsterdam, June 2017

PART ONE

ALWAYS RETURNING
2008

'So geographers, in Afric maps,
With savage pictures fill their gaps,
And o'er uninhabitable downs,
Place elephants for want of towns.'
 Jonathan Swift, *On Poetry: A Rhapsody* (II 176–80)

Descending through the Scottish Highlands, you pass along a range of dark, brooding hills. The road threads its way through a landscape of blunt peaks that squat like abandoned hulks, split by lochs of deep, glassy water in which silver clouds hover weightlessly. The valleys are broad and flat. They give the mountains breathing space, their breadth a testament to time's passage, to the fact that these rugged hills were once comparable in scale to what we see in the Himalayas today. The unrelenting weight of years has worn them down to blunted stubs.

The glens are aligned along the same north-east–south-west axis as the road, expressed in a series of fault lines and fissures that cut into the underlying strata. Once upon a time a warm sea ebbed and flowed here, leaving fossil beds that match up with those found on the east coast of Canada like two sides of a shattered puzzle. The evolution of trilobites, a kind of prehistoric scarab beetle, and other forms of extinct life found in North America are identical to those in Scotland. Around four hundred million years ago the Iapetus Ocean, as it is now known, snapped shut as the palaeocontinents of Laurentia and Baltica slammed sharply into one another, buckling and forcing the ground upwards into mountains thousands of metres high.

When I was growing up I had a friend whose father was a geologist. When people ask why, of all the things in the world, I chose to study the subject, I often tell the story of how my friend's father used to drive us out in his Toyota pick-up into the flat, empty lands around the city. He would read the landscape, picking up a pebble to explain how, once upon a time, there was a sea where we were standing. That mountains rose up and tumbled down into the water and all that was left were these stones, littering the ground around our feet. It was a fascinating moment and one that stayed with me. It was as if a new dimension had been added to the world, as if time had turned the landscape into a story. So now I see a thread running from these worn-down mountains to my childhood in Khartoum.

The fault lines are now marked by roads that in turn trace the ninth-century routes along which Vikings once dragged their longboats between the lochs on their way to Ireland. Further south the Highlands soften into lush green hills approaching Edinburgh. It is here that the first signs for Blair Castle appear. A popular stopping place, visitors, many of them with families, mill about in the parking area before wandering the grounds. In the front hall of the castle you are greeted by guides dressed up in alarmingly bright green tartan kilts who offer to direct you around. A panelled staircase lined with portraits creaks its way back up through nineteen generations of the family tree.

A handy pamphlet informs you that Blair Castle is the seat of Clan Murray and dates back to the thirteenth century. Work on the oldest tower began in 1269, in the absence of the Earl of Atholl, who was otherwise occupied in the Holy Lands, doing his part for the Crusades. Narrow hallways cramped with hardware are a nod to the castle's military history. The duties of the family regiment, the Atholl Highlanders, are purely ceremonial nowadays, but it remains the only legal private regiment in Europe, a kind of early precursor of modern security contractors.

It takes about an hour to tour the house. The slow-moving train of curious onlookers drifts gamely through one vast salon after another, examining centuries of accumulated treasures.

The whole castle feels rather like a time capsule, affording visitors a chance to step into the bygone age of glory and empire. None of these objects would fit into most modern homes. The huge carpets would have to be slashed into strips. The canvasses and oil paintings would cover entire walls. But while our living space has shrunk our knowledge of the world has grown. The privileged masters of this castle once held the globe in the palm of their hands. Ming vases from China. Lacquered boxes from Japan. Embroidered rugs from Persia. In one room hangs a series of enormous tapestries, each depicting one of the four corners of the British Empire. They show scenes of an exotic, benign world: men riding camels, bearers swathed in turbans, jewelled princes, ferocious tigers. All are passive in the face of imperial power. The gaze of today's visitor barely grazes the surface of these displays. In their pockets they carry devices that can summon swathes of information at a touch, flowing in from every corner of the globe in an instant. The world feels infinitely closer and yet in many ways equally distant and remote.

Taken together, the contents of the castle amount to a glimpse through the prism of a gigantic bauble, colourful and rich. Playful objects nag at our curiosity. They bewitch, fascinate, beckon to be taken up and examined at leisure. Objects cannot speak. They have no history other than that we ascribe to them. Men and women stroll through a tropical version of Eden, innocent and unselfconscious, while around them are creatures that once evoked wonder – zebras, giraffes, crocodiles and monkeys. They stare back at us, conveniently distant, silent objects in a vivid dreamscape, a lost empire of exotica. Figures in an imaginary homeland.

At the end of a long corridor cluttered with sheets of armour, crossed swords and halberds, and peppered with mounted deer antlers, the visitor finally arrives at a large ballroom. The sudden light and bright space is a relief after the dark and narrow confinement of the corridor. The contrast comes as a shock and many assume there is nothing more to be seen. They take a few paces, turn to glance around the hollow, empty room and make for the exit. I am about to do the same when some subliminal perception causes me to hesitate. It is an unsettling feeling of familiarity, something I know is here in this room.

Sunlight spills over the floorboards from high windows along one side of the room. The light lends the varnished wood a coppery glow. To the left of the doorway is a raised orchestra box suspended in midair. It is not hard to imagine fine evenings when the castle might have hosted elegantly dressed socialites dancing to foxtrots and waltzes. I move further into the room, drawn in by something I still cannot quite put my finger on. The walls on either side, I notice, are hung with objects. Dull, ragged garments hanging like ghostly drapes over the wooden panels. With their faded colours they resemble long, dirty shirts strung on poles. Scarecrows. Cut roughly, they are of a particular square shape, some ivory-yellow, others green, all distinguished by distinctive patches of a contrasting colour – black, white, red. I begin to circle the room. There are spears, armfuls of them, and shields of a rough shiny black leather that I know instantly is hippopotamus hide. And there are swords, with a characteristic bulbous swelling near the tip of the scabbard.

I come to a halt in the middle of the hall and gaze around me. I know these objects. These are war trophies, collected in the Sudan Campaign that lasted from 1896 to the Battle of Omdurman in September 1898. The British Reconquest brought to an end years of Mahdist rule in Sudan. Lord Kitchener, who led the campaign, was known to be arrogant and overconfident and said to be more popular among the Egyptian and Sudanese troops than with his own officers. His stern, cold expression later became familiar in the 'Your Country Needs You' recruitment posters of the First World War, apparently the result of his face and eyes being damaged by dust while returning across the desert from Aqaba in Jordan.

Kitchener, now ranked Sirdar, or Commander in Chief of the new Egyptian Army, had his own personal score to settle in the Sudan. Thirteen years earlier he had been in the advance party of the Relief Expedition that had made its way slowly up the Nile to save General Gordon. It fell to him to convey to the besieged general why they were taking so long to come to his rescue; they arrived in Khartoum in January 1885, just two days too late. The Mahdi's black flag was already flying over the palace. Gordon was dead, killed and decapitated.

The Battle of Omdurman marked the end of an era in more ways than one. It was the collision of modern industrial armoury with medieval warfare. The 'dervishes', as the British dubbed the Khalifa's men, got no closer than 500 metres before they were cut down. The British were equipped with modern artillery and, more importantly, the water-cooled Maxim machine gun. The Lee-Metford .303 rifles they used had a long range and were loaded with dumdum cartridges – the nineteenth-century equivalent of today's hollow-point bullet. Named after the arsenal in Calcutta where they were first developed, their tips were carefully filed flat, causing them to splinter on impact with bone, increasing the internal damage. Guns that could kill at a distance made modern man untouchable to the *Ansar*, the Mahdi's followers, who carried spears and ancient single-shot rifles. They wore the same medieval rags and chain mail as that lining the ballroom of Blair Castle. Thirteen years of isolation and sanctions had left the country and their arsenal in another age. An estimated 11,000 Sudanese died on the Kerreri plain that day, 4 September 1898. British casualties numbered a grand total of forty-eight. One young officer who observed the battle was Winston Churchill. The dervishes resembled the Crusaders in the Bayeux Tapestry, he wrote. Antiquated, dilapidated and hopelessly outgunned. To his credit, Churchill later denounced the Sirdar's orders to take no prisoners, a clear breach of the rules of engagement. Countless men were shot out of hand, the only good dervish being a dead dervish.

This confrontation sealed a new pact between Europe and Africa. Among those who sensed the dangers inherent in the jubilation that accompanied the military victories of the industrial age was Joseph Conrad, who sat down to write *Heart of Darkness* in the immediate wake of Kitchener's triumphant return to England. Engineering empowered the European, made him capable of anything, and Conrad saw that this power, the unrestrained ability to do evil to others, contained the keys to the undoing of the soul.

The collection of spears and *jibbas* that I saw in that sunlit room recalled the Khalifa's House, which I had visited many times as a child. It lay opposite the Mahdi's tomb in Omdurman and was a maze of muddy walls, low ceilings and sagging rope beds upon which the old warriors had once slept. In the entrance yard stood a rusty collection of ancient cars with iron wheels, along with a few rickety old rifles and flimsy shields made of hide that had warped with age to resemble dried-out turtle shells. The spears were so frail it was hard to imagine that they had once been capable of being wielded to kill and maim. The grubby glass cases and their dusty, neglected contents made war seem like a quaint tradition, a distant, forgotten memory.

*

At night, seen from the air, the city of Khartoum appears to float untethered in the dark void, a glittering tray of precious stones strewn across a sheet of obsidian. It seems to whirl out there, a lost outpost far off in space, reeling like an electric dervish on through infinity. Beyond the halo of light there is nothing, no hint of movement or life. Nothing but the utter and complete obscurity that invites you to trust what cannot be seen, to take a leap of faith and step over the edge of the known world. It gives a sense of just how fragile the city is, encased like that, within nothingness.

Hours before, taxiing along the runway in Frankfurt, the plane had jerked to a sudden halt. A moment later the captain's voice came over the public address system. Speaking in steady, accented English, he explained that there was a problem with the oxygen system. The calm voice of reason, he appealed to our sense of logic. 'It is not serious, but as I am sure you will appreciate, we do not want to fly down into Africa with a problem that cannot be fixed.' The news was received by the other passengers with understanding nods. It underlined the precariousness of the journey we were about to undertake. Nobody in their right minds would fly off into Africa without making sure they had the means to get back again.

The delay gave me time to ask myself once more what I thought I was doing. Had I really thought this through? The last time I had been in Khartoum was in December 1989, six months after the *coup d'état* that brought Omar al-Bashir to power. Then, people were saying, 'If they last six months, they will last six years'; a rule of thumb that had been established in a country that had known a succession of military takeovers. In this case it proved to be right. It was now nineteen years since they had come to power.

The self-styled Revolution of National Salvation (or *Inqaz*) marked one of the most divisive chapters in Sudan's history. The first ten years were bleak. The country plunged into a dark, oppressive era characterised by stories of horror and desperation. Nobody had ever seen anything quite like it. My parents had left soon after, deciding it was too dangerous to remain. They joined the growing number of Sudanese who had relocated to Cairo. My father had been running a newspaper, the *Sudan Times*, that was shut down in the severe crackdown on the press. Both of my parents had since passed away. Up until he died my father had been adamant that he would never go back home, alive or dead, while the regime remained in power, and so he was buried in London, much to the annoyance of his family.

As we sat on the runway waiting for the German engineers to do their thing, I looked out of the window. Like the captain and, I guessed, most other people around me, I was planning to come back to Europe. For over twenty years I had made my home here. I had a family here. Realistically, I didn't imagine moving back. Yet I had never made the conscious decision to cut Sudan out of my life. It was a part of who I was and probably always would be. If I felt a sense of obligation, it was not so much to my parents as to the idea of who I was. If we are the sum of our parts then Sudan was one part that I had neglected for far too long.

The situation felt somehow familiar and I found myself thinking of the parallels with my first novel, *Navigation of a Rainmaker*. Tanner, the central character, travels to his father's home country for the first time. Sudan as a country was a subject I had struggled with all my writing life, in novels, stories, essays – each one providing one more piece in a puzzle that still felt incomplete. The most immediate reason for choosing to go back now was the conflict in Darfur. It had stirred up the world. There were calls for direct military intervention, for it to be labelled a genocide. The president had been indicted for war crimes by the International Criminal Court in The Hague. As I followed all of this in the news, I realised that I had always believed in the healing qualities of writing. If there was one underlying theme to the work I had done, it would be the exploration of the idea of this country and where it had gone wrong. It was there in my first novel and ran through everything like a common thread. Now it seemed, that after all of these years and all of these words, I had achieved nothing. I needed to write about Darfur, and, to do that, I needed to go back.

That said, I realised, as we sat stalled on the tarmac, that this trip was a leap in the dark. The encounter in the ballroom at Blair Castle had felt like more than coincidence. It had stirred the bottom of some emotional memory that I had forgotten, perhaps on purpose. Now it was there before me, undeniably drawing me back. It wasn't nostalgia I had felt so much as the shock of recognition. After so many years abroad, making a life for myself among strangers, learning to accept alienation as a part of who I am, knowing that wherever I went I would never entirely fit in, here was something that had cut through all of that, leaving me exposed and vulnerable, and longing to reconnect with a world I had ignored for too long.

The captain's voice returned on the intercom, full of praise for the German technicians who had done such a fantastic job. We would be on our way as soon as we had a new departure slot: 'In the meantime, sit back and relax. Our cabin crew will try to make your delay as pleasant as possible.' But it was a false dawn. A moment later he came back on and announced that the problem had not in fact gone away and the marvellous technicians were on their way back to the aircraft.

As the ordeal dragged itself out I found consolation in the book lying on my lap that I had been unsuccessfully trying to distract myself with. *L'Usage du monde* by Nicolas Bouvier. I flipped through the pages until my eye settled on one line: '*l'essential est de partir*'.

At the far end of the dining room stands an enormous television set. I sit with my back to the screen, trying to ignore it, which proves impossible. There are high-pitched squeals and people shouting excitedly for attention. Eventually I yield, craning my neck to look over my shoulder. The set dominates everything with its oppressive, vivid presence. I squint at the images. I see a bright jumble of colour and lots of small creatures rushing about that I eventually realise are children.

The dining room is deserted. Other than myself there is no one, not even a waiter in sight. Just me and the screaming kids. On a nearby shelf stands a large bottle that might once have contained some kind of liquor, but is now filled with an odd blue liquid that resembles cleaning fluid, along with a bunch of wilted plastic flowers. A waiter appears silently. So silently that I know he cannot be Sudanese. He stands at a discreet distance and bows slightly in a gesture of respect that is both familiar and out of place. Very quietly he says good morning, so softly that it takes me a moment to realise that he is speaking English. I ask for tea and he disappears again without a word. It takes an age to arrive. When he finally returns, he sets the cup and pot on the table and then takes a step back and once again waits, watching me. He smiles as if expecting something.

'Where are you from?' he asks finally, his curiosity getting the better of him.

'From here. I used to live around the corner in Street 51.'

I find pleasure in just describing the address, which I realise has now become tangible again. After years of abstraction, it has meaning once more. We could walk there in five minutes. Instead of acknowledgement, a slow smile spreads across his face. Clearly he doesn't believe me. He chuckles lightly, as though I am trying to humour him. I don't look Sudanese. I am too light-skinned. I must be Egyptian. No, I tell him. I am not, I insist. He is Ethiopian. When I tell him I have visited his country he is very impressed and vanishes to inform the others working in the kitchen. One by one they appear in the doorway to take a look at me.

On the television screen the five-year-olds lie on the floor and kick their feet in the air as if imitating insects. They are deliriously happy for some unaccountable reason. They raise their hands high and wave. They run at one another and then fall down again, still screaming in a language I cannot understand. A man and a woman dressed in brightly coloured animal costumes with masks on are also very excited. They scream along with the kids.

I gradually take in more of my surroundings. The posters hanging on the walls display snow-capped mountains, cherry blossoms, and, oddly, a long, hairy phallus that turns out to be a ginseng root. A row of upright drums are mounted on high wooden frames. The skin of each drum is decorated with the ying–yang symbol – two interlocked commas – one red, one blue. Circling these are a series of ideograms. Three black bars symbolise the order of heaven; three rows of broken bars are the chaos of life on earth.

In its former life this was an old villa. After that it was known as the Wady el-Nil Hotel. I never visited it then, let alone rented a room. The reception area comprises a bare table placed underneath the stairs behind which sits Ali, who is always eager to talk. He greets me cheerily and invites me to sit with him. He enquires about my health and my family. We chat as if we have known each other for years. There is a complicity born of some kind of recognition. Ali is worried. Above his head a wooden plaque commemorates Sudanese–Korean friendship. A symbol of harmony. Perhaps it is the positive and negative forces that flow through all things in the duality of being that is getting to him, though I decide not to venture this notion. A Korean man wanders by holding a mop. It still feels like an African hotel, despite the Korean presence. This is the New Scramble for Africa, with Southeast Asia stepping in with a soft-shoe version of old-fashioned colonialism.

The fact is, Ali explains, as he finally comes to the point, there is a shortage of hotel rooms right now. There is a convention on in town and all the hotels are full. He went out of his way to give me the room. It would be safer if I pay in advance, he says, and goes on to remind me again just how lucky I am.

It strikes me as an odd story. What kind of convention would need to resort to a rundown place like this, so far away from town? They have a dozen rooms, all of them cracked, creaky and grimy with stories, and all of them occupied. None of the guests I have seen walking about the corridors look as if they just flew into town for a few days. I can't imagine them attending any sort of convention. They look more like the kind of guests who have been here for so long they can't remember why they came in the first place. They wouldn't know how to leave if they had to. As if to reinforce this, I encounter a woman with a slightly distracted look about her circling the upper floor with an aluminium teapot in one hand and no apparent purpose in mind. She wanders back and forth. From time to time she climbs the few steps to the roof terrace and gazes out across six lanes of traffic to the airport with an expression of longing.

Ali is right about one thing. The other hotels in town are completely full. To cash in on the oil boom they have pushed up their rates and now demand what a modest hotel in London or Paris might charge. The kind of traveller who visits Khartoum these days appears to be doing so on a very comfortable budget. The old hotels are being phased out like weary relics of a bygone age. The once sparkling Hilton looks dowdy and depressing, the unlit lobby of the Meridien is as cavernous as a tomb, with strange figures shuffling about in the gloom. At the other end of the scale, the new five-star Salam Rotana Hotel glitters with glib self-content. Other new ones are on the way. If you drive along the old river road your eye is immediately drawn, not to the majestic old Grand Hotel where Louis Armstrong once stayed, but to the giant white egg that is the Gaddafi-built Al-Fatih Hotel.

When you ask people what has changed about the city, they lament that it has become more African, which makes you wonder where exactly they think they were living before. Even the sincere ones, who genuinely appear keen to hear my opinion, I see their eyes glaze over when I start out telling them how much is unchanged. It's understandable. They have lived out their lives here, adjusting to every new element as it arrives. They want to hear that all these transformations are obvious. Gradually I change my tune. I find myself saying that of course there have been a lot of changes, a response that generally elicits eager nods of approval. All is well with the world. Time has not stood still all these years, as it sometimes appears to me. In its own way, it has changed, of course, but I came here looking for familiarity, and find it everywhere, even in the way the streets around the hotel are breaking down into dusty tracks; the asphalt crumbling into little tarry seeds. This, too, perhaps more than anything, strikes a chord; the ceaseless air of decay. The way time and nature persist in trying to push man's fragile constructions back into the ground; the struggle to keep things from sliding away. This I remember.

The main inconvenience of the Africa Hotel, I soon realise, is the noise. As the days go by it begins to weigh more heavily. Our old house was just around the corner from the room where I lie listening to the grumbling, hooting vehicles, but there was far less traffic in those days. The New Extension, as it used to be called, marked the southern edge of the city. Beyond us was flat, open ground, a military base, a public roads depot where they stored water pipes that we used to climb through, and after that unbroken sand stretching to the horizon. Now the empty wasteland has become cluttered with haphazard scatterings of buildings and mosques, streets, new neighbourhoods that have names I do not know.

At dusk, as the cinnamon light filters through the window above the narrow, squeaky bed, I listen as the din slowly diminishes. From two million inhabitants the city has now swelled to a possible eight – nobody really seems to know. People are constantly adjusting to this expanding flux. This is not Cairo, a city of around twenty million souls who have had decades of daily congestion to evolve an almost mystical understanding of the relationship between space and kinetic motion. There, cars brush past one another with barely a hairsbreadth between them. It is admirable to witness. They have an intrinsic understanding of economy of movement. Vehicles rush into impossibly narrow spaces, jiggle their lights and tap their horns before slipping by. The rules are unwritten in any handbook known to man, but they exist all the same. Tension is rarely unleashed and when it comes it is usually quickly dispensed with because anything is a distraction from the essential business of getting from A to B as swiftly as possible. There is a pragmatism in play that is at odds with the cliché of the excitable, temperamental Arab. In Cairo, life is work and work means motion. Salaries are so low that many people rely on at least two jobs. They can't afford to live downtown, so their lives depend on being able to shuttle back and forth through some of the worst traffic jams in the world. Drivers might curse and swear and argue, but the dispute is usually settled within minutes.

Here, the notion of traffic is a novel one. On average I count three accidents a day. Most of them are minor, but each brings the world to a halt. Everything stops. Every driver in sight gets out and strolls around the scene at their leisure. They call their friends. They appeal to witnesses, to Allah, to everyone and to nobody at once. Driving skills are in short supply. There is a tendency to barrel headlong in one direction only to lock the brakes abruptly and veer inexplicably left or right without warning. With the wheel of a car comes an assumption of propriety, not just of the vehicle but of the road itself. Since the cars tend to be moving slowly because of congestion, the accidents are generally not serious – there are dents and smashed glass and, occasionally, blood.

In a country of limitless open space, of empty highways and simple tracks, roads bounded only by desert and scrubland, constriction makes people nervous. Up until very recently few could afford a car here, but the oil wealth of the last decade changed that. There are assembly plants spewing out 500 new cars a month. The roads are crammed with new vehicles, bright and shiny, straight from the factory. Owning a car has become an end in itself. Cars and mobile telephones are life-fulfilling objects of desire. We have become a capitalist society.

On my way up to my room one afternoon I pass the same woman with the teapot, standing in her usual spot, staring across the busy road. Above the noise of the traffic are other engines that I have been trying to ignore. With jet engines and propellers whirring themselves into a frenzy, a trail of aircraft rolls through an unbroken dust storm. Between the commercial flights bringing in the odd tourist along with visiting engineers, Filipina maids and private jets taking executives to meetings in Shenzhen, Guangzhou and Kuala Lumpur, or hopping over the Red Sea to sample the temptations of Dubai, there are fleets of cargo planes. Their tails bear the logos of the organisations they serve: UN, World Food Programme, etc. They are a reminder that beyond all of this lies another, more urgent catastrophe. All day and night these planes take off and land. The WFP have 2.6 million people to feed in refugee camps in Darfur. The total cost of delivering a basic meal of sorghum porridge to someone in one of those camps costs more per head than it would to eat in the finest restaurant in Paris.

Now that I am back here, I begin to imagine what it must have been like for my parents to leave. This was their city, the place where they had made their lives and raised a family. When I left here I was going out into the world, to explore, to travel. To them, when they left, it would have felt as though they were losing everything they had worked for.

In Cairo they found themselves part of the exiled community of Sudanese expats, along with artists, painters, musicians, intellectuals, academics, politicians and journalists. It was difficult for my father, who had never been politically active, to find himself exiled from home at the point in his life when he should have been preparing to enjoy his retirement. A man who had adhered to convention all his life, whose advice to me had always advocated patience and caution, avoiding risk at all cost, now found himself ejected for trying to do what was right.

Like all exiles they took the decision to leave, thinking it would only be temporary. When they got together with others the conversation would be of rumours of life back home, of torture, secret imprisonment and death. The homeland, so near and yet so far away, seemed to have shifted in its frame. It was no longer the country they had believed in and worked for. My father and his friends were in a state of shock. Something had been broken. Omar al-Bashir and his Revolutionary Command Council did not come from the educated classes. They represented a resentment for everything that had gone before. They had turned everything on its head. As the novelist Tayeb Salih famously asked, 'Where did these people come from?'

Exile is an open-ended condition. For years my parents kept on the old house. They rented part of it out, moving their personal belongings into one room that was sealed up like a mausoleum. My mother went back from time to time to collect things, but my father never dared. I try to imagine what that is like, the gradual letting go, watching the life that you had built for yourself slipping through your fingers.

The quarter is known as Hillet Hamad, after Sheikh Hamad wad Mayroum, who was urged in 1898 by Kitchener, then governor-general, to encourage his people to move here. Skilled workers were needed for the railways and dockyard and the area soon became known as the *warsha*, or workshop, of the capital. The street name reads *al-Shallaliyya*, and means the people from the area around the first cataract close to Aswan – the word *shallal* means rapids, or waterfall. Many of those villages no longer exist; they vanished long ago beneath the rising waters of the Nile that came with the building of the High Dam.

I was unsure what to expect. After so many years away I wasn't even certain the house would still be there, or that I would be able to find it, but I recognise it as soon as I see it. The *neem* trees outside have grown to a decent size. They provide an idyllic touch to the old, rather ramshackle house, making it stand out from what is otherwise a stark, bare, unsurfaced street.

To my complete surprise, I hear my name being called as I climb out of the taxi. Nobody knew I was coming. I couldn't get in touch as I had no telephone numbers that still worked. And yet. It takes me a moment to locate where the shouting is coming from, and then I see him. Hammoudi, looking greyer, his shirt carelessly unbuttoned, standing on the corner watching the world go by. He's the closest thing I have to an uncle and I have fond memories of him riding me around on his blue Vespa when I was a little boy. He was the image of the independent young man back then – a man on the move, pursuing his destiny. He was a journalist, which suggested some urgent engagement with the affairs of the world. All of these things endeared him to me. It is almost seventeen years since I last saw him, and yet he recognises me across the street inside a moving car in an instant. He, although heavier and a little more lined, seems otherwise unchanged. He is still the handsome, slightly recklessly good-looking man I recall. There was always something enigmatic about him. It is an emotional moment and one that I am completely unprepared for. As he throws his arms around me I feel tears coming to my eyes.

Hammoudi still lives in one half of my grandmother's house, the house where my father grew up. It is very simple in structure,

and more or less as I remember it. The adobe walls have gradually
been replaced with brick, the yard used to be covered simply with
earth, which I recall was neatly swept every morning. It has now
been paved with a random pattern of broken tiles.

I remember it as a house filled with women. Haboba, my
grandmother, and her sisters, Zeinab and Mama; Mama, a plump,
smiling woman with tribal scars on her face who was always busy
cooking. I remember her sitting on a low wooden stool pushing
crispy slices of aubergine around a pan of oil bubbling on a charcoal stove. Of all my brothers I was the one who was closest to
this place. I used to come here alone when I was quite small and
stay for the weekend. I would bring a little suitcase – in actual
fact an old vanity case of my mother's that was white and had a
red lining. I would carefully pack my spare clothes, toothbrush, a
gellabiya for sleeping in and a metal hairbrush my mother would
insist on but that I hated and refused to use. I was fond of that
case and would carry it with great seriousness. I can still recall
the ritual, the damp, cool smell of the earthen floor when I knelt
down to place it under the high wooden bed where I slept.

In contrast to our more modern life on the other side of the
river, here I had a feeling of belonging and community, of pride in
where one came from. Also a sense of order, of how things were
done that, in our cosmopolitan life, seemed to be lacking. Among
themselves my grandmother and her sisters spoke not Arabic,
but Nubian *rutana*, a language that seemed to connect with some
ancient tradition that went far beyond me. The daily routine was
simple and timeless, centred around preparing meals, going to the
market, visiting neighbours. Although it was a bit of a drag to
be paraded around countless distant family members and friends
who lived nearby and generally fussed over, I also felt pride at
belonging.

On one side of the yard an opening shielded by a wall gave way
to the men's side of the house, which was really no more than a
small yard and a single long room. In the old days they would sit
playing cards all day, Hammoudi among them. Now, he occupies this side with his family. The toilet, too, I remember, was on
that side, with all the horror and fascination it exerted. It was a

raised cubicle in the outer wall rather like a watchtower. You had to climb several steps to get up to it. Inside there was a hole in the floor through which you would aim at a metal bucket down below – more difficult if you had to squat over it. The bucket would be emptied every night into the back of an open trailer towed behind a tractor. I can still recall the horrific stench if you ever got stuck behind it while driving back late at night.

Life here is lived in the open. Doors, where they exist, are never closed. People wander in and out, from house to house. The men now play cards in the little corner where the goats used to live. Hammoudi takes it upon himself to lead me by the hand around the quarter, just as he did when I was a child. There are about eight homes for me to visit, all of the occupants being in some way related to us. They will all, he assures me, be annoyed if I don't pay them a visit. From my grandmother's only brother, Adam, who must be in his nineties, through various cousins, nephews and nieces, I do my best to keep track and recall all the names and how we are related, but it is not easy. Some of those I remember have passed away or moved abroad. Small children I don't remember are now adults with jobs or are attending university.

Outside a two-storey house crushed against the perimeter wall we thump on a sheet-metal door decorated with black whorls of iron and stand in the sun waiting. Eventually a girl in her twenties appears. She stares at us through her spectacles, not recognising me. Then there is a cry from behind her and a large woman pushes her aside. This is my aunt Leila, larger than I remember but with the same dimpled smile. She throws her arms around me and kisses me on both cheeks. 'All week,' she exclaims, in a display of melodrama that is a form of heralding my arrival, 'all week my eye has been plaguing me. It means that someone is coming from far away. I thought, oh Lord, who could it be?' Where does the reference to the eye come from, I wonder, as she embraces me again. Old, pre-Islamic superstition that has filtered down from ancient beliefs? The third eye? The eye of Horus? Over the next few hours she repeats the story of a warning in advance of my arrival, touching a finger to her right eye. 'I knew it,' she says. 'I knew it.'

Whether it is true or not is irrelevant. It is a gesture. She is trying
to make me feel welcome, and I appreciate that. I am conscious of
all the years I have been away and have been negligent in keeping
in touch. It is not long before I am being reminded of the fact. As
the eldest son, I should have returned to sort out our affairs when
my parents passed away. Politics is no excuse. I didn't feel it was
safe for me to go back, but I could have done more. The matter of
the property and our belongings was left in the hands of a rather
fickle relative, of whom nobody has anything good to say. He
has since taken himself off to work in the Gulf, leaving chaos and
mystery in his wake. A call to Abu Dhabi results in an awkward
conversation and, as expected, complete denial on his part of any
wrongdoing. Leila clucks in lament. 'Your mother had so many
nice things. Paintings, furniture, all the photographs of that time.'

The photographs. My mother could be described as a keen
amateur, an avid snapshot taker who documented every friend,
every family visit, every social event. People often ask about her
photographs, but most of them are lost, all the pictures of our
childhood are gone, tossed no doubt onto a rubbish pyre to join
the ashen dust that envelops us.

Leila's husband, Abdeen, is a solid, quiet man with a commanding presence. He is a judge and is addressed by the respectful term, *Mawlana*. He has emerged as the patriarchal head of the
family and meeting him involves an audience of stately proportions. He receives visitors in his upstairs salon, or diwan. Two
rows of high wooden chairs are arranged like a gauntlet, facing one another. They are heavy and rather ostentatious in the
baroque style of Louis XIV, so beloved in the Arab world since
the days of Napoleon. At the far end stands a curious ensemble
of curved shelves that resembles an altar. A massive piece of furniture made of wood the colour of dirty ivory, it has been painted
to give it the appearance of stone. On an ornamental, neo-classical
pillar balances a sphere. On one shelf an elaborate page of Islamic
scripture is framed. Next to it an open Quran rests on a wooden
stand. Beneath all of this ornamentation sits the television set. I
discover there is a set in every room I visit. These remain on all
the time, although nobody ever seems to actually watch anything

in particular. Instead, the screens function rather like living, moving backdrops, animated windows on the world. The huge pictures on the walls of Blair Castle spring to mind. Here is their postmodern equivalent, another way of demonstrating one's grasp of the world in all its splendour and diversity. As we talk, ducks fly across northern European skies, or dive to catch fish in their beaks. Children dressed in winter clothes run past a medieval castle. Dinosaurs rip one another to bloody shreds. Not so much the world we know as a distant planet, filling up wall space with colour and life.

We talk about this and that. He is curious to know about my life, my children, my brothers, where they are and what they are doing. The setting, chairs stretching away left and right, make it feel like an audience. I think of caliphs and sultans. During the lacunae that loom in the conversation our gaze drifts back to the images of people running around a forest being chased by monsters. The sound is turned down, the story of no importance; what matters is that we have a distraction for our eyes whenever we are short of a topic to pursue. I ask about the state of the country. The *mawlana* frowns. Corruption is endemic. It goes all the way to the top. The flow of words stops and starts. It is his day of rest. In a few minutes he will begin preparing himself to go to the mosque for Friday prayers, washing and putting on a clean white gellabiya and imma, the long white cloth worn like a wobbly turban. The cloth is big enough to serve as a shroud to wrap your body in when you die.

The old manners have gone, he declares, a lament I am to hear again and again. With the influx of large numbers of people from the west of the country and the south, the city has lost touch with itself. Social life has changed, he says, with a nod at the television. Nobody goes out any more. In the early 1990s, when the regime's zealotry was fresh and fierce, the habit of visiting friends in the cool evenings was lost. People still drink, but they do it alone, at home, he says, shaking his head. They drink terrible things. They lose their eyesight, even their limbs. He seems to find the conversation taxing. The onscreen action insinuates itself between us, taking each hiatus and stretching it until eventually the conversation becomes the distraction. He draws my attention to a large framed photograph hanging on the wall in the corner. It is a picture of himself and my father, signing the papers at my brother's wedding. That was twenty years ago. I sense a note of disapproval. My brother is the respectable one who did the right thing and married early and locally. Instead, I went abroad, married a foreign woman and then got divorced, with all that that entails. There is something in my story that seems to make him uncomfortable.

It is easier to talk to the women, I find. Having completed my duty in the male diwan I descend the stairs and Leila takes me to visit Dehayba, another aunt. The house is unrecognisable as the place where we stayed as small children on a visit from England. I recall it less from memory than from the old 8mm ciné films that my mother took. Dehayba's daughter Rashida lives downstairs. A small, quiet woman, she greets me warmly and sits with great dignity. She tells me how she travelled the world in the 1960s when she was a trade union delegate. Another age. All around Europe, even staying in Copenhagen for a time. Her story sounds like a confession, a bid to place her life on the map of the world at large, to not be eclipsed by the passage of time. No longer seated in this enclosed room on the same narrow, dusty street where she was born. On the floor above is Nadia, her sister, and her brother Magdy and at the top is Maher's wife, Soad, who is losing her memory. She is light-skinned and keeps asking if I remember who she is and how my parents are doing – having forgotten they passed away ten years ago. In each room we are greeted by another television set, each one larger than the last. They all flash the same lost message from another planet and they are all ignored. They are like aquariums, blinking with brightly coloured, exotic species.

As Hammoudi and I wander back, circling through the hot streets, we come to a point where the houses end. A low wall encloses an area of uneven ground, dotted with flattish dusty mounds like molehills. Some bear small markers, others nothing. This is where they would have liked my father to have been buried, he tells me. The family was upset that we didn't bring him back. I try to explain that it would have been against his wishes, but I realise that this is not enough. However bad the situation was, people survived, they adjusted, they accommodated themselves to the regime. If you stayed away so long it was for a reason. And land means something here. Where you are born and where you die. These details are important. In the fullness of time regimes come and go, even one as enduring as the current one, but the place you come to rest is final.

Beyond the graveyard there was once a golf course without a blade of grass. The holes were smoothed over with fine sand and rolled flat. As a boy, my father would trail behind the Englishmen who played golf here, begging for a piastre in return for toting their clubs around the course. Instead of tees they made little cones of sand on which to rest the balls and were paid according to how many of these they managed to make. Looking at that dusty space now, it strikes me that this is where he belongs, not in the damp and completely random space of a north London cemetery.

London was to play a part in my father's life. Larger perhaps than he might have wanted to admit. During his years in England he adopted the habits and manners of the English. Throughout his life he cultivated a collection of alarming bow ties, vividly coloured, often with polka dots and stripes, which he wore with no self-consciousness at all. He had a collection of pipes and developed a fondness for tennis and Scotch whisky. In later life his antiquated manners and quaint expressions evoked bemusement in the rough informality of contemporary Britain. Like all ageing people, he was trapped in the circumstances of his own era, an age when conformity was a requirement for respectability.

He first arrived in 1949 at the age of twenty-four. He had never travelled abroad before then. The flight took two days. From Khartoum they flew north along the Nile to Wadi Halfa and Cairo. From there the BOAC Douglas DC4 would strike a course west across North Africa to Tripoli, where they descended for a break while the aircraft was refuelled. They took off again and as the sun was setting he would have watched the Mediterranean disappear beneath the wings as the North African coastline was left behind. They spent a night on Malta, in the port of Valletta. The next morning the plane carried on north, heading for Orly, south of Paris. Already the weather was changing. Banks of cloud cluttered the sky and pearls of rain slid down the glass through which he peered, eager to see what awaited him. After another refuelling break the plane slipped over the south coast of England to land, finally, at Blackbushe aerodrome near Reading.

It is difficult to imagine what must have been going through his mind. All he knew of Britain was gleaned from books and news-reels, from the Lombards mail-order catalogue out of which he had picked his suit. What he found was a flickering, far-off place of shadows and light. Britain was still recovering from the war. Eggs, butter and meat were still rationed. In those early years his mother would send him parcels of food from Sudan, includ-ing packets of meat that were seized on by customs officials. He worked at the cultural centre at Sudan House in Rutland Gate, just off Hyde Park. He always talked with great affection of his boss, Mr Hartley, and his assistant, Anne Clayton. In the closing stages of the empire a newfound relationship was developing between subjects and masters. As Student Welfare Officer it was his job to look after the interests of the Sudanese students who were being sent to Britain for education in the run-up to independence.

In London one could see black men and women working side by side with white people to rebuild the 'New Jerusalem', as the reconstruction of London was ambitiously dubbed. His educa-tion came while travelling up and down the country in search of digs for students. This brought him into close proximity with ordinary people. These Englishmen were no longer the remote officers of the Sudan Political Service he had known as a child, the Oxbridge 'Blues' whose golf clubs he toted around, but working-class men and women with whom it was possible to strike up a casual conversation in a pub or a grocer's shop. Being sociable came to him naturally. It was probably what saw him through those early, dark years, and it was a skill that was to help him all his life.

Back then it was not uncommon to find handwritten signs in the windows of boarding houses that read 'No Blacks or Irish'. Casual racism was something he took in his stride and I never heard him speak bitterly about the way he was treated. It was a sensitive issue, bringing Africans to live among the British as equals, and the Sudan Agency was well aware of the dangers that bad publicity could present to their work. They were preparing a generation to take over the country once they left. It was important that both sides emerged from this contact with a good impression of the other. It was a controversial issue and scandals, which were not infrequent, were to be avoided. My father's job included trying to soothe amorous landladies, outraged husbands, along with a gamut of heartbreaks, depressions, suicides, drunks, runaways. People who found it difficult to adjust to life in the UK. The students were picked from the Northern Sudanese elite, and almost exclusively they were men. Children of privilege, in England many found themselves out of their depth, unhappy, cold, homesick and lonely. Some reacted to their new freedoms by going overboard. Others withdrew, locking themselves away in isolation.

My parents made an unlikely couple. My mother worked at Sudan House as an accountant. Born and raised in Hendon, her mother was from Bradford and her father was German. It can't have been easy growing up in Britain during and after the Second World War with a German surname, and I wonder what part this played in her decision to marry my father and leave Britain to live so far away in Sudan, where she remained for forty years. My grandfather had come over between the wars and developments in Germany during the 1930s persuaded him never to go back. He broke with his brother, who had joined the Hitler Youth, and the two never spoke again. Instead he settled in Britain, marrying and setting up his own office machine company in London under his wife's maiden name – Parker Patents. When war broke out in 1939 he narrowly avoided internment; if he had lived in Britain one day less he would have been locked up. This, however, did not stop his mother-in-law from calling the Home Guard on a regular basis to report there being a German spy in the house.

It's hard to imagine what they had in common. My mother had a comfortable, middle-class English upbringing. My father was born in a house of mud bricks and received only a rudimentary education. His father had been a cook for Sudan Railways and Telegraphs. His grandfather had sailed a two-masted *dahabiya* up and down the northern reaches of the Nile. Perhaps it was the sense of being outsiders, of having been born between places, in a world that was changing rapidly. In photographs they convey a maturity that seems beyond their age. Their clothes look formal. In some they are with their friends, all dressed up in evening wear, as if they are about to go out. The men in suits and ties, the women in glamorous gowns that shimmer in the night air. They stand with cigarettes poised in angled fingers, exuding an air of elegant confidence, in themselves and their future.

They never talked about their marriage as something remarkable, and often seemed quite unaware of the fact that they were breaking centuries of taboo. A black man marrying a white woman. There were states in the US where it was illegal in those days, and plenty of other places in between where you could get yourself lynched. In an interview published years later, my father remarked, 'Our relationship started with respect for one another, because there was this feeling of absolute togetherness. I don't think she recognised that I was a different colour from her, nor did I think she was a different colour from me. We just felt that with increased contact men and women of different ethnic backgrounds overcome their inherent prejudices and fears and are inevitably drawn together.'

This was 1955. After the sacrifice and pain of the Second World War, the future looked promising. Old taboos were breaking down. Colonies were being freed. Independence promised a new era of hope. It would be naive to suggest they did not encounter resistance. My mother's family made no secret of their disapproval. Equally, many Sudanese felt it was wrong to break with tradition. Still, they bobbed along on a tide of optimism. The old chains holding the world in place were coming apart. In some way, their personal aspirations, creating a family out of opposites, was a micro-cosmic response to the great unknown that loomed ahead of them.

This city, which has occupied so much of my thoughts over the years, seems now like a dream I had almost forgotten. It comes back slowly, as if from a great distance, closing in, erasing the time that has elapsed. Seen from the air, or on a map, the outline of the city illus-trates the origins of its name. The Arabic word *khartoum* signifies 'trunk', and that is what the city resembles: the head of an elephant lying in the sand. There are other, less romantic explanations of the etymology, including the name of a plant in the Nubian language. When you trace the lines backwards, around the head, watching as they lose themselves in ever more complex abstractions, geometries that defy tangible form, you begin to glimpse the enigma that is this country. The head and trunk may be here, but the rest of the baggy creature is harder to define, buried out there in the sand.

There is a well-known Sufi parable in which all the inhabitants of a city are blind. A king arrives and the rumour spreads that he has brought with him a magnificent animal the likes of which nobody has ever glimpsed before. Everyone rushes out to exam-ine this wondrous creature and all return with a different account.

The first declares it to be wide and flat, like a rug. The second describes a hollow pipe of great destructive force, while the third maintains that it is sturdy and upright, built like a pillar. Each of them is partly right and all are completely wrong at the same time.

For centuries the elephant was a creature of myth, sent as a gift to impress kings and emperors as evidence of the marvels of the known world, a demonstration of the power the donor had at his disposal. Elephants abound in the tapestries hanging in Blair Castle illustrating the four corners of the British Empire, as do leopards and naked savages. Haroun al-Rashid sent one from Baghdad to Charlemagne in France. That elephant, Abu al-Abbas, eventually died, reportedly from drinking too much red wine – a barrel a day. And an elephant is said to have played a role in the Reformation: in the sixteenth century the King of Portugal sent a small white elephant to Pope Leo X in Rome where for a time it became a symbol of Catholic decadence to the furious Lutherans before it eventually died of constipation.

Like the elephant in the parable, this country seems to defy all attempts to describe it. Journalists, academics, writers, myself included, have tried to define that mythical beast, the nation. Many have come close, but none have achieved more than fragmentary success. The separate visions were destined to remain incomplete, disperse, divisive, never quite attaining the holistic totality that would be the fulfilment of the promise of independence.

The word city is almost too grand for this jumble of intersections and gaudy lights. At times it is hollow and deserted, at others it is drunk on its own resplendence, dazzled by its own audacity, drowning in the luminosity of its existence. I recall the moment of my arrival. As the plane floated down through the night sky towards the earth I felt a mixture of emotions welling up in me as I tried to imagine what awaited me. Compared to the nothingness of the darkness beyond, it is something. From within, the rest of the country fades into the distance. It dissolves in shadows and heat haze. It is easy to see how even urgent matters like the crisis in Darfur might become remote and irrelevant. To approach the city is to turn your back on that void. Once inside, all else is lost. The city draws you in, sucking the energy out of the vast surrounding expanse and channelling it into this tangled knot.

At the heart of the city lies the confluence, the coming together of the two great rivers that provides the reason for its existence. The Blue Nile, having tumbled down from the highlands of Ethiopia, meets the patient, sullen tug of the ponderous White Nile that has laced a sinuous course through the southern marshlands. The two need one another. There are 2,500 kilometres from here to the Mediterranean Sea and only 385 metres of elevation. It would take thirty minutes to walk up that height if it was right in front of you. It is only the two rivers combined that can make the long, dry run through the desert to the sea. If there is a purpose to this city, then, it lies in the alchemy produced by the fusion of these two currents, this subduction of difference, this blending of contrasts. And you can see it in the water: if there is one spot in the city that seems emblematic of the elusive enigma of nationhood, then it is there, at the tip of the horn in the Mogran Gardens. It is only there that the magical line produced by the two rivers folding into one another is made visible.

Mogran, the word used to describe the junction of the two Niles, may derive from the Arabic root *qarn*, which can mean to join, marry or to compare two things. It can also mean horn, as in rhinoceros, which might describe the shape of the point at which the two rivers meet.

It was around this bend in January 1885 that the Expeditionary Force arrived, only to find that the khedive's flag was no longer flying over the palace. Gordon was dead, slain by the Mahdi's overzealous followers, who clearly ran amok. It was to be thirteen years before the British returned to put their demons to rest. One of the boats that ferried them upstream in 1898 was the *Melik*, a small, metal-hulled gunboat that could be dismantled and dragged in sections up the rocky cataracts that bar the river between here and Aswan on the border with Egypt. In later years, the *Melik* became the club house of the Blue Nile Sailing Club, a grandiose name for a sleepy little corner under the neem trees where yachts and small motor launches were parked. One of these had been bought by my father and a friend. I have no idea what they were thinking. They owned it for years but we only ever went out in it on one memorable occasion.

In an age when water is becoming increasingly scarce, here is a city with a miraculous abundance. It is a wealth that the inhabitants might appear to take for granted, forgetting the hundreds of kilometres of dry land that extend from here in every direction. Of course, there have been songs written in celebration of the Nile, going back to the hymns of the Ancient Egyptians. Here, at the confluence, the coming together of the two rivers takes on a greater significance, not just as a geographic feature, or even a source of life, but as a symbol of the city as a point of inflection, the gravitational axis around which the country turns.

The irony of this is striking, now, at this moment when the country is coming apart at the seams. The current hiatus, the six years of peace that came into effect with the signing of the 2005 Comprehensive Peace Agreement, will terminate in a referendum that could bring about the secession of the South. That would mark the end of the dream of a grand Sudan, the largest country in Africa, microcosm of the continent, meeting place of north and south, east and west. There were great hopes that we would set a precedent for the rest of Africa. Why has it proven so hard to find harmony and peace? Looking at other sub-Saharan neighbours such as Nigeria, Chad or Mali, the old mammoth blocks look like throwbacks, species destined to be rendered extinct in the fullness of time. Break-up seems somehow inevitable, looking at the massed tensions collected within their boundaries.

Just along from the Mogran was the zoo. We went there countless times. A zoological garden (with the emphasis on garden), it

was a place for children to run about with all that energy in which
the young delight and their parents despair. You had to seek out
the animals, which were hidden away in sad little fenced-off enclosures. Dusty giant tortoises, flirty peacocks strutting beneath
shady trellises. The best thrill was waiting for you as soon as you
came through the front gate: a host of baby crocodiles in a cage
like a hatbox. You could, if your mother wasn't looking, stick a
finger through the wire mesh and touch their scaly flanks as they
sat motionless on the damp wall, narrow snouts wide, sleeping
with their eyes open.

I recall a tired, dusty-looking animal jailed behind a ring of
metal bars. Less bars than flattened staves thrust into the dry earth.
This melancholy creature, with its twitching tiny ears and myopic
gaze, always seemed on the point of keeling over in despair. It
exuded an air of noble resignation. I like to think there was dignity in the armed posture, that silent attendance. Denial, perhaps,
a refusal to accept the fact that instead of endless plains to roam
it was caged inside an area just big enough for a family of rabbits.
The white rhinoceros had inhabited the country for thousands
of years, certainly it had been around long before Tutmoses II
famously hunted one around the town of Shendi in the fifteenth
century BC. An old, old creature. At the dawn of independence it
was the national symbol. A little metal plaque attached to the bars
declared that the species was in danger of extinction. A tiny red
spot on a white map marked its dwindling heart. There was something poignant about having such a noble, almost extinct creature
as your national symbol. In later years it was abandoned in favour
of the much more pretentious and vicious secretary bird. I'm not
quite sure what that says about the country.

To get to the zoo we would drive past the Presidential Palace,
which stood, in all its white-painted splendour, on Nile Avenue.
The heavy eucalyptus and banyan trees, imported by the British
from India, formed a long, dark tunnel of mystery alongside the
river. For security reasons it was forbidden to stop and there
was always a thrill of danger as we approached, rushing through
all too quickly. You caught a brief glimpse of the palace guards
standing to attention on the veranda, dressed in their immaculate

white uniforms. On their heads, they wore Anzac-style bush hats with one side of the brim folded up and a black ostrich feather fluttering delicately in the air. It was both tantalising and enchanting. Between the two guards was an entrance, a dark arch that led inwards, to what we could only guess.

Although not the original building, the palace stands on the spot where Gordon met his end at the hands of the Mahdi's followers, one of the most significant episodes in the country's history. As the car cleared the gates on the other side and we flew onwards into the future, we did not yet understand that we were the privileged children of history's bloody sacrifice. All of it – the soldiers, the pristine white walls, the hidden interior of power – evoked something of the mystery that existed beyond our lifetimes, in what was known as the past. It had created the circumstances out of which we had emerged. History remained as unfathomable as it was vital.

The zoo is no longer there. The green fences and leafy gardens, the enclosures with their unhappy inmates were sold by a corrupt minister to be replaced by an enormous white helmet of a hotel. Built by Maltese contractors, this is Colonel Gaddafi's contribution to the regenerating city. The form of the hotel resembles a gigantic, armoured version of the silver dome on the Mahdi's tomb across the river in Omdurman. When he arrived here, to avenge Gordon's murder thirteen years earlier, Kitchener blasted a hole through the dome of the tomb with his artillery and tossed the Mahdi's bones unceremoniously into the river. Now it is as if the spell of the man who had plagued him for so long still lingers.

When Napoleon and his forces abandoned Egypt in 1801, after only three years, they left behind them a power vacuum that was helpfully filled by an Ottoman commander of Albanian origin named Muhammed Ali. In 1805 he declared himself Pasha and the independent ruler of Egypt. The French were happy to lend his enterprise support in their efforts to counter the greater threats from London and Constantinople. Muhammed Ali was a moderniser, a man who yearned to arouse Egypt 'from the sleep of ages'. He contracted Europeans and Americans to command his troops, to build dams and bridges. He conquered Syria and Arabia and drew over half of the Ottoman territories in the region into his own private empire.

An army led by Muhammed Ali's son Ismail was despatched up the Nile in July 1820. It was composed of mercenaries from a wide range of backgrounds: Albanians, Magrebis and Turks of one sort or another. To the Sudanese they were known collectively as 'Turks'. When the British arrived eighty years later, they too were known as Turks. Ismail saw his arrival as the dawn of a new era. He made one fatal mistake, however, by insulting Mek Nimr of the Ja'aliyin. Invited to supper one night, Ismail was drugged and then burned alive by his hosts. It was one of the very first acts of rebellion against the Turco-Egyptian invaders. Like many revolts over the coming years it was carried out with inferior weapons and little military experience. The rebels lacked a sense of unity to draw them together. Even then there was an inability to come together against a common cause. The Funj, the Ja'aliyin and the Abdallab all mounted their own separate revolts. There were massacres at Metemma, Halfaya was burned down, Tuti Island was razed and looted.

The following year the Turco-Egyptian army began training a new kind of troop for the task. The *Jihadiyya*, made up of freed Sudanese slaves, were trained at a camp in Aswan. Hundreds died under the harsh conditions but these troops were destined to man the garrisons in Sudan. The Irregular Cavalry, made up of Shaygiyya horsemen, was another force. It was at around this time that the military governor Osman Bey established a fort at the site of what was to become Khartoum.

The man known as the Mahdi was born Muhammed Ahmed Ibn Abdallah, the son of a carpenter and boatbuilder who turned his back on the family tradition. According to legend he claimed that his hands were too soft for hewing trees into hulls. With an affinity for spiritual matters, he was, by nature, an altogether more esoteric spirit. Against the wishes of his father and brothers he threw down his tools and joined the Sammaniya Sufi order. From early on he proved uncompromising in his dedication. He clashed with his master, accusing the sheikh of decadence in the lavish celebration of his son's circumcision. He was stubborn, too. Even when the sheikh forgave him for his insolence and lack of respect he refused to return to the fold.

By the 1880s bad feelings towards the Turco-Egyptian rulers had grown. Corruption flourished and the merchant class of central Sudan, the *jellaba*, were being squeezed by raised taxes. In the suffering he witnessed on his travels around the country, armed with nothing more than a begging bowl, the ascetic Muhammed Ahmed saw the behaviour of the Turks as symptomatic of a broader moral decay. For a time he sold firewood, until he learned it was being used to make illegal alcohol. On another occasion he refused the food being distributed at a mosque when he discovered it was paid for by the ruling authorities. But he could also be pragmatic. When he heard that a wealthy merchant was planning to marry a young boy, he went straight to the Turkish authorities to get them to put a halt to it.

Muhammed Ahmed settled on Aba Island just south of Khartoum where he built a mosque. News spread that the island was home to a powerful mystic. Men sailing by on boats and steamers would pause to bend down and pray out of respect. Rumours of his blessings, or *baraka*, spread through the land. Once his opposition to the authorities became known, the stories began to grow, miracles attached themselves to his name; a cloud was said to follow wherever he went, shading him from the sun; milk flowed from his fingertips. Finally, in 1881, he declared himself *al-Mahdi al-Muntazer* –The Expected One.

The idea of the Mahdi, or successor to the Prophet Muhammed, is more commonly associated with Shia Islamic tradition. In Sunni

Islam, it is linked to an obscure and little-known idea connected to the end of days. One prominent authority was Ibn Kathir, a disciple of Ibn Taymiya. Born near Damascus in the fourteenth century, where he died in 1373, his most famous work is a history, *al-Bidayya wa'al-Nihayya* (The Beginning and the End), a collection of references to the end of time taken from a wide range of sources including the Hadith – stories of the Prophet's life.

Ibn Kathir describes the appearance of a man who will restore Islam to its purest form. This Mahdi is said to be one of the signs of the final hour: he will arrive from Transoxiana; an army bearing black banners will rise from the east; he will distribute wealth freely; knowledge will decline and ignorance will grow; adultery and the drinking of wine will become commonplace; there will be smoke and landslides; the sun will rise in the west; the number of men will decrease and women increase until every man has fifty wives; the Mahdi himself will resemble the Prophet Muhammed – in behaviour, but not in looks; he will have a high forehead and a hooked nose. His task is to rid the earth of corruption and restore Islam to its former glory. He will bring justice to the world until the coming of the *Dajjal*, the false messiah, or Antichrist, then Jesus will appear and the final trumpet will sound.

The Mahdi's army was made up of the common people, men who had nothing to lose. They had little or no military training. To begin with they also had no weapons. They did not know how to fight. They dressed in the patched *jibbas* typical of the Sufi orders, similar to the ones I saw hanging in the ballroom at Blair Castle. These costumes symbolised humility, a shunning of material wealth. What they lacked in skill and experience the Mahdi's followers, the *Ansar*, made up for in enthusiasm. As his fame spread the authorities grew worried. The military expeditions sent to put him down failed to arrest or defeat him. They succeeded only in boosting his reputation.

In November 1883, an expedition led by Colonel William Hicks, a British officer working for the Egyptian government, was surrounded and cut to pieces. Ten thousand men were slaughtered in three days. It marked a turning point. With the weapons they captured the *Ansar* became a match for any Egyptian force.

The Mahdi withdrew to Kordofan, south-west of Khartoum, and settled around Jedel Qadir, which became known as a holy mountain. When finally they advanced on Khartoum nothing could stop them; it was only a question of time before the country fell to him.

It was at this point that Gordon entered the picture. Nobody knew what to make of the Mahdi, or how to deal with him. Was he genuine or a charlatan, using this message of doom for his own purposes? Speculation soon drifted into fuzzy myth-making. What remained clear was that something had to be done before the fanaticism spread further throughout the region. The question was what?

Egypt was ruled by the autocratic dynasty created by Muhammed Ali. They treated the country as their own private estate. Reckless spending and borrowing by Khedive Ismail had dropped the economy into the hands of the European banks. Ismail the Magnificent, he was dubbed. He dreamed of fulfilling his grandfather Muhammed Ali's ambition to create an empire stretching the length of the Nile, ruled by an Egypt that was the equal of Europe. To get the job done he employed Europeans.

Egyptian enterprise was driven by commercial interests, including slavery. During his first term in the service of the extravagant khedive, Gordon spent two years struggling to stamp out the trade and impose order in Equatoria province in the South. He resigned in despair and returned to England. The khedive begged him to return and eventually Gordon agreed, on one condition: that he be made governor-general. His wish was granted and by February 1877 he was back in Cairo. By then Egypt was facing bankruptcy and badly needed new revenue. In June 1878, Ismail was deposed, recalled to the Ottoman court by a letter addressed to the 'Ex-Khedive'. Gordon once more resigned in disgust, suspecting (rightly) that the country would be turned over to Ismail's son, Tewfik, and his foppish court of Europeans and pashas.

The antipathy was mutual. In the sophisticated salons of the Egyptian capital Gordon the purist was regarded with suspicion. His intense blue eyes and thick, fair hair were said to signify that he carried a light within him. There is a streak of vanity about Gordon, his sense of being driven by a higher calling. He was swept along on a tide of public fervour. He was a celebrity, spoken of in gentlemen's clubs and smokey restaurants as the man to restore Britain's lost dignity.

Gordon fled London for the quiet of his sister's house in Southampton where he nevertheless consented to be interviewed for the *Pall Mall Gazette* by W. T. Stead, a notorious journalist, spiritualist and purveyor of scandal. Gordon laid out his view plainly: the danger lay in the *idea* of the Mahdi, that it might be infectious, that it might spread: 'In all the cities in Egypt it will be felt that what the Mahdi has done they may do; and as he has driven out the intruder and the infidel, they may do the same.' The Mahdi's success had already stirred great 'fermentation' in Arabia and Syria. Posters had appeared in the streets of Damascus calling for the people to rise up against their Turkish rulers just as the Mahdi had done. What was at stake was control of the entire region. 'If nothing is done,' Gordon warned, 'the whole of the Eastern Question may be reopened.'

There were those who saw the Mahdi's rise as the outcome of British intervention in Egypt. To put down the revolt led by Colonel Ahmed Orabi against Khedive Tewfik in 1879, the British bombarded Alexandria and landed nearby at Tel al-Kebir. Orabi was banished to what is now Sri Lanka. The poet Wilfrid Blunt is one of the few observers who was critical of Gordon. He saw him as a knight errant on a fool's mission. Gordon himself drew the comparison to Don Quixote in his journals, referring to the hopelessness of trying to defeat slavery. Blunt also faulted Gordon for underrating the enemy, of failing to recognise the moral imperative of the Mahdi. This could have been rectified if Gordon had been able to communicate with the Mahdi properly: 'If he had gone to the Mahdi,' Blunt wrote, 'he could not have blinded himself to the elevation of the position the Mahdi claimed as socialistic reformer.'

Gordon's mission was confused. Even when he stepped up from the platform at Charing Cross station onto the train to carry him on the first leg of what would be his last journey to Africa, he had no real notion of what he would actually do once he arrived in Khartoum. The government had moved away from the idea of abandoning the Sudan, and instead wanted to create a buffer zone in Northern Sudan along the lines of the British-controlled kingdom of Sarawak in Borneo. There is a certain weird logic in the idea of taking what had worked in one part of the empire and applying it elsewhere. It is the kind of argument that only makes sense when the various parts of the world appear to be interchangeable. Still, it must have provided some consolation. Western and Southern Sudan would be left to the Mahdi but Egypt would be protected from the south. In Wilfrid Blunt's eyes Gordon was naive, deluded by the sense that his was a humanitarian mission in the name of the Lord, and blind to the political and economic aims of the statesmen he served.

The explorer Sir Samuel Baker was the leading authority on Africa. Baker wrote an article in *The Times* urging the government to take action and send in troops to save the Egyptian garrisons from the Mahdi. He was convinced that Gordon was the man for the job and Gladstone, the prime minister, was forced to take a decision. Public opinion demanded that Gordon be despatched. Lord Granville, the foreign secretary, suggested Gordon be sent not in a military capacity but as an adviser. This would give the impression of the government taking action without actually committing itself to the use of military force. The War Office had no desire to embark on a military campaign if there was any chance that a more expedient solution could be found. Gordon provided a neat political solution to a complex problem. Lord Wolseley, accompanying Gordon to the station, discovered at the last minute that he had no money on him and handed over all the cash he was carrying, along with his watch and chain. It was an inauspicious start for a man setting off to do battle with an idea.

The Mahdi was not Gordon's first encounter with religious troublemakers. Years before, in China, he had come up against the Taiping Rebellion, centred about the self-styled *Tien Wang*, or Celestial King. Through a mixture of evangelical teachings received from American missionaries and his own spiritual visions, the *Tien Wang* thought himself to be the Son of God and brother of Jesus Christ, whose mission was to establish the Taiping, the Reign of Eternal Peace on earth. Gordon was hired by a group of Shanghai merchants to command their private army.

In China, Gordon's legend found form. He acquired the status of a demi-god, striding in front of his men with only a cane for a weapon. Indeed, the Taipings so admired Gordon that their sharp-shooters were ordered not to take aim at him. Another aspect of Gordon's character made itself known during this episode. He was offended when his Chinese masters eventually murdered the Celestial King and subsequently refused to take their money for his services. In Britain he was honoured as nothing more than a notable public servant. This distaste for honours, for pomp and ceremony, and an antagonistic relationship with authority was to mark him throughout his life.

*

It was either on the train as he steamed down through Italy towards Brindisi, or else aboard the SS *Tanjore* crossing the Mediterranean, that Gordon arrived at the conclusion that an old adversary, Zubayr Pasha, would be the best person to install in Khartoum once the Mahdi was removed. This would have come as a shock to anyone who knew of the years Gordon had spent running down Zubayr's little slave empire in what is now southern Darfur. He must also have known that public opinion in Britain would have disapproved of a former slave trader being installed as governor-general. The press had built Zubayr into a terrifying monster.

In those days, middle-class Victorians ruled three-quarters of the globe. In their eyes, the world was inhabited by inferior beings. They felt morally superior to those to whom civilisation had not yet arrived in its completeness, nor had been touched by the Christian faith. You couldn't get much lower than a slave trader – cruel, inhumane, invariably Arab and Muslim. A man who beat and abused his fellow human beings, catching them and selling them like beasts of burden. The Abolition bill of 1833 outlawed slavery anywhere in the British Empire, although the practice persisted beyond that date with new forms of ownership.

Gordon was the embodiment of how the Victorians liked to see themselves. Well-meaning, self-sacrificing, a morally upstanding man who wanted to make the world a better place, he was drawn to the idea of the infinite soul, that there is more to us than what happens in this life. In England he sought out organisations and charities that worked with the poor. He read the Bible in an effort to unlock its secrets and had no time for 'novels or worldly books'. It is this asceticism that lends his character the aspect of a latter-day saint, a man devoted to goodness and justice, repulsed by decadence, by the hypocrisy of politics and the dishonesty that went with high office. Yet he was also known to explode into a fury, kicking and beating those working for him over the most trivial of matters with no warning or explanation. In *Eminent Victorians*, Lytton Strachey paints a portrait of Gordon as a paranoid, reclusive drunk who would retreat to his tent with a bottle of whisky and a bible, a hatchet and a flag planted outside to prevent him from being disturbed.

How Gordon planned to persuade Zubayr is not clear. There was no love lost between the two men. In the press he was described as living in splendour in his palace in the desert, surrounded by chained lions. Zubayr held Gordon personally responsible for the death of his son, Suleiman, who had been executed by Gordon's lieutenant Romolo Gessi. When they subsequently met in Cairo the two men could barely stand being in the same room and were unable even to shake hands. Still, Gordon later claimed that he was overcome by a 'mystic feeling' that he could trust Zubayr. It was precisely this sort of thing that made Sir Evelyn Baring, consul-general of Egypt, distrust Gordon, viewing him as unpredictable and an unsound man for the job. 'I have no confidence in opinions based on mystic feelings,' he wrote. The general was, in his opinion, 'quite unfit'. There wasn't much love for Gordon in Cairo and both the Khedive Tewfik and the Egyptian prime minister supported Baring. When no accord could be reached with Zubayr, another man, Amir Abdel Shakur, was nominated in his place. Shakur lasted as far as Aswan, where he abandoned the train along with his entourage and twenty-three 'wives'.

All indications suggest that Gordon's mind was in a state of turmoil. The Mahdi was an unknown quantity whom nobody really
understood, but it was believed that he represented an idea so
terrifying that it might cause the entire British Empire to unravel.
On the journey south, Gordon sent one telegram after another
back to Cairo, often contradicting himself. One has the impression he was making it up as he went along, inventing his own narrative even as he moved, slipping upstream, passing through the
landscape by train and then camel, deciding the fate of a country
as it came to him.

On arrival in Khartoum in February 1884 Gordon immediately
burned all records of debt and destroyed the Turkish instruments
of torture. This was to be a new beginning. He sent a message
of peace and reconciliation to the Mahdi. All prisoners of war
were set free. These measures were intended to win hearts and
minds. Above all he needed the locals on his side. He promised
more money: £100,000 and Indian troops rather than Egyptians.
By then, he had somehow managed to convince himself that there
was actually no pressing need to evacuate the garrison. After such
a warm welcome perhaps his presence alone would be enough to
thwart the Mahdi's ambitions.

Gordon's character seems almost to mirror the idiosyncratic
eccentricity of the Mahdi, the mystical premonitions, the impul-
sive behaviour. Indeed, in contrast to what others wrote of him,
in his journals he professed admiration for the devotion and
ascetic discipline of the Mahdi's followers. He was also keenly
aware of the ambiguity of his position: 'Who are the rebels? We,
or the Arabs?' he asked. He urged his officers to read Plutarch,
and secretly wished they would be more like his enemy: 'Islam
means resigning or devoting oneself entirely to God and His service. In other words, self-sacrifice. A true Christian is of the Islam
religion.'

During his first tour of service Gordon had raced around the
country by camel for months at a time, descending on startled
outposts to stamp out revolts that broke out like brush fires here
and there. It was here that his reputation was forged. Out of

the desert he would fly, they said, like a jinn. In movement he found the sense of purpose that evaded him in the rest of his life. When not moving he often slumped into the 'doles', as he called his bouts of depression. Isolated in his convictions, Gordon was celibate and, like the Mahdi, he prayed constantly. There is something remarkable about the way in which he committed himself to the task, believing that his faith would see him through. In that sense, Sudan provided the ultimate test for such a character, always seeking his limits; an empty canvas on which to paint himself.

Trained by the Royal Engineers, Gordon's passion was map-making. It served him well in China, allowing him to develop strategies to isolate the enemy, turning roads and waterways to his advantage. Besieged in Khartoum, however, he was out of his depth. The land eluded his grasp, dissolving into a kind of abstraction. His surveying skills proved of little use. He became confused by the similarity of local names: 'The city moves all the time,' he wrote in frustration of one place. This seems fitting, considering the crucial role mapping played in the creation of the country. Sudan's history might even be said to consist of a series of overlapping maps, starting with the old kingdoms and sultanates of Nubia, Sennar, Darfur, shifting spheres of power that eventually fell beneath the authoritarian grip of the Ottoman heir, Muhammed Ali and his descendants. The Anglo-Egyptian Sudan only came into being in the last years of the nineteenth century, the borders hammered out between Belgium, France, Italy and Ethiopia. Gordon was trying to find his way out of the labyrinth into which he had led himself.

The journals describing the last few months at Khartoum show a man going slowly out of his mind. He continued his habit of sending some twenty to thirty telegrams a day, despatching one as soon as a thought came into his head, only to cancel it almost immediately with another. Isolated and frustrated, he found himself held hostage, not so much by the Mahdi's forces, who were biding their time, but by his superiors, the very people who had sent him here, and by Kitchener, the useless messenger. Days became weeks and weeks became months. Gordon prowled the palace, prodding his lazy soldiers awake, using his telescope to spy out the enemy positions from the roof. He was starved of information. When he signalled with his bugle, the Mahdi's bugler across the river would mockingly echo the tune. They were toying with him. And while sending messengers out of town was relatively easy, receiving despatches was far more difficult. No one in their right minds wanted to enter a besieged town that was about to fall. 'You send me no information,' he writes to Kitchener, barely a fortnight before his death, 'though you have lots of money.'

The journals read at times like a stream of consciousness, comprising free associations of daily events and reports of enemy movements before spiralling off into raving monologues about the British press, or the vanity and cowardice of the officers on whom he had to rely. What was it all for, he asked? In ten or twelve years they would all be deaf and toothless, replaced by a new generation of Barings, Wolseleys and Gordons. They would vegetate in their London clubs. 'Better a ball in the brain than to flicker out unheeded.' He felt contempt for the Egyptian soldiers he had risked his life to save. They forgot his orders, they lied and could not be counted on in a fight. Still, he preferred being cut off in Khartoum than back in London: 'I dwell on the joy of never seeing Britain again, with its horrid dinner parties – we all wear marks saying what we do not believe, eat and drinking things we do not want and then abusing one another – I would rather live like a Dervish with the Mahdi than go out to dinner every evening in London.' Alone in his palace, listening to the distant drums, Gordon saw his life as a crucifixion of sorts. He imagined he was awaiting Armageddon. He shut himself up for days, refusing to speak to anyone. He wandered the empty palace at night holding conversations with imaginary interlocutors.

In the end it was the river that he so enjoyed gazing upon which was his undoing. In the early hours of 26 January 1885 the water level dropped low enough for the Mahdi's men to edge around the city's western defences. The *Ansar* rushed the palace, where they killed Gordon. When the Englishman's severed head was brought to the Mahdi he was furious; he had wanted Gordon brought to him alive.

Gordon could not have planned his death more perfectly. The ultimate act of self-sacrifice, to die as a martyr, isolated and alone, clinging to his beliefs, unwilling to abandon his principles, no matter what the price. In England he was a hero. Wilfrid Blunt, however, remained scathing in his judgement. 'If ever right triumphed in the world,' he wrote, 'it was at the fall of Khartoum.' As for the Mahdi, his victory was short-lived. Six months later he, too, was dead, by poison, disease or divine will, it is not known. A tomb was built with a shining *qubba*, or dome, in the distinctive manner of a venerated saint. It stayed there until 1898, when the tomb was dismantled and its contents thrown into the river. Rumour has it that the Sirdar held onto the skull, which he tried to present to Queen Victoria. The queen was scandalised and the skull ended up at the Royal College of Medicine in London's Gower Street for a time before it mysteriously disappeared from display, never to be seen again. It makes for a curious footnote and one that conjures up the image of the Mahdi's disembodied soul wandering London forever.

At the Khalifa's House museum in Omdurman, a visiting class of schoolchildren charge about, ignoring their teacher's efforts to convey the significance of the objects around them. There is only

a passing interest as they rush from one room to the next, giggling and shoving one another in their efforts to disrupt the educational process. You can't really blame them. The teacher is dull
and uninspiring. From his comments he seems barely to grasp the
history he is trying to convey. The children sense his insecurity.
They are more curious about the other visitors and wonder why
I am taking photographs of that strange contraption in the corner,
which turns out to be a printing press.

In the opposite corner, beside a photograph of Gordon, stand
two ornamental saddles. They draw curious stares from the children, and it is not difficult to see why. They were a gift, presented
to Gordon in thanks for his efforts in putting down the Taiping
Rebellion. The Chinese knew where he was being posted next
and had heard that they had camels in this part of the world.
Naturally, they assumed that, like all camels in China, the ones in
Sudan had two humps.

The noise of the schoolchildren recedes into the yard.
History, this story, means little to them. An anecdote, a faded
photograph of a *khawaja* and two odd contraptions. Like kids
visiting museums all over the world, the past is an amusement,
a distraction. How this odd man and the decrepit objects in this
house could somehow be connected to their lives, to the country they live in, the problems they face, the wars they fight, is
still not clear to them and may never be. For the moment it is
just a funny little house full of heavy old swords and shields that
look like the shells of strange animals. A spaceship would hold
more interest.

Like Gulliver in a strange land, I stride across town, amazed at how it has become a miniature version of its former self. Everything really does seem smaller. It takes no time at all to walk from one place to another. The streets are narrower. When you bend down to look more closely you notice that the old downtown area occupies only a fraction of the city. It also appears to have been abandoned. The streets are neglected and run down. The covered sidewalks are now peppered with itinerant merchants, many of them new arrivals. They spread their shoes and belts, shirts and underwear out on the same cardboard boxes that carried them from the South China Sea.

In the wake of Gordon's death Khartoum was abandoned. The Mahdi's successor, the Khalifa, established himself in Omdurman, across the river to the west. With the Reconquest in 1898, there was a determined effort to erase all trace of the Mahdi from the world. Gordon's spirit lingered over the ruins like a hallowed memory. The first layout for the city, designed under Kitchener, was a series of intersecting diagonals said to be based on the pattern of the Union Jack. The man who was given the task of restructuring the city and infrastructure was an engineer named W. H. McLean, who was later to redesign Jerusalem. When McLean arrived in 1906, Khartoum had a population of 25,000. A country of blacks ruled by Blues, as the saying went at the time, the Blues being the Oxbridge graduates who staffed the Sudan Political Service.

The Sudan Political Service was one of the most prestigious of the Overseas Administrative Services. Candidates were hand-picked, particularly in the early days, when they were considered of the highest calibre: 'The flower of those who are turned out of our schools and colleges,' declared Lord Cromer, governor of Egypt. Officers often wrote home about the difficulties they faced, the trials and tribulations of trying to improve their polo game, for example. In doing so they traced the pattern of their relationship to the people they governed. On the occasion of a visit by local dig-nitaries, one officer, Stephen Butler, writing to his father, described how the British would 'roar with laughter to see their faces when they saw the electric light switched on. Of course they all had to have a go at it, turning it on and off to the accompaniment of shrieks of delight.' This spectacle was only topped by what Butler

calls the *succès fou* of the visit, when the visitors discovered hot-
and cold-water taps in the bathroom. The dignified Arab sheikhs
were as excited as 'schoolboys on a visit to the capital'.

After 1882 Britain effectively ruled both countries. Ostensibly,
the British were only in the Sudan to help the Egyptians. The
awkward term condominium was chosen to allay French and
Italian fears about British expansionism in Africa. It also served
as an escape clause. Britain didn't really want full control; what
it wanted was the benefits without the responsibility. Specifically,
it needed to safeguard the water required in Egypt, the real jewel
on the Nile as far as they were concerned. Egypt's strategic value
stemmed from the Suez Canal – the gateway to India and British
possessions further east.

The new Khartoum was to be strictly divided according to race
and class. The three classes were British, Egyptian and 'Natives'.
The British were afforded the area closest to the river, with access
to water and gardens that were deemed 'necessary for the comfort
of Europeans'. By the time McLean left, in 1913, Khartoum was
described as 'an artificial enclave, European in appearance and tone,
well-tended and well-watered, more Mediterranean than African'.

As it emerges out of the blur of memory the differences are
subtle. You want it to be as it was, a part of you. Unlike those who
have observed every minuscule shift in time as an incremental
progression, day by day, the city to me has remained trapped in a
former age like an insect in resin that turns slowly to amber. Their
lives are inscribed in its decay and metamorphoses. It is a function
of who they have become, of what they once were. Every place
remains loyal to its own existence, to the belief that the universe
flows around the axis of the here and now. Where you have been
and what you have seen all these years is of no great significance.
What matters is what has taken place here in your absence. I am
astonished by the unexpected surprises, such as the sign over my
mother's shop, even though it closed long ago, that seem to have
been waiting just for me to find.

The old European downtown quarter was once occupied
by the traders who arrived in the wake of the Reconquest, and
even before that, in the days of Turco-Egyptian rule: Greeks,
Levantines, Armenians, Copts. They brought with them a touch

of the Mediterranean. A few of them are still here, because this is home and there is nowhere else to go, but most have gone. But even the city I knew is not the way it was in its heyday. A copy of the *Sudan Star* dated 7 November 1945 gives some of the flavour of the time: 'Drastic Laws to Kill Sudanese Custom', reads one headline, an article dealing with the custom of pharaonic circumcision. A new law being considered by the North Sudan Advisory Council would mean up to seven years in prison for any person performing what is now termed female genital mutilation. Further down the same page is an account of how plans to capture Hitler were foiled by the Führer's suicide. In Bavaria, the Americans are closing in on Berchtesgaden. Mussolini's body has disappeared. There is an advertisement for the Gordon Music Hall. A weekly column, 'The Hump', outlines the entertainment available in the capital: at the Coliseum and Blue Nile cinemas Bette Davis can be seen in Warner Bros.' latest hit, *Watch on the Rhine*.

Many of the old shops along Gamhouria Street are shuttered, others remain dark, depleted Aladdin's caves with old-fashioned signs and glass shelves that are bare. There are cases displaying fountain pens and briefcases. Objects no one really wants, or can afford. Sharp-witted boys are swift to step up holding sheets of cardboard to which they have clipped anything and everything to cater to your immediate needs: lighters, Chinese Uniball pens or scratch cards for topping up your phone. Who needs shops? This is a versatile market that thrives on immediacy. If something doesn't sell, they won't be back with it tomorrow. I spend days looking for a disposable fountain pen like one I once bought here. Now nobody recognises it. They take it from my fingers and turn it over in wonder. Where did you get it? Right here, I insist, a few months back. No, they shake their heads, can't be. They've never seen such a thing in their lives. Stationers, bookshops, newspaper stalls, street vendors. I wander back and forth but no one can help. They frown, trying to find a way of taking it to pieces. You throw it away? They shake their heads. You can't have bought it here. All memory of such an item seems to have vanished under the ebb and flow of daily life. Nothing is remembered unless it serves an immediate purpose. All that remain are fragments, like archaeological artefacts.

The straight roads and square buildings carry an echo of the image in which they were once built. The decaying structures, the shuttered doorways, the old cafés, all serve as a reminder of how that European vision did not hold. Their faded glamour looks sad; a memory of lost hope, a bygone age. Instead of renovating and revitalising, the city has expanded its perimeter, moving outward. Perhaps this, too, is a way of avoiding addressing the past; the discomfort expressed in relocating from one fixed centre to a pattern that is more diffuse and obscure. Instead of the rigid order of straight lines, there are pockets of activity here and there. Rows of shops and restaurants are clustered together, offices located in villas, in former residential areas that have no street signs and are hard to find. Either you know where you are going or you need someone to take you there.

The downtown area is only of interest to people like myself, as a curiosity, a dusty museum, a crumbling monument. All along the arcades people sit in empty stores and gaze out mournfully at the passing traffic, waiting for a customer who refuses to appear. The shelves they guard are run down and denuded, dotted with just a few remaining items, novelties no one cares to buy. Still the ceremony continues. Keys are sought and eventually found, glass display cases are slid open with care. The bookshops where I used to linger after school, searching for diversion, waiting for my mother to close the shop and go home, are quiet. A few tattered textbooks lie on display, their pages curled by the sun. A sports equipment store whose windows are filled, bizarrely, with muscular blonde women baring white teeth while toning their bodies on strange contraptions. It has the same rundown, timeless feel that I remember so well, as if the mere business of getting through the day is enough of a challenge.

My father worked in Barlaman Street. After school, I would walk in from the midday heat to be hit by a noisy blast of cold air. The office was lined with dark wood. I knew everyone who worked out there and they all knew me. If my father was in a meeting I would wait at one of their desks. I enjoyed listening to them chat among themselves, watching them at work. There was a drinking fountain that dispensed water so icy it made your head hurt. I was happy sitting there for hours. This was where all the big companies were located in those days. At night it glowed with the bright lights and logos of airlines and banks, the brightly lit signs and shady porticos. It was a stone's throw from the Presidential Palace and the river. It felt glamorous, connected to the world, unlike the rest of the city, which seemed tied to an ancient, forgotten rhyme and reason of its own.

Years ago people used to stroll here in the cool of the evening with their families, past the brightly lit shops with everyone dressed up, children eating ice cream. In the 1990s, the early years of the *Inqaz*, a curfew was imposed that made going out in the evening impossible. Men and women were forbidden from mixing socially, even at weddings. Cinemas were closed down and power cuts ensured that the lights went out in this part of town. The city never recovered. The electricity issue has been solved but the sense of insecurity still lingers. At night the streets are deserted now and unlit save for the strafing beams of fast-moving headlights. Itinerant figures slide through the shadows of the tall buildings seeking shelter; refugees, deranged war veterans, orphans. Homelessnes. Madness. Decay. Everything else is gone.

The old Athenée is still there, though only a hollowed-out skeleton of what it once was. The interior of the café has been stripped bare, the walls are grubby and the tiled floor is cracked and broken. Gone are the fancy high stools and the tables and chairs. I can still recall the taste of their vanilla ice cream. Dotted around the square are shops that specialise in handicrafts for nonexistent tourists, their windows crammed with the same crocodile-head ashtrays, snakeskin wallets, goatskin drums and wire-stringed *rababas* that I can recall. A procession of carved elephants trudges over an ivory rainbow. The centre of the square is cluttered with electric generators from the days when power cuts were a daily occurrence. Now people squat on grubby crates and three-legged chairs whose plastic weaving has come unstrung. There is an air of hopelessness about the place.

'Do people still buy these things?' I ask.

Babiker stands behind the counter of Folklore House. Above his head is a large framed black and white photograph of someone who could have been an earlier version of himself from back in the Swing era, dressed in a sharp suit cut in the style of the 1950s.

An assistant shuffles up, slides open one of the glass cabinets and
starts patiently working along a row of snakeskin purses of dif-
fering sizes. He takes each one down, dusts it off carefully with a
rag before replacing it on the shelf. Babiker shrugs: 'I warn people
they could get into trouble taking them into Europe but a lot of
them decide to take the risk anyway.'

He took over running the shop when his father, the man in the
picture, passed away. It is the oldest shop of its kind, not just on
this square but in the entire city. The family opened their first
shop in Omdurman in 1916, and this one followed in the sixties
when the area was just coming into its own. In the evenings there
was an excitement generated by the cool night air and the bright
neon signs illuminating the shops. People milled about expect-
antly. Babiker remembers how the square used to be a favourite haunt of local artists and writers. There was a gallery upstairs
above the Athenée, a glamorous place where people came to chat
over tea and Turkish coffee. It was here that many of them would
display their work. Nowadays, Babiker tells me, it is hard to find
artisans who are capable of doing work of such a high standard.
The carved ebony figures are of warriors, bare-breasted women,
giraffes, an ostrich with an egg. All look roughly finished and
clumsy. Many of the wood carvings are made in Kenya, where
the quality is better. According to Babiker, this coarsening is also
reflected in the quality of the visitors who arrive from abroad.
They are less and less interested in what is happening locally.
Technicians come here to do a job and leave; they tend to buy the
first thing they see. They are unlikely to linger and drink tea the
way visitors did in the old days and are generally more difficult to
engage in conversation. It all contributes to a lowering of expecta-
tions. People have changed, he says.

Babiker spent many years abroad, living in south-east London,
Lewisham and Deptford. Eventually he decided it was not for
him. He came home, despite his father's pleas for him to stay
away. This was in 1990, a year after the *coup d'état* that brought
Bashir to power – the year my parents fled. Those were the years
when the purges of the Revolution of National Salvation were
at their height and the future looked bleak. Artists suffered and

many of those who left have still not returned. Babiker is optimistic, however. He believes that the art world is coming back
to life. It is no longer centred around this old square, although a
young artist did recently stage an installation there. Nowadays,
like everything else, it is elsewhere. He is less convinced about
the state of the economy. The government is opportunistic. They
want to squeeze as much out of the country as they can now,
without a thought for the future. There is no long-term strategy.
If the stagnation of the old downtown area symbolises the end
of an era it also emphasises the current lack of coherence. It is
easier to throw up new buildings, mosques, hotels, even shopping malls, on a patch of unclaimed land somewhere than to work
on remodelling the old. The past serves only as an example of
what no longer works. The city has broken out of its mould but
is struggling to find a new form.

Officially, I am a foreigner here. Travelling on a British passport
means I have to register as an alien, which involves the usual filling out of forms, photocopying everything countless times and,
more to the point, paying in hard currency. They are squeezing all
they can out of the oil boom and see no point in making life easy
for visitors. Before any of this process can begin, however, I have
to find the place. The office is not downtown, not in any of the
various ministries or government compounds. Instead it is somewhere out in Burri, about twenty minutes' drive from the centre.
The taxi driver sets me down by the road and points confidently
at a gap between two houses. 'It's over there,' he says. Foolishly,

I set off walking. It is a windy day and the dust is blowing around me in all directions. I come to the end of the street and see nothing that looks like a police station. I ask an old man, then two girls, then a little boy in a shop selling chewing gum and telephone cards. I have a feeling I am completely on the wrong track. Eventually I am directed across an open patch of waste ground equipped with goalposts, to a house on a side street that looks like a police station but where nothing much seems to be happening. I stand patiently by the barred window and wait for the officers inside to finish what they are doing. They have just arrested a young man and are busy shouting at him while he empties his pockets. One of them records a list of items. This proves to be a slow and laborious task. Each object is double-checked as it is written out painstakingly in longhand on a scrap of paper: cigarettes, lighter, wallet, keys. Eventually things calm down enough for them to notice me, but when I ask about alien registration they shake their heads and wave off into the distance. Nothing to do with them.

Twenty minutes later I find myself at a police training college that they have not quite finished building. No one there knows anything about alien registration either. Finally, a man with two stripes on his sleeve tells me it is down the road. By the time I get there they are closing for the day and not admitting more people. It would in any case have been a waste of time. I learn that I also need someone in possession of a *butaqa*, or national identity card, to vouch for me, which is not as easy as it sounds, as most people don't have one. Why not? 'It's more trouble than it's worth' everyone assures me. All of this is by the way of a reminder that the only way to get things done here is to have someone with you who understands how the system works. It is only some weeks later that I eventually find someone who knows somebody who is willing to swear that I am who I say I am, even though he has never met me before.

The Alien Registration Office is an unlikely setting for any kind of bureaucracy. Surrounded by high-walled villas, the garden of a large white house is crowded with Chinese, Malays, Indonesians and Filipinos, along with the odd European, dazed and sweltering in the heat. Each has a personal entourage of helpers, drivers, agents and lawyers, all trying to get close to the one photocopier that is set out on the terrace. It is operated by a demure, expressionless girl in a hijab wearing an excessive amount of make-up. She stands coolly at the centre of a cluster of men who watch with respectful fascination as she performs her task without a word, without even raising her eyes to the person in front of her. We stand there with our documents held out, waiting for her to pick a hand. Over and over she repeats the same sequence of movements: money in one hand, document swept across the screen, hit the button, and then return copy and document to the outstretched hand. She carries on patiently, oblivious to the urgency of the men.

Having a foreign passport used to be something of a privilege, but it has become commonplace and I see plenty of Sudanese clutching US, Spanish, UK and a variety of other national documents in their hands. Further over, another scrum has formed around a window covered with wire netting that has been conveniently slashed open to allow you to reach in through the jagged slit to hand over your documents in the hope they will be accepted and not thrown back with a demand that you go back to your hotel and get them stamped, which is what happens to the person in front of me. It is what you pray will not happen. The slightest mishap will cause you to lose another day. I push my way in. Through the torn netting I glimpse a row of nine people, eight women and one man, sitting alongside one another in the gloom. They are patiently copying out details into ledgers, in a manner that evokes the image of scribes in an ancient court. It is the kind of time-consuming, thankless toil that can only make sense when you are within it, concentrating on the task in front of you. Once you step back the futility of it all becomes obvious. The ledgers are destined to join the heaps piled up at the back of the room, slumped in chaotic disorder, gathering dust and dead beetles. Nobody will ever be able to find anything in there, and all of this work serves less for keeping a record than for maintaining the impression of order. In that sense, it is no more than a theatrical farce. It is still amazing to watch. One person affixes the sticker. The next uses the stapler. Then comes the stamp. Finally, all the pages are placed in a folder. They work with production-line efficiency and with complete disregard for the information being processed. None of the details are scrutinised or queried, unless some detail has been omitted, some box left blank. It is a matter of complying, of fulfilling the demands of each stage in the process. I catch a brief glimpse of my passport rising to the surface only to vanish again. A blur of names and faces wash over one another. There is nothing to do but wait patiently until your name is called. The names are repeated, passed backwards by the crowd huddling around the delivery window. Expediency is in all our interests. The faster each person is processed the sooner your time will come. Eventually, when your name emerges like an echo from within, it sounds like a stranger being called. But finally your passport is passed back over the heads, from one hand to another, until miraculously it reaches you. The image resonates in my head, capturing perfectly how your fate lies in the hands of others. As an individual you are helpless.

As thanks for the help I am buying lunch. We cross the river to Omdurman and one of the most famous fish restaurants in the capital. It is not much to look at: a patch of sand dotted with fishtails and bones, scoured by skinny-ribbed stray cats. A sheet of corrugated iron provides the shade and the men (no women in sight) sit on low stools around *siniyas*, wide aluminium trays that act as tables. The fish is Nile tilapia, or *bulti*, and bream, *bayta*. Dexterously, a young boy slices off the scales on a high table, scraping them into a silvery pile using the flat edge of a knife the size of his forearm. He splits the fish open, strips them and throws them into a basket. From there they are dipped in flour before being dropped straight into a great wide vat of bubbling oil. Flecks of silvery scales stick to the boy's face as he concentrates on his work. The walls of the kitchen are blackened with wood smoke from the fires under the vats. The fish float in the golden oil, stirred by a man with a handsome face and a long fork. He flips them over deftly. Sweat pours down his forehead as he takes care of about thirty fish at a time, all bubbling on the surface. When they are done he scoops them into a bowl and they come out to the counter where an old man shakes salt and a generous sprinkling of cumin over them. You tell him how many you want and the fish are wrapped in paper. Two or three is normal, some ask for more. A pink plastic bag of bread, along with sliced onions, lime and chilli powder, are all the acoutrements you can hope for. It's a stone's throw from the river and the best fish you will ever taste. Just along from where we sit are the softly rounded mounds that are all that remain of the walls built to defend the city against Kitchener's Expeditionary Force in 1898. Hardly anyone pays them any attention. They look almost like natural features, having grown into the surrounding riverbank over more than a century.

Nadir, the man who helped me through this bureaucratic ritual, has swiftly become one of the most important contacts I have made here and not just because he knows where to eat fish. Our fathers grew up together in the same neighbourhood and we knew one another as children, though in the intervening years saw nothing of each other. When we met again I found it was easy to connect. He lived through the difficulties of the last decades and so his experience is like the flip side of mine. As we drive back across the river Nadir talks about his time in prison. 'You weren't here,' he says. 'You didn't see how it was.' He was arrested for working on a student newspaper and imprisoned in a house in Baladia Street in the middle of town. Since it did not feature on any official register, he simply vanished from the world, with no record of ever having been arrested. You became a ghost, which is what these places were dubbed – *Bayut al-Ashbah* – ghost houses. This one was divided into two halves. In one part the prisoners were confined all day and only let out morning and evening. In the other half they were allowed out of their cells to get exercise. There was a garden that they would flood with water. They would force the inmates out and hose them down. 'What are your links to the communist party?' they asked him. 'I have none.' The officer who beat him happened to be an old schoolmate. They used to be in the same class. He was the *teesh*, the dunce, who always came bottom of the class. Now he had his chance to get even. There was no point to the torture. Nadir had no political links at all. 'Dark days,' he mutters now, shaking his head.

The first time he was arrested they arrived outside his house and ordered him into a 'box', a converted pick-up, to join several other people whom he had never seen before. They were all

blindfolded and driven around for hours before they arrived at
the military compound at the centre of town in the old neighbourhood of Hai al-Matar, which used to be university staff accommodation. I recalled staying there one summer as a child in a simple
villa surrounded by lush gardens and hedgerows. It was requisitioned by the military and ringed by concrete walls. The complex
is dominated by a number of ugly, Soviet-style buildings that date
back to the 1970s when the president, Nimeiri, was going through
his socialist phase. On the roof they had constructed a number of
flimsy cells that were exposed to the sun. Nadir was placed in one
of these and left to stew in unbearable heat for twenty-one days,
after which they let him go with no explanation and no charges.
Three months later they came back in a Toyota Cressida. They
blindfolded him again and drove him round. This time they took
him to the ghost house.

After two months, one of the guards who knew Nadir arranged
for him to be transferred to the other half of the house where
you were at least allowed to move around during the day and to
use the toilet when you pleased, as opposed to being let out of
your cell only twice a day. For years afterwards he was plagued
by nightmares and had trouble sleeping. He was one of the lucky
ones. Many others received much worse treatment. One man he
still remembers was kept for three months and beaten daily. When
he was finally released, he was spotted wandering along the road
in the same clothes he had been wearing throughout his incar-
ceration with an unkempt beard and long hair. An old friend who
happened to be driving by recognised him and stopped his car.
He burst into tears when he saw the state of his friend. Shortly
afterwards the man died.

'I saw things I never imagined I would. Some were beaten and
tortured so badly they died. You would see men crawling along
the ground on their hands and knees to the toilet because their
feet were broken.' Nadir doesn't like talking about his experiences. Most of the people he knew then have left the country, and
many of them have not returned. It's hard to estimate the damage this episode did to the national spirit, what it did to political
development. Perhaps it goes a long way to explaining the apathy

today. Although many have returned, there are still millions of Sudanese in exile who will probably never recover from the experience of those years and will never trust the current regime enough to come home. They have new lives in Europe, the Far East, or America. A generation of young men and women, educated and talented, that has been wiped away.

And as we come down off the bridge we have a clear view of the building site of the Al Sunut Development project. This is what the future looks like. On paper it resembles something out of a science-fiction film. A four-billion dollar, 160-acre business district replete with glass towers, hotels, offices, duplexes, shopping malls with an adjoining residential zone including apartment blocks, a marina and a golf course. The local equivalent of what can be seen across the Red Sea in the Gulf: Dubai on the Nile. This is what the new class of oil-rich businessmen dream of. There used to be a forest of silver acacia trees that stretched along the riverbank at this spot. What remains of the forest is home to all the thieves and bandits in the city. If your car has been stolen, this is where you might start looking for it. So the new wealth of the country is to be separated from the lawbreakers by a reinforced wire fence. This modern mirage seems to have leapt out of another dimension. What will happen to us when this is reality? When our eyes are filled with the blinding reflection of thousands of glass mirrors, aimed at the sun? I wonder at the significance of the fact that it is built on the very same spot where, just over a century ago, the Mahdi's men crossed the river and breached the city's defences.

Gladstone was seen as the man who had failed Gordon. Even the queen expressed her dismay, and the prime minister was forced to resign in June 1885. His replacement, Lord Salisbury, saw the defeat of the Mahdi as a victory for Christianity and the civilised world. He described the Reconquest as a victory over the 'false religion' of Islam. The very word reconquest echoes that of another *Reconquista*, the expulsion of the Moors from fifteenth-century Spain. Salisbury was in favour of Christianising the entire country. He viewed Mahdism as 'a formidable mixture of religious fanaticism and military spirit ... which Islam alone seems to have the secret of conferring upon its votaries'. This stood in stark contrast to the views of the liberal Gladstone, who described the Sudanese rebels as 'a people struggling rightly to be free'.

The role of Christianity in the wake of the British victory was a delicate one. Evelyn Baring, later Lord Cromer, the British Agent in Egypt, forbid missionaries from proselytising in the North. Rumours that the British were planning to convert the entire country to Christianity could easily have sparked another revolt. The missionaries found more fertile ground in the South where the Dinka were tired of Islam and Arabs generally – they came promising protection and friendship but ended up raiding and pillaging, carrying off women and children into slavery. Not that the enlightened Christians did not come bearing their own prejudices: 'The mental capacity of a Denka [sic] at the present moment is very small and full of cow and corn,' appraised the Rev. F. B. Hadow in 1906.

Since religion was such a touchy subject, the British opted to transform the mores of Sudanese society by nurturing a Westernised elite. The main tool of change was to be a college of further education – an Eton on the Nile – the Gordon Memorial College. Gordon's spirit was to hang over the country for some time to come. The British public overlooked the Royal Engineer who tried with deep sincerity to do a job for which he was temperamentally and technically unsuited. Instead, they remembered Gordon the romantic, the Christian martyr, an adventurer guided by divine presence. It was an attractive myth; and one that the new college would carry forwards. It was to be sponsored by donations to the Gordon Memorial Fund, a fitting testament to his devotion and, indeed, sacrifice. It would create a new class of administrators, people who would run the country under the firm hand of the British governor-general and his district commissioners.

This new class of Sudanese were known as effendis. As they began to emerge, another problem became apparent: by educating the Sudanese, making them more Western in outlook, more amenable, they also handed them the means to question the British presence. While hoping to foster the creation of a new class closer in thought to their rulers, the experience of being brought together also fermented a new sense of solidarity among the students, and the emergence of a common identity. For the first time they began to see themselves collectively as Sudanese.

There is some irony in the fact that it was only when they came into contact with the British, when they saw how they themselves were viewed, that the newly educated class of Sudanese began to perceive themselves as a nation. They began to downplay archaic notions of tribal roots, and replace them with the modern concept of a national identity. By 1928, graduates were insisting on being described as 'Sudanese'. Being pushed together with people from different regions and tribes, all of varied physical traits, customs, habits and languages, forced these young men to seek some other basis of establishing mutual bonds. Their experience was unique and largely restricted to the elite, educated class. Brought together under the gaze of a higher power, the effendis forged national sentiments and began to overcome their own prejudices about their fellow countrymen. It was an experience that would prove impossible to extend to the population at large, an oversight that would dog the Sudanese intelligentsia for generations.

In their quest for modernity the Sudanese elite were quite selective in what they took from their contact with the West, but it was a touch more intimate than the British were comfortable with. As the divide between native and master in language and dress dissolved, the British administration worried that their own aura was being eroded. The new elite was becoming altogether too familiar with their rulers. The Sudanese effendi could now talk, walk and act like a good Englishman. By the 1920s his presence was beginning to resemble a serious threat to the theory of indirect rule. Many British officers openly despised the African equivalent of the Indian babu – the Europeanised native. Dress codes were changed as a consequence. Sudanese were forbidden from wearing Western clothes; pupils at the Gordon Memorial College were sent home to change their shoes for more traditional slippers. Medical arguments were raised, suggesting that the wearing of European clothes was detrimental to the health of an African, causing, among other ailments, bad teeth, lung problems and lowered fertility. Instead, they were obliged to wear 'native dress', the imma and gellabiya they had always worn. The British began to encourage difference rather than dispel it. And it wasn't just their dress code. The policy in education was to favour existing hierarchies. The sons of sheikhs were given priority, regardless of their academic abilities. Segregation of North and South was also imposed. Rather than being educated in Khartoum, promising Southerners were sent across the border to Makerere College in Kampala, Uganda.

Independence came more quickly than anyone expected. According to Sir Gawain Bell, a former Sudan Political Service officer, none of those who set out for the Sudan in the 1930s imagined the country would be independent before they reached retirement at fifty, but already British administrators were being replaced by Sudanese. There were several advantages, not least of which was the fact that you could pay a Sudanese less than half of what you had to pay his British, Egyptian or Lebanese counterpart. By the end of the Second World War, the end began to look inevitable. At the 1947 Juba Conference it was declared that Sudan would become independent, and that it would remain a single unit. The Southerners were not consulted on the matter.

From 1953 to 1956 great haste was made to get the country ready. The days of colonial rule were now numbered. The world that emerged from the war was very different from the one that had gone into it. Everywhere you looked European empires were crumbling: French Indochina fell in 1954 and the insurrection that would eventually become the Algerian war of independence had already begun. Britain had the largest and most complicated empire and the costs of maintaining it were beginning to outstrip the benefits. The Commonwealth was designed as early as 1931 to act as a buffer to slow down the drive towards independence, in itself a tricky business. Indian independence in 1947 had resulted in millions of deaths. War had broken out in Palestine after the British withdrew in 1948, and the Suez Crisis of 1956 underlined the new world order. Nasser emerged the victor of that fracas and Britain suffered a humiliating lesson in its loss of authority and lack of the military power needed to maintain its colonial presence. The Suez Crisis also ushered in the new age of Soviet and American dominance, both intent on dividing up the rest of the world between them as a wave of dismantlement swept around the globe.

The heavy traffic that rushes all day long along the university road, cutting through the centre of town, barely has the time or the inclination to notice the Ethnographic Museum that lies undisturbed on a leafy corner of Mek Nimr Street. Thousands of vehicles, cars, buses, taxis, minivans and donkeys and rickshaws speed headlong down the leafy avenue in an unstoppable torrent of urgency. The boys hanging from the open doorways of the minibuses yell destinations frantically in a bid for more passengers. People squeeze in and out, dropping to the road to take off running. The air is thick with the honking and hooting of these infernal machines, spewing out noxious clouds of exhaust, ferrying their loads to and from the city. Day in and day out.

Even those passengers who might have noticed the museum would be baffled by what purpose it might serve. In its sad, neglected state it gets few visitors. The pieces on display are moth-eaten and worm-ridden. Frames are cracked, cases lie mysteriously empty. As you step through the gate in the high tamarind hedge all sense of haste and motion comes to an end. Nothing has changed in forty or fifty years. A weary gatekeeper hovers, ushering you into his little niche – it's not really an office – and insisting that you sign the visitors' book. He is adamant about this, as if collecting evidence to prove that his presence is not redundant. Inside, the artefacts are tacked onto the wall in a lopsided, haphazard fashion that suggests little thought went into the task. By the door a heavy wooden case looks like it belongs in a museum itself, let alone the map it contains. There is nothing to indicate that anything has been renovated for at least forty years. The neatly typewritten cards and descriptions have a discipline about them that appears at odds with the disordered context in which they are placed. They are a testament to a period of this country's history: the black and white photographs, accounts of tribesmen, their customs and traditions, were gathered and written up by British ethnographers in the early twentieth century.

A white man and his wife, both in their sixties and clearly that rarity of rarities, tourists, wander along gamely behind their guide trying to summon up some enthusiasm for this sorry sight. Their half-hearted remarks make the visit seem an act of courtesy, a desire to show respect and polite interest, but they cannot hide their disappointment. Their guide, a young man in his twenties, has clearly never been inside this building before in his life. He does his best to humour them, feigning excitement for certain objects in the room, which are clearly meaningless to him. He is keen to appear to be doing a good job, but his eagerness to please results in a frivolous attitude that clearly displeases his charges almost as much as the state of the museum itself. 'This is a cow,' he says, pointing at a large fetish of a bullock that stands in the middle of the room. Made of mud, blood and urine, according to the label, it is an impressive object, standing waist-high from the floor, mournfully facing the door as if longing to walk straight out of there. The visitors wait patiently, hoping more information is forthcoming, but the young guide is a city-dweller, a Northerner, and the objects displayed in the cabinets around us might as well have come from Mars for all they mean to him. They smile politely, as it is becoming clear that his every utterance only confirms his ignorance anew. Giving up all hope of his assistance, they turn instead to a hefty guidebook they have brought with them, which they consult avidly, searching for clues to try and fill in the blanks left by the scant information provided by the cards on the wall. Bored and deciding he has done his best, the young guide wanders outside for a cigarette as they squint at the arrows and adornments, seeking some hidden significance.

The fact that the museum is still here is no doubt due to some bureaucratic oversight. Perhaps they have forgotten it still exists. Perhaps it is protocol and an instilled sense of respect for learning that has saved it from being turned into offices, or a parking space for oil executives. It is a relic of bygone ambitions. In the early years of independence there were many working towards the idea of Sudan accepting itself as an African nation. To the Northerners, and the educated elite in particular, the idea there could be anything linking them to these men and women who walked around naked and worshipped bullocks made of mud went against everything they believed about themselves as civilised Muslims, and worthy inheritors of the new nation from their European masters.

The foreign couple have seen enough and decide it is time to move on, which leaves me alone. Two female curators wander back and forth from room to room, leaning on the walls as if they were at home, while conducting a long, involved conversation about unreliable men. They are oblivious to my presence. They stretch and yawn and wonder what to do with their day while all around them the rather ancient and irreplaceable objects crumble slowly into dust. You can almost hear the woodworm and other assorted insects crunching their way through the national heritage. There are bows and arrows, shelters, a model of a Rashaida camp. A splintered wooden frame holds a photograph of an Englishman wearing a pith helmet alongside a group of almost naked men.

Although they started out as a means of documenting the primitiveness of the 'native' to the British colonial scholar, each cabinet now seems ironically to mark the closing of a door on the diversity of this country. These fragments are reminders of a way of existence that has been largely extinguished. There are no signs or pictures to indicate that life has continued in those places since the thirties or forties when these artefacts were gathered. No modern masks or bracelets innovated out of waste plastic or tin, nothing to describe the lives of the descendants of those figures in the pictures in the present day. It's as if they were cut off and abandoned. As if this museum is a testament to another world, an ancient kingdom far away that has no connection to the country we can hear passing by outside, beyond the hedges. The sense of extinction is palpable.

Of course, to the effendis, the ruling elite, the people in those pictures were as alien to them as they were to the British academics, perhaps even more so. The Sudanese aspired to become modern, to be accepted as members of the civilised world. To do so they adopted Western clothes and manners. They learned their languages, read their books. They took up tennis, smoked pipes and drank whisky. They did everything, in short, to distance themselves from the primitive way of life represented in the images and artefacts displayed here. No one wanted to be reminded of any naked savages. It was all something of an embarrassment, part of what they were trying to get away from. To join the modern world they had to distance themselves from tribal behaviour, from the very nature of the nation they were trying to form.

How is a country to make sense of itself when it refuses to recognise its own people? By turning its back on its own past it was closing the door on achieving nationhood. The compulsion to impose a racial polarity on the country dates back to at least the 1930s when colonial administrators and academics tried to make sense of the racial spectrum of their native subjects. The memory of the Mahdi was still fresh and Islam was taken as the deciding factor. The dangers were spelled out by Winston Churchill in *The River War*, his recollection of the Reconquest of 1898: 'The qualities of mongrels are rarely admirable, and the mixture of the Arab and negro types has produced a debased and cruel breed, more shocking because they are more intelligent than the primitive savages.' The increase in intelligence was, according to Churchill, what makes the Sudanese prone to become 'without exception, hunters of men'.

By the 1960s the message had been toned down, but was basically unchanged. The historian P. M. Holt called it 'the indigenous tradition'. He cited it as one of three factors that would characterise the emergence of the nation and determine the country's future, along with the withdrawal of Egypt and Britain, and the shared experiences of the people, living through the Turco-Egyptian Empire, the Mahdist revolt and Anglo-Egyptian rule.

In an ideal world this museum would be a celebration rather than a mausoleum, which is what it resembles now: a tomb for diversity, for the country that might have been. I wander through feeling a growing impatience and despair. The rooms are infused with a melancholy air, a sense that what this place is really preserving is a lie, but it is a lie that we need, no matter how fossilised and moth-eaten. A lie about order and progress and the succession of knowledge over time. It is a lie that we continue to venerate because the alternative would mean addressing our assumptions in ways that we are not prepared to do.

In a hall at the back a row of empty display cabinets looks as though they have been recently ransacked. As I return to the street and the mad cacophony and fumes of mid-morning traffic, I feel as though I have been released from a spell. But there is no escaping the past. Out of half a century of independence Sudan has seen forty years of civil war. It is no coincidence.

'Janjaweed is an attitude,' sighs Halimah. She is just back from five days of being jolted around Darfur in the back of a Landcruiser and needs to see her Chinese acupuncturist as soon as possible to relieve the pain. In the meantime she consents to have lunch with me. In an Indian restaurant in Souk Two she orders for us both in fluent Hindi. At the age of sixteen her father, a rather broad-minded civil servant in the service of Sudan Railways, decided to send her abroad to study, in Bombay. Halimah (not her real name) was not keen on leaving her family. She recalls sitting in the aeroplane alone, crying. India gave her the independence she feels now, even though she found it a challenge. 'We Sudanese don't find it easy to live in intimate contact with other people.' Things like sharing bathrooms and so on she found particularly unpleasant and would prefer to use the toilet in a public place like a cinema rather than in the house where she was staying. Her time there left her with a good impression of the Indians. 'They don't interfere. They keep to themselves.' She soon managed to learn the language, translating for the old woman she was boarding with. She had never lived away from her family before.

Why did she agree to go? Perhaps because she already felt different in some way, apart from her brothers. At the age of six she was circumcised. She remembers it vividly as one of the most traumatic events in her life. 'It wasn't the worst kind,' she says now. It was done at the house of her grandparents; her parents were afraid that she would hate them for it. Her father was against it, but bowed eventually to the pressure from the rest of the family, particularly her mother, whom she never felt close to.

One of the most important things she learned in India was the ability to live with people who are different from you. It was this, above all, which she brought away. It politicised her. In India she experienced discrimination for the first time. People looked at her and asked what tribe she was from in Africa. This was unexpected the assumption that she came from a more primitive background than they did. Up until that point she had taken her social standing for granted, never questioning her Shaigiya background, nor the privileges that came from belonging to one of the most prominent Northern Sudanese tribes.

When she returned home in the late nineties, Halimah felt more cut off from her brothers than ever. She realised she no longer needed them to do things for her. In politics, too, things had changed. She had witnessed a democracy in fully working operation in India. By then Sudan had been transformed by seven years of hard-line Islamist rule. Adjustments had to be made; even travelling by public transport was no longer easy for single women. She found it difficult to adapt. For a time she considered moving to Cairo. A lot of her friends went to the Gulf to work, to Doha, Bahrain, in search of good jobs. Halimah considered doing the same, but she didn't like the Arabs generally and felt she would be looked down upon. In the end it was her ability in English rather than her academic qualifications that secured her work with *Al Ayyam* newspaper.

At the paper, Halimah worked at all manner of jobs, from typing to translation to advertising. Gradually she found herself drawn to the vocation of reporter. She began to write and soon had established a reputation for herself as an unconventional girl. Her social life was sacrificed. Marriage, the usual course a woman was expected to take, was avoided. She was aware that she was being observed, and, moving in a man's world as she was, aware that all contact with the opposite sex had to be proper if she was to avoid gaining an unwanted reputation. She fell in love once, while in India, with a Sudanese man, but it led to nothing. Halimah knows it is very difficult to find a Sudanese man who will suit her. Sudanese men refuse to change. Perhaps this explains why so many women seem to be involved in trying to bring about change, whether it is in Darfur, or in the treatment of Southerners, or in human rights. Men in general do not feel that their lives are infringed upon, that there are restrictions imposed on their movements or behaviour, even the way they dress. Perhaps it is only once you experience those kinds of limitations that you begin to question the world around you.

Halimah's experiences in Darfur are still fresh in her mind. The road trip was to investigate government claims that people are returning to their homes. The results were not encouraging. People are afraid to go back, she says, afraid of what they will find. On the outskirts of one village that had been burned to the ground they came across a woman hiding in the bush. She had tried to go back home, she told them, but the people who had come and burned the village down were now living there. They found a similar situation elsewhere. There was no sense that it was safe to go back and no one had any confidence in the government protecting them.

In the camps, Halimah avoids meeting the sheikhs. She goes straight to the women, 'because I know they don't have a political agenda'. The sheikhs were growing aware that their importance was increasing with all the outside attention. Dealing with them had become more complicated.

There are other tangible signs of the impact the crisis is having on the local environment. There are nine camps, around seventy organisations and consultancies. Foreign aid workers have started to have an influence on local culture and not everyone is happy about this. Girls see Western women wearing trousers, walking around like men. And there is more money floating around. Towns such as El Fasher or Nyala have become more expensive than Khartoum. Everything – rent, bottled water – is three times the price it used to be.

The long-term consequences of this conflict are unknown, but the damage to the social fabric is clearly devastating. Women who have been raped, sometimes in front of their husbands, feel their marriage has changed. Divorce is frequent. And then there are the children who are the outcome of rape. Children without fathers. They look different. When they are small they are often picked on by other children because of their looks. Halimah recalls a girl of sixteen who already had two children by different fathers. She gave birth to the first when she was thirteen. Two years later she was raped again.

The walls of the Africa Hotel are a dirty white. From time to time an acrid bubble of gas rises up the tubes in the bathroom and fills the room with the stench of rotting water. The furniture is flimsy and unconvincing, as if none of it was really meant to be used, but is simply a collection of stage props. The coat stand is made of tubular metal. It has green arms with yellow spheres on the end protruding from every side. As soon as you try to hang anything on it, a shirt, say, it keels over. The whirr of the fan drowns out the buzz of the neon light.

In the early hours the sound of the *azzan* echoes from a great distance as the mosques compete in their call to prayer. There is no order to them as they scramble over one another in a jumble, rolling on and on. Each has his own distinct style and tone. Some are more melodious than others. Some are simply painfully out of tune. The sounds float on the wind, rising and falling beneath the moan of aircraft engines. The noise from the planes is a constant howl as they take off and land continuously. The big jets make the glass rattle in the windows while the rumble of the heavy cargo planes heading out to feed the refugee camps is a reminder of what is happening in Darfur. Whenever their thunder fades the birds swarm through the trees chirping in confused fashion. The *azzan* gives way to a boy reading from the Quran. You fall asleep again and wake to the plaintive thump of a solitary hammer somewhere nearby. The main road outside used to be a simple, unlined two-lane strip of tarmac running south. Now there are eight lanes, all separated by high pavements so that it resembles a cattle run or a bowling alley. It appears to have been designed by a certified maniac. Perhaps an engineer who believed that authority must be literally imposed on society. Cars swerve wildly, trying to find the right lane. Pedestrians remain stranded on these barriers waiting for a break in the endless stream of flying metal to fling themselves across.

The streets of the New Extension, or *Amarat* as it is called, used to be well-dressed tarmac, with kerbs and concrete pavements to hold them in place. But time has undone this order and they now resemble withered tracks winding through a rural village, staggered by enormous potholes and stony ruts. Desultory goats trudge along through the dust. Many of the houses have been converted into offices and now house non-governmental organisations (NGOs) and obscure subdivisions of the UN, the only ones to whom never-ending disaster spells opportunity. They sweep by imperiously in bulky SUVs that bounce through the trenches with ease, enormous fat wheels crunching what is left of the tarmac into a peppery black gravel. They chase after one another through clouds of dust as if this was just another section of the Dakar Rally, leaving ordinary cars stranded on turtle humps, their tiny wheels spinning hopelessly in the air.

As the days go by I begin to have a growing feeling that I am losing all sense of purpose. I am being sucked into an inertia that takes me back to my listless years as a teenager, when life appeared to lack purpose and nothing ever seemed to happen. Trapped in the ennui that seems to be the natural state of existence in this place, it is a struggle to get anything done at all. The hopelessness is insidious and seeps into your being, leaving you with a sense of unmitigated despair.

I had been hoping to find a way out to Darfur, to see what is going on there for myself, but my plans fall through. The Oxfam press officer in London had been enthusiastic when I contacted her. She thought she could get me out there and put me in touch with her counterpart in Khartoum, who turned out to be an elusive disappointment. Contacting him proves a fruitless waste of time. When we do manage to meet up he is cagey. We sit and drink tea at O-Zone, a chic café frequented by expats. From the outset he is determined to demonstrate how at ease he is in this country and spends several minutes chatting idly on the phone with one of his drivers, apparently for my benefit. I begin to think that perhaps Oxfam was a mistake. This is a difficult time for NGOs generally in this country, and for those with a Christian background it is even harder. My recommendation from London now carries little weight. I struggle to understand where the lack of trust stems from, but the conversation is clearly going nowhere until eventually he comes clean: 'I really know nothing about you,' he admits finally. 'You could be with the security services as far as I know.'

Maybe I was getting in the way of his saving the country. A similar experience awaited me at the British Council where, after a long wait, I was subjected to a tedious, self-serving list of platitudes by the rather condescending director. I wanted to talk about the translation of local writers into English, but this was not of interest. Literature generally was not of interest. The library I recalled fondly had disappeared along with the old premises. In its place was a single shelf of books on language, economics and computers, along with a clutch of Nick Hornby novels. The British Council has become a glorified business school, a travel agency trying to stir up business for colleges in the UK seeking lucrative foreign students as their clientele. He even managed to get in a complaint about the French. Perhaps it is the English abroad, or maybe I have manoeuvred myself into the same position as the effendis a century ago; too familiar with British ways for them to be comfortable with me.

There is more suspicion waiting for me in the lobby of a downtown hotel, a cool, dark enclave in the midst of the hot, bright labyrinth of streets around the Arab market, the Souk al-Araby. This is traditionally where traders arrived over the centuries, bringing their goods to exchange. A tall man wearing the traditional white gellabiya and imma along with an incongruous set of sunglasses is waiting for me. He could be a trader in the market, but he is a lawyer. He looks up as I approach. I am five minutes late, but he looks ready to leave. He looks at me incredulously when I produce my voice recorder.

'Are you really going to use that?'

'Why not?' I ask.

'No reason,' he shrugs. 'If you are not afraid.'

His tone implies that I reconsider. The Plaza Hotel feels like a narrow, enclosed space, cut off from the world by smoked glass that sits awkwardly in warped aluminium frames. Outside, the street is noisy and crowded. People mill around, microbuses, auto-rickshaws and donkey carts bump past one another along the hot, uneven streets. In contrast, the lobby is limpid and motionless. Nothing moves. I have heard that most hotels are swarming with security agents and informers, but this one looks dead and deserted. Facing me there is a mirror that runs the length of one wall and is intended to give the impression of space. I can easily watch everyone in the room without turning my head. Nearby is a group of Arab businessmen.

'I didn't want to meet you,' the lawyer mutters unhappily. If it wasn't for a mutual friend of ours he wouldn't have come, he says. It also explains why he chose this place, neutral ground. There is something straight and no-nonsense about him. I get the feeling that he is a busy man who doesn't like to have his time wasted. He sits close to the arm rest of the long sofa and I place the Sony next to his arm. It is a discreet little machine and will only attract attention if someone is looking for something out of the ordinary.

He represents a network of Darfur lawyers stationed in Khartoum. They are concerned, broadly speaking, with defending human rights violations in Nyala, El Fasher and Geneina. They deal with cases of rape, land appropriation and culpable homicide and provide their assistance free in the form of legal aid. Most of their clients are internally displaced persons, or IDPs. Much of their support comes from foreign NGOs. This puts them in a vulnerable position. Receiving money from Western donors lays them open to the charge of being agents of foreign powers. The legal procedures involved are further complicated by the fact that the accused are often National Intelligence and Security Service

(NISS) operatives who have immunity; even if they have committed a criminal act, you can't prosecute them. He cites one recent case in Geneina in which a man killed two people in one afternoon, in broad daylight.

'How did he kill them?' I ask.

'He shot them with a Kalash,' he says casually, glancing quickly over his shoulder.

The culprit was arrested, but there followed an attack on the prison and he was liberated. At the nearby police station nobody even went outside to see what was going on. Today the same man is free to wander around the market in Geneina with his own bodyguard.

'We have so many cases of rape where the victims have clearly identified the rapist.' Nothing can be done. 'A thief stole a camel. They caught the man with the camel and took him to prison. A group of armed men came and got him out.'

There are too many weapons, no security and no law. If armed robbery and violent crime are hard to prosecute, cases involving land claims are even more complicated. A law was passed giving anyone the right to settle on land from which people had fled. And trying to make a case about land rights is a good way to get yourself killed. I ask him how he came to be involved in such a dangerous field. He holds up his hands. 'I can't say no,' he shrugs. When someone comes asking for help he feels obliged to try, but it isn't easy and the results are not encouraging. Someone in West Darfur approached him claiming that his sheep had been stolen. The victim identified the culprit and a case was opened. One night three men turned up and simply killed the man.

'A colleague of mine working in the US pointed out to me that there are actually no crimes in Darfur, because effectively there are no laws being enforced on the ground for people to break.'

The police have outdated weapons. The other side have more powerful guns, heavy-calibre mounted weapons, like Dushkas and Garanovs. You can't fight them with a Kalashnikov. At a meeting a few days ago someone came up to him and told him that they had found 15,000 weapons in their village. All of this means that, even if the conflict were to end tomorrow, the business of restoring social order would still take a long time and a lot of hard work. As for the Janjaweed – the notorious militia blamed for much of the violence in Darfur – they are hard to track down because they travel on horseback.

'They wear khaki and carry government identity cards. You can't touch them. They come from the army. They get a salary. They are hired on a very haphazard basis, given a gun and about eight hundred rounds. They are told to come back for more when they run out.'

He himself was born near Geneina, which is one reason why he feels very close to the people in Darfur. And he was once in government himself. In the mirror behind him, I notice one of the receptionists circling, watching us closely.

'Where do you begin to solve a problem like Darfur?' I ask.

'You need time. There is no security. This is the first step. There must be security.' The people have to feel safe, protected from the Antonov bombers and helicopter gunships, as well as from the Janjaweed on the ground. The Janjaweed have to be disarmed and relocated to a separate area. A peacekeeping force has to show they are as strong, if not stronger, than the Janjaweed or else people will not stay. And there is another problem: the rebel militias themselves.

'I say this and I am in opposition to the government; but unless these groups come together with a united political aim, peace will never be achieved.'

The Janjaweed are no longer as homogenous as they might once have been. Now their ranks include people from Chad, Burkina Faso, Cameroon and Senegal. As there were not enough Janjaweed locally others were brought in from further afield. People led their tribes across the borders from Chad and even as far away as Nigeria and they paid them. The leaders of the Janjaweed are known to be here in Khartoum, like Musa Hilal, who owns a building in Manshia reputed to be worth two billion old Sudanese pounds – about two million dollars. There are parts of Khartoum North that are allegedly inhabited by former members of the Janjaweed militias. The big names can no longer stay in Darfur because it is too dangerous for them.

'This is a trans-African problem,' the lawyer tells me. After five years these Janjaweed fighters are given Sudanese nationality knowing they can settle on the land they have helped to 'liberate'. His own village south of Geneina has been occupied by settlers from Chad. They have taken it over and are now planting in the fields. And it's not just the border tribes now. One day he noticed a man in one of the markets wearing a cowboy hat; 'I thought the hat was funny. He looked interesting, and I wanted a photograph of him, so I asked someone to take a picture of me standing next to the man.' They started talking and he realised from his accent that the man was not local. When he enquired where the man was from he turned out to be from the Mahameed in Niger.

'When I asked what had brought him all this way, he said that back home they were told that the land here was unoccupied, that cattle were wandering around free for the taking. So they came.'

The western region remained independent for longer than any other part of the country. It is something the people there are proud of. Darfur only joined the Sudan in 1916. Neighbouring Dar Masalit was an even later addition, incorporated in 1922. The Sultanate reached its zenith at the end of the eighteenth century when it ruled both Darfur and Kordofan, and with the decline of the Funj to the east it became the leading trading partner with Egypt. The Sultan controlled everything in those days. No one could enter the country without his knowing.

The land was divided into twenty-two *hakura* – traditional divisions that were abolished by the People's Local Government Act of 1971, which replaced them with local councils whose boundaries cut across old tribal lines. The idea was to devolve power away from the centre to the regions. In actual fact it simply stripped authority from local leaders and replaced them with centrally appointed administrators. Two decades later, the current regime introduced another novel twist by declaring that the land really belonged to Allah and that ownership would henceforth be decided on the basis of religious allegiance. The new areas were given Islamic names. In their bid for complete control the current regime felt it had to do away with all previous systems of rule. And so the old figures of authority – the omda, the sheikh, etc. – were replaced by another means of control and the land was divided up into smaller units, thereby reducing the sphere of influence even further.

By now my legal source is growing restless. He glances around him and again mentions our mutual friend, the man who put me in touch with him. 'If it wasn't for him I wouldn't have come,' he repeats. I follow his eye and find the same receptionist, still watching us in the mirror as he moves around the room, picking up ashtrays and replacing them in an apparently pointless exercise, drawing ever closer. 'There's the reason,' he says, rising to his feet abruptly. He shakes my hand briskly and turns. I watch him disappear through the smoked-glass doors, his white gellabiya swallowed up by the billowing clouds of dust and cotton blowing through the busy market streets.

Darfur's celebrity status is no better summarised than by the image of French *intello* Bernard-Henri Lévy sitting amidst the ruins of a village that has been razed to the ground. There is nothing but blackened earth, broken pots, ashes. It is a charnel house, the site where men, women and children were murdered, raped and driven from their homes. Against the backdrop of this brutality the Rive Gauche *penseur* poses in an immaculate white designer shirt. It is not simply the paradox of this elegantly dressed man in contrast to the setting that strikes me, it is the assumption that the photograph is meaningless to his audience without his presence.

He lends gravity to the situation. There is something nauseating about the whole idea of cloaking vanity, moral rectitude and outrage. The ruins of a simple hut that had no running water and no electricity before it was burned to the ground. The white shirt is a distraction begging further interrogation. Did he bring it with him for the occasion, donning it swiftly before the photo shoot? Or has he simply managed to make the journey, over land, sea and air without ruffling his clothes?

Bernard-Henri Lévy's breathless account of his journey, published in May 2007 in *Le Monde*, reads like an updated outtake of *Beau Geste*. He races across the desert while talking into his satellite telephone to contacts in Paris. He is here to bear witness, he declares, and that is exactly what the great man literally does: 'I witness it: the paraphernalia, the big guns, and the smell of a hot war and large-scale crimes against humanity. It's all there.' The grandeur of the telling makes the actual event shrivel. Still, to be fair, Lévy, for all his immaculate indignation, does avoid falling into the ditch of explaining the conflict as marauding Arabs preying on innocent Africans, fanatical Islam versus the world. But still, how did this happen, how did Darfur become a cause célèbre?

'The most vicious ethnic cleansing you've never heard of' is how columnist Nicholas Kristof introduced the conflict to readers of the *New York Times* in March 2004. It announced the start of mainstream American media interest, which soon took off on its own trajectory. That same month, Mukesh Kapila, UN coordinator for the Sudan, declared that Darfur was the world's greatest humanitarian crisis. His statement, timed to coincide with the tenth anniversary of the genocide in Rwanda, where Kapila had previously been stationed, sent the media into a frenzy. The 'angle' had been found, writes Gérard Prunier in his book on the subject, *Darfur: The Ambiguous Genocide*: 'Darfur was a genocide and the Arabs were killing the Blacks', a shorthand version of what was happening, but effective in terms of sound bites. In June 2004, the US House of Representatives passed a resolution urging President Bush to call the atrocities in Darfur 'by its rightful name: genocide'. In July, the United States Holocaust

Memorial Museum in Washington, DC, upgraded their 'genocide warning' to a 'genocide emergency', making explicit the
connection between the Holocaust and whatever was occurring in Darfur. In September of that same year, the movie *Hotel
Rwanda* was released, feeding immediately into the heightened
sense that history was repeating itself before our very eyes. The
film's star, Don Cheadle, metamorphosed into a high-profile
activist for the cause. Along with John Prendergast, former special adviser to the Clinton administration on African Affairs,
Cheadle wrote a book on the subject, *Not On Our Watch: The
Mission to End Genocide in Darfur and Beyond*, which became
an immediate bestseller. The title came from a note scribbled
by George W. Bush in the margins of a report into the lack of
American action in Rwanda during the Clinton era. The connection between Darfur and Rwanda was now firmly established in
people's minds. In April 2006 a crowd converged on the historic
Mall in Washington – the organisers estimated that between ten
and fifteen thousand people were present. They demanded an
end to the genocide in Darfur. It was a remarkable expression of
collectivity, a coming together for the sake of the plight of their
fellow man in a place most of them would, until recently, have
been unable to find on a map. The irony was that by that point
the killing was more or less over.

There was no way of stopping it. Darfur was a runaway train.
Grassroots activism ensued on an unprecedented scale. All over
the United States people became involved, from Jewish organisations to college students, everyone felt the urge to be a part of
it. Mia Farrow and Angelina Jolie put their backs to the wheel,
flying into the region, dragging the spotlight of the world media
on their heels. I felt as if I was watching a heightened, updated
version of the 1984 famine. Soon somebody would release a song,
which they did, of course; a re-recording of the Band Aid anthem,
'Do They Know It's Christmas?'. It felt as though time had stood
still for twenty years.

In 2004, the UN International Commission of Enquiry
described Darfur as a region inhabited by tribal groups that could
be classified in different ways, but without clear-cut distinctions

between them. Conflict, particularly in the previous twenty years, had increased the polarisation. The distinction between Arab and African was less a matter of ethnic or racial difference than a question of which side of the conflict you stood on. There were Africans fighting on the government side and Arabs opposed to the Janjaweed.

In August of that year, the US Congress unanimously passed a resolution declaring it a genocide. This wasn't a first. In June 1999, Congress had condemned the Sudanese government for waging 'genocidal war' in South Sudan. Still, it was a significant moment. The following month, September 2004, Secretary of State Colin Powell appeared before the Senate Foreign Relations Committee declaring that, even though it was a genocide, the US had no plans to act.

The claims were disputed by those working on the ground. According to Jean-Hervé Bradol, president of Médecins Sans Frontières, the word genocide created confusion. 'The situation is severe enough to be described for what it is – a mass repression campaign against civilians.' MSF teams working in Darfur since December 2003 had not witnessed 'The intention to kill all individuals of a particular group. We have information about massacres, but never any attempt to eliminate all the members of a specific group.' There were other considerations. MSF wanted to keep working in the region, doing what it was created to do, helping those in need. Designating the conflict a genocide would risk provoking the government into refusing them access.

There were suggestions the Bush administration was trying to divert attention from the deepening crisis in Iraq. This theory was later confirmed in a *Panorama* programme for the BBC in July 2005, when former US ambassador to the UN John Danforth stated that the characterisation of the conflict as a genocide was intended for 'internal consumption' in the run-up to the election in 2004, when Bush was duly re-elected for a second term.

By this point a popular movement had spread through colleges in the United States. On YouTube hundreds of homemade patchwork videos were posted, overlaying images of suffering and death with sentimental rock music. It wasn't long before the bands themselves were getting in on the act, wandering in deserts singing about rising up and working-class heroes.

The point being that it was no longer about Sudan. Darfur had become an American issue. It had more to do with America's need to understand itself, to see itself as a world leader, as the needle on a global moral compass. The discourse replaced comprehension with emotional rhetoric. Gore Vidal once wrote that Americans continually euphemise; they can never call anything by its name. Saul Bellow put it differently, claiming there are no Tartuffes in American literature, 'No monster hypocrites, no deep cynics.' Instead, America has 'virtuous myths' that are applied with imbecile earnestness. 'Our own experience as a people has become a source of ecstasy. And here am I, doing it, too,' he added.

Darfur offered the chance for America to believe in itself again, after the dismay of Iraq, which was fast becoming a catalogue of disaster. Here was a chance to do the right thing. Three key lobby groups provided the backbone to the activist movement. Each of them saw their own fate rewritten on the blank page of a distant land. To the Black Caucus, this was a case of Arab militias trying to exterminate black Africans. There's nothing new about government use of proxy militias to further their aims. Exploiting ethnic tensions is a well-established tactic. In the Bahr al-Ghazal region in the 1980s they were called the Murahileen. Like the Janjaweed, they preyed on civilians, razing villages to the ground. Christian organisations had a long history of saving Africans from predatory Muslims. For decades a number of congressmen had been urging support for the Sudanese People's Liberation Army (SPLA) in their fight against the North.

The term genocide carries certain legal parameters and obligations attached to it. Samantha Power summed up the issue in her book on the subject, *A Problem from Hell*, in which she writes: 'There is no simple equation linking Darfur with Rwanda and hence with Hitler.' The definition in the UN treaty suffers from what she terms 'the numbers problem': there is no consensus as to how many people have to die or be expelled from their homes for ethnic cleansing to qualify as a genocide. The problem is that if you define a percentage you would immediately grant perpetrators free rein up to that tipping point. More importantly, the law would be unable to protect anyone if it could only be applied *after* a group had been largely eliminated. In the end a broad, 'intent-based' definition was arrived at. Estimates of casualties in Darfur proved as disputed as in Iraq, with numbers ranging from around 70,000 to a high-end figure of 400,000. By 2007 mortality rates were estimated to be marginally better than they were before the war and, significantly, also lower than in parts of Khartoum. Nobody was particularly interested in the underlying historical causes and what this might mean for the country's future. If all the focus is on explaining the violence as racially or ethnically motivated we risk missing other essential factors, such as climate change, which played a key role; with delayed and insufficient rains forcing herders to move onto farming land earlier than normal, breaking the interdependence between the two groups. Without addressing this issue we run the risk of perpetuating the conditions for other similar conflicts to arise in the future.

Darfur's exceptionalism is also explained by the fact that it does not conflict with American interests in the region; on the contrary, it reinforces them. American companies had recently invested in a $3.7 billion oil deal with Sudan's western neighbour Chad, including a pipeline leading through Cameroon to the Gulf of Guinea, but no inroads had been made into Sudan, where 60 per cent of the oil concessions belonged to China. In March 2007, an open letter signed by some of the most prominent writers in Europe, including several Nobel laureates, called on the EU to intervene and impose sanctions on the leaders of Bashir's regime: 'The Europe which allowed Auschwitz and failed in Bosnia must not tolerate the murder in Darfur … We must not once again betray our European civilization by watching and waiting while another civilization in Africa is destroyed.'

Detaching the conflict from political and economic interests allowed Darfur to be seen, like Rwanda in 1994, and Eastern Congo in 1998, as yet another inexplicable outburst of internecine violence of the kind that regularly convulses the African continent. Most of the time they happen in the shadows; Darfur, conversely, was taking place under the spotlight. A pseudo-liberal agenda emerged whereby it was possible to simultaneously oppose the war in Iraq and support the invasion of Darfur. It fed into the conviction that Western impotence was due to a confused sense of values generated by guilt over European imperialism, slavery and racism.

In Ted Braun's 2007 film *Darfur Now*, Don Cheadle explains how, visiting Africa for the first time some years earlier to film *Hotel Rwanda* (2004), he had been struck by the similarities between that story and what was happening in Darfur. It made the conflict personal. In February 2005 Cheadle visited the IDP camps as part of a congressional fact-finding mission. In the film he travels to China and Egypt with his friend George Clooney trying to raise awareness, and one gets a sense of how this became a personal mission. They return to address a press conference at the UN in New York. 'Someday this will end,' Clooney solemnly informs the assembly, 'and then we will ask where were these United Nations at the time?' Towards the end of the film we see Luis Moreno Ocampo, Chief Prosecutor for the International Criminal Court, standing in The Hague smiling wistfully to himself. He imagines what it would be like if the people of Darfur could be in the courtroom to observe the guilty parties being tried. His is a civilising mission. Darfur is a metaphor for the world gone bad. 'If we succeed,' he says, 'Darfur will be like Argentina; not perfect, but at least people are not killing each other. If we fail, in twenty-five years the world will be like Darfur.'

PART TWO

A HISTORY OF LOST CHAPTERS
2009

'We shall stand as a lighthouse for peace,
tranquility and compassion in this world.'
Ismail al-Azhari
Sudan's first prime minister, 1956

'The enemy is within. It is us.'
Mansour Khalid

The National Museum stands a stone's throw from the Mogran, where the two rivers meet. The last time I was here, six months after the 1989 coup, the upper galleries were chained shut, barring centuries of Christian Nubia from public view. This was Islam at its most inward-looking and intolerant, in denial of history. Anything that came before the word of Muhammed was worthless. Closing a wing of the museum illustrated the level of pious hysteria that reigned at the time. Merely allowing people to see such objects might expose them to accusations of idol worship. There were rumours that holes had been drilled into the sides of the towering basalt figures outside the entrance to the museum. Idols being anathema to Islam, the holes would neutralise any powers they had. It seemed like a bizarre thing to do, one paranoid superstition to overcome another. It was to be another twelve years before the Taliban dynamited the fifty-metre-high Buddhas in Bamiyan, and more still until Daesh, or Islamic State, went on the rampage in Nineveh, Mosul and Palmyra, but the drive is the same: to erase the existence of any truth other than the one you subscribe to. This narrow view holds that museums serve no purpose other than to illuminate modern Muslim existence as the culmination of history.

To fully make sense of a country you have to understand its history, and here we have a problem: in the absence of written sources, the passage of time goes unnoticed. Kingdoms rose and fell, civilisations came and went, having no apparent impact on the progress of mankind. They vanished almost without trace. Each successive century wiped the slate clean.

A few historians challenged this view. Prominent among these was Basil Davidson. To overcome the lack of documentation, he believed it was necessary to work 'intuitively', which is to say that certain assumptions were made for which there was no hard evidence at the time, in the belief that archaeologists would eventually uncover the truth.

Africa was seen as an unknown quantity where history had never been recorded, at least not in the way that convention deemed it should. In 1830 Hegel declared that 'Africa is no historical part of the world', a confirmation of this absence of documentation. This goes some way to explaining why nineteenth-century European powers viewed Africa as little more than an opportunity, a vacant piece of property to be divided among themselves.

Egypt was the exception. Europe's fascination with Ancient Egypt was triggered by Napoleon Bonaparte's extraordinary expedition in 1798. But everything south of the Valley of the Kings was ignored. The best-documented region of Sudanese history has to be Nubia, the area straddling the border between Egypt and Sudan. Linked to the pharaohs for centuries, Nubia was powerful enough to rule Ancient Egypt in the fabled 25th Dynasty, yet it remains largely an enigma to this day.

Islam, along with Arabic, arrived with the decline and fall of Christian Nubia in the early fourteenth century, and was only consolidated with the emergence further south of the first Muslim dynasty in Sennar, the Funj Sultanate, in the sixteenth century. Over that time the Nubian Christians maintained a treaty with the Egyptians that lasted for six centuries, paying a tribute of slaves every year in return for gifts of grain. The Nubian script was transcribed using a modified Greek alphabet, much as the Copts did,

but it remains largely impenetrable. Without a Rosetta Stone to shed
light on the language, the history of Nubia vanished into oblivion,
buried under rock, sand and, eventually, water, the final page of this
lost history being written by the completion of the Aswan High
Dam in 1970. The subsequent flooding of the Nile Valley erased a
vast tract of land some 500 kilometres long, covering what was buried there under water. The dam was needed for the modernisation
of Egypt and so the past was traded for a brighter future.

Pot shards and unfinished stories – the blank pages of a history
that will only ever be fragmentary, despite recent efforts to understand it. On the Sudanese side of the border the archaeological
sites were abandoned to their fate. It is still not uncommon to
come across statues, shattered figures, objects lying about in the
sand as if discarded only yesterday: a hillside strewn with granite
rams, a basalt foot on a pedestal.

The ancient history of these lands, of the civilisations that
evolved and thrived here, drinking from the same river that flows
past the museum today, is almost completely absent from the education curriculum. I learned nothing about Sudan's past at school.
History lessons were limited, and then, bizarrely, we studied
things like Bismarck, realpolitik and the bombing of Hiroshima
and Nagasaki. Interesting though these things were, they weren't
exactly pertinent to our immediate situation. History, the books
seemed to be telling us, was a European concern, and not something we needed to worry about. That is probably the real reason
the archaeological sites are so neglected, and, even now, rarely
visited. The distant past is to be distrusted, not embraced. And
where does that leave us?

The little girl weaves between the rows of stationary cars as she pushes her sister in a wheelchair. The odd thing about them is how carefree they both seem. Their faces are bright and cheerful, as if this was some kind of a game, racing between the cars. They stop beside each window and hold out their hands. The eldest is about twelve. The girl in the chair is a little younger. She looks thin but healthy, except for the fact that she has no legs.

The traffic lights at the bottom of Mek Nimr Street have the honour of being known simply as *al-Stop*. It is the slowest junction in town. The narrow tree-lined streets, originally designed with sleepy donkey carts and the occasional colonial officer's automobile in mind, are now choked with vehicles of every shape and size. As the drivers sit and while away the minutes, young men slip between the aisles of stalled vehicles hawking the most unlikely objects: ironing boards, lighters shaped like giant yellow matches, mirrors, plastic washstands adorned with Mercedes-Benz emblems, padded mountain jackets in case a blizzard suddenly descends, fluffy pink acrylic dogs and wall clocks. No one ever buys a clock, time being one commodity everyone seems to have plenty of.

All of these goods look new and bizzarely out of context. They all came in by container from the country of modern wonders; from factories in places like Guangzhou, made by workers who might be surprised to see their goods here. The statistics say that in the Pearl River Delta an estimated 40,000 fingers a year are lost or broken in factory accidents, that China has the highest rate of cancer in the world, and that, out of an urban population of 560 million, 500 million do not have access to clean drinking water. It is normal to work seventy hours a week for less than a dollar a day. And here we are at the other end of the rainbow, where, if you suggested working seventy hours a week, you would be laughed out of town. Cheap, disposable goods make everything affordable, not just to a small elite, but to the impoverished masses. Here are the luxuries of the world laid before you at an affordable price. A magical carpet of modern miracles, China is irresistible to Africa. The roads, railways, dams, power plants that are springing up all over the continent are replacing antiquated colonial relics and ponderous Cold War gifts. Until the Chinese came along there was no way to do this. The downside is visible on every street corner where carts are loaded high with imported fruit and vegetables. Local farmers are in trouble. Many of them owe money to the banks and if they default on loans they can lose their land. Those who are working have a hard time competing with the boxes that arrive daily from the Far East.

The two girls move aside as the cars shuffle forward a few metres, only to come to a halt again. I wonder how the little one lost her legs. Was it a shell, or a bomb dropped on her village? Up until the late nineties the Sudan Air Force was so badly equipped they would resort to rolling 100-kilogram bombs straight off the loading ramps of antiquated Antonov cargo planes.

The girls are a vivid reminder of the war, and the Comprehensive Peace Agreement that ended it in 2005. The CPA closed the book on twenty-one years of conflict between North and South and set out a complex process of steps intended to lead to the consolidation of peace. A six-year interim period was laid out during which the country would be ruled by a Government of National Unity, with power shared between North and South. We are in the middle of that period now. At the end of that time two things are meant to happen: multi-party elections and a referendum to allow Southerners to decide if they wished to break away and form their own independent country.

To my taxi driver the Southerners are an unwanted problem. 'They have no business here,' he says angrily, hunched morosely over the wheel of his Korean-made microbus, known locally as an *amjad*. 'We have nothing to do with them and they have nothing to do with us.' The sooner they all go back to where they came from the better. 'What if they don't want to go back?' I ask. It is a question many people are asking. What will happen to the Southerners who have been settled here for decades – an estimated two million refugees who made their way north to the capital during the war? How will they go back, where to, and what awaits them there? Many have made a life for themselves here. They are city people now. Why should they want to move back to towns and villages with no electricity or running water? 'That's all taken care of,' the driver assures me confidently; the CPA gives them six years to sort things out. After that they are on their own.

This interpretation of the Comprehensive Peace Agreement should be of concern. Instead of taking it as the start of a lasting collaboration that will heal the wounds and cement the bonds between North and South to prevent war from flaring up again, it is commonly seen as a solution to what is often referred to as the 'Southern problem'. So much for unity and justice for all. The driver feels he has nothing in common with the Southerners – there is no sense that they belong to the same nation as he does. While the CPA recognises the existence of different cultures, it contains nothing about the task of reinventing Sudanese identity in such a way that would move towards achieving that parity. As we drive on, finally clearing the junction, the two girls settle themselves down under a tree on a patch of dust they have made their own, to wait for the lights to change and the cars to halt so that their work can begin again.

At around 5 p.m. on 30 July 2005, a Russian-made Kazan Mi-172 helicopter lifted off from Entebbe airport in Uganda. Aboard was the first vice president of the newly instated interim Government of National Unity (GNU) and president of the Government of South Sudan (GOSS), John Garang de Mabior. Altogether, including crew and entourage, there were thirteen people on the aircraft. It was late in the day to be setting out. Light was already fading and the weather forecast did not look good. The flight to the SPLM headquarters at New Site on the Ugandan border should have taken just over two hours. They never arrived. The helicopter went down in the Zulia Mountains only a short distance from their destination. Everyone on board was killed.

A commission of investigation was launched in both Sudan and Uganda. The helicopter belonged to Ugandan President Museveni. Both the flight data recorder and cockpit voice recorder boxes were the property of the Ugandan government. The investigating commission included members from both North and South Sudan as well as a US Homeland Security officer; ballistics and explosives specialists, pathologists, police officers and aviation experts. The commission travelled to Moscow to question the technical staff at the International Aviation Centre as well as the makers of the Kazan. They visited the site of the crash, they interviewed eyewitnesses and people connected to the flight and the first vice president. Satellite images of the crash were requested through the Ministry of Defence. They put together a reconstruction of what had most probably happened.

It was raining that evening and the sky was overcast. The helicopter had been recently overhauled and updated in Moscow. It had been back in operation for little over a week, clocking only twenty hours' flying time before the crash. The Ugandan pilot and co-pilot were experienced and well-trained. The explosives and ballistics team concluded that no firearms or explosives were involved. At the nearby SPLA camp of New Cush, a commander reported hearing the sound of a helicopter and wondered why anyone should be flying in such bad weather. He was relieved when he heard the helicopter veer right, away from the clouds. Later on, he saw a light in the distance but it wasn't until the next morning that a search party found the wreckage of the helicopter, still burning.

The flight data recorder was damaged by fire, but on the cockpit voice recorder the co-pilot can be heard urging the pilot to climb as the helicopter lost altitude. They were facing mountains that are 2,000 metres high. Shortly after that it would appear that the machine started to become unstable in the bad weather and there ensued a discussion about diverting to another landing site. Up to nine minutes before the crash occurred the helicopter was still on course. Seven minutes later, with less than two minutes to live, they appear to have decided to descend, thinking to fly under the cloud. At this point there is some indication of an error. A discrepancy was later found between the two GPS devices on board, indicating that at least one of them had been set to the wrong altitude at the start of the flight. Was this simply error on the part of one of the pilots, or something more sinister? Resetting a GPS to an incorrect altimeter reading is quite easily done. As a method of bringing down the aircraft, however, it hardly seems reliable, even factoring in the bad weather. The cockpit recordings give no indication that the crash was intentional, that it was a suicidal plunge by either pilot. The report suggests the simplest conclusion of all, that the most likely cause of the accident was a combination of bad weather and human error.

Despite the apparent rigour of the investigation and the lack of any obvious signs of foul play, many will never accept that it was a simple accident. There was too much at stake. At that precise moment in history, after two decades of war and the victory that the CPA heralded, this was the dawn of a new age, and Garang was the man who had brought it about. The country was finally united and he was there at the top as vice president, just as he had promised he would be. As one man who was close to him put it: 'It hasn't been proven *yet*.'

Certainly there was no doubt in the minds of the thousands who ran riot through the streets of Khartoum when news of his death broke. The disturbances lasted three days. Officially, the number of people who died was put at twenty-four, unofficially 130, but others say there were many more. Damage to property, to shops, homes and cars was considerable.

The fates could not have conspired to time Garang's death more poignantly. It has all the air of a Greek tragedy: the exiled king returning to take his rightful seat on the throne only for death to intervene, snatching him away in his hour of triumph. For over two decades he had fought to liberate the country from tyranny. Over a million people turned out to greet him when he arrived in Khartoum to be officially instated as vice president of the interim Government of National Unity after twenty-one years of war. He had been in power for twenty-one days when he died.

John Garang was a complex figure, to some a messiah, to others an authoritarian who would not abide dissent. This intransigence led, in the early 1990s, to a major fracture within the SPLA. A number of commanders broke away, deciding they could no longer serve a man who refused to allow them a say. To many in the South he was a father figure, a beacon of hope who promised freedom and dignity. In the wake of his death, a process of beatification began. 'It is the body that has gone,' his wife declared tearfully on the radio in an attempt to calm the anger. 'His spirit, his vision, his programme – we're going to implement them.' It was a claim that proved to be short-lived. It soon became apparent that he must have been among the last of those who didn't favour secession.

Garang had been in pursuit of a myth, that of becoming the first Southern president of the country, not just the South. His notion of a 'New Sudan' envisaged the inclusion of all the country's marginalised peoples. On the day he died he was scheduled to meet representatives of the Sudan Liberation Army and the Justice and Equality Movement, the two main rebel groups in Darfur, a conflict he had vowed to resolve as his first priority. Unity had been his goal right from the moment he took up arms against Khartoum back in the 1980s. It was the cause of his strife with many of his comrades in arms in the 1990s. Along with unity went the aim of liberating the country from the oppressive centralist and sectarian politics that had dominated the arena for so long. It was an audacious dream, whatever you thought of the man.

Born in the town of Wangulei, in Eastern Twic, part of the Jonglei region, Garang was a Dinka. His parents were simple farmers with no education. They had seven children, of whom John was the second youngest. He did not finish secondary school in Rumbek, going off instead to join the Anyanya rebel army, which had been fighting for secession since 1955. It was a short-lived war. Garang had only been a captain for six months, four of which were spent in training, when the Addis Ababa Accord brought the end of the First Civil War in 1972. He never experienced battle nor the hardships of life in the bush. At first he actually opposed the peace agreement, claiming that the time was not ripe for peace.

He only accepted it when he realised that he was in a minority and there was no real support for his position within the Anyanya movement.

With the end of the war, the Anyanya forces were absorbed into the national army. Garang moved swiftly up through the ranks, going on to Fort Benning, Georgia, for advanced training. Described as a studious young man, his head always in a book, his mind filled with big ideas, he graduated from Iowa State University in 1981 with a Ph.D. in agriculture, a subject that remained a lifelong interest. Farming, he believed, would transform his homeland. He even taught for a spell at Khartoum University's Agricultural College in Shambat.

The remarkable achievement of the Addis Ababa Accord was to last ten short years. By 1983, Nimeiri was busy unravelling all the good work he had done. In a deep economic hole, he was desperate to get his hands on the rich oil fields in the South and made the decision to replace Southern troops in the Bentiu area with Northerners. Predictably, the result was mutiny. Nimeiri compounded his error by sending Garang to deal with the problem. Garang went to Bor, listened to the grievances of the mutineers and decided to throw in his lot with them. Nimeiri, used to dealing with the grumblings of the increasingly toothless old Anyanya leadership, had been lulled into a false sense of security. And so, in May 1983, the Southern People's Liberation Army was born and the Second Civil War began.

The SPLA headquarters at New Site lies right on the Ugandan border. The helicopter struck the ground at an altitude of approximately 1,650 metres at a position of 04° north. The symbolism is striking. There he was, the exile returning to reclaim his kingdom, poised on the edge of a new era, flying along the borderline of a vast expanse of a country that stretched all the way up to 22° north, a full 18° of latitude rich in diversity and variety, which until now had been entangled in internecine conflict, fractricide, unending suffering and oppression. To Garang, as he floated down over those misty green hills, it must have seemed as though everything was finally in his grasp, as if he were literally standing on the threshold of infinite possibility.

The first time I set eyes on Yasir Arman I was immediately struck by the short, powerfully built man. There was something quite unsettling about his intense, unwavering gaze. Here was a man who had seen death and it had left its trace on him. Arman is that rarity, a Northerner who had fought in the SPLA alongside Garang for twenty years, rising through the ranks to become one of his close friends and trusted commanders.

This makes him an interesting choice as presidential candidate,[*] which is what he is the second time we meet. It's a sign that the Sudan People's Liberation Movement (SPLM) is trying to distance itself from the idea that it is exclusively a Southern movement. It's a hard sell, trying to convince Northerners that they can benefit from Garang's vision of a pluralist Sudan. Elections are set for April and the day we meet is the closing day of their annual conference. I wait for him in the garden of the party offices in the New Extension – another converted villa. After days of cancelled appointments and phone calls back and forth from one intermediary to another, he sweeps in, only an hour late and trailed by

[*]The presidential elections were delayed and eventually held in 2010 when Arman came second to Bashir's 68 per cent, with 22 per cent of the vote.

his entourage. This time I see a different man. Polished, smooth, immaculately dressed in an expensive suit, this is Arman the politician. People greet him as he walks in. Cars wait in the street with their engines running. Before we talk he offers to show me around.

As we move briskly from room to darkened, deserted room – it is late in the evening and everyone has gone home – Arman flicks on the lights to reveal, over and over, rows of photographs lining the walls. The subject of each and every one of them is John Garang. A man for all people. The Unifier, the great Liberator. Many capture the moment of his triumphant return in early 2005: a sea of faces stretched out beneath the podium, as far as the eye can see. It's hard to overstate the significance of that moment. The crowds who turned out to hail him were an ample demonstration that the capital was no longer exclusively Northern. Here was the unity he had fought for, displayed in all those young, hopeful, upturned faces.

That afternoon I had watched Arman at the close of the SPLM annual general conference. In itself it was a chaotic affair. Journalists crowded into a room cluttered with bulky tables and chairs, chattering among themselves, taking pictures of one another to pass the time. An hour dragged by, and then another. Nobody was sure who was going to appear. Finally, a small man in an oversized suit stepped forward. He wore a canary-yellow shirt with a bright red tie that hung down to his knees. This was Deputy Chairman James Wanni Igga. 'Rome was not built in a day,' he announced ponderously in English. There followed a series of long-winded statements, commitments to the CPA, to the idea of unity, to combating corruption. Throughout this, Arman sat on stage, stiff-backed and silent, an intimidating figure, his powerful bulk buttoned into a tightly fitting shark-grey suit – different from the dark one he appeared in later. What the SPLM really needed at this point was a decent tailor. Arman, while not speaking for the most part, seemed keenly aware of everything around him, but also acutely uncomfortable. He smiled when the rest of us smiled.

In his book, whose title translates rather awkwardly as *A Presence in the Tsunami of His Absence*, Arman evokes comparisons with Mandela and Mahatma Gandhi, whose non-violent struggle and self-reliance were, according to Arman, an inspiration. Arman's narrative seeks to place Garang within a broader global context. In this version he was fighting not just for the rights of the Sudanese people but for Africans in general. This places the SPLA's fight alongside the great liberation struggles of history, from civil rights and Martin Luther King, to Stokely Carmichael and the Black Panthers, to the ANC and, more curiously, Bobby Sands, the IRA gunman who died during a hunger strike at the Maze Prison in 1981. The sticking point in the matter of creating a national identity lay in the idea of the so-called 'Southern Question'. What we had to do, according to Arman, was start thinking in terms of the 'Sudan Question'. It was important to look at the national framework rather than stigmatising the South.

Arman's real education began in prison after he was arrested as a student activist while studying law at Khartoum University. A less romantic version of this story claims that he went on the run after being involved in the death of a National Islamic Front supporter who died in a clash during a demonstration. In either case, some months later he was en route to Addis Ababa. There, near the Itang refugee camp, home to some 200,000 Sudanese refugees who had fled the fighting, he was trained comprehensively. The first time they met Garang took him aside and told him: 'I want you to shake hands with every one of the men who will be fighting alongside you.' There were 3,000 of them. In twenty-one years in the jungle, Arman tells me, Garang never, ever considered the idea of secession. According to Arman there are over 570 ethnic groups in the Sudan and more than 130 languages, and a history that goes back 7,000 years. Garang offered a new political model that would encompass all of them.

Garang was a child of the sixties. Born in 1945, he arrived in the United States in time to be caught up in the anti-war movement. In Africa, these were years of optimism, dominated by colossal figures such as Kwame Nkrumah and Julius Nyerere. The talk was of Pan-Africanism, of fraternity and cooperation between the newly independent states. This struck Garang as ironic; before you could begin talking about African unity surely you had to address the question of unity within Sudan itself?

Arman describes the long march through the bush of Eastern Equatoria when he became close to Garang. This was the rainy season in the autumn of 1988. Between bouts of malaria, heavy rains and the hot winds of the *simooma* they talked about the old civilisations of the Nile Valley: Cheikh Anta Diop's Afrocentric take on Ancient Egyptian history. Identifying the inhabitants of Nile Valley civilisation as black Africans provided Garang with an argument that placed the Sudan he envisaged at the heart of a long and diverse history.

There is no question about the country's need for a new model. Beyond the combined total of thirty-seven years of war in the South, unrest spread to the Beja in the East and to Kajjabar in the North where protests against the Chinese construction of the Hamdab Dam near Merowe have resulted in deaths. And then there is Darfur – a further symptom of the same dysfunctional malaise and Garang's top priority at the time of his death.

'Before we are Arabs or African,' Garang liked to say, 'before we are Muslims or Christians, before we are Northerners or Southerners, we are Sudanese.' But convincing the Northerner that the SPLM has something to offer them is not going to be an easy task. The movement is associated with the struggle in the South. When the vice president, Ali Osman Taha, negotiated the Comprehensive Peace Agreement with John Garang, unity was the goal towards which both of them were working. The clause stipulating the South's right to hold a referendum was included at the last minute as a mere formality, a concession to the secessionists in Garang's ranks with whom he had long been at odds.

Yasir Arman's eyes gleam with fervour in the harsh white incandescence of the neon strip lighting that lines the garden walls of the yard. 'Stability is a paradox,' he declares, as bottles of water are placed in front of us. 'It is very far and very close at the same time. We can go to heaven or hell. We are on the edge.' The country has reached the point of make or break. 'Sudan is now a Shakespearean theme,' he says, warming to the task. 'To be or not to be.'

It's fair to say the SPLM is finding the transition to peacetime politics something of a challenge. Arman's awkwardness in his tight suits, his obvious discomfort in facing an audience, make perfect sense when you consider that he spent decades fighting a bush war. These are men of violence, more at ease in combat fatigues. The loss of their leader leaves the SPLM toiling with the lack of a figure of Garang's stature and charisma to carry their ideals forward. Garang envisaged a nationwide uprising, with people all over the country rising up to join their brothers in the South, but that was twenty years ago.

The New Sudan that Garang had in mind was one where the imbalance of power between centre and periphery was overcome, where the sectarian, elitist elements that dominated Sudanese politics were replaced by a climate of mutual respect that would assure unity and justice for all, regardless of religion, sex or ethnicity. The term 'New Sudan' first surfaced at peace negotiations in 1986 at Koka Dam. At the time, the SPLA had been in a strong position militarily and Khartoum felt threatened. The then prime minister, Sadig al-Mahdi (the great-grandson of the original Mahdi), derailed the peace deal. It cost him the support of his generals, who were weary of war. They were also afraid of losing their authority to the informal local militias that had been created to propagate war on the cheap. Sadig didn't last much longer. Three years later, in June 1989, he was displaced by a Revolutionary Command Council of military officers led by Omar al-Bashir, but the opportunity for peace was gone and the war was to continue for another sixteen years.

Whether Garang would have been capable of delivering that vision of a country of equality and peace is a question that will never be answered. Rather than a successor to Gandhi or Mandela, however, Garang was a survivor. He displayed a chameleon-like ability to change with the times. In the 1980s when his support came from the Stalinist regime in Addis Ababa he declared himself a Marxist. In the 1990s he allied himself with the West where he was seen by Israel and the Christian right in America as a champion in the struggle against political Islam. Some twenty million dollars' worth of military equipment passed through

Eritrea, Ethiopia and Uganda to Garang and his men. Perhaps it is naive to assume that it is possible to remain true to one's ideals over such a long time. Either way, the question remains as to what values Garang really could have committed to by the time he arrived in power.

According to Arman, Garang's vision remains 'very much alive and present'. Still, after so many decades of war, centuries of slavery and oppression, believing in the possibility of a New Sudan, a country united on the basis of citizenship and equality demands a profound leap of faith, particularly now, without Garang. In his own way, however, Arman is right. The moment of truth has arrived: the Comprehensive Peace Agreement is the best chance this country has to come together, to consolidate the national unity that has proved so elusive. There are six years in which to try and heal the wounds. We are already more than half-way through that interim period and there is little sign of any real effort being made to restore trust or consolidate unity. If it fails the country risks coming apart at the seams. This time, very possibly, with armed struggle in the north, east and west, as well as in the south; a maelstrom deeper and darker than anything seen before.

For two decades, out in the bush, 'Doctor John' encapsulated the spirit of possibility: the exiled king whose return would restore life, happiness and prosperity. Now that he is gone, Garang's ghost hangs over the country like the shadow of what might have been.

The papers are full of large advertisements aimed at convincing people that the government is injecting new life into the economy. There are new initiatives, such as the Mahaseel Agricultural Investment Fund. They are trying to raise a billion dollars for a large cooperative agricultural venture between Beltone and the Kenana Sugar Company – one of the largest sugar schemes in the world. Bashir likes to refer to this as his 'Green Revolution'. The Mahaseel scheme is an attempt to latch onto the trend for vast agricultural schemes that has been taking place all across the continent. A series of high-profile foreign investors have been looking for land and water to grow the food they need. Saudi Arabia, UAE, South Korea, are all busy setting up projects here.

One of the largest of these is Jarch Capital, run by Philippe Heilberg, a former commodities trader with top New York firms like AIG and Salomon Brothers. Heilberg has leased a vast area of land in a partnership deal with Gabriel Matip, a rebel leader labelled a 'warlord' by the Western media. When an attempt to secure an oil block with the government of South Sudan fell through in 2005, Heilberg went directly to Matip. It is still not clear whether Matip had a genuine claim to the land he was leasing to the American as he was in conflict with the Dinka-dominated goverment; by din't of his being from the rival Nuer. In January 2009, the chairman of South Sudan's Land Commission claimed he only knew of the deal through media reports. Gabriel Matip set up his own company, Leac, which controlled agricultural land rights for 4,000 square kilometres of land ruled by his own militia. This area is projected to more than double in size, to some one million hectares. Heilberg, who owns 70 per cent of Leac and plans to invest over a billion dollars in the coming decade, has given assurances that 10 per cent of all profits will return to the local population in the form of investments in education, healthcare, infrastructure and so forth, but he makes no bones about the fact that he is not driven by altruistic motives. 'We are not an NGO,' Heilberg declared in an interview. 'We do this to make money. We would give back to the people because it is the right thing to do and we also want to see people prosper because, if the people prosper, they will like us to remain.'

There seems little doubt that, for those interested in making a profit, Africa offers opportunities where the return far outweighs the risk – what is known as the 'alpha factor' – which all investors are looking for. Funds like Emergent Asset Management explain to potential investors the huge gains to be made from investing in African agricultural projects. The land is fertile and cheap, and by applying modern farming methods they expect yields to treble. Investors come from all across the board and everyone is at it – large agricultural projects are a big thing, attracting a range of clients from Deutsche Bank to Goldman Sachs and Morgan Stanley. All are busy gathering hundreds of millions of dollars from clients interested in investing in farming developments not only in Africa, but also in Russia and China. An in-depth report by the *Observer* in March 2010 suggested that in the last three years an estimated fifty million hectares – an area the size of Spain – spread over twenty or so countries across the African continent has been bought up for large-scale agricultural development. The report identifies the motivation for such schemes to be found in the rising cost of petroleum, an increasing lack of water and a worldwide shortage of food. In Ethiopia, a country in which thirteen million people are dependent on assistance from foreign NGOs, the Saudi billionaire Sheikh Al-Amoudi plans to employ 10,000 people in a project to develop half a million hectares. Another enterprise, Karuturi – one of a number of Indian companies now running agricultural projects in Ethiopia – leased 300,000 hectares in 2008, but provoked some local protest.

There have already been accusations of land grabbing, forced displacements and the kind of exploitation already familiar in Kenya around the flower-growing farms in the Naivasha area. It has been described as the 'new colonialism'. Opinion is divided as to whether such projects will benefit Africa or make life worse for small farmers and consumers alike. A report by the organisation Action Aid draws a direct correlation between increasing hunger and the drive to meet an EU target of 10 per cent use of biofuel by the end of the decade. To do this Europe needs to cultivate 17.5 million hectares. To fuel its clean cars, argues the report, Europe is forcing people in Africa towards starvation.

In the end, it seems, it all comes down to how such projects are implemented and coordinated with local needs, and the degree to which the benefits are balanced against the use of natural resources such as water, and the impact on the environment, not to mention the rights of the workers and land owners, etc. This new development presents the very real but equally absurd scenario of people starving in one part of a country, while at the other end they are exporting rice, grain and other hard-currency crops to contracted buyers abroad. In itself there is nothing new about such paradoxes. According to an Oxfam report in 1985, during what was described as the worst famine in living memory, the poorest countries in Africa paid twice as much to the West in interest on loans than they received in aid. It puts the successes of campaigns like Band Aid and Live Aid in a rather bleaker context.

Gabriel Matip's father, Major General Paulino Matip Nhial, a member of the Luac board, played a leading role in one of the most vicious episodes in the civil war. At the end of the 1990s a power struggle broke out over control of the oil fields in Western Upper Nile/Unity State. Paulino Matip played a key role in stirring up inter-tribal conflict. It was part of Khartoum's strategy to divide the Southern rebels, and it worked. In June 1998, Matip's Khartoum-backed militia attacked, looted and burned the town of Ler, along with dozens of surrounding villages, causing relief agencies of Operation Lifeline Sudan to pull out of the area. Around 25,000 people were displaced. Ler became a ghost town.

In February 1999, the warring tribes were brought together at Wunlit. Paulino Matip's Bul Nuer was the only group not to participate in the reconciliation meeting. The chiefs of the Dinka, self-styled 'masters of the fishing spear', and the Nuer 'earth masters' gathered round as a tethered white ox was slaughtered to cleanse the bad blood between them. Political and military rivalry was to end. There would be no more raiding, destroying villages, abducting women and children, etc.

Peace between Nuer and Dinka, or between the Nuer and the *jallaba* Arabs, who also laid claim to the area, would have sabotaged government plans to divide the South and take control of the oil fields. By the end of the decade the government was close to achieving just that. The Chinese had almost completed a 1,600-kilometre pipeline that would funnel the oil up to the Red Sea coast in the north-east. A new refinery was being built on the outskirts of the capital. Finally, it looked as if the regime would see some benefit from decades of exploration. Estimates of the oil reserves were multiplying rapidly, eventually surpassing one billion barrels by the end of 1999.

And so petroleum became a cause worthy of jihad. Bashir called on young men and women to volunteer for the mujahideen brigades, to go south and defend the oil fields in the name of Islam. In May 1999 the government launched a fierce two-month scorched-earth campaign, incorporating aerial bombardment and helicopter gunships. Paulino's forces played a part in that assault. His efforts to drive people off the land were brutal. There was looting, of cattle, but also of grain, along with the destruction of granaries, livestock and villages. People were forced to run or be killed. Women were raped, boys as young as nine or ten were put to work as porters, while older children were forced into fighting as soldiers. Those who fled walked for a week to reach safety in Dinka land. Many drowned or perished along the way from hunger and disease.

In the absence of a clearly regulated land act in South Sudan, Heilberg is banking on the fact that, whatever the future brings, his local partners will retain their hold on his land. It is a carefully calculated risk for which Jarch Capital counts on a number of high-level specialist advisers on its board, including ex-CIA officers and retired advisers on African and Middle Eastern affairs, among them Joseph Wilson, former US ambassador and husband of outed CIA operative Valerie Plame. It was Wilson who questioned the Bush administration's claim that Iraq had procured yellow cake uranium from Niger, a key piece of evidence in the case for the invasion of Iraq of 2003. None of them seems particularly troubled by the morality of working with war criminals as their local allies.

Heilberg appears to have chosen a particularly risky corner of the country to invest in. Mayom lies in the north-west sector of

Unity State – a contested creation of Nimeiri's back in the 1980s; his attempt to redraw the map so that the oil reserves would remain part of the North. It was one of the root causes of the Second Civil War. The area was a disputed part of the border-line between North and South. Heilberg's strategy, going into partnership with a militia leader at odds with the government, might be best understood as a form of insurance. Taken to its logical conclusion, it is an investment in the belief that the state will eventually break up into feudal territories run by warlords like Matip.

This concordance between warlords and economic interests feels like a distant echo of the state of affairs at the close of the nineteenth century. Zubayr Pasha ran an area just to the north-west of Heilberg's African empire with his own private army. Zubayr might have become governor of Sudan if Whitehall had not baulked at the idea of employing the services of a notorious slave trader. It's not difficult to imagine that he would have felt quite at home today. Nothing much has changed, apart from the weaponry. The West is still sending confused signals. On the one hand, the president is wanted to stand trial for war crimes, while at the other end of the country another man accused of war crimes is signing multimillion dollar deals, and nobody bats an eyelid.

The real question, the one underlying all the pain and suffering, concerns the roots of this conflict. As I wander around the city, it

comes to me that my childhood years were an exception, a brief hiatus. Identity is never a given, but must be seized, claimed, demanded and, on occasion, fought for. What do people want, after all, if not justice, the right to live in peace, to have an opportunity to prosper? Everything I see around me seems to confirm that the struggle to create a nation here has failed. No lessons have been learned. But why, and was it always destined to be this way?

When you turn back to face history the picture becomes increasingly fractured. The unforgiving landscape makes movement a matter of life and death; access to fertile land, to grazing pastures, to water. It's all about freedom of movement, and yet so much of the history of this country is concerned with imposing restrictions, creating boundaries, defining difference.

The academic and former minister Francis Deng, writing in the optimistic days following the Addis Ababa Accord of 1972, suggested that, so long as we accept the ethnic, cultural and religious linkage underlying the history of South–North relations, 'No clear cut racial or cultural dichotomy can be drawn between the two parts of the country.' The fact of the matter is that the entire country is characterised by transgression, a heritage of criss-crossing cultural hybridity and racial intermarriage that is evident in the country's manifold diversity. It is not a country of blacks so much as one of many shades of grey. The North is not as Arab as it might wish to think, and the South is not as non-Arab. The common notion of a Muslim North and a Christian South assumes that faith has geographic and racial limitations. It reinforces notions of ethnic division, implying that some are genetically more inclined to the cross and others to the crescent. Such generalisations only serve the outsider looking for patterns, and laws of separation, which are the keys to divide and rule, to creating the conditions for subordination. To grasp something is to have a handle on it, to be able to control it.

The pattern was set by the colonial mindset. Three British academics in particular, H. A. MacMichael, J. S. Trimmingham and P. M. Holt, created between them a scholarly landscape that sustained an Orientalist view of the country and its inhabitants. These stereotypes were passed on, through the British

administration, to journalists, development workers and decision makers, and ultimately, to the Sudanese themselves. This
line of thinking placed all Sudanese within a context of classical
Arabic scholarship, a hierarchy in which Sudan figures as a place
of degenerate, racial impurity – impoverished both culturally
and religiously. Recognising Islam and Arab culture as genuine
and worthy relegated anything that lay beyond, as MacMichael
put it, to 'a monkeydom of nations'. All of this tied in with current perceptions of a pseudo-Darwinist nature. To MacMichael,
pre-colonial Sudan was a land of chaotic savagery inhabited by a
'human detritus', the outcome of the Arab penetration of Africa.
Islam gave the Arabs moral superiority over what they discovered
there. The pre-historical civilisations were dismissed as irrelevant.

This view was convenient for a number of reasons, most immediately in that it legitimised the colonial project. This is not to say
that notions of racial and cultural superiority did not exist prior to
the arrival of the British, but one could certainly argue that colonial scholarship lent authority to a perception that accentuated difference within the newly minted framework of the nation, thereby
making the achievement of national unity all the more difficult.

The British social anthropologist E. E. Evans-Pritchard conducted the definitive study of the Nuer people. He declared in the
1950s that there were no 'true Negroes' in the South. The closest
he could come to describing the Nilotic people was as 'Negroid' –
that is, displaying Hamitic-Caucasian elements, linguistically,
physically, culturally. In their beliefs, the Nuer and Dinka, the
two largest ethnic groups in South Sudan, show a closer affinity to
northern influences than to sub-Saharan ones. The burial rites of
the Dinka, the presence of pyramids, even the curve of their bulls'
horns, shaped by the owners, echo those seen in the wall paintings of Ancient Egypt. Religion, both North and South, is rarely
free from local traditions and beliefs, with animist or pagan rituals
incorporated in a syncretic blend. Instead of viewing this as a key
that might offer a fascinating insight into the evolution of the Nile
Valley, such links are commonly suppressed. Simplification is the
foundation of myth-making.

There are broken clocks everywhere I go, as if the concept of time has ceased to be relevant. Is it that no one ever bothers to change the battery? Many of these wall clocks bear the logo of one company or another: Nile Petroleum, Union Carbide, Sudan Airways. All of them were no doubt received as promotional gifts from airlines and insurance companies. When they stop they just hang there in the air, waiting.

A party has been arranged for me in my grandmother's old house. The names and the faces begin to blur. Some come back to me from behind a forgotten door in my memory. Heaps of sandwiches and peeled fruit stand ready, all covered in plastic shrink wrap. Ishraq is now a handsome woman in middle age; decades have passed since she was that little girl with her hair in plaits that I used to chase around.

Strong women predominate in this family, I realise, as people talk around me. I find myself withdrawing, imagining a parallel life. What might have happened to me, say, if all those years ago I had elected to stay? As the sun goes down and the yard swells with the watery glow of a single electric bulb burning over the front door, I feel suddenly at home, drawn back to the safety of childhood, when I used to fall asleep in this very yard to the sound of the women talking softly into the night. For a time it is comforting, but there are constant interruptions as people keep arriving. I am the distraction. It's torture really. They pause, clutching my hand, making me guess who they are. It is all part of the game of letting you back into their lives after so long an absence. It should not be easy. Beneath the warmth and hospitality there flutters an unstated unease about my presence. Sixteen years away is a long time, but more than the issue of lost time it says something about your priorities. It says that your concerns are elsewhere.

Ishraq's life has not been easy, she tells me. I remember her father, Aamer, a loquacious, charismatic man who used to make us all laugh. He would tease me, calling me Jimmy. I remember a generous uncle. They remember a father who walked out on them when things got tough back in the 1980s. He went abroad in search of work and settled in Saudi Arabia where he made a good living for himself and, more to the point, started a new family. A certain bitterness creeps into her voice as she recounts how she lost all her savings through unfair taxes and high rates. She and her husband had a number of financial ventures that apparently did not work out. They went abroad for a time, to the Gulf, where they found some success and returned with money to invest. They opened a supermarket and built a three-storey house. How they lost everything is another matter. The details are not clear. They had to sell everything and are now forced to rent.

It seems like such an intimate story, this confession of personal downfall, that I'm not sure how to respond. Perhaps they think I have a fortune somewhere and can help them. But I have nothing, not even a reciprocal tale of woe to offer. While she manages to keep it in check, you can feel her bitterness swirling just below the surface. Life has dealt her the kind of blow from which you do not recover easily. I wonder if this heartfelt confession has something to do with her father; if seeing me has brought back memories of when we were young and she was a pretty, precocious child, the apple of her father's eye. I wonder if my arrival has triggered this urge to explain herself. All I can do is listen and make sympathetic noises. If there was something I could do to help, I would do it, but I can't see how. She doesn't mention money, and neither do I. She's a strong, proud woman and would be offended if I mentioned it, and, besides, I'm a struggling writer not a philanthropist. As she gets up to go, I feel a sudden sense of loss. It strikes me that her purpose in coming here this evening was just this, to tell me her story. Not to ask for help or to demand sympathy, just to say, this is who I am, this is what life has done to me.

As I watch the vibrant green outfit disappear through the muddy wall I feel moved, and the inexplicable touch of sadness at seeing something precious vanishing, perhaps forever.

I am drawn into conversation with Alawiya, who is eager to tell me how bad things are at the university where she teaches. Soon after it came to power in June 1989, the new regime decided to reform the education system in the name of the *Inqaz al-Watania*, the Revolution of National Salvation as they dubbed it. Thirteen new universities were invented in the space of no time, with more to follow. It was a popular move. Education has always been highly respected in this country and not just as a means to a good job, a better life. It's about class mobility. Now it was to be available for everyone. Academic standards were lowered. If you couldn't get into one of the main universities you were bound to get into one of the new ones. The reforms touched all levels. Schools began teaching children to recite verses of the Quran, while cutting back on basic skills like languages and mathematics. Alawiya's undergraduates sometimes don't know the difference between centimetres and millimetres. She represents part of the dwindling lower middle classes. Educated and progressive, their skills are no longer valued. They can't even afford to give their own children the opportunity they had, namely a good education. Nowadays, students arrive driving big fancy cars, a consequence of the oil boom and the nouveau riche who have moved in.

In the 1960s this country was renowned for its progressive attitude. Women (such as Fatima Ahmed Ibrahim, who founded the Women's Union in 1952) played a prominent role in the trade union movement and the communist party. Egypt's first lady Jehan Sadat would cite the country as a model for women throughout the Middle East. Today, the situation has changed. For many women, university is simply a means to an end. More specifically, it is a way of finding a husband. It's not easy: men tend to avoid woman who are better educated, or have a strong character. Intelligent women, or those who earn more money, are also out of the running.

It is not uncommon for a mother to approach her daughter's lecturer as a potential suitor. Male lecturers receive love letters pushed under their doors. Age is not a concern. Marrying a man who is twenty or thirty years older is not unusual; the goal is security, not love. This has given rise to the phenomenon of the second wife, an idea that holds appeal for both older men and young women in search of a little financial security. This, too, was encouraged by the new regime. A trend was started of men marrying the widows of martyrs killed in the war. It was even permitted to marry a woman who was already pregnant by her absent husband. The fact that the martyred widow chosen was often both very pretty and very young was deemed irrelevant. It was an act of self-sacrifice, a kind of charity, taking responsibility for the family of a martyr who had fallen in battle.

Since it is common for people to marry their cousins first time around, the second time they might choose a secretary or junior colleague who comes from a poor family; someone who is quite happy to live alone in a flat and wait for her husband to visit her at night. Another tendency is to marry abroad. Women who are not willing to compromise find it very difficult, while men are spoilt for choice. Subsequently they are increasingly inclined to divorce their ageing wives in exchange for a younger one. Women who haven't finished university are appealing for a number of reasons. The younger they are the less chance there is of them having become involved in romances with other men. This doesn't imply they have been sexually active; merely the fact of having been in love with another man is unpalatable.

Professionals like Alawiya see the system caving in all around them. People are promoted because they have a connection in the

National Congress Party. Good teachers, women with education and training, are forced onto the streets, setting up tea and coffee stalls because they need the income and can't find work anywhere. Two days ago I happened to pass the women's prison in Omdurman as a group of inmates was released. Women are often arrested for making alcohol in the less affluent parts of town. They are fined and flogged, then locked up overnight. Often they are caught selling their goods in a neighbourhood where they haven't bribed the right police officer.

There is bitterness to these tales of how society appears to have lost all sense of direction. With all its talk of religion, the Muslim community, family values and so forth, the fact is that society has become more uneven. Over the last two decades Islam has been unable to deliver real social equality. People no longer believe there is any hope of being rewarded for their work; they have no faith in the fairness of the system.

Suddenly everyone in the yard is joining in the conversation. They all have stories to tell. I can't catch them all. Later, when I come to write up my notes, one sticks in my memory. Because it was an odd, rather trivial story, and because so much importance was attached to it: a local boy absconded from a nearby shop with the day's takings. The story was conveyed with weary resignation, offered as a sign that the world has taken leave of its senses. Nobody, not even the boy in your local grocer's shop, can be trusted any longer. It is a sign of the times; the sense that something essential has been lost and will never be recovered.

When people ask where you are from, they often use the word *jins*, which can mean race or gender as well as nationality. It really means which part of the country are you from, what is your tribe. In a country of mixed heritage it is a reflection of that obsession with placing people, and belonging. My father's family are Nubians, often described as a distinct but intermediate race; darker than the Egyptians, lighter than sub-Saharan Africans. Their facial features and hair also differ. Their language or *rotana*, the language my grandmother spoke, survived long after the arrival of Arabic in the Middle Ages.

To the pharaohs of Ancient Egypt, Nubia was a treasure trove of slaves, ivory and gold, tucked away in thick seams inside the broken, rocky hills east of the Nile. The slaves were brought north along the old roads to provide exotic domestic help in Egypt and further afield, across the Mediterranean, along with ivory, ostrich eggs, feathers, leopard skins and ebony. Nineteenth-century European fascination with Ancient Egypt bordered on a mystical belief in its provenance, the fact that it appeared to have sprung up on the banks of the Nile out of nothing. There was no evidence of civilisations before 3400 BC. Herodotus dubbed the people living south of Elephantine Island, today's Aswan, *aithíops*, the Greek for 'The Burnt Faces'. He was not entirely wrong, for Ethiopia is where they originated, some 2.6 million years ago. A million years later *Homo erectus* was making his way north along the Nile. The earliest remains in Upper Egypt date to around 80,000 years ago. By the first centuries BC it is estimated that between Aswan and Khartoum there were between 30,000 and 50,000 people altogether, spread across hundreds of settlements. Estimating the size of the nomadic population is more difficult.

In 1948, an excavation commenced on a mound of earth north-east of the railway station, close to Khartoum's main hospital. Crowned by a sayal tree (*Acacia spirocarpa*) the mound was strewn with fragments of red brick – all that remained of a mosque that once stood there. It was one of two main cemeteries in Khartoum. It was first discovered by a British gunner who had spent the Second World War sitting in a trench on that very spot manning an anti-aircraft gun for the Sudan Auxiliary Defence Force. While he scanned the skies for Italian bombers flying in from Abyssinia he had plenty of time to examine the debris around him and soon realised that he was sitting on a Stone Age settlement. The gunner's name was A. J. Arkell, who, in civilian life, was an archaeologist. After the war he sought permission to undertake an excavation of the site. A surface layer was unearthed, containing flakes of quartz and rhyolite along with hard red pottery sherds and grindstones, hammer-stones, broken sandstone rings and fossilised bone fragments. It appeared to have once been the location of a Neolithic village. A metre-thick layer of occupation debris revealed harpoon spears with four barbs, previously unseen in the area, as well as microlithic crescents, trapezes, all indications of a Stone Age culture new to Sudan. There were also the shells of land snails (*Limicolaria flammata*), a species no longer found there, and the seeds of *Celtis integrifolia*, a tree that today grows only as far north as Sennar. These finds indicate that the average rainfall then was around three times what it was in the middle of the twentieth century. Snails need at least 400mm of rainfall a year and by 1948 it had fallen to only 164mm. Today it is around 100mm.

The excavation work was carried out by trained diggers; *quftis* were imported from Egypt (the word derives from Qift, the location of the first excavations undertaken by Sir Flinders Petrie in 1895). Along with horns and the teeth of large mammals they dug up ostrich-shell disc beads and the bones of hyena, porcupine, antelope, black rhino, elephant, leopard, warthogs, hippopotamus and zebra, as well as the Egyptian wolf-jackal. These creatures testify to a great diversity of fauna in the Khartoum area, of which only a tiny fraction survives today.

Aside from reflecting the effects of climate change and urban growth, Arkell's research provides evidence of the city's original inhabitants. Racially, the human remains were characterised as a Negroid race with a short, wide skull (mesaticephaly) that is distinct from the Nilotic skull-type. This suggests that Khartoum's earliest occupants were similar to those found today in the Jebel Moya region – 200 kilometres to the south. Their way of life was very similar to that of the Dinka in Bor district today, another 500 kilometres further south. They spear fish and harpoon hippos. When the floodwaters rise they are forced back to higher ground. Unlike the Dinka today, they did not have cattle or other domestic livestock. They survived by fishing and hunting and when the pickings were slim they ate the Ampullaria snails. In the South today the snails are traditionally used as bait for fishing and not usually eaten. They hunted with bows and arrows. For the larger game they used traps, digging pits for buffalo, elephant and rhino to fall into. Arkell believed this evidence supported the theory that the Ancient Egyptians originally came from the south. In 30 BC Diodorus of Sicily described the Egyptians as the first people; that they came from the south was, according to him, an established fact. All of this places the current presence of Southerners in the capital in a very different light. They have more in common physically with the earliest recorded inhabitants of the city than we Northerners do. In a sense, we are the outsiders and they the original settlers; the city belongs to them.

The sun is high overhead and I am the only person on foot. Nobody walks in this part of the city any more. This is the old route we used to take to school every day in my father's car. A long queue of vehicles stretches out beside me. Long ago, I remember people walking. People with donkeys. People on bicycles. Not any more. Now the streets are empty but for cars. Everyone sits behind the wheel of their brand new, locally assembled car.

The new breed of Korean microbuses means nothing to me. Tiny, high and unstable, they resemble overgrown toys. Some of them run on propane gas. Several people have warned me that they have a tendency to explode. This could be just hearsay, but the gas-driven models are rumoured to have been banned from import. Some have large signs on the dashboard warning you not to smoke – often accompanied by an ominous whiff of gas. I begin to look out for the signs whenever negotiating the price with the driver. But business is brisk. One young driver explained that he had paid off his taxi in only six months. He had expected it to take years. He put twelve million Sudanese pounds down as a deposit, money he had borrowed from an uncle who worked abroad. Now he was making one and a half million a month and only had three more payments to make before the car was his. What would he do then? He hasn't really thought about it. Perhaps sell the car, which is less than a year old, and buy a new one.

This confidence contrasts sharply with the dour outlook of another driver whose pessimism extends to the state of the country. Unity will not last, he grumbles. The Southerners want to cut the country in half, with the border as far north as Kosti. There is an unhappy set to his mouth and he drives in quick, nervous jerks, hunched aggressively over the wheel. The Southerners are bent on stealing the country. It's not the first time I have heard the charge. Did he take part in the violence against them when Garang died? He gives me a furtive look: 'Of course. You don't think we are going to just stand aside and let them do what they want?'

Millions of Southerners, men and women, fled north during the war. Over the last twenty years they have tried to make a life for themselves in the capital. They lived in shanty towns that were regularly flattened by government *kashas*, or raids. They worked as labourers on building sites. They stood on street corners hawking shirts, cigarettes and whatever else they could get their hands on. The women found work as domestic servants. To be Southern in Khartoum is to suffer prejudice and racism at the hands of Northerners who look down on them as *abeed* – the old term for slaves. They live the homeless, stateless existence of the internally displaced.

Garang's death created a flashpoint, an implosion of tensions that had been building up in the city for years, and a warning of what lay ahead if these issues were not addressed in some way. People took to the streets unable to believe that his helicopter crash could possibly have been an accident. They vented their frustration on the capital, smashing shops and attacking anyone they came across, pulling people from their cars. It had to be a conspiracy, an assassination by the regime. Reprisals followed, with Northerners attacking Southerners. The Southerners have absorbed the memory of centuries of hatred, the driver continues. The long shadow of history has bitten into them hard. 'The younger ones have never heard the word slave before,' the driver sneers, 'but they are convinced their skin works against them.'

The Peugeot 404 and the Hillman Minx, these are the cars I remember. Old Humbers and heavy Russian Volgas. The yellow taxis with the hand-painted green stripe along the side that are now little more than museum relics. There are still some around, trembling on street corners or parked in the shade under neem trees, hoping against hope that someone will be desperate enough to ask to be taken somewhere. Coming out of the university one morning, I find one waiting and without hesitation I jump in. I am not going far, but I am late and it's a temptation I cannot resist.

What happened to the old taxis, I ask the driver; why are they all in such a bad state? They are all on their last legs, scrappy bits of metal with sharp edges protruding. He laughs; yes, they are all dying. The drivers can't afford to buy new ones and there are no spares left for these old models. As if on cue, the car starts to wobble and splutter. The white-haired man pulls over and climbs out to lift up the bonnet. I wait while he struggles. Finally he manages to get it started. We manage another fifty metres before it stops again. This time I go round to join him and we both stand there staring at the forlorn engine that stubbornly refuses to return to life. The driver is solemn, barely able to speak, utterly stricken by a sense of embarrassment and shame, ineffectively dabbing the engine with a dirty rag as if comforting an ailing loved one. At first he refuses to take any money. I press it into his hand. He needs it more than I do at this point and, besides, the sentimental value of those few minutes in the back of his yellow taxi are worth more than I can pay him.

The holding camp lies at the far end of Omdurman – the road is surfaced only intermittently. You bump up and down, on and off the tarmac, passing through parts of town that are new, most of them still unrecognised officially. One carries a sign proclaiming it as *Madinat Al-Nakhal*. The Town of the Palm Tree, a name given by its inhabitants. This is the geography of necessity. The urgent creation of occupied spaces out of the void. From a distance they appear similar, dusty open ground covered by a harvest of urban debris – plastic bags and flattened bottles. Startled, skinny dogs scramble out of roadside ditches where they rummage for food. When the rains come the whole place disappears under a tide of water that can take weeks to subside.

The task of the International Organization for Migration is to help people who want to leave the capital and return to their homelands in the South. The IOM camp consists of little more than parallel rows of long canvas tents behind a high wire fence. There isn't a tree in sight. In the middle of the compound stands a simple shelter that serves as a cooking area, where people can light fires to make their food. Another one serves as a bathroom and toilet area. It doesn't look big enough to cope with the size of the camp, even though right now it is not close to being filled to capacity. On the far side is another area with a tent where medical examinations are carried out and two others from which rations

are distributed. Beyond this are several huge Magirus-Deutz
trucks. They spend two days gathering those who are preparing
to leave. On the third day a convoy of lorries heads off to the
south. The trailers are piled high with the returnees' furniture,
their personal possessions and luggage. A stack of rolled-up mattresses and plastic garden furniture, chairs and tables. A couple of
bicycles. It doesn't look like much to be starting a new life with.

Raja is a journalist with the *Citizen* newspaper. She tells me
that people leave because life in the capital is too hard for them.
Finding work is not easy. Civilians began streaming north to get
away from the fighting after the outbreak of war in 1983. In addition, the IOM has been flying Southern refugees in from camps in
neighbouring countries: Uganda, Kenya, Ethiopia. In Cairo, Raja
met disaffected youths who had turned to crime. They are violent
and suspicious of everyone: the UN, the Egyptians, even their
own people. They have to deal with racial discrimination as well
as all the rest that goes with being a displaced refugee.

Young Southerners in Khartoum have faced something similar. A grey-haired man appears outside one of the tents with his
eighteen-year-old son. The boy is tall and thin, able-bodied and
eager to work; his father looks tired and frail, leaning his weight
on a staff. His name is Marar Goj and he has spent more than
fifteen years in Khartoum. He is going to Konabei. All he needs,
he says, is enough to tide them over for a while, and a net. He's a
fisherman by trade. 'Just give me a bit of salt with my food and
I am happy.' He repeats this over and over again, like a mantra.
A net to work with. He doesn't look strong enough to haul a net,
let alone undertake such an arduous journey. There is a blank, distant look in his eye. A picture of desperation. A man who believes
his life depends on one little wish being granted. Going home.
The boy doesn't know the homelands. His head darts nervously
from side to side as he talks. He was a small child when he came
here, but his Arabic is still rudimentary. Does he know anything
about fishing? No, but his father will teach him. The attention is
making him nervous. There is an air of impatience among them,
eager to be rid of this city now that they are committed to going
back. After two days in this camp they are keen to be on their

way. The boy can barely stand still. He has no idea what lies ahead of him. The women are more resigned. There is nothing left for them here. They have had enough of the city. They all have similar complaints. They are tired of washing clothes for a living, their hands sting from all the soap powder they have to use every day. A slim woman in white wanders back and forth aimlessly, a small child on her hip. She speaks to no one, just paces up and down as if she is already gone.

A desolate wind blows through the wire round the camp, stirring up the dust. All the returnees are given enough provisions to last them for fifteen days. In the Non-Food Items tent they present their identity cards, which are checked against a list before they are handed a large nylon sack containing a length of plastic sheeting, a couple of blankets, two plastic jerrycans for collecting water, six mats for laying on the ground at night to sleep on and fifteen bars of pink soap. Each family struggles out of the tent with their sack. In the tent opposite they go through a similar procedure and receive in return a fortnight's food rations: a bottle of cooking oil, a bag of high-energy corn-soya meal. There are also sacks of split lentils from Japan.

What kind of life awaits them back in the South, so far from the capital? It is hard not to conclude that they will be disappointed. It's not difficult to see why many of those who go home end up returning again. Like all migrants everywhere, they have had years to forget the reality they left behind and to fill in the gaps with romantic notions of the return to an idyllic homeland. It strikes me how young they are, all of them. A tall, striking woman with fine features stands to one side cradling a small child. Her family is alongside her. The husband is silent. Her twelve-year-old son has never been to school, she smiles. Their government has failed them. This city has failed them. They would rather take their chances out there in the wind than stay here. The canvas flaps around us in the empty tent.

Outside, a minivan draws up. A primly dressed Northern woman, her head covered with the obligatory brown scarf, climbs out. She is accompanied by a tall, goofy-looking man. They represent an organisation called Jasmar, a government agency for raising awareness about landmines. They prop a sheet of hardboard with a poster attached to it against the side of the vehicle. The people in the compound glance over but nobody pays much attention. No effort is made to summon them, or even to mingle and talk to the returnees. There are no available figures for the number of landmine victims, but there are estimated to be several thousand. For twenty years both sides have been busy planting the devices, without a thought as to who will retrieve them. Digging mines up is a lot more complicated than burying them. Along the borders with Chad and Egypt there are still mines put there by the British during the Second World War.

I walk over to examine the poster. The display shows thirty-five different types of landmine, from heavy anti-tank devices to light anti-personnel mines that resemble colourful toys. There is another list of UXOs – unexploded ordnance. The girl repeats the words several times, in English – apparently there is no Arabic equivalent – as if they are a magical incantation whose significance will become apparent to us in time. Rusty shells is what she means. When I ask if she has figures for the number of mines there are out there, roughly, even, anything at all, she shakes her head. She has no such information and repeats that her job is simply to raise awareness about the existence of mines and unexploded bombs. No statistics. No idea what is actually out there. She hands a few more leaflets to us and smiles, her job done. Not one of the returnees has come over to see what the minivan is doing there. No one has come up to ask for a leaflet. Satisfied she has done her job, she fixes her scarf and climbs into the back of the van, out of the sun, sliding the door closed behind her to shut herself in.

The leaflet explains in English and Arabic that landmines are dangerous and usually hidden and are to be avoided. I wonder how many of the people who are about to go back to their mine-infested homelands can read – in any language. If in doubt, it says, ask for help. It doesn't tell you who you are supposed to ask out there in the bush. Mined areas have no visible signs, it reads. The presence of dead animals may indicate a mined area; some zones are marked with painted signs or 'stones piles sticks'. 'Most dangerous areas in Sudan are not marked or have signs; do not assume an area is safe if it is not marked.' It doesn't sound very reassuring.

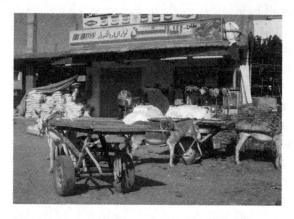

Oxfam finally allows me to see part of their operation. On the outskirts of Omdurman, beyond everything, a smattering of clay houses rises out of the ground. This is Dar al-Salaam, the 'House of Peace'. People began to settle here back in the mid-1980s, when floods hit western Sudan. Over the years the shelters became houses, built in the traditional style. Bricks laid out in rows to dry in the sun provide evidence that they are still building. It never stops growing. In other new neighbourhoods they have now got electricity and water and are slowly being absorbed into the city proper. But here this still hasn't happened. The government appears to be hoping that one morning they will just get up and go back to where they came from.

Although it is their project, the Oxfam people give the impression of having little idea of what is actually going on there. Every fact is corrected by Ayesha, a representative from a local women's group. A sprightly young woman who all but disappears inside the red *tobe* she wraps around her, she is so full of energy it is exhausting just to watch her in action.

At one of the Urban Project Centres – a bare room with an earthen floor, a table and a few chairs – I meet four women. One of them, Soumaya, hails from Gawa in the north-western corner of Kordofan. There, she explains, traditionally they make salt by digging wells fifteen to twenty metres deep. The water is saline. They pour it out and leave it to dry in the sun. To them salt has magical powers. It cures any ailment. They wash in it to protect themselves. They sell the salt in El Obeid. Here there is no salt. Here they have fresh water that is delivered on a donkey-drawn wagon and sold to them by the jerrycan.

Water is key. In 1989 it was estimated that between a half and two-thirds of the city was without water, a sign that the city could not cope with the demands being made on it even then. This was symptomatic of a broader, national malaise. Since then the capital has expanded in leaps and bounds, each successive wave triggered invariably by a crisis elsewhere in the country. In the 1980s it was drought in the west, in the 1990s and later in 2002–3, it was war in the south. The population almost doubled. Urban crisis was an expression of national distress. Faced with death, abandoned, or even persecuted by their government, the people flocked to the only place they could go, the centre. Whenever the capital failed to deal with their problems out there, they came here, and they would keep on coming.

Now they long to return. All the women have a similar story to tell. They feel trapped out here in the middle of nowhere. If it was up to them they would go home tomorrow, but their husbands are earning money in town – a source of income they are reluctant to lose. The women feel no connection to the city, which is a good forty minutes' drive from here, and they are cut off from Kordofan, which they long for and, after twenty years, still consider home. People have a better life there, they all agree. They have televisions with more stations. Very big televisions, says Soumaya excitedly. They have telephones and electricity. Life there is good, Hawa adds, the children learn instead of sitting in the street all day as they do here. There are tasks for them to do there, looking after the animals, tending the fields – here there is nothing. The Oxfam people are surprised to hear that there are new arrivals from Darfur. Darfur is the back of beyond. Beyond Kordofan, rather, which is only five hours' drive away by truck or bus. The men from Kordofan travel home regularly to visit

their herds and tend their fields. They come and go with the seasons. They take their sons with them. Often they go there to get
married.

Ayesha, the sprightly Rizayqat woman, smiles a lot and talks
more than the other three women combined. She takes over, toss-
ing out figures so fast that it leaves the Oxfam representatives
struggling to jot down notes for their files: 1,800 houses in their
square. Ayesha is responsible for twenty-eight squares in all. An
average of six people in each house, though often there are ten
or more. Thirty-two thousand people in the southern half and
37,000 in the northern half of Dar al-Salaam. She takes us to visit
her house. A large dairy cow and a heifer are haltered within a
mud-walled enclosure by the front door. The Rizayqat traditionally raise cattle, and this scheme provides them with cows as a
means of making money. For a time we all stand admiring the
cow. The Oxfam people and myself are clearly city-dwellers who
can barely tell one end of an animal from another. The cow produces milk and possibly one calf a year. It is self-perpetuating:
money is lent to the women, at a rate of 2 per cent a month, which
they can pay off by selling the milk and the calves.

There are no proper streets here, although the houses have
been laid out with some sense of order. In the distance a brick
tower stands out starkly against the desolate landscape – the
beginning of a project by one of the new start-up universities
that stalled at some point. It is not hard to see why Ayesha and
the other women long for their homelands. From here the city
appears bleak and unforgiving. There are ditches filled with stag-
nant green water. Plastic bags of all colours form a faded rainbow around the houses where people have tossed their rubbish.
Goats huddle together against the dusty wind. A dead dog lies
in a breach between walls. But the women are cheerful and have
plenty to say. They all talk at once, about televisions and children,
the need to work, to improve their situation. The nearest hospital
is far away. There are small medical centres run by NGOs such as
the Red Cross. Life here is not easy, yet they manage.

In comparison to Ayesha's optimism the man from Oxfam
seems perpetually glum, apparently still undecided on whether or

not to trust me. I wonder how he managed to wind up in a place like this. Whatever motivation he finds in doing this work it does not seem to give him any real satisfaction. In the course of an awkward, stuttering conversation I learn that he was previously based in Ramallah. How was that? 'Fantastic,' he says quickly, as though recalling a particularly enjoyable holiday. As we drive back towards the city he asks the driver to drop him off in Omdurman. I watch his tall frame disappear, the same mournful expression on his face, wading into the crowd like some modern-day apostle looking for a cause worthy of him.

Osman brings news of Darfur. He has just returned from visiting the IDP camps to see conditions for himself. In Kalma there are hundreds of thousands of people who have lost everything, family, home, loved ones, along with fields and livestock. All they have left is a strip of canvas in the middle of nowhere. There is little chance of them going back to their homes. The violence has abated, but the gunmen have taken control and it is unsafe. To drive from one town to another you have to pay off the various militias that control each section of the road. Everyone pays these 'highway taxes', as they are dubbed. Darfur has suddenly become an expensive place to live. A newspaper costs twice as much as in the capital. But I am curious. 'Why has it taken you so long to go there and see it for yourself?' I ask. The conflict has been going for five years.

'I don't like to get into politics,' he says warily. Such caution is perhaps understandable in a country where journalists walk a dangerous line. Most of the time he writes about cultural matters.

Journalists became an endangered species back in the 1990s. Even those who published their work outside the country risked being arrested for criticising the government. Many were imprisoned, tortured or killed. The lucky ones made it into exile. The fact that Osman has finally made the trip at all says something about how things are changing. People are no longer as afraid as they once were and there is a growing sense that time is running out for the regime.

Nowadays, the union of journalists is pretty much aligned with the powers that be, but there are a few independent-minded people for whom the freedom of the media is worth fighting for. Slowly, others are finding the courage to speak out. Osman's view of the situation has been changed by what he saw. The authorities would like people to believe that foreign press reports exaggerate what is happening out there, but what he has seen confirms that the situation is worse even than the descriptions in the international press.

On another level, it was a chance for Osman to get to know a part of his country he had never seen before. He visited the old palaces and took photographs of the ceremonial outfits, red and blue, that were used whenever the Sultan made a public appearance. If he came out wearing blue he would be distributing gifts; if red, it meant someone was about to be punished for something. Osman was pleased with this discovery. It gave him the kind of angle he could use, a cultural memento of an old world order that has disappeared.

Some two centuries earlier, in 1803, another visitor to Darfur, Muhammed bin Umar al-Tunisi, was astonished by what he saw. He noted a strong female presence and how women were more independent than anywhere he had visited in the rest of *Bilad al-Sudan* – the Lands of the Sudan, meaning, in those days, the entire width of the continent south of the North African coastal strip, stretching from the Atlantic coast to the Red Sea. The conservative al-Tunisi was amazed at how women were able to move around with complete freedom, in particular the princesses, or *marujan* as they were known, who followed the liberated way of life of the Sultan's mother.

Just over a century later, H. A. MacMichael described the house
of Sultan Ali Dinar as:

> a perfect Sudanese Alhambra. The Khalifa's house in Omdurman
> is a hovel compared to it. There are small shady gardens and
> little fish ponds, arcades, colonnades, store rooms and every
> type of building. The floors are strewn with fine silver sand.
> The thatch on the roof is the finest imaginable and looks as
> if it has been clipped with scissors. The walls are beautifully
> plastered in red, and the interiors of the halls are covered with
> great inscriptions from the Koran in handsome calligraphy or
> with chess board designs. Only the best birsh (straw mats) or
> bamboo has been used in the roofings. Trellis work in ebony
> is found in place of interior walls and the very flooring in the
> women's quarters, under the silvery sand is impregnated with
> spices.

Darfur lies at the midpoint between the two great rivers of
Africa, the Nile and the Niger. In his speculations on the source
of the Nile, Herodotus describes it as flowing west to east in the
heart of the continent, confusing it no doubt with the Niger, as
did many travellers, including Ibn Battuta in the fourteenth century. In the famed Tangerine's imagined geography, the river he
saw in Mali was connected to the land of the Nuba, known to him
at the time as a Christian kingdom. He envisaged a line connecting him to Dongola and the cataracts on the Nile as a boundary
marking a division between the 'negro' territories of sub-Saharan
Africa and the start of Egypt.

There are other stories, legendary tales of a journey across the
desert made by an exile from Spain; a Morisco expelled by the
fervent Christians, who somehow wound up deep in the midst of
the vast African continent, as far as possible from every coastline.
How much truth there is in this is difficult to tell. Myths seem
to blow themselves into the country's history, to linger there like
cobwebs, neither dispelled nor proven.

The emptiness of the map gives a false impression of Darfur
being without history. There are many ruins to disprove this, such

as the city of Jebel Uri and the graves of the Daju people. There are buildings made of red brick that include at least one Christian church and a monastery. In the 1920s, A. J. Arkell described the hills of Jebel Furnung, six hours' drive north-west of El Fasher. Beyond the wadi of Ain Soro the land flattens westward across Wadai where a path drops down into a valley to rise on the hill of Jebel Uri. A zigzag causeway leads to the summit of some one thousand metres. Inhabited for some four centuries, built with stone and no mortar, the structures are still intact, two or three metres high.

Uri may have been the headquarters of the Kanem administration, during the expansion of that empire in the thirteenth century under Dunama Dibbalem. Here was a relay station on the route that linked the Niger with the Indian Ocean. Arkell believed that Harkhuf of the 6th Dynasty of Ancient Egypt (2400–2600 BC) reached here by camel along the Forty Days' Road – still in use today. There are so many similarities between the institutions of the kingdom of Darfur and that of Kush that Arkell suggests it is possible Darfur may have been founded by a royal family exiled from Meroë after its fall – sometime after AD 350.

Twenty miles south of Uri lies Ain Fara, a smaller city of circular stone dwellings, crowned with the remains of a fine red-brick monastery and church of Christian Nubia. Tenth-century pottery, including terracotta ornamented with fish, doves and crosses, proves this. These buildings were transformed with the arrival of Islam in the fourteenth/fifteenth centuries into mosques. The monasteries became palaces or seats of government. Islam may have been introduced by Mai Idris Alooma, who ruled the Kanem-Bornu Empire from 1571 to 1603. Darfur became independent after him and the local Fur sultans of the Keira dynasty built their palaces and mosques in the Furnung hills. The last of these was Sultan Ali Dinar.

MacMichael visited El Fasher in 1915, despatched from neighbouring Kordofan in his capacity as a British intelligence officer. Darfur was not incorporated into the Sudan until the following year and Reginald Wingate, the governor-general in Khartoum, was worried about it getting out of hand. Less than twenty years after the British Reconquest had taken Khartoum from the Khalifa there was still a real fear that another Mahdi might rise up. The other worry was that the Sultan of Darfur, Ali Dinar, would be drawn into the First World War on the wrong side, fighting for the Turks. The problem, as Wingate saw it, was sending a small, Christian-led force 'into a little-known country against a population inclined to bouts of fanaticism'. Interestingly, the British settled on a strategy that would be echoed decades later by Bashir's regime: they decided to arm local militias. Three hundred rifles were given to the Rizayqat of Southern Darfur to stir up their problems with the Fur. Two hundred more were handed to the Kababish. MacMichael was instructed that it was imperative to give the impression that the British were taking action as a result of the 'Sultan's attitude', and not simply because they had decided to interfere.

The irony is that the Sultanate of Darfur was created by intermarriage, between the rulers of the Keyra clan of the Fur with Arabs. The founding figure was Suleiman Solong in 1640. The word *solong* translates as 'the Arab'. It is possible that he came from the Benu Hilal, though P. M. Holt calls this is a glorification of the facts, saying it is more likely they were from the local Fazara nomads, or else connected to the Wadai royal family in Kordofan. In either case, Solong married a Fur princess and thus founded the dynasty that ruled over Darfur and neighbouring Kordofan and from the end of the eighteenth century, with the demise of the Funj Sultanate to the east, became the main trading party with Egypt. This was the zenith of the Darfur Sultanate and it was to last until 1874, when Zubayr moved in from the south. This was the same slave-trading Zubayr who found himself up against Gordon.

Osman has returned in optimistic mood and has a new job with the SPLM daily, *Ajras al-Hurriyah* (The Bells of Freedom). The paper backs Garang's vision of a pluralist Sudan, not just in the south, but also through armed engagement in the Nuba Mountains, and, more recently, though less successfully, in Darfur. Real unity seems a long way off and secession still remains a very real possibility. The six-year period of unity ushered in by the

Comprehensive Peace Agreement in 2005 will soon be over and it's not clear what will happen when it ends.

We sit at a tea stall in a narrow street one evening. Actually, it is no more than a patch of dusty ground in front of a row of houses. A single neon strip over what might once have been a garage but is now an all-purpose shop provides scant illumination. Amid the laughter and debate a woman crouches behind a low table with rows of glass jars containing the spices, sugar and tea and coffee that she mixes deftly. Beside her a blackened kettle sits on a charcoal stove. Seating is provided by a couple of plastic crates taken from the stacks outside the store. Another woman serves the tea on a tray with a bowl of shelled peanuts to accompany it.

When I ask Osman if he really believes there are grounds for hope in the future, for reconciliation between North and South, he tells me there are more links than many people realise, here in this city. His own brother married a girl from the South whom he met while working in Wau. The chairman of the SPLM, Yasir Arman, is married to a Southerner, and there are plenty of other examples of mixed marriages, though it usually only works one way, with Northern men marrying Southern women. The other way around is far less common. A discussion ensues between Osman and a friend, Ubeid, who joins us. Ubeid is studying translation at Ahliya University for Girls. In the old days there was more intermarriage, she says. Osman corrects her, pointing out that in those days it was not through mutual consent. The women were taken as slaves. The children had no heritage rights.

In the harsh white flare of the neon light, I glimpse the silhouette of a man smoking a pipe. It is pitch-black by now. Cars start up around us and drive past, flooding the air with toxic fumes. The tea is sweet and the plastic crate is hard and uncomfortable.

Osman lived through the early years of the *Inqaz*. He was forced to do his military training in the mountains west of Omdurman. They taught him to run, crawl and to shoot. His wife to be was also forced to train. Osman was lucky; when the time came for him to do his military service he was allowed to work as a teacher. Others he knew from those days were sent to fight in the South and never came back. Often the body was never returned, something that is particularly painful in a society where tradition demands the dead be washed by relatives in preparation for the hereafter. 'In those days they would come to the house as if it was a celebration. Your son has become a martyr, they would say. He has gone to heaven.' High-ranking military officers would make an appearance – even Hassan al-Turabi, the scholar whose ideas fuelled the drive for national salvation, would turn up to celebrate the marriage of the deceased with his *houria* brides in heaven. They brought gifts, crates of soft drinks and sacks of sugar, a sheep to be sacrificed. 'Some families would welcome them because, well, what else could they do?' shrugs Ubeid. But others did not and confrontations would sometimes take place.

Every Thursday evening state television would broadcast a programme dedicated to the martyrs fallen in battle. On their way to battle men were given little keys to hang around their necks: to open the gates of paradise if they died as martyrs. The television show would open with a cannon salvo. Videos would follow: each soldier was required to make one before they went off to fight. Ubeid remembers the experience well. 'Every week we used to gather round the television, the whole family, to see what had happened.' Some returned home minus an arm or a leg. Today these veterans are to be found in the military hospital by the main railway station. A few months ago, in protest at the abysmal conditions, they came out and occupied Omdurman Bridge. The crippled and the maimed. They lay down and blocked traffic for several hours.

By the end of the decade the zeal of the early years was waning. People would laugh when Turabi, the great ideologue, solemnly declared that those who had fallen in the war were actually not martyrs. No one had really believed all that nonsense in the first place. It was a pathetic end to a tragic era. To deal with all that pain, to heal the wounds on both sides, requires a serious, concerted effort, which is nowhere in evidence. Is it reasonable to imagine reconciliation between North and South? Ubeid is sceptical. What would happen to the memories, the suffering and sacrifice? Would all that simply be forgotten? Osman, the idealist, argues that of course it would not just be swept under the carpet, but he has no real answer for how, in a newly united Sudan, the past will be dealt with.

Assistant Professor Munzoul Assal's office is on the first floor of the Sociology Department at Khartoum University. The sunlight filters through a long row of high arches that resemble pairs of ivory tusks propped up on the floor. From Darfur himself, Assal has been documenting and analysing the situation for years. He is appalled by the lack of any kind of real strategy.

'The government could resolve the conflict if it wanted to do so,' says Assal. He accepts that a share of the blame must be carried by the rebels, though mostly for petty infighting and putting the personality of individual leaders first. 'The longer the conflict goes on, the more chance there is of other conflicts springing up.'

The real threat to stability stems from the failure of government to face unresolved issues. Another source of concern is the matter of the various factions of the security forces that are at odds with one another. Each is well armed and answers only to itself. It is part of a strategy to prevent any one section becoming too big a threat. The idea is that they balance one another out. The *Haraka al-Shaabiya*, the People's Defence Forces, are the main group, but there are also paramilitary forces like the Special Reserves, the *Ihtiyat Markezi*. Each group has a distinctive uniform and shoulder flashes of their own. The president has his own special guard. The Janjaweed leaders also live here in the capital, with their own protection, and along with them are the rebel groups. All in all there are a lot of people with guns.

As time goes by and the conflicts go unaddressed, there is an increasing risk of them being brought to the capital. Sudan has one of the highest rates of urbanisation in the world. People are draining away from the rural areas and flooding into the cities. In a paper on the impact, Professor Assal uses the term 'pathological urbanisation' to describe how people live together without any form of social integration. On the eve of independence in 1956 Greater Khartoum had a population of a quarter of a million. By the early 1990s this had grown to nearly three million. By 2005 Khartoum was estimated officially to hold 4.5 million. Unofficially, the figure now is seven million, an estimated two million of whom qualify as internally displaced persons. All over the country a similar pattern can be witnessed, though on a smaller scale. The wealthy now live alongside impromptu squatter sites and IDP camps. The rise in luxury accommodation and investments by foreign companies adds another layer of complexity to the already fractured sociopolitical landscape. It seems ironic, not to say tragic, that, as rich and poor rub up against each other, the gap between them is wider than ever, certainly greater than anything I can ever recall.

The fear of outsiders dates back to the 1980s at least. The prime minister at the time, Sadig al-Mahdi, warned of the dangers of a *zanj* (black) ring springing up around the city. A tightening belt of disenfranchised, poverty-stricken migrants. These fears were realised with the unrest that flared following the death of John Garang in 2005. Thousands went on the rampage. Not only Southerners participated, as Munzoul Assal points out, but people from every corner of the country. The violence lasted for three days. People were targeted according to their ethnic origin; some were pulled from their cars and beaten to death. Shops and businesses were ransacked and burned to the ground. It was the outpouring of years of frustration and anger at their Northern brethren whom they saw around them living comfortable lives while they in turn had lost everything, starting with their homes, their land and their families. Consequently, many of the settlements were demolished and the inhabitants relocated further away.

With the Comprehensive Peace Agreement came the notion that it would encourage people to leave the capital and return to their homelands in the South, the Nuba Mountains and the Blue Nile area. But this proved not to be the case. Those who did go home often discovered that poverty, the lack of infrastructure and investment, meant Khartoum remained an attractive proposition, drawing them back. More significantly, rather than the migrants adapting to the city, what happened was the opposite; the new immigrants ruralised the city, bringing with them networks and community self-help systems to allow them to adapt to their new urban lives. Munzoul Assal stresses that this kind of transformation is a form of democratic participation and marks their integration into the political system. It's an interesting point, democracy versus metropolitanism, one that applies to many parts of the world.

The rapidly expanding city is here to stay. The government, of course, remains in denial. So far their approach has been one of containment, with high levels of security and the penetration of civil society organisations through the creation of their own National Congress Party fronts. Rather than integration and democratic participation, the prospect of the entire country being represented within the confines of the city poses a threat: 'The danger is that regional problems will now be brought into the capital.' Surely it is not a bad thing, I suggest, for the government to be made aware of the problems they have been ignoring for decades? The danger, Professor Assal explains, is that now, if the issues are not solved, then the wars of yesterday, which took place thousands of kilometres away, will now be fought out here in this city.

Bashir is flitting around the world trying to improve his international profile these days, in the run-up to the ICC's expected announcement. He appears on television in a live video conference with Louis Farrakhan, leader of the Nation of Islam. In a mosque in Detroit, he answers questions from the audience: 'The problem is that Darfur began long before we came to power,' he explains, in the voice of reason. 'There is an effort by a number of countries to get rid of us – the American–Israeli lobby wants to remove me from power.' When in doubt, deflect the issue.

Can the massacres in Darfur, the decades of brutal violence in the South, in Bahr al-Ghazal, in the Nuba Mountains, can all of this be explained as a consequence of imperialist violence, handed down from master to slave? Thinking of the accounts of Belgian brutality in the Congo in the nineteenth century, the use of the chicotte – a hippopotamus-hide whip – and the amputation of hands, suggests something more than imperialism was at work, some brutal and fundamental trait that stems from the profound depths of human nature. An instinct, which, when combined with power, comes into its own, creating the horrors we have seen, then and now.

In Conrad's rendering, Africa became a metaphor for the cruellest places in the human soul. In his book *Exterminate All the Brutes*, Sven Lindqvist examines the phrase that terminates Kurtz's report into the civilising project of imperialism. Lindqvist first read *Heart of Darkness* in 1949, at the age of seventeen. The Holocaust was not ancient history, it had just happened. He quotes the historian Herbert Spencer who wrote, around the same time as Conrad, that imperialism had served civilisation by clearing the inferior races off the earth. Hannah Arendt went further, arguing that the groundwork for the Holocaust was laid down in episodes of imperial genocide in the colonies. The decimations of local populations in the Congo and South Africa, in which millions perished, prepared the way for what was to come in Europe. The Germans, Lindqvist tells us, 'have been made the sole scapegoats for ideas of extermination that are actually a common European heritage'.

Hegel maintained that what distinguished man from animal was his ability to sacrifice himself for a higher cause, such as was demonstrated in the French Revolution. Imperialism, the glories of exploration that fed imperialism, was just such a noble cause; finding the 'blank spaces' on the map, as Conrad put it. A contrasting perspective was provided by Frantz Fanon. 'The colonised man,' he wrote in *The Wretched of the Earth*, 'liberates himself in and through violence.' Fanon applied logic to dismantle prejudice: slavery was abolished on the basis of human dignity, ergo, the black man was, after all, a human being. He describes his problem as that of being displaced from history. This displacement defines his disempowerment. The violence we see is that of those who have overthrown their victimhood to become masters of their own lives. The anthropologist Mahmood Mamdani writes that the laws of war are generally perceived to apply only to wars among the civilised; in the colonial wars it is the laws of nature that apply. There is no noble cause.

Displacement from history is also how Mansour Khalid, author and former government minister, characterises Sudan's problems. In his introduction to the speeches of John Garang, Khalid, the man who engineered the Addis Ababa Accord of 1972, writes, 'The entrenchment of Arab–Islamic culture in the Sudan was the great achievement of two purely African Sudanese Kingdoms – the Funj and the Fur.' In other words, the modern sense of Arab and Islamic culture in Sudan has been detached from the actual history out of which they evolved.

Khalid is an erudite and outspoken critic of many previous rulers. He is also a survivor who has been in and out of favour with successive rulers. An air of danger surrounds him and the powerful, sleek cars parked outside his front gate are ready to leap into action at a moment's notice. For decades he has managed to tread the tightrope, staying close to the throne and yet avoiding the fallout when there is a tumble. Under Nimeiri he was a cabinet minister. More recently he acted as a presidential adviser after the signing of the CPA that ended the Second Civil War. He somehow fits into the profile of the solitary, dedicated man, with no wife and children to encumber him. Drivers and bodyguards watch the gate while a troupe of aides shepherd in trays of tea and refreshments, summoned by a portable console that he presses discreetly. The gadget suits the surroundings, which could be the set of a James Bond intrigue, with glass walls, zebra skins on the walls and split-level rooms, fountains and cool basins of water adorning the garden. The house was designed in the 1970s by one of the country's most original architects, Abdel-Moneim Mustafa. With its statues and African art works it resembles a cross between a modern art museum and a Californian hideaway built by Frank Lloyd Wright.

When he talks, he often smiles knowingly, which suggests that he is holding back slightly. He has been in this game for a long time and is a prolific author of books on the subject of this country's political turmoil. He hails from a family of religious scholars and Sufi devotees, but there is something particularly irreverent about his personality. The North's persistence in waging war with the South, he once wrote, was explained by 'a sense of perverted nationalism'. One could argue the same in relation to Darfur, or, indeed, to any part of the country that finds itself at odds with a regime that sees itself as having the sole right to define national identity, in this case in the form of a rigid and intolerant vision of Islamism.

Having known most of the key figures personally, Khalid is familiar with their foibles and the petty weaknesses of Sudanese politics. Marginalisation, he says, is the first element to be addressed, by class, by region, by gender. Someone like former prime minister Sadig al-Mahdi thinks only in terms of ethnicity, but there are many other ways in which people are marginalised and these have to be seriously addressed. The second crucial issue is the separation of state and faith. 'You never see a state that prays. The state does not go on the *haj* [pilgrimage].' What we have witnessed, he insists, is the 'sanctification of the state'.

'Those who called for secession in the past have been prompted by a sense of despair,' Mansour wrote, more than a decade ago, 'rather than a desire to see their country divided.' It is this despair, this inability to find a way forwards, to believe in the elusive goal of a country of equals that has been key in the country's undoing.

Even Garang could not see beyond the tactics of 'the oppressor', who managed to divide the nation into 'Muslims and Christians, into Arabs and Africans'. As a call to war perhaps it works, but as a solution to the country's ailments it leaves something to be desired.

Back in May 1877, at the start of his second term in office, this time as governor-general, Gordon declared that his first priority was to stamp out the slave trade. Every hero needs a worthy opponent and in Zubayr Pasha, 'Chinese Gordon', the Victorian idol, had found his. In the British press Zubayr was portrayed as a monster, a mercilessly cruel man who embodied their dark fears. His private army of 500 was despatched to capture men, women and children, to burn villages to the ground. His rise hastened the end of the Darfur Sultanate's two-and-a-half-century reign. By 1874 Zubayr had effectively conquered Darfur with his private army. His horsemen travelled for hundreds of miles through the interior, raiding and seizing slaves as they went. Zubayr himself lived in luxury, with carpeted diwans to receive guests, uniformed slaves to wait on him and lions chained up around the palace.

Gordon entrusted the mission of dealing with Zubayr to Romolo Gessi, one of the few Europeans in whom he had confidence. In 1876 Zubayr had travelled to Cairo to seek a Firman from the Khedive Ismail, a decree that would establish him as the legal governor of Darfur. Zubayr worried the khedive, who had him imprisoned instead. In his absence Zubayr's son Suleiman took charge of his little empire. Gessi managed to capture Suleiman, and had him put to death, something that was later to complicate matters for Gordon.

In Gessi, Gordon saw a latter-day Francis Drake whose only failing was his Italian background: 'What a pity you are not an Englishman,' Gordon declared at one point, causing Gessi to storm out. In fact, Gessi's father, born in Ravenna, had acquired British citizenship while working in London and later became the British vice consul in Constantinople. It wasn't the same thing. Like Gordon, however, Gessi was a bit of a nowhere man. Born in Constantinople, or, rather, on a ship bound for there (or possibly Malta), where he was baptised, the family moved to Bucharest, where he grew up. Later he attended military college at Halle in Germany. Gessi met Gordon during the Crimean War, and although he spent hardly any time in Italy he was later adopted by the Italian fascists as a hero, the man who marked the start of the Italian exploration of Africa. After his death his remains were exhumed from Suez and reburied with full honours in Ravenna. Gessi had his own extraordinary adventures. Travelling back to Khartoum, his boat became lost in the Sudd marshes and drifted in circles for three months. There were stories of cannibalism, of men going insane.

One of the few insights we have into Zubayr's personality comes from a remarkable interview with Flora Shaw, a British journalist and writer, in 1887. After being placed under house arrest he was exiled to Gibraltar. The series of interviews with Shaw were published in the *Contemporary Review* and did much to redeem his reputation as a notorious slaver. Shaw had established her reputation writing for *The Times* in London, eventually becoming colonial editor, which allowed her to travel widely throughout the British Empire. The *Montreal Herald* described her 'indomitable spirit and trust in the innate chivalry of the race', as she travelled alone along the Yukon to interview miners. 'One of the remarkable women of the age,' wrote the paper. Shaw was the epitome of the English lady, it continued, 'Quick in all the sympathies of her sex but endowed by nature with the power of will, of observation and of expression'. Shaw became an authority on questions relating to the development of the empire and was on the verge of becoming a celebrated public figure in her own right. A close friend of Cecil Rhodes, she was later to marry Lord Lugard, governor of Hong Kong and the first governor-general of Nigeria. Shaw is credited with coining the name Nigeria for what was previously known as the Royal Niger Company Territories.

In the winter of 1886, Shaw arrived on Gibraltar, 'That meeting point for travellers from India, Morocco, and Spain, where one knows and feels, that when his foot touches the soil he is in England again.' What most did not know was that high above the perpendicular marble cliffs lay a windblown cottage built on a ledge, and in this sat one Zubayr Pasha, in lofty exile from his distant lands in western Sudan.

Quite why the British decided that Gibraltar was the place for Zubayr is not clear. His influence was obviously so strong that he was deemed too dangerous to keep anywhere remotely within Sudan's sphere. For four months Shaw visited 'the Pasha', as she refers to him, once a week. She describes him as a tall, dark man clad in the draperies of Eastern dress, smoking a pipe of hashish. It sounds like an Orientalist fantasy, something Victorian readers might expect from a novelist. Indeed, the entire interview reads rather like a tale from the *Arabian Nights*.

Each afternoon they would talk until the sun began to sink over the sea, and it was time for prayer. Among the Arabs, Shaw informs her readers, a man is not held to be of noble birth unless he can trace his ancestry back to a connection with the family of the Prophet Muhammed. Zubayr claimed direct descent from Abbas, the Prophet's uncle. This linked him to the Abbasid dynasty that had once ruled Spain, ironically, now visible from his clifftop eyrie.

Zubayr's family hailed from Cairo. They moved to Khartoum, where he grew up. As a boy he dreamed of exploring the south in search of adventure, rather like Conrad's character: 'Some portions were described as gardens, in which every sort of fruit grew wild; others as deadly swamps, where nothing but crocodiles and venomous insects could live. Dwarfs, giants, gnomes, and white races with long silky hair were among the inhabitants of the wilds.

There were the horrors of cannibalism to face, the excitement of big game to hunt.'

Shaw's imagination seems to have been hard at work, or perhaps she was simply filling in the gaps left by an incomplete translation. Zubayr himself spoke no European language and her interpreter, 'Achamet', was not only unqualified ('His patience was as great as his stock of English was small'), he was also unfamiliar with the context of Zubayr's story. Shaw admits it was given to her in so many pieces that 'they could scarcely fit into each other'. Nevertheless, she gives it a good whirl.

Zubayr's tale begins in 1857 when he was sent to fetch a cousin who had gone ivory hunting in the region beyond Bahr al-Ghazal. He sailed up the White Nile to plead with a merchant named Ali Imouri to let his cousin go. Instead, Zubayr found himself forced to join their expedition: 'And thus I started, poor as a slave.' The journey took more than four months, during which time the captive Zubayr had nothing to do but read the Quran. Out of boredom, he decided to join a caravan that set out to explore the interior. In the region of Makua they were attacked. Zubayr managed to shoot the chief and save the merchant from death. Imouri was now in his debt and Zubayr was given respect along with new clothes, food and arms. He was even allowed to drink coffee.

Zubayr gradually began to take charge of Imouri's business, changing its style, imposing strict military discipline on the men. When Imouri returned to Khartoum he left Zubayr in charge. For four months he acquainted himself with the customs of the locals. He learned their language and discovered they were not cannibals, that they had a sense of justice and could distinguish between the truth and a lie. He realised that any merchant could trade with them so long as he treated them fairly, and so he did. In exchange for beads he acquired feathers, ivory, gum and skins. This combination of firmness and fairness endeared him to the locals who, according to Zubayr, even named their children after him.

At this point, Shaw's sympathetic portrait seems at odds with the picture painted of Zubayr previously, whereby he regarded all blacks as cannibals, savages, adulterers, and therefore legitimate fodder for his slave-trading enterprises. Zubayr went on to explain how he decided to try his luck alone. In 1858, taking his money back to Khartoum he invested in trading goods and a boat. This time he went further west, towards the Nyam-Nyams – a pejorative term for the Azande people. According to Jules Verne, no less, the name comes from the sound made while chewing human flesh. The Azande, Zubayr explained, had no god, no prophet, no law: 'One man worshipped a tree, another his chickens, some fire, some water, some the buffalo, some the serpent.' Cannibalism was rife.

Shaw's account of Zubayr's life veers at times into fable along the lines of *Gulliver's Travels*, or, indeed, something by Jules Verne (*Five Weeks in a Balloon* was published in 1863). When James Bruce returned from his exploits in East Africa in the eighteenth century, he was ridiculed by London society and famously dismissed by Dr Johnson as a fabulist (Johnson may have had his reasons, since he himself had recently published a novel on the subject as well as a translation of Joachim Lobo's *Travels in Abyssinia*). The stories Bruce told were simply too incredible to be true. Almost a hundred years later, Zubayr's story must have sounded equally fantastical.

At the height of his power caravans were arriving three or four times a week from Syria, Tunis, Tripoli and Morocco. He dealt with Prussian, French and Italian merchants. He was earning £12,000 a month. Among the Azande it was customary to keep any prisoners taken in war for food. When he saw fine and serviceable young men being slaughtered this way Zubayr thought it a pity. He suggested to the king that they be bought for a few beads or calico and trained as soldiers. He started a trend and soon, instead of eating their young prisoners, neighbouring tribes would offer them for sale.

In one story Zubayr and the king entered a village to find it entirely deserted, but for a good supply of beer that had been left out in every house. Zubayr urged the men not to touch it, but they ignored his warnings and fell upon it. So incapacitated were they by drink that when the chief's army returned they were easily overcome and slaughtered. Zubayr managed to protect King Tikima, but was badly wounded himself when a spear pierced his right lung. Wisely, he refused to have the spear pulled out until they were safely home, fearing he would lose more blood, and instead had the shaft cut off.

While being nursed back to health for forty days, Zubayr asked for the grateful king's daughter in marriage. His wish was granted. Once recovered, Zubayr went back to work and eighteen months later had amassed two shiploads of ivory, tamarind and gum. It was while transporting this haul back to Khartoum that Zubayr's ships became hopelessly lost in the vast, shifting marshes of the Sudd. Like Romolo Gessi, and countless other explorers, they were unable to find their way. They ran out of drinking water and food and went round in circles for weeks. Some of the men died, others went mad. The story takes on the hallucinatory aspect of a dream as they drift hopelessly through myriad channels, between floating islands of papyrus and reeds, completely disorientated.

Zubayr emerges from the interview as an exiled noble, a man of character with a most remarkable story to tell. He was surely aware that through Shaw he was addressing the British nation, the Queen of England, even. Sudan is an Oriental fable: the stations filled with ostrich feathers, tamarind, honey, wax, gum Arabic, along with lion skins, leopards, elephants, antelope and rhinoceros – from the horn of which it was believed, Shaw informs us gravely, poison cannot be drunk unperceived, just as in Marco Polo's day. Zubayr's tale complemented the Victorian sense of awe at the marvellous world that lay within their grasp.

For Zubayr, the interview gave him a chance to redeem himself, to clear the shadow hanging over him as Gordon's arch enemy. Indeed, he was freed from exile shortly after the interview was published. His charm clearly worked on Shaw, who perceived in him, perhaps, something of a voracious imperialist spirit: 'He had all the enlightened trader's faith in trade as a civilising medium,' she wrote. 'He believed that were trade to flow unimpeded, peace, order, knowledge and every blessing of organised society must follow in its train.' The Pasha humbly confirms this view; the suppression of slave-hunting was only incidental to the opening of the roads, but it was absolutely necessary. Shaw goes on: 'It was a curious experience to hear Zubehr [sic] Pasha speak of the same things [as Gordon], as not only the ideal, but in some degree the accomplished work of his lifetime.'

This embracing of commercial enterprise as the redeeming quality in a renowned slaver puts the whole anti-slavery movement in a different light. Was Zubayr being kept as a potential ruler of Sudan? Even the morally upright Gordon had no qualms about proposing him to replace the Mahdi: 'He alone can ride the Sudan horse.' A slave trader, in other words, was preferable to a Muslim with a mission, even if he had the country behind him. When Shaw read passages from Gordon's journals referring to him as a slave trader, Zubayr promptly began to sing the praises of the fallen hero, the man he held responsible for the death of his son. The man whose hand he had refused to shake in Cairo when Gordon was on his way to save the garrison in Khartoum. Now, he described Gordon as having the character of a saint. A man who cared more for the poor than for the rich. Gordon had two weaknesses, according to Zubayr: he imagined that all men were at heart as good as himself, and he did not speak Arabic, which meant he was easily deceived.

At the time of the interview both Gordon and the Mahdi had been dead for two years. Sudan was in the hands of the Khalifa Abdullahi. Gladstone had been forced to resign as prime minister as a result of the public outcry over Gordon's death. His replacement, Lord Salisbury, made no secret of his distaste for Islam. Mahdism, he said, represented 'a formidable mixture of religious fanaticism and military spirit' unique to Islam. He subscribed to the fear that Mahdism would spread, that a resurgence of Islam threatened the entire region and that this might lead to the revival of the Ottoman Empire and a Pan-Islamic confederation ruled by the Caliph in Constantinople. For his part, the Khalifa boasted that he planned to continue the Mahdi's mission, sending his armies through Egypt to the Holy Land, cleansing the Islamic world of decadence and corruption. This particular pipe dream culminated at Toski in 1889, when the Egyptian army fought off an attempted invasion by a weakened and demoralised force.

The British, nevertheless, decided to proceed cautiously. For ten years they practised a policy of containment. Sanctions were imposed, watchtowers were posted on the Egyptian border at Wadi Halfa. During those years, wrote the war correspondent and popular historian Alan Moorehead, the interior of the Sudan was as remote as Tibet. A series of accounts of life under Mahdist rule emerged, all of them carefully structured and aimed at turning public opinion in Britain – 'one of the vilest despotisms' ever seen, according to Salisbury. Written by Europeans who had escaped captivity, the most famous of these books was by Father Ohrwalder and Rudolf Slatin. Translated and embellished by the head of military intelligence in the Egyptian army, Major Reginald Wingate – later to be governor of Sudan – they offered a vivid picture of the cruelty and barbarity of life under the Khalifa. The work done by Wingate's industrious intelligence service eventually paid off in 1896 when an Expeditionary Force was assembled in Egypt under the command of Kitchener, who had an old score to settle.

From time to time stories emerge, hinting at dark currents stirring beneath the surface. A newspaper editor was kidnapped outside his home and held for several days. The motive was not clear. Eventually, his body appeared in a cemetery. He had been decapitated. A grim picture was to be found, like so many horrors, on the internet. The perpetrators were caught. They claimed to be professional killers and had been paid three million Sudanese pounds, around $1,500, by people from Western Sudan. Fifteen people went on trial. The judge ruled that the press be forbidden from taking notes – they weren't even allowed to bring pen and paper into court with them. The killers boasted that they had had a little fun with the dead man after they cut off his head. 'If you are a man,' they taunted him, 'let us see you try to put it back on again.' Soon another explanation surfaced. There were claims the editor had published a story about girls in Darfur being corrupted by foreigners working for international organisations – corrupted being a euphemism for having sex with them. Some took this as an insult to the honour of Darfuri women that had to be avenged. Yet another explanation went further. In this version, the editor was working on a story of corruption and money-laundering involving members of the ruling NCP. Truth becomes so fragmented that eventually it doesn't matter which story is true. All of them tell us something. Together they create a composite of a society that is splintering.

Back in my room that evening I find myself unable to concentrate on anything. Flipping through the channels the alternatives soon break down into themes: religious programmes – lengthy accounts of why the Quran is right about everything, and how all prophets since the time of Adam were actually Muslims. In other words, before the arrival of Islam, people were carrying out the will of Allah even though they were not even aware of His existence. Then there are news bulletins, which endlessly repeat the same information. A couple of Egyptian films show people helpless in the grip of romantic love – the eternal balm to soothe the pain of the present – the actors gazing blankly into one another's eyes as they wait for the next bit of melodrama to fall from the sky. A couple of studio debates, where, again, religion figures strongly. It strikes me how many Islamic channels there are in English nowadays, each one doing its part to hold together the threads of the modern, globalised Islamic community, or *umma*. Bearded men face the camera and deliver a rendition in poor Arabic, which they then proceed to translate into quite incomprehensible English for their no doubt confounded, but enlightened audience. A science programme so old-fashioned it evokes a sense of nostalgia to hear them explaining organic chemistry in such dull, pedantic terms. My schooldays come back to me. Hours of copying notes from the blackboard without understanding a word. Even here there is a linguistic paradox. The explanations are given in Arabic, while the terminology and the fragments of text read aloud are in English, which seems to illustrate the conflicted dependency of the East on the West. Another impatient jab of the finger brings me with an unexpected jolt back into the world I am living in.

The film *The Four Feathers* is being shown on one of the plethora of Americanised channels broadcast from the Gulf. It is the seventh remake of the novel by A. E. W. Mason. The earliest was a silent film from 1915. The most famous is Zoltan Korda's 1939 version, which was so popular it formed the basis for a 2002 remake.

What is it about this story that continues to exert such fascination? This most recent version opens on the playing fields of England, where a group of officers are forging the bonds of comradeship that will see them through life. We watch them playing roughly on a muddy rugby pitch, and then transformed into proper English gentlemen wearing their dress uniforms at the regimental dance. Good men whose honourable intentions will shortly be tested when they find themselves in the desert surrounded by bloodthirsty fanatics. So far, so predictable. I am attentive, trying to discern some complex post-colonial theme. The director, after all, is Indian. Surely he might bring something new to this chapter of colonial history?

On the eve of departure, Harry Faversham decides he only joined the army to please his father and is really not cut out for war. He would much rather settle down and enjoy married life. He resigns his commission. His friends respond by symbolically sending him the eponymous feathers of the title, denouncing him as a coward. Our hero spends the next ninety minutes proving that, naturally, he is far more courageous than any of his friends. What is the point of all this, I ask myself aloud?

As he waits for an opportunity to redeem himself, Harry goes native, working alongside the camp followers, the 'tribe of slaves' who fetch and carry. Here, we witness our hero degraded by the cruel Arabs, brought down to the level of the black slaves who surround him; even lower. This, I conclude, is some kind of wish-fulfilment; the white man emerging as the long-suffering victim he truly is, which in turn is all about reverse racism – something like that.

The English troops ride into an unnamed village. A sniper picks off one soldier and a pursuit ensues. The devoted fanatic naturally refuses to surrender, in the manner of your average fanatic, and in an act of zealous conviction raises his gun in hopeless defiance, only to fall in a hail of superior firepower. Is this some veiled justification for the use of excessive force; people get killed because they are beyond reason and want to die?

Next we are introduced to the Noble Savage. We've seen the soldiers at work and at play, we have seen them drunk and in courtship. We consider them to be people, vulnerable human beings, no different in fact from you and I, as it were. The natives, on the other hand, remain obscure. The sniper shrouded in rags as he fires on them from a concealed position is clearly fairly devious. Now we meet Abou Fatma, quickly dubbed Abou by the soldiers – rather like the pet monkey in Disney's *Aladdin*. Unlike Korda's 1939 film, which was shot in Sudan with Sudanese extras, it's not clear what Abou's ethnic affiliation might be. My guess would be a contemporary dance troupe in Camden. He has tattooed animal and star figures on his chest – freestyle innovations on the theme of Dinka and Nuer traditions perhaps? I suspect these particular motifs would be novel to them. Being the only native in sight capable of uttering more than grunts, it falls upon Abou to carry the burden of indigenous representation all on his lonesome. His motives remain obscure. Why he would risk life and limb for an Englishman he happens to meet in the desert remains a mystery. 'God put you before me, so I have to help you,' he explains helpfully, leaving most of us in the dark. Abou is a good Muslim, except that he appears to say his prayers backwards. Abou's purpose is clear – to help Englishmen. The rest of the country is occupied by fanatics. On occasion they gather around the lone white man and play games in the familiar manner of simple, friendly natives everywhere on the dark side of the planet. This raises them to the level of playful primates.

This, I realise finally, is not a story about Sudan, but about the confusions of today's Britain, seen through a darkly exotic glass. Harry defends the robust Abou when he is abused by the Egyptian NCO, who is (naturally) more racist than the British. He defends a slave princess from the South, played by super-model Alek Wek, who an enterprising and evil European (French, of course) is taking *south* to sell, obviously having not heard that most slave markets lay to the north or across the Red Sea to the east. The Mahdi's name comes up several times, usually with the words 'fanatic' or 'Mahometan' tagged on for good measure. This is not a film about the brutal cost of building an empire, or the darkness of the human soul, nor about what motivates people to take up arms against foreign oppressors. But, equally, it cannot be dismissed as just an innocent piece of escapist fantasy. This kind of representation has consequences. Erasing history means something. However obscure the country and its history might seem, Sudan is not a blank canvas upon which it is possible to write anything. Painting over fact in this way adds opacity to the confusion. It is either wilfully ignorant, or knowingly condescending. I can't decide which. We can only speculate on the director's motives. From the first strains of Pakistani Qawalli music over the opening credits this film tells us that, in some kind of multi-cultural rainbow-worldview, our stories are interchangeable, and thereby insignificant. We count only as background colour. The lack of specificity renders us irrelevant, lost in a blur of distant exoticism.

Made in 2002, this film also seems to endorse the simplistic equation linking the Mahdi and Osama bin Laden. At the end, our heroes, restored once more to a cosy fireside in England, can have a civilised drink and deliver the comforting message that what motivated the British conquest of far-off places was not nationalism, nor an idea, or a flag, or a country, but the man to the left of you and the man to the right of you. 'And when the armies have been scattered and empires fallen, we remember that moment when we stood side by side.' It's a nice thought, but it excludes many of us. All over the world we watch these movies. In living rooms and starlit yards, in Chad, on street corners in

Bamako, in my grandmother's house, faces are illuminated by a glow emanating from far away, telling us who and what we are, defining our limitations. If you do not tell your story, others will do it for you. In despair, I push the button and the screen goes dark.

PART THREE

DIVERGENT CITY
2010

'All about him, the city was yielding its forms. Houses seemed to turn into liquid and to flow away before he reached them. A horse in the distance became a mist when he got there. Fountains dissolved into fragrances. Palaces became empty spaces. [...] It suddenly seemed odd to him, but the solid things of the city seemed like ideas. And ideas, which were alive in the air seemed to him like solid things.'

Ben Okri

'The Nile flows quietly ...
Seeping through the city's silence
And the burning sorrows of villages.'

Al-Saddiq Al-Raddi

I move into a small flat in a new building. My room is on the ground floor; the ones upstairs are more expensive and reserved for foreigners. The room has no windows and no view. It feels cramped and claustrophobic. A little kitchenette only makes me long for home.

The building is set back from the road, rising out of what appears to be waste ground. The land has been parcelled off and sold to developers, but the government has no plans to put down tarmac and streets until all the buildings are finished. To reach the front entrance you stumble over uneven heaps of rubble. Out of the forgotten piles of rounded pebbles, broken bricks and all the rest of it, the seven-storey construction rises cleanly. New apartment blocks mushroom out of the rough sand left, right and centre with no apparent coordination between them, no grid on which to relate to one another. Every few blocks or so a shiny new mosque looms to provide spiritual consolation. Some of these take rather innovative, even bizarre, shapes. Proliferation seems to encourage architectural experimentation. Funding appears to be limitless.

This was once known as Street 15 but it has another name now, one that nobody ever uses. The Revolution of National Salvation replaced numerical street numbers with names that celebrated the glories of Islamic history. Al Quds Street for Jerusalem. Another is named after the martyr Wad al-Nejumi, one of the Mahdi's most famous generals. Still, this faux nostalgia for an Arab past never really fitted. The new names never caught on. Ask anyone what street you are standing on and you will always get a number in reply, even if the old signs are long gone.

The New Extension was built as part of a masterplan for the city created back in the late 1950s by C. A. Doxiadis, a Greek architect and town planner. We have him to thank for this rectilinear grid of streets and villas, which sits awkwardly on the edge of the old town. Doxiadis was quite a daring choice at the time. A man of vision, he proposed the idea of a science of human settlements, which he called Ekistics. There were five guiding principles, or elements: nature, anthropos, society, shells (buildings) and networks. A successful human settlement, one that abides by these five principles, would create harmony between man and his constructed environment. He believed he was designing the city of the future. I grew up in this very same neighbourhood and knowing this makes my childhood feel as though it was part of an experiment.

Doxiadis, who lived through the age of fascism in Europe and witnessed the military dictatorship in Greece, believed that architecture was the cure that would restore our humanity. He saw the inevitable fusion of all the cities of the world into one gigantic Ecumenopolis – a city that stretched across the planet. He might perhaps have been content with the way Khartoum has spread outwards, away from the old centre. He saw the expansion of the city as inevitable. We have to embrace change rather than ignore it. I wonder what he would make of the state of his project today. The rigid rectangular grid is breaking down. The streets have become soft and rounded, the tarmac broken and covered in sand, the edges worn away.

The house where I lived for most of my upbringing was a simple villa of cracked walls and dust-blown verandas. I remember a strip of crabby lawn divided by a car port where an ageing Vauxhall Viva would sit. Over the years the garden flourished, becoming thick with vegetation as my mother crowded it with trees that she tended religiously. Watering the plants in the after-noons was a daily ritual that she never missed. There were flat-leaved papayas, swathes of bougainvillea, an enormous lime tree that eventually towered over the house and a guava tree into whose slim but sturdy branches we would climb. The fruit never had a chance to ripen fully before they were plucked and eaten. During the afternoons we had the world to ourselves. Being as quiet as possible so as not to disturb the adults who were sleeping inside, we picked through the hedges for tamarind fruits, green spirals that contained a bittersweet white pod inside.

I spent my formative years in that house, whiling away long, dead afternoons in the living room reading. Novels that often I barely understood. The Mexico of Greene's *The Power and the Glory*, Durrell's Alexandria Quartet, the philosophical rumina-tions of Octavio Paz, the poetry of Dante, James Baldwin's essays, the labyrinthine workings of Borges, along with the stately homes of P. G. Wodehouse and Agatha Christie. I sifted through them all, looking for connections, for clues as to how the world was, and how it might perceive me. It took me a long time to real-ise that this place, this sleepy little town in which nothing ever seemed to happen, could be the source of stories, just as much as anywhere else.

What remains is the memory of those nights, the stars and the voices, talking long into the early hours. We always slept outside in those days. The world felt open and at ease with itself. Every evening we carried our mattresses out and unfurled them onto the metal bed frames that stood there. One thing I can't get used to in this new place is sleeping indoors. The new architecture is all about hermetically sealing you off from the world. Apartment buildings don't allow for sleeping outside. I would lie in bed lis-tening to the comforting sound of voices carrying over in the night sky – sometimes from the neighbours across the wall at the back, but often from the front of the house when my parents had visitors. These were the sounds I fell asleep to.

Both my parents were socially outgoing and popular. My father's circle of friends included many intellectuals, people he had met during his early years in Britain when he knew them as students. His natural gift was his ability to handle people. It was a note of pride for him that he had never had to ask for a job in his life. He was sought after. Although he took little interest in reading anything beyond current affairs, he often professed a respect for journalists and writers, people of learning. It was the respect of an outsider, one who knows his limitations, whose personal ambitions have now been channelled into his sons. That's where I came into it.

There can be nothing more frustrating for a child growing up than the knowledge that your father has the answer to everything. He knew how the world worked. Not only how, but who made it work and how they got there. I made the mistake of telling him I was interested in studying philosophy. I must have been fourteen or fifteen. I was going through an Eastern phase, spurred on no doubt by overexposure to Kung Fu movies and was stuck on Confucius, Zen Buddhism, and, in particular, the Taoists, who appeared to embody a wisdom and detachment from the world that seemed entirely in tune with nature. My father would hear nothing of it. To make a success of a career as a philosopher, he told me, you had to be really smart to begin with, and then write lots of books – the clear implication being that both of these qualifications excluded me.

I wonder if this is what nudged me towards writing. I am pretty certain that everything about my father's conventionality increased my affinity for the obscure, in literary tastes as much as anything else, which probably did me untold damage. I gravitated towards whatever social fractions, whatever margins I could find. At school I rejected football, volleyball and basketball to take up judo, which at the time was the preserve of a small sect-like group under the tutelage of Father Charles, a tall, austere man who was a keen amateur. For a time it became an obsession. Later, I shifted my attention to mountaineering, nearly killing myself in the process. It was an unconscious effort, seeking distraction, but the underlying current always led away from what was expected.

This applied to my reading, too. I was fascinated by Robbe-Grillet's *Jealousy* and William Burroughs's *Naked Lunch* – the weirder they were, the better I liked them. I preferred Thomas

Pynchon to Virginia Woolf and Thomas Hardy. Books about in-betweeners like myself, Ralph Ellison's *Invisible Man* and Thomas Berger's *Little Big Man*, exerted a mystical attraction, speaking across barriers of time and race. Arabic fiction was almost nonexistent in our house, for my father hardly ever read anything that was not taken up with the Middle East, current affairs and so on. Made-up stories could never compete with the real thing. Arabic was the language of the president's endless speeches that swallowed up entire evenings of television viewing. It was the language of the Arab–Israeli wars, of Nasser and Sadat, and the suffering of Palestine. What novels we had were by Naguib Mahfouz and, of course, Tayeb Salih, whose books I first read in English. This in itself was a revelation. The shock of seeing them alongside Soyinka and Sartre. The notion that this place where we lived could be the setting, the source of something so alien as a novel seemed quite hard to grasp.

Perhaps this too accentuated the appeal of literature, an inner world that remained closed to him. My father was blessed with a gift for storytelling. He could keep an audience enthralled all evening long with his amusing anecdotes. He was most proud of the problems he had solved, the people he had helped. The rich and the powerful came to him for advice. In his later years he would occasionally mutter about writing his memoirs. My mother would encourage him and there were times when he seemed quite taken with the idea, but writing wasn't something that came naturally to him. Sitting alone in a room with his thoughts bored him. What he enjoyed was the attention storytelling brought him. So long as he had an audience the stories would flow and the people in them came alive. Alone with a sheet of paper and a pen they did not. I tried to get him to record some of his stories, but when he sat down with a tape machine in front of him he would become self-conscious. His manner changed. The relaxed, natural tone was replaced by an awkward formality. It was a torture, somehow bringing back his shortcomings, his lack of education. The act of setting down the old stories seemed to freight them with a weight and responsibility they could not bear. He attempted to add and embellish, to construct a literary shelf on which they could sit. It was a disaster. At one point I bought him a small tape recorder and urged him to speak into it when the mood took him, thinking that perhaps my presence was the cause of the problems; my son the writer. It didn't work. Instead, he used the machine to make terrible recordings off the television of Hassan Attiyah singing, or the sermons of Egypt's most popular imam, Sheikh Metwalli Sha'rawi, who would appear every Friday to air his interpretation of the Quran, and tales of his mystical encounters. My father's stories were destined to remain absent from history's record.

I inherited my love of reading from my mother, just as she in turn had from her mother, a strange, unhappy woman whom I did not know well. Then I would picture my English grandparents like characters out of a novel Dickens never wrote, living in their rather grand and gloomy old house in London. A daunting and reclusive figure, my grandmother slept in a bed that was surrounded by books, lurid, dark tales of murder and betrayal. She seemed to have no understanding of, or sympathy for, children and lived a secluded, somewhat pampered life, waited on by her unmarried sister Dora, whom she picked on maliciously.

In the downstairs workshop my grandfather would be busy building his office machines. The business enjoyed some success, but by the time we came along it was in decline. The old factory and workforce had been reduced to a single room and Trevor, his Trinidadian assistant. The noise of machinery drifting up the cold wooden staircase, the hum of typewriters and smoky wisps from soldering irons lent the house a touch of sorcery. There were long work benches covered in mysterious dials and scales, drills, measuring callipers and boxes filled with every shape and size of spring and gleaming screw imaginable. Curled iron filings like silver worms and the smell of damp earth and machine oil.

My grandmother occupied a room that was really just a little alcove curtained off with heavy damask drapes off the narrow hall that connected the big living and dining room with the kitchen – a dark, unhappy place infused with the clinging smell of burnt lard and tinned peas. Ranged along the window ledge were rows of plastic yoghurt pots crammed with congealed frying-pan fat that was stored in a habit dating back to the war. Her living space was fenced off by rows and rows of books stacked up on

all sides on the floor, like mah-jong tiles. Cheap paperbacks: John
Creasy, Leslie Charteris, Dick Francis, Marjory Allingham, Ellery
Queen, Dorothy L. Sayers. Characters like The Saint, The Baron,
The Toff. She used to send me Agatha Christie novels by surface
post, wrapped in brown paper tied with string, and accompanied
by tiny reels of brown magnetic tape bearing audio letters. We
would sit and listen to her voice, watching the clear plastic spools
slowly turning in the machine. It felt like a message from a distant
galaxy.

In the reception area one morning I find Jaafar sitting behind his
desk. He is the co-owner of the building. In his thirties, Jaafar
assumes that I have come home in search of investment opportunities, drawn by the oil money and the loosening of restrictions.
Most of the people renting his rooms are businessmen. He is optimistic about the current situation and asks about the oppurtu-
nities in Spain, where I live. For a time, we talk about Spanish
products – ceramics, about which I know nothing, but also cars
and lorries. For about five minutes I try to convince myself that I
might be able to go into some kind of commercial enterprise. I am
pretty sure I would be terrible at it. Nevertheless, I am intrigued
by how it works, and, besides, it is a way of getting Jaafar to talk.
He himself recently returned from six years in the United States.
Moving back wasn't easy, he says. It wasn't his first attempt. By
1992 he had grown disenchanted with life in Philadelphia, and
with his American wife. He longed for home, but those were difficult times. The regime was still in its hard-line phase and the place

was swimming with radicals: Afghan Arabs, Pakistanis, Iraqis, Iranians, Egyptians. They all had offices and training camps here. That era came to an end with the split between Bashir and Turabi at the end of their first decade. The country needed revenue. In the late 1990s oil exploitation began to get serious and, in a burst of pragmatism, the zealots were nudged aside.

The oil money has fuelled a land boom. It is the fastest way to new wealth. Property prices have tripled in recent years. Jaafar and his brother bought this plot of land for 200,000 LS per square metre – around US $200. That was seven years ago. The next-door plot has just sold for three times that. The gaps are filling in quickly and business is good. Jaafar's clients are technocrats from Europe and the Gulf, information technology specialists from Oman who fly across the Red Sea for two or three weeks at a time. There are still problems, he claims, obstacles in the way of the honest entrepreneur trying to make a living, and the government sets taxes too high.

Jaafar's cheerful optimism starts to wither under the weight of my questions. I suspect that I have overdone my interest and now it sounds as if he is trying to discourage me. I have come to resemble a threat, a potential competitor, or maybe he is trying to justify his prices. I've still not adjusted to how expensive Khartoum has become. Most hotel rooms start at around $150 a night. Here, that kind of money seems strangely ludicrous. Jaafar is impatient to recover his investment. It is a sign of the uncertainty that characterises this boomtown desperation; tomorrow the bubble might just burst.

Relenting, he offers to drive me into town. On the way, he relaxes a little and explains that the government is incapable of providing even basic services. If the road outside your house needs resurfacing nothing will be done until the residents can afford to pay for the work themselves. They gather up, say, twenty million (just under $10,000), most of which subsequently disappears. We make a detour to drop off his young daughter at her kindergarten, a brown-walled house with a high metal gate that has been brightly painted to distinguish it from the others in the street. The lack of public schools means private institutions have sprung up all over the place. Parents struggle to pay the necessary fees. The same applies to healthcare. There are new private hospitals everywhere. The public sector has withered away. We pass a group of pupils from a nearby government school, dressed in their blue camouflage outfits, a paramilitary hangover from the days of National Salvation and its vision of a militarised Islamic Republic along Iranian lines. Thousands of black chadors were imported from Tehran for women in the public sector, as well as whips for the morality police to chastise offenders. But it takes more than a few uniforms and renaming of streets to create a revolution.

This desire to erase the old affected money in a direct way. A combination of zeal and inflation gave rise to a confusion of currencies. At one stage there were three: the old pound, the new pound and the dinar, all jostling for supremacy. When paying for something you might get all three back, mixed together in a grubby handful, even in a bank. In restaurants the menu might be marked in dinars or new pounds, but was always quoted in old pounds, multiplied a thousand times, which creates its own kind of confusion.

When they came to power in June 1989 the country was deeply in debt. Oil deposits were not much more than a rumour. According to senior military officers the war in the South was unwinnable, but no effort was made to broker a peace deal. In the first six years the currency fell against the US dollar, dropping from 12 to 700 LS. The economy was in disastrous shape and the war was costing around a million dollars a day. Now, in the midst of this boom, all of that is just a memory that everyone is eager to forget, just like the signposts on street corners that no one pays any attention to.

To face the river is to turn one's back on the landscape: the river road with its dark canopy of thick banyan leaves, the cool breeze that blows by the palace, the vegetation that thrives there in the grey silt and blue water. All of this is a distant memory only a few hundred metres away down what was once known as Victoria Avenue, now *Sharia al-Qasr*, Palace Road.

Even as the Blue and White Niles come together, merging into the main artery that flows north from here, the capital seems to splinter, fragmenting around the point of confluence. By nature this city is plural, a conglomerate of three towns: Khartoum, Khartoum North (or Bahry) and Omdurman. *Al Asima al-Muthalatha* – the triple capital. This multiplicity hangs over the city as a stark reminder of the country's nature: diversity, plurality and the potential of unity. This is geography as metaphor.

It continues to duplicate itself, multiplying, spreading outwards in ever-expanding rings into new quarters, neighbourhoods, places that have appeared literally out of nowhere. Houses have sprung out of the ground, mud walls rising up, unfolding themselves from the dust to be dubbed with a host of invented names. This is the shape of Doxiadis's City of the Future. As a metaphor for urban expansion in the twenty-first century, it tells us what is in store for Khartoum. The struggle against indifference, anonymity, the submergence of individuality under a flood tide of demographic growth. This is what most people mean when they talk about change. The torrent of people from out there beyond the horizon, from the great wide nowhere. In the long run, this influx may be the only hope this country has of surviving.

At night you find yourself enmeshed in a transit hub that looms out of the dark. Buses, cars, taxis and minivans churn around trying to find their way, spreading drapes of mineral dust that glitter like murky wings in headlight beams. The city has swollen, overflowing its banks. Out of a sense of wonder, people offer to drive you as far as the Sabaloga Dam to prove to you how far the urban sprawl extends. It is as if they themselves do not quite believe what has happened to their city, what is happening before their very eyes. At independence in 1956, it was less a city than a small town. The population of the entire country was put at ten million. Today, the capital alone rivals that figure.

Night and day, minivans and tiny microbuses hurtle along Africa Road, urgently ferrying people to and from the centre. Crossroads wrap themselves like snarled rope around points of convergence. There are stalls with hot tea and snacks. Oil lamps hiss and two-tone horns sound bursts of exuberance. Jagged fragments of music spill from passing windows. Lively food stalls, roadside vendors and market shacks have materialised to feed the needs of thousands of passing strangers daily. Young boys rush around calling out the destinations of places that have just been invented – you won't find them on any map. They lie further out, quarters you have never heard of until you arrive.

Junctions like this are springing up around the city, jumping-off stations before you reach the darkness and all points beyond. The roads trail off into the distance and then drop away abruptly, tarmac giving way to sand. After a short gap, another strip might begin, or not. There are no street lights, of course. It's too soon for that. The only illumination comes from passing cars and the flicker of oil lamps. The new quarters adopt names that reflect the state of the world at the time of their birth. There is Dar al-Salaam and El Fatih, Angola and Mandela, as well as a Naivasha – named after the Rift Valley town in Kenya where the Comprehensive Peace Agreement was signed in 2005, ending the Second Civil War. There is even one called *Allah Maafy* – meaning 'Allah is not in', or maybe 'God doesn't exist'. In ten years' time, perhaps less, this virtual city will come to define the capital by the sheer volume of its inhabitants.

By day this geography of necessity comes to light. A stratigraphy of invention. Dusty waste covered with the ground-down detritus of plastic bags and bottles – flattened and curled like curious seashells. It is constantly growing, a steady, timeless accumulation. Rows of adobe bricks lie baking in the sun. The clay-rich earth is mixed with water and straw and then poured into wooden moulds before being stacked and left to dry. The grey-brown colour matches the landscape, rendering the walls indistinguishable from the earth. You drive towards what looks like nothing, only to find yourself suddenly surrounded, as if a dusty sheet has been whipped away to reveal rows of houses. The western edge of Omdurman is now said to reach almost to the border of neighbouring Kordofan province. Nobody knows what is out there. It all folds into the blurred conglomeration of rumour and fear. Some quarters have been here for over twenty years, but are still not officially recognised as part of the city. They are not connected to the power grid or sewage system and water is delivered by two-wheel donkey cart with a rusty tank on the back.

The fear of the incursion of outsiders, the so-called 'Black Belt' of refugees, dates back more than twenty years. This was the fear that the new arrivals, full of anger towards their Northern rulers, would one day rise up from their shanty towns and take their revenge, murdering the good citizens of Khartoum as they slept in their beds. To counter the spread of mud huts, the newly wealthy, pockets plump with oil revenue, have turned their backs on the horizon. Towers are going up all over the place. Ten, fifteen floors or more, far beyond what the infrastructure can bear. In leafy, residential Souq Two the old villas are knocked down with sledgehammers and gardens laid over as cement skeletons rise into the sky and stay there, unfinished. Everything is done in stages. First you buy the land, then you build the framework. The flats are completed only when they are sold. The two cities, the horizontal sprawl and the vertical spiral, are like diametrically opposed universes.

In 1820 Khartoum was no more than a permanent military camp. It only became the functioning seat of Egyptian rule around ten years later. John Petherick and George Melly, two British travellers who visited the town in 1846 and 1850 respectively, make it clear that Khartoum was a place of considerable importance. Both men noted the primitive architecture, the irregular construction of the town, the narrow, winding streets; a constriction relieved only here and there by empty spaces resembling squares, etc. By 1862, when Sir Samuel Baker passed through, the town was still labouring to redeem itself. He recorded it as a miserable, filthy, unhealthy spot whose economy was driven by the slave trade.

Only twenty years on, another visitor, the South Tyrolean Father Ohrwalder, was struck by the pleasant gardens and shady groves of date palms. Perhaps it was all in the eye of the beholder. With the fall of Khartoum to the Mahdi in 1885, the city was abandoned. Everything of value was ferried across the river to Omdurman, where the Khalifa made his base. The mission house, the arsenal and parts of the palace were all that was left standing. Ohrwalder, a Catholic priest who was held captive for ten years, claimed that the building of opulent houses was forbidden by order of the thrifty Khalifa, who feared that it might lead to people hiding money in them. Houses then were not understood as being something permanent. Traditionally built of mud, they could be abandoned and rebuilt at the drop of a hat, much like the settlements on the city's outskirts today. Anything more solid was viewed with suspicion.

After the Reconquest in 1898, Kitchener set about rebuilding his new city, driving linear streets straight through the rubble. The British deemed Omdurman as hopeless, condemned to remain a rabbit warren, where walls were built 'at every conceivable angle and irregular curve'. The streets broadened and converged with no sense of order; at times they simply gave out into a dead end, big enough in places for a battalion to march abreast and in others barely the width of two people standing side by side. It remained largely unchanged from half a century earlier, when Petherick and Melly, exasperated and suffocating, were lost in the maze that is Africa.

W. H. McLean, author of the first urban plan for Khartoum back in 1910, wrote that a new and splendid city had been raised from the ruins left behind by the Khalifa. By 1960 Khartoum covered an area of seven square miles, with a population of around 15,000, all contained within the loop of the railway line that ringed it to the south and over which it was to spill in the coming years. Those living outside this iron arch outnumbered those within fourfold. Omdurman was the largest bazaar town in the entire continent, containing, according to McLean, 'specimens of most of the North and Central African races'. Khartoum, with its planned streets, remained obstinately 'European'.

Across the river in Khartoum North, Nubians were arriving from the area around Aswan, among them my father's family. They raised the number of inhabitants to around 25,000 officially, although, since the figures were not reliable even then, the real number may have been much higher. In common parlance, Khartoum was the 'office', Omdurman was 'home' and Khartoum North, with its growing industrial area of factories and dockyards, was known as the 'workshop'. The business centre of Khartoum had an Arab and a European market, the Arab being more 'Oriental' than 'African' in tone.

The city was certainly more cosmopolitan in those days. At that point a quarter of the population was made up of Europeans, the rest being Egyptian, Syrian and Sudanese. There was a 'Levantine' sector of rather wealthy traders and businessmen from Syria and Lebanon, and a quarter known as 'Little Greece', which began in Abu Tulieh Avenue and extended west to Victoria Avenue. Here there was a colony of middle-class Greeks, with their clinics and social clubs, shops and grocery stores, bakeries, bars, schools and churches, all serving a sizeable Greek community. There were street signs that added Greek names to the more common Arabic or English names. Today, there remain few traces of the Greek presence. The Greek Orthodox Church is secluded behind high walls and large iron gates, chained and padlocked. More commonly there is Papa Costa's bakery and restaurant, where writers still meet to read their work and talk.

At the furthest extreme of the southern end of the city, across the rail loop, lay the New Deims, a colony of mud houses laid out in a gridiron pattern around two large cemeteries that are still there today. These were low-income families who lived in fairly bad conditions, with underground pit latrines. The transverse streets were built wider than the longitudinal to provide shelter from the prevailing north–south winds. South of the New Deims were shanty towns made of tin sheets and wood where the Fellata, who had arrived in search of work from West Africa (particularly Nigeria), lived in less comfortable conditions. In this context, the current expansion of the city seems, in part, like a continuation of what went on before. The old European sections in the centre have faded out, taking with them the cosmopolitan diversity they represented, while the old dynamic between the classes remains.

Am I trying in some way to define myself through understanding this city? How, then, to describe it? The Incomplete City. The Unfinished City? The Broken City? Of course, it's not one city at all, but fractured. It is defined less as a city than by the rivers that flow through it, giving it life. The rivers divide the capital into three lobes. Perhaps there is a clue in this multiplicity. It is young, compared to Cairo, Baghdad or Damascus. It has no Omayyad architecture, no ancient temples or precious libraries. Two centuries ago there was nothing here but a simple fishing village. An improvised city, growing in the disorganised fashion of today's expanding globalised cities everywhere. Mutating. Out of control. There is no narrative here of metropolitan grandeur. This is not a playground for the wealthy, like Dubai, say. Nor

an industrial pole of the world such as Shanghai. It is not struggling to hold onto past glory, as some Western cities are, to avoid
being turned into gleaming, decrepit icons, of real value only to
tourists and real-estate speculators. To write about the cities of
Europe or America is to write of places that, as Toni Morrison
puts it, the disenfranchised inhabit but have no claim to. Here
there is a similar contest in play, as the new inhabitants arrive to
face the country's rulers and lay claim to its future.

The question I keep coming back to, perhaps the real reason
I came back here, is: what claim do I have to this city? A shared
history? The formative years of my life? A sense of heritage, of
belonging? Perhaps, but is that really enough? I didn't come here
to find myself, but to come to terms with what this country means
to me, and the truth is that all I really only know of it is this city.
I have always lived in cities. Despite a longing for solitude and
nature, rural areas make me nervous. I love the anonymity of the
city. The sense of equality it brings. Nobody can fully claim the
city because its true nature confronts us daily with our otherness.

We like to think we have a hold on those cities in which we
have spent part of our lives, but we don't, not really. If we are
lucky we might be able to glimpse some unchanged spirit that
remains constant in our lifetime, but even that is largely a prod-
uct of our own imagination. Cities change just as people change.
Much as I enjoy revisiting old haunts, it takes more than a few
visits to restore that bond; it takes commitment.

In describing Paris, Baudelaire wrote of the joys of losing oneself in the crowd. In Joyce's Dublin, Bloom notes, 'Everything
speaks in its own way.' Here, too, it comes in scraps, fragments,
glimpses. I struggle to find a way to hold on to what I see around
me, to bring it together, to set it in a frame that holds, not just
here, but one that resonates out there in the world. My position
is uncertain. Unlike Saul Bellow's Augie March, who declares
himself an American with conviction, I have only doubt. That
was another age. Augie March's exuberance is contradicted
by the alienness of New York in another of Bellow's works;
the New York of Mr Sammler is a city that is beyond his control, but that points towards the way the world is today. The

subcultures and 'panic waving' colour that wrestle the city from his grasp are somehow familiar, even comforting. This is where Hanif Kureishi's Karim Amir comes in, 'an Englishman born and bred, almost'. None of these examples is adequate, none of them quite fits my situation.

All cities are sacred, rising out of the ground to reach for the sky. The first settlements were burial grounds; they began when it became important to preserve our own presence through our ancestors. We started to take ourselves seriously. Our passing was worthy of record. Necropolis. Biopolis. The City of the Dead and the City of the Living. Wittgenstein once wrote that language is like an ancient city, a maze of streets and houses, the old and the new. Perhaps the corollary of this is that all cities are unfinished stories, trying to invent a language in which to express themselves.

Richard Sennet, strolling through Manhattan with Hannah Arendt, observes that the exile's voyage to citizenship entails the loss of the self – the gradual diminishment of the 'I'. This loss of identity, this commitment to our new belonging, takes place in the city, the matrix of modernity, somewhere, as Baudelaire observed of nineteenth-century Paris, it was possible to become bored. To the poet, escape from boredom lay before his very eyes, outside, in the encounter with otherness. To lose oneself in the crowd was to find one's individuality as a poet. This is the contradiction of cities, to belong is to be reminded of your outsiderness. To many, of course, this is a reason to fear the city, where one is faced with the possibility of encountering the Other: people who are not like you, who do not look like you do, do not share the same cultural references, or religious beliefs.

In the last three decades, Khartoum has become that place, where the otherness of the country has come face-to-face with itself. An accumulation of evidence of the government's failure to resolve the nation's problems. If in the past Sudan's problems were historically associated with conflicts that were far enough away to be out of sight and thus out of mind, the present situation promises that they are now unavoidable, close enough to touch and smell. Once it was possible to ignore what was happening out there. Now, it is right in front of you, at the crossroads. And there is something about this predicament that is both universal and very modern, a sign of the times we live in.

In the 1930s, Hannah Arendt had worked for the establishment of a Zionist state, which she envisaged as a place of freedom, 'a place so charged with history that it could belong to no one'. She imagined it would be a shared place of differences. Arendt became disillusioned when she realised that what was envisaged was the establishment of a nation, which would simply be compounding the 'European national error', as she put it. Having witnessed Hitler's rise to power, Arendt knew what nationalism was capable of. Her fears echo down through history to the present day when nationalist sentiments are being posited as a defence against spiralling globalisation and the influx of migrants. All too often, the notion of nationhood being touted by politicians in Europe today offers nostalgic longing for a distant vision past in place of a real of collective identity. Turning inwards, winding the clocks back, to render the nation as a fairy-tale fantasy. It is, essentially, an admission of failure, of our inability to embrace our collective otherness.

In *The Human Condition*, Arendt writes of the rebirth, or 'natality', as she calls it; the emergence of the will to remake oneself as an adult. This, to her, was the essence of politics; to change the world from the way it was inherited. The exile, or migrant, must find grounds for a common life among people who do not share the same story. We must learn to identify with the Other in order to find empathy for those who are not like us. As the world grows smaller and more crowded, the notion of stable, impermeable frontiers retreats into myth.

Another writer who struggled to reconcile his own experience with the segregation of his age was James Baldwin. I first read his essay 'Down at the Cross – Letter from a Region of My Mind' in a battered Penguin edition of the book *The Fire Next Time* that I still treasure, on one of those dead afternoons in the old house in Street 51. Addressing the racial problems of the United States at the height of the civil rights movement in 1962, Baldwin wrote that the only solution to the predicament of 'negroes' in America lay in the recognition, by both whites and blacks, that their fates were tied together to a common destiny. Baldwin describes the moment of his disillusionment with the Church at a young age, something that saved him from a life of delinquency. About a year after becoming a preacher he experienced 'a slow crumbling' of his faith when he discovered that religion was divisive. Salvation stopped at the church door: 'When we were told to love everybody, I had thought that that meant *everybody*. But no. It applied only to those who believed as we did, and did not apply to white people at all.' He goes on: 'The passion with which we loved the Lord was a measure of how deeply we feared and distrusted and, in the end, hated almost all strangers.' It is impossible not to hear in Baldwin's words an echo of our current predicament. In order to realise ourselves as a nation we have to accept ourselves *as we are*, rather than as we would like to see ourselves. In other words, to achieve our identity we need to recognise each other's existence.

The UN estimates that the slum population of the world is increasing at the rate of twenty-five million inhabitants a year. In his book *Planet of Slums*, the anthropologist Mike Davis wrote, 'Forty years ago [around the time James Baldwin was writing] ideological warfare between the two great Cold War blocs generated competing visions of abolishing world poverty and rehousing slum dwellers.' Now both sides appear to have abandoned this goal. The disregard with which the less wealthy parts of the world are seen is matched within the urban centres themselves. Davis has written extensively about the growth of Los Angeles in the early twentieth century, when roads and railway lines were constructed to separate the rich from poor neighbourhoods. This trend continues but the gaps are growing smaller and the spaces more crowded. For the first time in human history the urban population of the world now outnumbers the rural. A watershed in human history, as Mike Davis calls it, comparable in impact to the Neolithic or Industrial Revolutions. We have become an urban species, no longer capable of sustaining ourselves but wholly dependent on the services that provide us with food, water and power. In the urban environment humanity becomes tangled in an inextricable web of giving and taking, each wheel inventing itself in the shadow of its surroundings. Today's Dickensian characters are to be found in the favelas of São Paulo, in the Makoko slums of Lagos, in shanties from Mumbai to Addis Ababa and Khartoum, where these informal inhabitants make up to 99 per cent of the city's population.

The problem of securing the inner cities has now become a major priority for the military. The issue now is containment. With increasingly invasive high-tech surveillance systems to guard borders, it is the slums, with their disenfranchised populations, that present the greatest threat. In the wake of the humiliating 'Black Hawk Down' episode in Somalia in 1993, the Pentagon turned its attention to urban warfare. Tomorrow's battles will be fought in cities, they believe. In turning their attention to urban populations, the Pentagon and other military forces are following suit, learning to dichotomise – to distinguish friend from foe. They are being trained by Israel, a leading exponent of this type of warfare, having practised it for years on the Palestinians in the Occupied Territories.

Khartoum was an invention, a convenience, an outpost at a bend in the river, chosen less for its climate than for its strategic worth. 'How often,' asked McLean in 1910, with an air of weary resignation, 'do we find in the tropics arrangements which are clearly only suited to European conditions?' Kitchener's planned layout for the new city comprised a series of Double Street Crossings, adjacent blocks modelled on the pattern of the Union Jack, with diagonal lines as well as vertical and horizontal axes meeting at one central position. The design was not simply cosmetic. It lent itself to the strategic defence of the city – one machine gun at the centre could control all the surrounding streets. At the bottom of Victoria Avenue in front of the palace stood a statue of Gordon mounted upon a camel, long since relocated to Aberdeen. There was also a statue of Kitchener himself, on a horse named Democrat, which stood before the Ministry of Finance. That, too, has gone. But Kitchener's rigid geometrical order remains in place, steadily wilting under the increasing weight of traffic. The state's GIAD factory assembles 500 cars a month. When stuck in gridlock, you realise it is 500 too many.

Global cities today often have more in common with one another culturally than with the countries in which they are located. There is something, in other words, which connects the cosmopolitan inhabitants of Cairo, Chicago or Cape Town more closely to one another than with their compatriots in the Egyptian *rif*, the wilds of Kansas, or the shanty towns of Johannesburg. Goethe, writing in 1787, coined the term *Weltstadt*, or 'world city', to denote the cultural centres of the world. The Weimar poet yearned to discover a lost, ancient world in the neo-classical remains of Paris and Rome. Two centuries later and shorn of romanticism the term has come to signify the economic centres of the world and their isolation from the rest of the world. The wealthy isolate themselves not so much by borders as by private security contractors and gated communities.

We think of European cities as inherently ordered, though this is not how they came into being. They grew in awkward leaps and bounds. The 'urban revolution' was experienced at first hand as almost senseless growth. London had no central government until 1888. The real decisions were made by entrepreneurs, land-owners. The same is true of many European cities. It was money that determined change. The homes and shops of poorer people were torn down to make way for the wealthy. In 1910, the richest 1 per cent of Great Britain owned 70 per cent of the country's wealth (today it's around 55 per cent). The poverty and deprivation described by Dickens was the flip side of the pomp and glory of empire. The imperial magnificence of Edwardian London, 'the modern Rome' of Henry James, was built on the wealth coming from the vast empire that lay at the far end of the telescope. London swelled as the rural population diminished, reaching its zenith at the close of the nineteenth century. But already things were accelerating; it took London forty years to grow to the size that Rome had needed 600 years to attain.

The sense of order that informed the layout and structure of Europe's grand cities has come undone. The modern skyline juxtaposes ultra-modern megaliths alongside relics of past glory, from Nelson's Column to the Shard. We derive comfort from the sense of progress, although at times it feels as though society is sinking under the weight of all this freight, the past and the future, struggling for coherence in the present.

In Africa, the present wipes away the past at a faster rate, erasing it to make way for what is to come. In 1969, the Aswan High Dam flooded 300 kilometres of the Nile Valley, swamping hundreds of centuries of history under Lake Nasser. The present flows over the past, smoothing over gaps in the record like muddy water. Dig through the earth in Soba, just south of Khartoum, and you discover the remains of the kingdom of Alodia that emerged from the break-up of Meroë in around AD 500. Already Soba, which used to be a distant hamlet, is being absorbed into the expanding capital. In May 2005, more than thirty people were killed in clashes with police when thousands of IDPs were evicted from a shanty town in Soba Aradi. It is now the location of the new American embassy, which, according to a report in *Al Hayat* newspaper in March 2007, will also be the CIA centre for East Africa, something that would have been unthinkable ten years ago. Four hundred sealed shipping containers of equipment were brought into the country, bypassing customs inspections.

The old kingdoms blur into one another. Little remains of Kerma, though in the third millennium BC it was a threat to the pharaohs of Ancient Egypt. There were Kush and Meroë, and the sultanates of Darfur and Funj. All rose and fell back into the earth, worn down by sun and wind, leaving little trace of their passing. In the nineteenth century, the city of Suakin was a magnificent complex of gleaming buildings on the Red Sea carved of coral. Today it is a mound of rubble.

When I first came back here, I had no idea what awaited me. I expected the city I once knew to have been swept away by time. I thought I might come across a few vague traces scattered like fossilised relics, but they would be minutiae of little meaning to anyone but myself. I was astonished at how much had *not* changed. Underneath the time-worn decay was the city I remembered. As I walked around, fragments of lost memory began to surface, as if I had simply left them on such and such corner only to rediscover them again. Streets and squares, cinemas and shop signs, including my mother's old shop. All still intact. Even faces, people who remembered me. I began to experience a strange sense of guilt, having been absent for all those years, taking for granted that somehow it would all still be there for me, the city that had lived on in my imagination as I was busy writing about it, reconstructing it, inventing streets and corners, places and people. I felt intense gratitude to those who remembered me, friends and relatives who took me in as though no time at all had passed, as if a fissure had opened up, allowing me to peer through the crack in the earth and look back in time.

An odd couple walked into the shop one day hand in hand, her leading him, as my mother put it, like a pair of children who had stepped straight out of one of Grimm's fairy tales. She, a tiny, wizened figure in her seventies. He, a magical bean shoot, a giant rising into the sky – half-naked – his only concession to the ways of the city being a skimpy pair of red nylon shorts with the number eight on one leg. The woman led him forward like an overgrown child, her prize. A string of curious followers trailed behind them, like human breadcrumbs. They thronged the doorway, shoving one another in their impatience, their boxes of chewing gum and strings of lollipops hanging limply from senseless fingers while others pressed their faces to the window, hands cupped around their eyes to cut out the glare.

In the few years since it had opened, my mother's shop had become something of a refuge for strangers. It exercised a mysterious attraction. People walked in and buried themselves in the jumbled chaos. They would turn up to pass a few hours drinking tea and coffee, gulping down frothy glasses of sugary lemonade; the occasional tourist, engineers in transit, expat wives looking for ways to pass the day. The shop had become a reference point, one of those stopping-off places when you needed to get out of the sun or had an hour or so to kill downtown. In the evenings families would drop by on their nightly promenade.

They came in all shapes, sizes and colours. My mother had the ability to make all these wanderers feel welcome. It might have been the heat, or the fact that they were so far away from home, or maybe it had something to do with finding an Englishwoman in the midst of this foreignness. Cultural attachés, engineers, visiting professors, technocrats, volunteer teachers, sharp-tongued novelists, deposed monarchs from mountain kingdoms you couldn't find on an atlas, would-be Lawrences who had just loped into town on a camel, amateur artists, journalists, photographers, all looking for someone to help make sense of what they had found here. They came and went with the seasons, and she listened to them all.

If my mother managed to adapt so well to this alien environment it was because she possessed a generosity of spirit that stemmed, I believe, from a fundamental belief in the goodness of people. Like my father, she was amused by the quirks and eccentricities of individuals. Neither of them had a head for business, but they were both social creatures. If she had been born a decade or so later she would no doubt have become some kind of hippy, although there was nothing remotely bohemian about her; apart from that one time when I saw her sitting on the floor at a grown-up party puffing on a black Sobranie. It was the only time I ever saw her smoking and the sight shocked me to the core, revealing as it did a hidden sensuality that I had never seen before. She was interested in the rights of women and, growing up, I would browse through her stacks of the feminist magazine *Spare Rib*, with curiosity and not a little bafflement. Throughout her life, she remained committed to her life in Sudan. If she complained it was about the stupidity or short-sightedness of individuals.

On most days I would walk over from school and sit in the back of the shop doing my homework. Overweight ladies would squeeze through the narrow gap and disappear into the shaded booth where a modern machine awaited them. Pads and Velcro straps were attached to their fleshy parts that – hey presto! – by the miracle of modern science would disappear. That, at least, was the idea. I would listen to their snores competing with the unperturbed hum of the machine. They never looked any slimmer when they emerged, which perhaps explained why their husbands eventually grew tired of paying for a treatment whose only visible reduction was to their wallets. The machine was our star attraction, but we had other products such as biscuits that helped you to diet. People would pick these up and turn them over slowly in their hands. It doesn't look like much of a meal, they grumbled. They were right. We kids were fed the broken packets, the ones with little teeth marks on the cellophane where a mouse had tried to get in. When the desperate housewives of Khartoum waddled in and slumped down in front of my mother, imploring her to find a cure for them, she offered them Greek spaghetti that contained no starch and tasted like gritty string. As my father often declared, whenever a damaged packet found its way onto our table, you would be better off boiling the cardboard box it came in. There were preserves and marmalade that contained no refined sugar. These proved popular, not least with the customs officials in Port Sudan, who delayed every shipment just long enough for a few cases to go missing.

The glass sign over the doorway displayed the silhouette of a rather svelte female form – the goddess whom the good wives of our sleepy river town came to worship. The sign read 'Slimming' in English. In Arabic the G was replaced by a ق in the Arabic language, which transformed the name roughly into 'Salamanca'. It was a dreamy sound that evoked far-off, mysterious places like Samarkand or Camelot. It had nothing to do with anything, but it did have a ring to it.

But legends are sometimes not enough, and with time it became clear that people were not overly concerned about their weight, or at least not in sufficient number. Heart disease and diabetes

were plentiful, but being plump was perceived as a sign of wellbeing. Only poor people were thin, and there were enough of those
about to confirm the fact. Custom dwindled, my parents argued
and gradually the expensive imported products gave way to local
handicrafts aimed at the more discerning traveller.

It was this that had drawn our celebrity visitor, who turned
out to be none other than Leni Riefenstahl. The fierce little
septuagenarian dug her way furiously through every item, my
mother in hot pursuit. She did not take lightly to having her
goods handled in such cavalier fashion and was clearly having a
hard time restraining her temper as a cascade of leather boxes,
clay pots, amber necklaces, glass beads and hefty Bedouin
silver bracelets were sent flying. The energetic little German
lady made her way through the shop like a furious demon,
disturbing everything, ricocheting from one side to the other,
knocking over lamps, copper bowls, stacks of coloured bas-
kets, burrowing into the clothes rack like a ravenous predator.
Shoving hangers aside, she scrabbled through the collection of
gellabiyas and dresses. Then, to everyone's horror, she began
pulling her dress off over her head, revealing an enormous pair
of underpants. Horrified, my mother tried to stop her. The
gathered audience howled in response, their patience rewarded.
They clutched one another and fell about. Others went shriek-
ing wildly down the street. Wide-eyed kids turned to stone,
Chiclets tumbling from gaping jaws, not quite sure what they
were witnessing as my mother tried to guide her customer out
of sight. There was some debate over the price, but all that mat-
tered was ending this transaction as quickly as possible, and my
mother, who normally drove a hard bargain, gave way without
a fight. And then she was gone, vanishing through the doorway
forever, her entourage yapping at her heels, waving cigarettes
and caramels under her nose.

It was only some years later that I learned who Leni Riefenstahl
was. Her film *The Last of the Nuba* and the book of photographs that followed contained epic photographs of semi-naked
Nuban wrestlers covered in body paint, ash and blood. In her
essay 'Fascinating Fascism', Susan Sontag examined the German

filmmaker's career. Riefenstahl had made two documentary films for the Nazis in the 1930s; *Triumph of the Will*, in 1934, transformed the Nazi Party Congress at Nuremberg into a visually captivating classic. In 1936, she filmed the Berlin Olympics for *The Olympiad*. The aesthetics of these films, according to Sontag, allows them to 'transcend' propaganda. Riefenstahl had been a film star who had caught Hitler's eye. In her film on the Nuba, Sontag argues, Riefenstahl saw beauty and death, two themes that ran through all her work. In *The Last of the Nuba*, the defiant, semi-naked primitives await their imminent extinction. This was already underway. To Riefenstahl, the Nuban wrestlers fought not for material gain, but for 'the renewal of the sacred vitality of the tribe'. What awaited them was the corruption of their noble savagery by the trappings of modernity: clothes, money, jobs, and, of course, war. Riefenstahl was fascinated by the beauty of the wrestlers in the same way that she was drawn to the beauty of the Nazi soldiers. It is this objectification of the African in the European gaze that detaches the suffering on the continent from its political/historical context. It was one of those strange jump-cuts when time seemed to fold in on itself like a fan closing. History lay dormant in black and white photographs in our school textbooks. There Hitler was, riding along with the top down, hand held high in stiff-armed salute. And here she was in living colour, a little old lady trying out dresses in my mother's shop.

The dark figure of a nightwatchman sits motionless outside a house, leaning back against the wall on a broken-legged chair. His gaze is fixed with rapt, undivided attention on a group of teenage girls who sit inside a white SUV parked on the dusty apron nearby. A world away, they chatter and laugh among themselves, unaware they are being observed. Behind the glass, trapped in the glow that illuminates the interior, their brightly coloured headscarves bob like exotic plants. Al-Mufti Street is ablaze with flashing lights. A man staggers across the road with two beds under one arm. The jagged neon strips cut the darkness like glass rainbows over the line of sandwich stops, fast-food restaurants and juice bars. There is a party on at the Al-Watany club and the singer's voice echoes up into the hot night air over the lights. Passing *rukshas* with sound boxes attached rattle past in a high-pitched stutter, the music thundering in their wake. A little girl of about twelve, in a long white dress that is far too tight for her – she can hardly move her legs – stumbles across the uneven road in high heels balancing a tall stack of Styrofoam boxes containing someone's takeaway supper. It is Friday evening and this is where people come to have fun. The gardens of the cafés along the street are rich with the aromatic smell of shishas, the fragrant tobacco flavoured with peach, banana and apple.

At an intersection where people have great trouble crossing, one of the notoriously unstable three-wheeler *rukshas* was hit by a pick-up. Five people died. A crowd gathered and the *wali*, or governor, of Khartoum rushed to the scene as things began to turn nasty. Within days they were pulling up the road and installing a new set of traffic lights. It is a mark, people say, of just how nervous the regime is. The story is repeated everywhere I go.

In other ways, too, the government is hurting people, through outrageous taxes that make work unviable. Carpenters who can no longer afford to work because of the rates they are forced to pay. They close their workshops and carry on working from home, but the quality is not the same. Farmers are suffering, too. Normally, they are advanced loans from the Agricultural Bank against the coming harvest. If they default on their payments they go to prison. Many end up losing everything. Greed has produced new levels of hardship and is changing the manners and mores of the Sudanese. Stealing has become commonplace in a country once proud of its honesty.

Outside the O-zone Café tall, bony figures climb out of an SUV, silhouetted by sweeping headlights. These are the new urban cosmopolitans, the children of the Southern elite now installed in city palaces. No longer the construction workers of old, but the architects of the New Sudan. Their future lies in the closing stages of the CPA, which stipulates that the South has the right to hold a referendum on self-determination. If nothing is done to counter the general trend the South will secede a year from now. Apparently oblivious to their precarious situation, the kids take their seats under the trees, and wait to be served cappuccinos by Filipina waitresses. Dressed in the latest LA fashions of their rap heroes, they seem a long way from the bush where their fathers fought for twenty odd years.

Elsewhere, solitary Landcruisers emerge from the desert carrying silent, desperate men, their faces wrapped, their eyes wild, their clothes covered in dust after the long journey from who knows where. They circle the city at night. No one knows who they are, how they got here or why they came. In a quiet street they pull up and the men climb out to disperse into the shadows. When the cab light comes on it reveals the interior is loaded with weapons.

Alone in my room, I find myself going back over my notes on Zubayr Pasha. So much of Sudan's character is pinned to the figure of the Mahdi. Visionary leader, religious zealot, the man who drove the infidel out, his role seems oddly disproportionate. The Mahdi was in so many ways a one-off, an enigmatic presence driven by spiritual conviction and virtue. He was dead within six months of defeating Gordon. His legacy lived on, through the sect he founded and the Umma political party that emerged from that, and through his descendants, who form a kind of aristocracy in the absence of such a thing. His great-grandson, Sadig al-Mahdi, was ousted from his post as prime minister by the 1989 coup.

Slavery has left a more enduring legacy on this country than the Mahdi's brief passing, and nobody represents that history better than Zubayr. Unlike the Mahdi, he lived on into his eighties. As a slave trader, Zubayr might be seen as the diametric opposite of the Mahdi, driven not by divine guidance or a noble mission, but by pragmatism, and old-fashioned capitalism. He created an empire the size of France on the southern edge of Darfur.

Appalled by slavery, British officials were advised not to interfere too much, not to come between masters and slaves. It was deemed unwise to antagonise the rich and powerful slavers. When Samuel Baker arrived in Khartoum in 1862 he noted that the city's thriving economy was driven by the slave trade. Merchants would sail south and overrun villages, burning and looting, seizing men, women and children, placing them in wooden yokes, crowding them together in tiny, cramped spaces below decks before bringing them north. Ivory and slaves went hand in hand; the ivory funded the transport of slaves.

The earliest record of slaves being traded dates back to AD 652 and the treaty between Christian Nubia and Muslim Egypt, pledging an annual tribute of slaves to be paid in exchange for peace. No doubt the trade was not new even then. Between the sixteenth and nineteenth centuries the Funj Sultanate of Sennar established a tradition of armies of slave soldiers. This was continued by the Ottomans after the Turco-Egyptian invasion of 1820, with the Egyptian *Jihadiyya* battalions, made up of branded

Southern soldiers – similar to the Turkish Janissaries. Domestic slaves became widespread and official raids were undertaken on a massive scale, always into non-Muslim territories.

All of this naturally left deep traces within society by the time independence arrived in the twentieth century. According to the historian R. S. O'Fahey, Sudanese slavery, particularly the domestic form, created what he described as a 'very peculiarly Sudanese form of racism'. O'Fahey had studied the situation in Darfur, where anyone not wishing to convert to Islam would flee south to the fringes of the sultanate where they could live as pagans. To the Fur in the north of Darfur, this made them legitimate prey, a reference to this even finding its way into one of their traditional songs: 'The people of Dar Fertit are slaves, and yet they go free.'

This process goes some way towards explaining the rise of origin myths that supported the suppression of an 'African' identity and the emergence and legitimisation of an 'Arab' one in its place. Ethnicity, religion, commercial self-interest all combine, along with the notion that Islam overrides ethnic bonds or erases them, clearing the land for habitation by the true believers.

In the mid-1990s, a number of Christian organisations began to mount a campaign to draw attention to a revival of the slave trade. Chief among these was a Swiss-based organisation called Christian Solidarity International (CSI). During the Cold War they used to smuggle Bibles across the Iron Curtain. In the post-Soviet Union era they turned their attention to Africa. In

1995, CSI began buying back slaves in so-called 'slave redemptions', using Arab middlemen to arrange the deals. In the US, the American Anti-Slavery Group launched a campaign to raise funds to support CSI's activities and increase awareness. By then Sudan had achieved the dubious reputation of being the world capital of militant Islamism. Listed as a sponsor of terrorism, it was viewed by the West as a rogue state, which made it increasingly isolated and easy to demonise. It was a script that played well with potential donors. The highly emotive nature of the issue, particularly in the United States, stirred up interest. In four years CSI claimed to have bought the freedom of nearly 8,000 slaves, paying between fifty and a hundred dollars apiece. In 1998 a class of schoolchildren in Colorado founded an abolitionist movement that drew a tremendous amount of media attention. They amassed a total of $50,000 from around the country.

Several commentators pointed out that local villagers and several organisations opposed paying redemption fees on the strength that it rewarded the slavers, and spurred them to take more. Slavery in some form had existed for centuries, and the government was fuelling this by exploiting local animosity in its use of militias. Encouraging indiscriminate prejudice against Arabs and Muslims was counter-productive. To many of Bashir's supporters it confirmed the notion of a Christian–Zionist conspiracy against Muslims. And while it might ease the conscience of a few well-meaning people, buying back a few slaves was not going to solve Sudan's problems.

The media nevertheless picked up on the campaign. Soon politicians and pop stars were stepping in. Michael Jackson declared, 'I want this slavery ended, now and forever.' Celebrities chained themselves to the railings outside the Sudanese embassy in Washington, DC. The thought that Christians were being forced into slavery by a rogue Muslim state touched a lot of nerves in the nation's capital. A number of congressmen became involved, including Susan Rice, then assistant secretary of state, and new legislation was passed allowing partisan aid to be fed to the SPLA.

Invited by the House of Lords to prepare a report on the subject, Lord McNair presented his findings in 1997 in which he

declared that much of the material he had seen struck him as con-
trived. That the government in Khartoum was guilty of all manner of human rights violations was not in doubt, he wrote, but
playing up certain aspects of the conflict did not help resolve the
situation; on the contrary, the harder they pushed the more these
groups actually strengthened the government. McNair concluded
that stories of organised slavery were sensationalist attempts to
distort what was happening. Paying tens of thousands of dollars
to middlemen in order to free 'slaves' risked making the situation worse. There were stories of SPLA men being dressed up as
slavers to meet the buyers, and of redemption money being directly used to fund Garang's forces.

McNair also heard stories, both in Kordofan and in the Nuba
Mountains, of people, mostly children, being abducted by the
other side – up to 10,000 male minors were reported to have been
inducted into the SPLA since 1991 and forced to become child
soldiers – a horrific statistic that put any of the CSI accusations
in the shade.

By the 1990s the war in the South had become sharply polar-
ised along ethnic lines. Leadership conflicts with the intractable
Garang had sharpened tensions. In the age of automatic weapons,
global power struggles and geostrategic interests, old tribal ani-
mosities acquired a heightened, internecine pitch.

The Second Sudanese Civil War, as it is sometimes called, began
with attacks on the oil camps in Bentiu in 1983, shortly after it
was announced that petroleum had been discovered. Nimeiri, six
billion dollars in debt, was badly in need of the revenue. Before it
could be exploited, however, rebels had attacked and killed three
Chevron workers in the area. Bentiu lies in the Nuer heartland.
The attacks were a resumption of the war that had ended with the
1972 Addis Ababa Accord, an agreement many of the old Anyanya
rebels had never really trusted. Their struggle had been seces-
sionist right from its beginnings in 1955, months before Sudan
itself was declared independent. The new rebels styled themselves
Anyanya II and were largely drawn from the Nuer tribe.

Ideological differences between Garang, a Bor Dinka, and the
Anyanya II rebels soon degenerated into ethnic conflict. Some of

the Anyanya preferred to join their enemies on the government side rather than submit to the authoritarian Garang. Nimeiri, and later Bashir, attempted to raise a Nuer militia to counter Garang's SPLA and safeguard the oil fields. Their opportunity came in 1991, when Garang's leadership was challenged by his own commanders. The subsequent confrontation was particularly vicious in areas where Dinka and Nuer had traditionally lived together, such as along the Duk Ridge. Riek Machar, one of the commanders who led the rebellion against Garang, engaged the use of Nuer beliefs, prophecies and prophets to help his cause. He raised a *decbor*, or 'White Army', who used razor-sharp spears and machetes to murder their victims. They covered themselves in white ash and with sheets they believed to be bullet-proof. After the 2014 Bor massacre, a series of raids that resulted in about 2,000 deaths, Garang's forces staged a counter-attack. The list of war crimes levelled at both sides in this period is long and horrific – raiding and looting civilian property including livestock, along with rape, abduction, abuse of prisoners, summary executions. The damage done to the social fabric was devastating. An estimated 14,000 men, women and children were abducted in that time.

The fall of the Mengistu regime in Ethiopia in 1991 robbed Garang of his strongest supporter. As a result, hundreds of thousands of Sudanese refugees were forced to leave the camps in Ethiopia and cross the border back into the war zone. Thousands died along the way. The government bombed them and used Chinese MiG fighter jets to strafe them with machine guns. The exodus precipitated a humanitarian crisis that was to continue on and off throughout the decade.

Operation Lifeline Sudan (OLS), a coalition of more than thirty NGOs formed under the umbrella of the UN World Food Programme, poured two billion dollars into the region over more than a decade and in this way relief aid became a weapon. Controlling its flow became an important strategic goal in the war. Khartoum restricted the issue of flight permits, which effectively meant that it decided whether civilians dependent on aid should live or die. This left the relief organisations with a dilemma: to break the embargo meant going against the government; not to do so meant letting people starve to death. Neutrality is a hard line to hold. For their part, the SPLA refused to let food into towns where government troops were besieged. They also requisitioned aid shipments for their own use. Both the SPLA and the government used their own militias to prey on civilians and steal their cattle and food. The outcome was a man-made disaster: famine accounted for the vast majority of fatalities in the war, close to two million. OLS was finally allowed into Upper Nile province in 1993. They estimated that 1.5 million people were in need of humanitarian assistance. In the 1998 famine in Bahr al-Ghazal around 60,000 people perished.

In the end it was greed that healed the rift and brought them back together again, united in one cause: to prevent the North from exploiting the South's petroleum resources. Sixteen militia commanders previously aligned with Khartoum turned against the government. A peace conference was arranged to resolve the differences between Nuer and Dinka.

Ethnic differences and oil reserves are a bad mix. A 2003 Human Rights Watch report details the complex interactions between companies working in the area and the ongoing conflict. The report concludes that oil exploitation was a key factor in triggering violence and human-rights violations by all sides. There is some suggestion that oil companies were complicit, or at least turned a blind eye to abuses, allowing government forces to share facilities such as airstrips. Witnesses claimed that government forces were using an oil company airstrip at Heglig to refuel their bombers and helicopter gunships between attacks on civilian targets. A 2003 report by the European Coalition on Oil in Sudan repeats the allegations of collusion. For their part, the oil companies have claimed to be committed to upholding the protection of human rights and the environment.

The high-profile media campaign highlighting complicity in slavery, along with allegations of a link between forced displacement and the exploitation of oil resources, culminated in the Sudan Peace Act, an act that was a declaration of intent, both denouncing war crimes and the abuse of humanitarian aid, as well as a commitment to lasting peace negotiations to end the war. It was widely supported on both sides of the US House of Representatives and was eventually passed in October 2002. The Greater Nile Petroleum Operating Corporation began exporting oil from Sudan in 1999. It was the beginning of a new era and marked the start of a new age of prosperity for those close to the government.

Across the road from the university, in the grounds of the Museum of Natural History, couples seek refuge on benches under the trees. Such courtship is a vital part of young people's lives, especially since marriage is an expense few can afford. A cage over on one side seems to have been placed there almost as an afterthought. A pair of very old and weary crocodiles lie in the sun. The pen they share would be a fair size for a couple of healthy rabbits, but not much more than that. They lounge in the filthy water morosely awaiting their own extinction. On the other side of the yard stands a row of taps for prayer ablutions. Propped against the wall, as if dropped there casually, is a metal sign bearing rather clumsily painted lines from the Quran. It's not clear why they are in English, perhaps to enlighten foreign visitors: 'Allah creates what He wills. For verily Allah has power over all things.' A reminder that, despite this being a museum devoted to natural history, Darwin's influence stops at the gates of the museum.

The intellectual mastermind behind the Islamist fervour that was introduced with the 1989 coup was the charismatic Hassan al-Turabi. He first came to prominence in the wake of the popular uprising, or intifada, of October 1964, but it wasn't until 1989 that he really got his chance. Turabi had struggled for years to find the right formula that would deliver the success he craved. His detractors claimed that his prime motivation was not so much ideological as personal. There was a touch of vanity about his appearance. People close to him did not trust him. According to a former colleague, there was some doubt concerning his commitment to an Islamic state. There were those who felt that what he really wanted was power.

So much of this country's history is dominated by idiosyncratic figures, and Turabi is up there with the best of them. Born into the ruling elite, his father was a *qadi*, a judge, and so he attended Gordon Memorial College along with all the other sons of sheikhs and *qadis*. He arrived in Britain in 1955 to study law at the University of London. In 1959 he chose to go to Paris to do his doctorate at the Sorbonne. Even this decision was, in part, determined by a desire to defy the norm. He wanted to break the monopoly of the English language, 'to learn another language, another culture', as he put it. The British were not keen on Sudanese studying in France in case it gave them ideas. For Turabi, this was all the more reason to do so. At the heart of the conundrum that is Hassan al-Turabi there lies a contrariness. His dissertation compared British and French colonial models through their actions in a state of emergency. He returned home to teach in the same Faculty of Law at Khartoum University that he was later to run into the ground.

Turabi helped to found the Islamic Charter Front (ICF) as an alternative to the Muslim Brotherhood, which he felt was not a good fit for Sudan. The Brotherhood, or Ikhwan, was marginalised from mainstream politics. Until 1965 they were opposed to the idea of a national state. What they aspired to was an echo of the old caliphate that had once united the global Muslim community from China to the Iberian peninsula, undivided by the borders inherited from colonialism. When Nasser expelled the Ikhwan from Egypt, they set up shop in Sudan. Essentially, Turabi opposed all available options. Not only Hassan al-Banna's Ikhwan, but even Sayyid Qutb's brand of salafist fundamentalism.

None of them, he felt, truly addressed the question of how to replace the regime you were fighting. Even the Iranian revolution had been thwarted in his view, prevented from achieving its full potential thanks to dogmatism.

Turabi disliked the prominence of the traditional sects in Sudanese politics and in particular the place afforded the Mahdi, whose mission was unorthodox and broadly unacceptable within the tenets of conventional Sunni Islam. Turabi was a vain and egocentric character. One suspects that he envied the long shadow the Mahdi cast over Sudan's history and politics. Sudanese Islam, with its superstitions, its syncretic African blend, its Sufi tradition, was all too idiosyncratic for a man who was looking for a pragmatic, workable model of political Islam. At the root of Turabi's discontent lay a personal grievance, the sense of having been slighted. Despite all the years he had spent learning about the West, the interest was never reciprocated. 'The West knows so little about Islam, generally,' he once explained in an interview. 'Muslims know a great deal about Christianity because it is part of their historical heritage and tradition of Islam.'

In 1985, as attorney general, he oversaw Nimeiri's dismantling of the legal system, replacing it with the cruel and inhumane version of Sharia known as the September Laws. Turabi defended his work as being in the spirit of Islam. Emergency courts, he argued, were based on *ijtihad* – religious reasoning – and therefore the closest thing to Islamic courts. Like many of his more eccentric rulings, this baffled Muslim scholars.

His role in the 1989 coup was not immediately clear. He spent the first five months in prison, along with all the other politicians, before he emerged as the ideologue behind it all. It was a strange partnership. The Sorbonne-educated scholar and Omar al-Bashir, the garage mechanic and delivery boy, later to become a military officer. Not content to be a mere political leader, Turabi saw himself more as a visionary spearheading universal change in the Muslim world. In interviews, he often claimed to represent a new, mature wave of global Islamic awakening. Fending off comparisons with Khomeini, he lectured the Africa Subcommitee of the House of Representatives in Washington, DC, on Islamic 'fundamentalism' and how the 1991 Gulf War had transformed the political dynamic in the Middle East, creating new regional alliances. Traditional enmity between Sunni and Shia, he claimed, no longer applied; evidence of this emerged in the close cooperation between Sudan and Iran.

Turabi set up the Pan-Arab and Islamic Conference (PAIC) in an attempt to breathe new life into the eclipsed notion of Pan-Arabism, which died out in the 1970s. Islam was to replace nationalism as the new driving force. The PAIC was aimed at curbing American imperialism and placing the Islamic Republic at the centre of the Muslim world. The General Assembly provided an umbrella that recognised and supported groups from Tajikistan to Burma and the Philippines, taking in Kosovo and Bosnia along the way. Turabi was in touch with them all: Islamists in the former Soviet republics in Central Asia, Kashmiri and Afghani mujahideen, even Louis Farrakhan's Nation of Islam in the United States. 'I know every Islamic movement in the world, secret or public,' he boasted in 1994. The fall of Kabul in 1992 meant that veteran Afghan Arabs were looking for new battles to fight. Some went to Bosnia, others arrived in Sudan to answer Turabi's call to take Islam deep into the continent, now that the civil war in the South had been renamed a jihad.

Here, finally, was his hour of glory. Turabi spoke of an Islamic renaissance. Nationalism had damaged the Islamic community by dividing Muslims, he claimed. He saw his mission as being to reunite them, to restore Islam to the glory of its golden age when the caliphate extended across continents, from Sumatra to Spain.

Examining Turabi's statements at the time, one is struck by the incongruity between his claims and the reality of the country. This new version of Islam was held up as a rejection of Western amorality and hypocrisy, yet women and children were left to starve in the refugee camps in the South. The Sudanese are Arab in culture, Turabi insisted, despite the colour of their skin. The First Gulf War was a blessing in disguise, he declared, for it had galvanised the entire Muslim world. It exposed the weakness of those who bowed to the Americans, such as the monarchs of Morocco and Saudi Arabia. The Pan-Arab Islamic Conference would bring together Islamic banks and charities, investment companies, missionaries, educational institutes, insurance and business enterprises.

To the outside world Turabi remained a beguiling figure. He spoke eloquently, if disparagingly, of the West. Charming and erudite, with a rather childish grin, he would come across as an impish uncle in comparison with the glowering ayatollahs in Iran. No one knew what to make of him. His elliptical statements made him hard to pin down. He was dubbed the *éminence grise*, the shadowy figure behind the throne.

For a time Khartoum became the new Kabul. The Egyptian press reported that Osama bin Laden's second in command, the paediatrician Dr Ayman al-Zawahiri, had opened training camps in Shendi, Khartoum North and Omdurman, where hundreds of jihadis were being drilled, many of them having arrived there from other camps in Iran and Yemen. The Pasdaran, the Iranian Republican Guard, provided more than thirty million of Tehran's dollars to help out. Children were rounded up in the shanty towns on the outskirts of Khartoum to be taken to special *khalwa* schools where they were chained up, beaten and forced to learn the Quran by rote. They were given Muslim names and when they reached the age of fifteen were entered into the militias and sent south to fight.

The constitution had been abolished. A state of emergency prevailed. All political parties were banned. A new national security order allowed people to be detained for up to six months without judicial review. Torture, disappearance and unlawful detention were all commonplace. Fifty-seven judges were dismissed. The press was heavily censored. Newspapers were closed, journalists arrested and many fled abroad. My parents joined the exodus, settling in Cairo in late 1990. The old traditional political parties, the Umma and the Democratic Union Party, were both severely curtailed, their property and mosques confiscated. The Popular Defence Forces were formed, militarising civilians with very little training. Participation was obligatory for all civil servants and university students, forty-five days of compulsory military training to increase religious fervour and to prepare them to go and fight the jihad in the South. Mass weddings were arranged to push the frontier of Islam southwards. Videos of martyrs were broadcast on television every week. High-ranking military officers would arrive at the family home to celebrate that the fallen had gone up to paradise and his waiting virgin brides.

For ten years Turabi reigned supreme. His removal from power in December 1999 was a declaration that the national experiment with Islamism had failed. To begin with it had been imposed by force, accompanied by broad political repression. A new elite was created that siphoned off the profits. The gap between rich and poor had not diminished but widened. Revolt was breaking out everywhere. The campaign of Arabisation and Islamisation had instilled the people of Darfur and the Nuba Mountains with a renewed sense of their own separate identity. The regime controlled less of the country's territory than any previous government. The SPLA was gaining ground, moving up along the Blue Nile towards the Roseires Dam and the capital, picking up support as they went.

Islam's arrival in the country, late and by a somewhat eccentric route, via travellers, mystics and Sufi wanderers, came in a very particular form. Syncretism was key; the religion embedded itself through the incorporation of indigenous elements, habits and superstitions that were already established. The mix can still be seen today, in the Sufi *tariqas*, or schools, in unorthodox traditions like the *zar*, or the use of leather amulets, or hijabs to shield one from evil. Rather than the imam, or learned scholar, it was the *feki* who reigned supreme. Part healer, part medicine man, part magician, the *feki* was more akin to a local saint. He would read to his congregation with the Quran in one hand and a bowl of *merissa*, the local beer – a traditional source of nutrition – in the other. He would cure his patients by making them drink the ink washed from the wooden tablets upon which sacred verses had been inscribed. He had the power to banish evil spirits, to protect people, even from flying bullets, with his magic amulets containing hair, nails, herbs and Quranic verses (a practice still seen today in Darfur and Kordofan). It is perhaps easy to understand the urge to distance oneself from such backwardness, from superstition, to embrace the conventional orthodoxy that is associated with Wahhabite Islam. If the history of this country has taught us anything, it is that we have turned away, time and again, from alternatives that might have provided us with a solution to our problems.

Turabi's rather dull, purist drive ignored other, more imaginative attempts to adapt Islam to local needs. The most notable of these came from Mahmoud Mohammed Taha. Considered one of the most original thinkers in the Islamic world, his *The Second Message of Islam* offers a possibility of a 'third way'. While not a secularist, Taha envisaged a line that would allow Muslim and non-Muslim to live together as equals, offering a platform on which Northerners could share power with the non-Muslim South in a way that was acceptable and less offensive than a secular, non-religious government.

Taha's thinking stemmed from an original interpretation of the Quran that is still widely admired, albeit disputed by more orthodox Muslim thinkers. According to this, the Quran can be divided into two parts. The Meccan suras, although chronologically earlier, are usually placed at the end of the book. These are shorter and characteristically elliptical. Often rich in poetic images and mystical allusions, these are the verses that are most open to free interpretation. The later verses were received in Medina, the town that became the cradle of the Muslim community that was to spread around the world. The Medina suras reflect the Prophet's efforts to outline a prescribed social order. According to Taha, this was intended within the context of the seventh century, and should not be taken as a guide for life today.

Taha uses a quotation from the Prophet Muhammed: 'Islam started as a stranger, and it shall return as a stranger in the same way ... Blessed are the strangers.' In other words, Islam is an outsider by nature and does not seek political authority. The true meaning of jihad is the daily spiritual struggle, the effort to strive, to deal with new challenges, to rise above temptation. Who are the strangers, the Prophet was asked. 'Those who revive my *sunna* [way of life] after it has been abandoned.' In Taha's reading, Islam is constantly renewed by the present and makes no claim on the past. The juridical implications of such a radical approach would be far-reaching, which might explain why they are so controversial. Constant renewal would undermine any claim to clerical authority.

It is perhaps significant that Taha was born, not in the North, but on the Blue Nile south of Khartoum, in the town of Rufaa. He grew up in Heglig in South Kordofan, in what is the centre of the country, an area now heavily occupied by Chinese oil-rig workers. He graduated as an engineer from the Gordon Memorial College in 1936. He was arrested in 1946 after founding the Republican Party in opposition to the British occupation. Released, he was then arrested again, this time for starting a revolt against the British in his hometown. It was during his two years in prison that Taha began the meditative study of the Quran that would prove crucial to the development of his ideas. Through prayer and fasting he arrived at the conclusion that the sacred text contained messages that would only be revealed in the fullness of time; Allah will grant knowledge of what a person does not know to those who act in accordance with what they do know.

After his release in 1951, Taha began to transform the Republican Party, turning it away from its secular political line towards becoming a vehicle for his particular vision of Islam. From his earliest writings it is clear that Taha was against the notion of Islamic rule. Imposing Sharia law would be divisive, he believed. He was opposed on all sides. Traditionalists were fiercely critical of his ideas, while military rulers such as General Abboud rejected his suggestions for a constitution.

The first time Taha was accused of apostasy was in 1968. He refused to appear in court and the charges were dropped. When Nimeiri came to power in 1969 Taha was granted a little more breathing space in return for his support for the regime's bid for national unity. In 1973 he was banned from public speaking. Ten years later Nimeiri's so-called September Laws – his cruel and highly controversial implementation of Sharia law – produced a definitive split. Taha was held in prison for nineteen months without charge. On his release he published a pamphlet entitled *This or The Flood*, demanding the repeal of the harsh laws. A Southerner, Taha argued, was entitled to full rights as a citizen. The September Laws made this impossible, placing non-Muslims under the guardianship of Muslims. These laws were a distortion of Islam, Taha declared, and a threat to national unity. On 5 January 1985, Taha and four other Republicans were arrested and charged with sedition, undermining the constitution and inciting unlawful opposition to the government. The Republican Party had maintained a line of non-violent protest. When the police blocked their marches they sat down in the road, in the spirit of Gandhi.

At one point during the trial, when the judge managed to tie himself in knots trying to disprove the unorthodox views of the defendants, Taha helpfully explained that the term he was searching for was the offence of *ridda*, apostasy. He was calling his bluff. The judge knew that to do so would be controversial and refused to use the word apostasy in his final ruling. This did not prevent all five of the accused being sentenced to death. Even Nimeiri in his public address talked only vaguely about the theory of apostasy in Sharia law without mentioning it by name. On Friday 18 January, Taha was led up the steps of the gallows, whose iron girders protrude over the top of the walls of Kober (formerly Cooper) Prison. He is said to have smiled and uttered the affirmation of Muslim faith, *la illahah il Allah* – there is no god but Allah, before the hood was placed over his head. A helicopter was standing by to whisk the body away to a secret location in the desert where he was buried in the sand with nothing to mark the spot.

A dishonesty hangs over the whole underhand process – the trial, the accusations, the execution and, finally, the subterfuge with the body. His killers were aware that they were going against all the rules, that they were breaking a taboo, hanging a man in the name of the very religion that he clearly believed in and defended. It was a turning point in the country's moral history.

The story goes that the president returned to his office one day after Friday prayers to find a copy lying on his desk. Nobody knew how it had arrived there, nor where it came from, or who had written it, nor how they had managed to get their hands on the government statistics and information it contained, nor indeed how it had been distributed so swiftly and efficiently. But the real question, the one nobody dared to speculate on, was what it could possibly mean, what the consequences of the Black Book might be.

The *Kitab al-Aswad* was an anonymous production. It first began to appear outside mosques in May 2000, distributed in photocopied sheets by earnest young men. As the story of the Black Book spread so too did the scope of its contents, until it took on the aspect of an avatar, lending itself to whatever shape was in your mind. To those opposed to the regime reading it was like discovering that one was not alone. The message it contained was really no more than a confirmation of what many had suspected for years.

Within days of its appearance the Black Book had spread all over the country. In popular legend it acquired a life of its own. It contained everything and nothing, people said. Its pages were blank. It was written in a language unknown to man. The stories grew more outrageous as they spread. Everyone had an idea of what they wanted it to contain. The Black Book had touched a nerve. It was immediately copied and recopied ad infinitum, passed on as soon as it had been read. In fact, there was nothing new about what it contained. It simply stated what everyone had always known, backed up by official facts and figures: wealth and opportunity were unequally distributed, according to race and ethnicity. This was hardly news. It was the kind of claim that had been already told, in countless litanies, an injustice passed on from father to son over generations.

The aim of the authors was plainly stated on the first page: 'This publication unveils the level of injustice practised by successive governments, secular and theocratic, democratic or autocratic, from the independence of the country in 1956 to this date.' Official documents and statistics turned the book into a catalogue of betrayal, a frank account of the true state of the nation.

In itself it was a radical moment, bringing the nation face-to-face with its own self-deception. There was no equality. There never had been. The Black Book also marked the end of the grand project of the *Inqaz*, the Revolution of National Salvation. It shattered the illusion that Islam was the great leveller. If anyone had laboured under the misguided impression that religion could end class-ridden nepotism and elitist dominance, that it would lead to increased social mobility, justice and equality, then here, at the end of the decade, was clear proof that it would not.

Hassan al-Turabi, the ideologue behind the 1989 coup, always claimed that his Islamic movement stemmed from the grassroots of the country, but the notion of the National Islamic Front as a populist and democratic movement was contradicted by the authoritarian practices of the regime: the widespread repression, the torture and arbitrary arrest of politicians, journalists, artists, musicians, and the broad suppression of women in general, in a country that once led the way both in trade unionism and gender equality.

The Black Book exposed how people from the Northern region, a mere 5.4 per cent of the population, had occupied almost 80 per cent of political posts since independence. Not even among Northerners was there broad representation as three ethnic groups dominated (the Shaigiya, the Jaali and the Danagla). A substantial portion of the book is devoted to demonstrating how the *Inqaz* showed no significant improvement on previous regimes. The book condemns the nepotism that decided the posts of minister of justice and attorney general. It attacks the media for presenting the culture of Northern Sudan as a national culture. It analyses distortions in documentary films made by the Popular Defence Forces that imply that the majority of the mujahideen who fell in the war were Northerners, when the opposite was true: nearly twenty times as many of those who died came from regions like Darfur and Kordofan, in the west and south of the country respectively. Even the 'weddings' of martyrs were recorded according to a perceived classification of citizenship – first, second and third class, with Northerners occupying first place. Development schemes, employment (even down to ministerial drivers), wealth distribution, privatisation of public enterprises, water and power, agricultural services, and a host of other sectors were analysed, and all demonstrate the predominance of the same three Northern tribes.

The last chapter of the Black Book is devoted to 'unevenness in the balance of justice' – the prime consequence of which, it claims, is loss of government credibility. The *Inqaz*, it concludes, 'affirmed the ethnic and regional domination of the north over the rest of the country'.

For a long time there was speculation as to who might have written the book, and how they had managed to get hold of the statistical material. Numerous people were fired from government posts, even within the Presidential Palace. The intelligence services searched high and low, interrogating journalists, writers, university lecturers, all to no avail. If anyone knew who had done it, no one was talking, which probably tells us more about how deeply the Black Book managed to touch people. In a country of high illiteracy, news of the book spread by word of mouth. You didn't have to have read it to know what it was about. Reading it was painful for some; to know that the system had failed for so long and that injustice was so deeply engrained. For most people, however, the statistics confirmed what they had always suspected, but had never been able to prove.

In time, the fog cleared to reveal that the Black Book had not one author but fifteen. One of them was a former state minister, others were university graduates who hailed from the west of the country. The documents were carefully pieced together using official sources. Working individually, they had to be careful not to be caught by the security forces and not to give away any of the others. The government's immediate reaction was to ignore the message it contained and try to catch those responsible.

The Black Book signalled a shift in Sudanese understanding of their political reality. In his analysis, the anthropologist Abdullahi Osman El Tom summed up the meaning of the book when he wrote: 'Behind the glow of the nation-building project and its discontent there exists a tragic tale of social, political and economic exclusion.'

Terence Ranger once described how, at the very moment when Europe was struggling to control Africa, from the 1870s to the 1890s, there was a growth of invented tradition in Europe. The founding of an empire forced Britain to ask what exactly it was itself. In that sense one might say that Europe was invented by Africa. In Africa there was no imperial state in place for the colonisers to assume control of, such as there had been in India, say. To the Europeans, the continent was an emptiness, a void, a blank page upon which history could be written. In return, the British offered the Africans an imperial monarchy to worship. In 1902 Flora Shaw, by now Lady Lugard, observed the Coronation Day celebrations in Nigeria. As the band played and the African servants shouted 'God Save the King', she reflects, 'I was struck by the thought as I looked down the table and noted the fine type of Englishman's face which presented itself in rows on either side, that it really is a phenomenon of our Empire that we should be able in the heart of Africa to bring together for dinner twenty well-bred English officers of as fine a type as you would hope to meet in the most civilised centre of London.'

Ranger reminds us that there was a basic misconception on the part of the Europeans. Having arrived with their own invented traditions, they expected to encounter an equivalent in Africa: societies ruled by deeply conservative traditions that would not change. It was here that the notion of a traditional or 'eternal' Africa began to emerge. Those Africans who did change, adopting European norms and fashions, creating hybrid identities, such as the *évolués* of the Congo, or the effendis in Khartoum, seemed somehow less admirable than real 'authentic' Africans who remained unspoilt, inhabiting their own traditional universe. Territorial boundaries that reinforced ethnic and social divides were somehow deemed necessary to keep that 'eternal' world intact. And in turn it provided the contrast needed to show just how modern and advanced European civilisation really was. Nobody wanted a blurring of the lines. The authors of the Black Book were up against something similar. So long as the vast majority of the country remained unaware of what was happening, the small ruling elite could continue to think of themselves as superior, naturally endowed with control of the country and its resources.

There was also another motivation: working from within the National Islamic Front, the authors took three years to gather the information needed, in the hope that publicising the data would draw attention to the plight of people in Darfur. By the time their work was complete, however, they realised they were never going to get what they wanted by peaceful means, and so the Justice and Equality Movement was born, one of the two main rebel groups in Darfur. They attacked a government air-force base at Golo, marking the start of the violence. If ever proof were needed of the link between that conflict and the ongoing national crisis, here it was in black and white. It cannot have made pleasant reading for the president or anyone else around him, since, essentially, the Black Book was the obituary of the Revolution of National Salvation.

The religious posturing that emerged from Nimeiri's late, Islamist years ran unhindered through the 1980s to culminate in the hard-line crackdown of the *Inqaz* at the close of the decade. Since then the religious message has gradually been watered down. Today it is just a means to an end – a substitute for a viable ideology. Membership of the ruling party is simply a way of increasing one's personal wealth. It has become dogmatic, concerned with superficial details. All new government buildings must have a mosque attached. Employees have the right to go and say their prayers. Even the very values that Islam prides itself on, such as, *tahara*, purification, whereby the soul is purified through the cleanliness of the body, seem to be challenged. There is little purity involved in the construction of the state now being built here. There is also a growth in the spread of *tasayyub*, the social malaise that could be translated as laziness, or neglect of one's duty. People simply no longer take pride in doing their job well. They have stopped caring. The legal profession and the judicial institutions themselves are also suffering. There is a sense that the country is on the brink of breakdown.

In 1989 Turabi had envisaged an Islamist revolution that would coil deeper into Africa and, for a time, Khartoum became the hub of a movement that he hoped would spread across the Red Sea into the Middle East as well as south into the interior of the continent. At the Pan-Arab Islamic Conference in Khartoum in April 1991, Turabi called for support in waging war in the South, now relabelled a jihad. They were engaged in a battle against Christian and Zionist crusaders, Turabi explained, and this concerned all Muslims everywhere. By the end of that decade the dream had been extinguished.

My sense of those years, growing up around here, is one of dislocation, of being separated from the events of the world. We had time, time to get bored, to stare out through the garden gate, time to think, long, dead afternoons spent reading, trying to imagine the places those authors were describing. Everything felt far away, as if we were suspended in a kind of limbo. We had a big old black Bakelite telephone. Every time it burst into life felt like an event and we would rush to answer it. My mother had a handful of music cassettes by artists we knew nothing about. I read reviews of films in *Newsweek* that I had no chance of seeing and developed the habit of trying to create those films in my head, based on a picture posted in the article. Nothing was given; you had to build your own path into the world.

In the afternoons, when the adults were sleeping, the streets had a magical feel to them, as if a spell had been cast over the world and only children were free to move around. I had a bicycle in those days, a Phoenix, made in India, which we could afford because it it was cheaper than the Chinese models. I stripped it down and customised it myself. I removed the chain cover, the rack and mudguards; I turned the handlebars over to give it the feel of a racing bike.

I can recall a proprietary feeling of ownership, riding around the streets in the afternoons when the adults were nowhere to be seen and the neighbourhood belonged to us. You would see things, as if the world had loosened its stays, revealing its intimate mysteries. Shopkeepers slept outside their shuttered doors. Taxi drivers dozed in their cars. Prostitutes leaned in the gateways of their houses, or got into scandalous scraps. The barriers came down, also between ourselves and kids from very different backgrounds. On the open, dusty squares we ran barefoot, kicking ragged old footballs around, often stuffed with newspaper, or so worn down the rubber bladder would poke through the stitching.

We were further out than where I am now, at the less affluent end of the Amarat. I'm not sure where the boundary was, but we rarely came this far into town. Nothing ever seemed to happen, except once, when the Saudi embassy was besieged. I must have been around twelve at the time. A group of Palestinians from the Black September organisation rammed a car in the driveway during a reception. They took the American ambassador and nine others hostage. We cycled as close as we could, stopping at the police barrier. There was nothing much to see. The embassy was a big white villa and there was nobody to be seen. There weren't even that many onlookers.

Black September was born out of King Hussein's expulsion of Palestinian fighters from Jordan in 1970. They were responsible for the attack at the 1972 Munich Olympics in which eleven Israelis were killed. Here they were calling for the release of Palestinian prisoners held in Israel and Jordan. When President Nixon declared there would be no negotiation with terrorists they murdered the three Western diplomats. The other hostages were released. A picture appeared in the paper showing the basement where the massacre took place. I remember feeling shocked that something like that could happen right in front of us. The rural simplicity of home was hit by the enormity of what was going on in the world.

The most notorious terrorist at the time was Carlos the Jackal, as he was nicknamed. He was Venezuelan and his real name was Ilyich Ramírez Sánchez. His picture appeared so regularly in the papers that he became a figure of fun. We used the name to describe people at school. It was easy to joke about such things when they existed only at the abstract level. As a terrorist, Carlos was hardly proficient. The list of bungled attacks and failed assassinations conveys a character who is a far cry from the lethal killer depicted in Robert Ludlum's Bourne novels.

Many years later, Carlos settled for a time in Khartoum, which seems almost surreal. He was to be seen strutting his stuff at wedding parties, or sipping coffee in the rather drab lounge of the Hilton, in those days the only spot in town that could make a claim to luxury. Eventually he was given up by Sudanese officials, sedated and traded off to French military intelligence in exchange for satellite photographs of SPLA camps in the South that the government was interested in bombing.

'Where we are is less important than where we think we belong,' Essam tells me. I don't really know what to make of him. I knew him vaguely as a child. He's a little younger than me. He spent several years in Britain and then came back with an English wife and two children. There is something about him that I can't put my finger on. It's as if he is playing along in a manner he assumes I will recognise, or even support. The breezy, casual demeanour is undermined by his nervous behaviour. He goes to all the parties and tends to drink too much. People steer clear of him, I realise, which is perhaps why he homes in on me so often. Usually he is alone. His wife, when she is with him, seems resentful towards her surroundings and everyone about her. He also skitters from one job to another. Now he is a journalist and seems to be gravitating towards some kind of creativity. I suspect this is why he is keen to talk to me.

'Isn't it more than just a matter of believing you belong?'

'I'm not sure,' he says, looking at the people around him, 'where this place is.'

At heart there lies an enigma, the conundrum that is the defining note in this country's identity. It has sustained forty years of civil war, along with a handful of minor armed conflicts along the way. War over what? Until the last decade or so, we had no real wealth to fight over, yet the fighting continued.

If it is an enigma, then it is also my enigma. A subject that has concerned me over the years. Not through some misguided belief in a personal mission, but because, wherever I go in the world, I am met by the same blank stares and furrowed brows. To constantly have to explain who I am is to engage perpetually with the same mechanisms of identity, denial and alienation. It's not just about the country, it's personal, and it has informed all of my writing.

I never showed my first novel to anyone while I was working on it. It was a slow, painful process and one that I found physically and emotionally challenging. I was using a manual typewriter and A5 paper – the sheer scale of an A4 sheet being simply too daunting to contemplate. I cautiously tapped out every word, every single-spaced line. Every page felt like an eternity. It took me two years. That first story was an exploration of identity that worked on two levels. The central character was in search of that part of himself he did not know, and that he believed he would find in his father's country. He travels there from Britain for the first time and soon becomes caught up in the country's civil war – its own struggle with identity. The publishers showed me a report that described it as the most misanthropic novel the reader had ever come across. I felt the pessimism was justified. We had just gone back into civil war. It was an intractable conflict created by the fact that the country could not accept its true nature. It could not reconcile itself to the fact that North and South were two halves of the unrealised whole.

I had spent five years living in Britain by then. I understood that the world I came from, the place I called home, did not exist to most people around me. Writing that book, I felt I was introducing myself and the place I came from to the world. There was no conscious decision to write about identity. I simply set out to try and describe someone like myself – with certain essential differences, but nevertheless. In order to tell the story I had to ask myself what kind of a place I came from.

The act of writing went against everything my father had planned for me. At least that was how I saw it. He and my mother had worked hard all their lives to give their children the university education they themselves had never had. Most of their friends, the men and women they had met in their early years in London, were educated. My father admired them. They became the first generation of a Western-educated elite. It was something to aspire to. These were the founders of the newly independent state. He wanted his children to be a part of that, to contribute, to join the effort to make Sudan a great country.

We never really talked about the book. When it finally appeared I think he was so surprised by the fact that his son had done such a thing that he was completely taken with the object itself. A book. The content was hardly an issue. He wrote to my editor, without asking me, telling her that what she had done was a wonderful thing, and that people would be very proud to see this book. It was touching to see how supportive he was, although in return I had to endure countless lectures on how to conduct my career as a writer. I saw the pessimistic outlook in the book as a constructive act, a political denunciation; if we were to create a new country we had to see it clearly, warts and all.

My father and his generation saw themselves as modernisers. They threw off traditional clothes and dressed themselves in tweed. They learned to drink Scotch whisky and to play tennis. Some of them even married Westerners (although the reverse, of Sudanese women marrying foreigners, was much less common). They had to do this in order to be taken seriously. There was no negotiation on cultural values. This was part of the transition process. Nurturing an elite class with a fondness for Britain made a lot of sense and Sudan was not the only place where it happened. It had become clear that native rule was unavoidable, but it was imperative that it was the right kind of native. The next best thing to having an empire was holding on to your colonies through soft power, creating a class of effendis to do the work for you.

Often, when we talk about the past it always seems somehow more solid than the present, as though time has settled around it like hardened mortar, giving shape and substance to what was once fluid. Of course, time itself is an invention, the calendar a record we created to make sense of our own existence. We write books, build museums, construct links that connect what was to what will be in a projection of how we see ourselves. The past is a continuous struggle to try and make sense of the present. That, after all, is why I came back; not to find the past, but to understand the present.

I stumble back along the uneven road in the dark. There are no street lights. The gloom is broken by the occasional flare of white neon from the entrance of yet another shop stuffed with tottering stacks of plastic bottles, crates, cardboard boxes and humming refrigerators. Everywhere you look men sit around with nothing to do, as if the highest aspiration in the world is to find a chair to sit in. They loll about idly under trees watching the world go by through heavy-lidded eyes. At the Goethe Institute the doorman sits upright and fast asleep, eyes shut, mouth open as you walk by. They sit and scratch their necks as they watch the traffic go by. Passing headlights pick out solitary figures standing motionless on street corners. They are waiting for a friend, for a ride, for something to reach out of the darkness and claim them.

The steady drift of young men to the capital has been going on for decades, an outcome of the lack of interest in the provinces. Men who were once busy in their homelands came to the city to find themselves out of work. The process carries on. A steady haemorrhage of people seeking a better life. At home the work is seasonal, but there is always something to be done. In the city, their lives lose focus, the men grow idle. They wander, squatting in makeshift shelters, eking out an uncertain existence. They become *hamishiyya* – spirits who have lost their grip on the physical world.

Visiting a friend one evening the headlights of the car settle for a time on the neighbour's gate, outside which sit three armed men. One of them leaps to his feet and comes over to yell at the driver to switch off the lights. He eventually stalks off. The house belongs to the Popular Defence Forces militia. The current occupant is a government minister who, rumour has it, once absconded with a large quantity of money from a bank he was running. This is the 'New Sudan'. Not the one Garang had in mind, but one where dishonesty is rewarded, provided a respectable face and a handful of thugs to safeguard it. There are hundreds of this type of men, all from dubious backgrounds. They make up the hard core propping up the power structure.

The spirit of optimism that followed the signing of the Comprehensive Peace Agreement in 2005 has evaporated. The government signed a federalist accord, something that might seem obvious in a country whose problems stem largely from an imbalance between centre and periphery, but implementing this accord has been problematic. In 2007, the man appointed to be in charge, Ibrahim Moneim Mansour, was sacked from his post – he was trying too hard. The truth was that there was never any real intention of improving conditions in the outlying areas. Bashir himself had laid it out bluntly in Naivasha during the CPA negotiations: 'We will not respect any regional demands, other than those made with by force of arms.'

For years the North has lived under the comforting delusion that the South would never break away; that, no matter how badly they were treated, the Southerners would prefer to take their chances in the North than be subject to domination by the larger tribes, most notably the Dinka who make up 40 per cent of the South. This notion of inter-ethnic animosity being the greatest deterrent to Southern independence has long been a source of comfort to the North's ruling elite. It also explains the lack of serious effort being made to convince Southerners that there is a place for them in this country. A few half-hearted placards by the side of the road proclaiming 'Our Strength is Our Unity' are not going to do the trick.

Perhaps it is because racial and cultural purity are so hard to come by that there is an obsession with defining oneself as being distinct from everyone else. We cannot deal with fluid, open-ended existences, which is why citizenship, once severed from racial and cultural markers, requires such faith. Freedom demands limitations. In a country of in-betweens – Arabised Africans and Africanised Arabs, all floating along freely – there is an existential need to cling to the slightest vestiges of distinction.

I knew before I came here that the crisis in Darfur wasn't about Darfur. It was the outcome of the same imbalances, the same malaise that had plagued the country since independence – the construction of a common identity. Under British rule the three southern provinces were given special status with a view to eventually being detached and incorporated into their other East African colonies. The Closed Door policy, as it became known, was designed to remove Arab officials and prevent trade or other contact between north and south. Missionaries introduced Christianity and the English language into the equation. It created a barrier that lasted for the best part of half a century, a barrier that was never really overcome. Nationhood will never be achieved without going beyond the rigid definitions and prejudices of tradition. To break out of the cycle of violence and destruction, Sudan has to step out of its own history.

As if on cue, a lanky Southern man steps languidly from the shadow of a looming building. Splayed out in his huge hand, like a deck of playing cards, are three cartons of American cigarettes. He addresses me politely, but I can't think of anyone who smokes. Some of the vendors construct towers out of the flattened cigarette cartons, interleaving them ingeniously for strength. They rise into the air in columns of red, white and gold. Elsewhere, faces are lit up by the blue glow from the screen of a mobile telephone as they crouch in the dust. I can recall how people used to sit outside their houses so as to read by the street lights. There has always been a great thirst for learning here, perhaps related to the fact that this city was host to one of the oldest and most respected universities in Africa. The image of a young man I saw on the plane returns to me, rocking back and forth with the blue airline blanket shrouding his head, two books open in front of him, turning from trigonometry to the Quran, as if the sacred and the profane were in conversation, seeking consolation from one in the other as the cataracts slipped away beneath us like prayer beads on a *sibha*. At the Petronas station all the workers are dressed in green polo shirts, nearby a group of mechanics in blue overalls squat around a bowl of *ful medemas*. A motorcyclist rides up wearing a pair of ski goggles. Every now and then something happens to prick the surface and what seemed tranquil and immutable suddenly flickers and comes awake.

Bureaucracy has become an end in itself, a self-perpetuating organism that seems to have been created to turn the slightest procedure into an arduous, time-wasting ordeal of duplicate and triplicate forms, days of queueing up, etc. No one goes through it if they can avoid it, but to avoid it you need someone to help you through the system, someone on the inside.

I have the right to an expatriate card, issued to nationals who hold foreign passports, of which there are now many. It will make entering and leaving the country easier, but they are not easy to get. One day I am introduced to Awad (not his real name), an operative in one of the branches of the national security apparatus. A plainclothes officer, he is one of tens of thousands of agents who roam the capital. A large, unassuming man with a cautious air, he is coy about what he actually does, deflecting any direct questions. Still, he is curious about me and so, true to his promise, he gets me through all the doors to the offices where decisions are made and documents are issued. It becomes a matter of pride to him to demonstrate what he is capable of. Wherever we go there are greetings all around, though these appear to be more out of professional courtesy, one colleague to another, rather than signifying any personal connection. Behind the barricades of glass and shutters, within the inner circles, bureaucratic efficiency is an empty desk, cleared of all problems. A large woman in a blue uniform appears. A commanding presence, she gives the orders. Hands are shaken, tea is served and the formalities are dispensed with quickly. The picture of me as a baby on my birth certificate extracts sighs and chuckles, particularly the mass of curls compared to my current lack of hair. It emerges that I am short of a document, my father's birth certificate: to prove your nationality no longer depends on whether you were born here or not. What is in question is the matter of your paternal heritage. I am ushered in to sit for a moment with a senior officer and, after a brief discussion, this formality is waived. I am vouched for and everything proceeds smoothly. In minutes papers are stamped and sealed and the matter is resolved. No bribes are asked for, or offered. It seems like a small but significant triumph.

Afterwards, Awad says he wants to introduce me to one of his colleagues and I feel obliged to accept. A few days later I find myself spending the afternoon with the two of them. Akram is a small, curt man with a narrow, angular face and a rather dapper moustache. He is quite pleased with himself and both men eagerly claim that he is the pride of the department because of his language skills. His command of English, they tell me, is so good that he is often mistaken for a native speaker. This seems unlikely, but it dawns on me that this is the true purpose of the meeting, for me to judge just how good his English is. Later, I realise that they have no doubts about Akram's abilities; what is really at stake is whether my English meets his approval. It is a curious situation. His English is slow and halting and speckled with dated mannerisms. For him English is an exercise in belief. He has never been abroad, to Britain, the United States, or any English-speaking country. English is as theoretical to him as astrophysics might be to me, or an ancient, dead language spoken by the Etruscans. Most of his colleagues, including Awad, speak no English, and they are proud of his abilities. Akram can fool anyone, they say, letting drop that he even drew praise from some visiting colleagues from the UK, presumably the British Secret Intelligence Service (MI6) – though they refuse to go into any further detail on that point – who the visitors were and what exactly they were doing here. None of that matters. The point is that they gave their stamp of approval to Akram's English. Since it is clearly not good enough to pass for a native speaker, I have to assume it was a courtesy on the part of the SIS, for the sake of furthering cooperation, or whatever.

'There is so much you could do for your country,' Awad tells me. 'We need people like you.' For a moment, I consider the idea of a career as an intelligence officer and decide to take the invitation as an opportunity to enquire further into what exactly Awad does. But he is coy about the details. He holds out a special walkie-talkie that has a squawk button on the side. 'If I am in trouble all I do is press that and people will come from every direction.' Not exactly the kind of enlightening insight I had been hoping for, but not to be lightly dismissed either. I can recall that even when I was at school it was an option people talked about. The thought of being inside the system is a powerful incentive. The authority that goes with having a gun and a radio with a panic button. Nowadays the National Intelligence and Security Service is more powerful than the military. The notion of becoming a secret agent floats temptingly before me before, inevitably, fading.

Akram talks obsessively. He believes he can do anything he sets his mind to, he tells me. I get the impression that the English language is not something that came easily to him, but was acquired through sustained effort and dedication. He hails from quite a humble background and was not born into the country's elite. To an extent this explains some of his insecurities. Perhaps sensing my scepticism, he repeats his claim that many foreigners have congratulated him on his English. I have been careful to congratulate him, too, but his harrying suggests I wasn't convincing enough. He is a harsh critic, quick to judge and pedantic to the point of being tedious. Somewhere underneath the jocular, teasing manner I sense there lurks a frustrated authoritarian. Insecurity makes his brows swell up when he encounters resistance to his opinions. Clearly he is on his best behaviour, having just been introduced to me. Awad insists on playing a game with him. Guess where he is from, he asks, referring to me, hinting that I might be attached to a foreign agency, that I am actually American or British. Akram swallows the bait and concedes that my Arabic is not bad. He has met plenty of Western intelligence agents. Some of them speak Arabic very well indeed. The astonishing thing is the level of the conversation. There is a moment of absurdity as they discuss the difference between the words 'investigation' and 'interrogation', as if such confusion occurs on a regular basis. I imagine that to be interrogated, or investigated, by either of them would be to enter a mirrored maze of misunderstandings and confusions. I want to ask more about the details of their work, but they are too conscious of the line over which they will not cross, not this time at least. Awad, while playing the easy-going, more relaxed one, nevertheless remains vigilant. He is warm and friendly, but every now and then, when I glance across, I catch him watching me. It makes me wonder what is really going through his mind.

We eat lunch and spend the afternoon talking. Later, as I make to leave, I pass through another salon where Awad's brother is sitting with his young fiancée. She is covered from head to foot, which is something of a shock. Nobody in my father's family dresses like that. Her face is covered by a veil. When I greet her, paradoxically, her behaviour is playful, even flirtatious. Giggling and wriggling about on the chair as if it were all a joke. I can only see her eyes and the scene puts me, oddly, in mind of a Victorian novel. There is something absurd and theatrical about this obsession with covering up, as if it makes the sexual impulse disappear whereas, in a way, it simply underlines the allure of the unattainable. It all seems unnecessary, since as the Quran (24:30) itself makes clear, responsibility lies with the man to 'cast his eyes down' rather than with the woman to cover herself.

As we make to go our separate ways, Awad informs me that there is heavy water in the Nile. This is a dense form of water used in nuclear reactors. It contains higher than normal amounts of deuterium, a hydrogen isotope. Groups of experts have examined the point where the two rivers come together. It strikes me as absurd. A far-fetched notion that belongs in science fiction, yet from his tone it is something they take very seriously in terms of national security. Is he implying that there are those who might be interested in harvesting this water for a nuclear weapons programme? The conversation has slid into the realm of fantasy. The poetry of that line of confluence, the point where Blue flows into White and both Niles meld into one, suddenly dissolves. In the Meidob Hills in the north of Darfur everyone is radioactive, they tell me. The Geiger counter needle goes off the scale. The hills are full of uranium. Maybe another reason the world is so interested in Darfur. Once you start looking, there is danger everywhere.

PART FOUR

LINES OF SEPARATION
2011

'It had ceased to be a blank space of delightful mystery. It had become a place of darkness.'

Joseph Conrad, *Heart of Darkness* (1899)

'As an artist the nuance is your task [...] not to simplify but to impart the nuance, to elucidate the complication, to imply the contradiction. Not to erase the contradiction, not to deny the contradiction, but to see where, within the contradiction, lies the tormented human being. To allow for the chaos, to let it in.'

Philip Roth, *I Married a Communist* (1998)

There is a rodent waiting for me when I move in. It scuttles across the wall and scrambles through a brick lattice as we climb the last stairs to the top floor. Adil, the landlord, gives an exasperated sigh. 'That mouse is driving us all crazy,' he says as he rattles the padlock, which stubbornly resists, before finally yielding. There is a barred outer gate that resembles a prison cell door and beyond this another of solid metal. A long sliver of excrement sits in the middle of the floor, but the culprit has vanished. It feels like a firm declaration of propriety.

For the next few weeks we are to share this living space, each with our own designated areas. The mouse remains in the kitchen, where it seems to be chewing its way steadily through the plywood cupboards and drawers. It gnaws away persistently, night and day, apparently hollowing out the entire structure. I hardly dare go in there for fear that slamming a door too hastily or leaning the wrong way might bring the whole room tumbling down on me. My space is primarily the bedroom, which is spacious and ventilated by a refreshing breeze that flows around the building. The reception area by the front door is neutral ground, but it is too narrow to be much use – guests have to sit facing one another with their knees almost touching. The best feature is the terrace, which covers the whole roof and looks out over the river to the south. It is a pleasant place to sit at sunset when the sky slowly drains of light. I am almost directly opposite the spot where Gordon spent his last days pacing the roof of the old palace. There is nowhere else in the world where the light fades in quite the same way. In the other direction I can see the Sayyid Mirghani mosque, the slim minarets pencilled in against the sky by white neon strips. To the left is the mosque of Hamad Wad al-Maryoum, the Mahas sheikh who was asked by Kitchener to bring his people from Nubia to settle in this corner of the new city at the end of the nineteenth century. All the original inhabitants of this quarter come from there, including my grandmother, whose old house is a stone's throw away.

With the British in 1898 came a number of Armenians, Syrians and Greeks who settled here. They were traders and money-lenders. There were more Jews in this neighbourhood than in Khartoum itself. Names like Sassoon, Cohen and Murad used to be commonplace. They owned shops stocked with all manner of goods brought in from Egypt. The area known as Musallamiya was occupied by Christians who had their own church.

From the other side of the roof, I have a view of the mural inset high in the cream-painted walls of the Coptic church of Girgis – St George, as he is known elsewhere. His image is to be found all over the Eastern Mediterranean and down into East Africa as far as Addis Ababa, where he is depicted with the typical oval features of an Ethiopian. In this case, however, St George appears distinctly alien, as does the armour he wears. Even the dragon he is slaying looks Western rather than Oriental.

At dusk the birds flit frantically between the trees and the muezzins begin their rolling, discordant chorus. As the sun fades over the city it brings a sense of calm that I cannot remember having experienced for a very long time. I stand on the roof, barefoot in the rising dark. The warm wind and the smell of the dust feel old and familiar. The sky above seems vast, bigger than anywhere else in the world – or so it feels. There is something comforting about this hour that makes me feel at home.

The sound of a singer echoes up from a wedding in a nearby street. In the mid-1990s, Bashir's regime decided to stamp out popular music, which it perceived as incompatible with the moral values of Islam. Of course, the regime was going against the tide of centuries. The Sudanese love music, and the only way to ban it was through violence and intimidation. Wedding parties, the most common venue for live music, often going on for days, were broken up with tear gas and riot police. Musicians were beaten, their instruments confiscated or destroyed. In a country where such things are expensive and hard to come by, breaking someone's violin is more than a crime. In November 1994, a teacher wandered into the musicians' club in Omdurman and stabbed several members. Said later to be mentally deranged, the usual apology for such actions, he was only subdued after he had killed the singer Khogali Osman and wounded Abdel Gadir Salim and another musician. Still, the idea of eradicating music was quite absurd, and so it is back, climbing into the night air as the singer moves seamlessly from one song to the next.

This view of the river is not going to last. Just across the street the open ground, once covered by rich, green neem trees, has been fenced off by hastily erected cement walls. It is now owned by a Qatari development company (the same one that built the Shard in London) whose plans include erecting a 130,000-square-metre complex of luxury apartments and leisure centres where now there is only sand and trees. It used to be the site of the local school, until someone in government realised the potential of this prime riverside plot and sold it for sixty million US dollars, just over half of which was used to build a new bridge that now brings this part of the city within ten minutes' walk of the downtown area. There is nothing left standing of the old structure but a few solitary walls. The pupils now have to commute to their school's new location. When it is eventually finished, the view from this terrace will be obliterated by the new buildings.

As the sun sinks, a bank of garish white flares across the river marks a Chinese building site. Another towering edifice. A square ramp of fierce arc lights rises into the sky. At twilight, a new skyline emerges, dominated by the hulking constructions that loom over the town like awkward temples in a new age. The towers are dark, hard outlines against the indigo sky. Who is going to live in them, I wonder? In this landscape, which is flat and open, towers seem incongruous.

Encouraged by the civil unrest that has shaken up the Middle East, there is cautious optimism that popular uprising here might deliver what political stagnation has failed to do. Khartoum, people proudly tell you, has a long tradition of civil uprisings – in April 1985 when Nimeiri went, and in October 1964 – a popular revolution that has achieved legendary status. So far nothing has been seen on the streets of the capital to suggest any such revolt is imminent.

The political inertia is partly explained by the fact that over the last six years the CPA has produced a period of stability and economic growth. Oil exports reached some 475,000 barrels a day. High prices on the world market and foreign investment in the country meant that GDP growth climbed at a rate never seen before, peaking at 10 per cent in 2007. If there is a strange absence of revolutionary spirit about, it may be due to the fact that prosperity is a new experience and nobody really wants to rock the boat.

The boom years produced a new class of Sudanese who did well out of the unfamiliar wealth in circulation. They found themselves able to afford a comfortable lifestyle. New cars soon clogged the streets while fancy restaurants and chic cafés proliferated to serve sumptuous feasts and frothy cappuccinos to the new cosmopolitans. The influx of a foreign labour force brought much-needed service skills to the capital and reinforced local perceptions of authority and power.

The referendum changed all of that. On 9 July 2010 thirty heads of state and 160 dignitaries gathered in Juba to observe the raising of the flag of the newly independent South Sudan. The break-up is already visible here in the absence of Southerners, who in recent years had become an integral part of the city's population of ambulant street vendors, while many of those who were due to return to the South are still waiting at collection points for the transport that was promised them by the SPLM. Having given up their homes, they have spent months squatting in wasteland with no amenities or shelter. Tens of thousands are trapped further south in Kosti, waiting for boats that never come.

There is already tension both along the new border and within the world's newest independent nation, although the fear that war would immediately break out again between North and South appears to be receding. Khartoum knows that the world is watching, and Bashir's National Congress Party is interested in maintaining the trust and interest of the international community, particularly in Washington. The new US embassy in Soba, just south of Khartoum, is the largest in East Africa and says something about American interest in this country.

Those concerned about the resurgence of North–South conflict include George Clooney, who has stepped in to sponsor a satellite vigil of the 2,000-kilometre borderline, a paparazzo in the sky, as he smoothly puts it, bringing his own authority on the subject to bear. But all indications suggest the new frontline will serve only to divide Sudan's problems into two parts. The problems in the North are well-documented, from the high-profile conflict in Darfur to lesser known, but equally serious, issues in the Nuba Mountains and the Upper Blue Nile province, both in the central part of the country. There are too many arms and militia groups, disbanded sections of the SPLA, which now find themselves on the wrong side of the new border. In the South there are the old tensions between Nuer and Dinka.

The North will lose out from secession. If that wasn't clear to those in power before the referendum, it is becoming so now. Aside from a hard-line minority who believe that, without the infidel South, a truly Islamic state is now finally achievable, most people realise the consequence of the fact that 80 per cent of the country's oil reserves lie in the South. Some revenue will continue to come in due to the fact that the oil has to pass through the North along a pipeline to refineries and the Red Sea. There are rumours of other deposits in the North but they remain just that, rumours. It is too late now to invest oil revenue in the economy. That ship has sailed, and, without the South, the North risks falling into an economic trough, compounded by political isolation, which Bashir is desperately trying to fend off.

The average citizen is already beginning to feel the economic contraction caused by secession. Many can't afford to eat meat or fish more than once a week. The middle class is struggling. To pay medical expenses they sell their furniture, belongings, or car, if they have one. Talk of the Arab Spring is tempered by concern about the possibility of war, such as we are witnessing in Yemen and Libya. There are meetings being held, debates and public forums about what is going on in the broader region. 'The longer it takes the more momentum it will gain,' a human rights lawyer tells me, 'and the more bloodshed there will be.' By his account the regime is dwindling. He points to division within the ruling National Congress Party. Hasaballa Omar, a senior NISS (National Intelligence and Security Service) officer and adviser to the president declared on public radio that if there was agreement between the political parties to abolish Sharia law, then it should go. Why he made such a reckless statement is not clear, but it went against the party line and he was instantly declared an apostate and forced to resign. His suggestion annoyed the party because it implied that Sharia was not a driving principle of the ruling party, merely a choice.

The regime knows it is in trouble. For the last ten years it has lived without a thought for the future, busy milking lucrative service companies to cash in on the oil boom. These are now being jettisoned. They are all losing money and cuts are being made to reduce overheads. Privatising them is the easiest way of dealing with the failing market. Property prices around Khartoum have started to fall, compounding the already slowing economy. An over-reliance on oil money, combined with a lack of initiative, investment in institutions, education, healthcare, infrastructure, etc., has left the country in a vulnerable state of inertia.

A quick drive past the old, tree-lined lanes of Hai-al-Matar, which were once villas for university staff, reveals a military fortress that just keeps on getting bigger – high concrete walls and watchtowers, neon lights and smoked glass. The purpose of it is not clear, but defence has become an end in itself, and the recipient of 70 per cent of the national budget. 'They listen,' I am told, when I ask what all of these buildings are for. Who is listening? And what are they listening for? The compound is reminiscent of the fortresses and towers of medieval Cairo. There is a long history in the Middle East of rulers building walled cities from which to rule the masses.

A man in a grubby orange T-shirt sits in the road beside an enormous SUV. There is someone in the car. Huge red brake lights glow fiercely in the sun. The man on the asphalt has a truncated form. The scene resembles a parable of mobility. The car, big and powerful, is designed to repulse outsiders, to insulate its occupants from the heat, dust, sunlight, poverty. All evaporates in the face of wretchedness and misery. The car doors remain closed, the windows sealed. The chrome-plated exhaust pipe emits a thin, noxious stream. The man on the ground manages to retain his dignity by remaining patient. He sits and waits, his gaze turned upwards towards the smoked windows. What else is he to do? Heavy buses rumble closely by. Light three-wheeled *rukshas* flutter past, swerving in alarming fashion, just missing him.

From the waist up he appears to have developed normally; it is from the waist down that his existence has twisted itself into an awkward spiral out of which he will never disentangle himself. I thought at first that he had lost his legs, in an accident perhaps, or in the war, but, no, they are there under him, wrapped together in the manner of a master yogi who is unable to extricate himself from a complex position. To move he propels himself along the road at great speed, pressing his large hands against the tarmac and lifting his body to swing it forwards through the arch of his arms. He is obviously a local character. People call out greetings as they go by, and he answers in spirited fashion. There is a cheerfulness in his mood and he shows tremendous energy, rushing from one side of the street to the other with little regard for the traffic.

But now he sits and waits. It looks like a stalemate. The windows of the SUV remain closed. The red lights burn furiously. The exhaust pipe putters away and the car sits motionless. Others appear, hawking boxes of paper tissues and shirts and tennis shoes. They step around the man in the orange shirt, who steadfastly keeps his spot. It's hard to keep sight of him in the chaotic melee. Whenever a flurry of cars goes by I think he must be hit, but he isn't. When the view clears he's still there, stubbornly gazing up at the smoked panel of glass, waiting.

There used to be a term for the ragged people who wander the city's streets – *shammasa*, meaning the disorientation induced by long periods wandering the streets without shelter; those touched by the sun. The heat induces a daze that is akin to a heightened spiritual state, rather like the dervishes in Omdurman in their patched *jibbas*, who weave in circles in the dust reciting the *dhikr* over and over, striving to overcome the self and rise up into a state of oneness with God and the universe.

This huge gap in wealth is new to me. There are stories about money in circulation of which no one knows the origin. Not oil money directly. An example is the building of a university for the police force. Early on in the self-styled period of National Salvation, the *Inqaz*, there was a bid to provide education for all. Universities sprang up everywhere, all of a low standard. It was quantity not quality they were promising. But to many this was good enough. This one promised increased social mobility. A professor told me that funding was arranged through a simple phone call to the Ministry of Education. Whenever they ran short, cash would be sent straight over. Up to a billion Sudanese pounds at a time. No questions asked. No receipts or paperwork. So much for transparency.

Another, often quoted, example is the Burj Al-Fateh Hotel (now the Corinthia), the white dome that resembles an armoured version of the Mahdi's tomb and now dominates the skyline. It was Gaddafi himself who made the deal, not his son. The old zoo was in a decrepit state. The animals were in dire need of attention. The land belonged to the state. It was bought by an official for a nominal sum and sold on to the developers at a profit of four million dollars, no questions asked.

I cross the street to the offices of *Al Ayyam* (The Days). They occupy the first floor of a nondescript building above a butcher's shop. Through the open doorway you can watch them wrapping strings of sausages, twirling them round on wide steel tables and slinging them over hooks hanging from the ceiling. There is nothing to indicate that the rather grubby doorway and narrow staircase is the entrance to the paper's offices. No sign over the door, no plaque on the wall. You would have to know it was here to find it. A battered desk sits under a tree where three or four people often congregate. Some stand, some lean against a conveniently parked car. Everyone is waiting; for someone to come, for time to go. Time is the one commodity everybody seems to have plenty of. A woman squats on a plastic crate with a charcoal stove in front of her on which a kettle steams over white ashes. A row of glass jars and pots filled with tea, mint leaves and sugar are spread before her. Orders drift down through the open windows and a young man moves up and down the stairs, his long legs taking them three at a time to deliver refreshments and round up the empty glasses. The staircase is dirty and unswept, though everyone takes the time to stop and shake you by the hand. Upstairs the visitor is greeted by empty rooms, bare tables. It seems like something of a small miracle that a newspaper emerges from such desolation each morning, and yet it does.

There are around twenty-five dailies in circulation in Khartoum, all competing for a limited number of readers and for scarce advertising revenue. Despite the vast quantities of cash that are swilling around the city these days, none of it is coming this way. Running a small newspaper is a desperate, day-to-day business. Despite what one might expect, there is generally a good degree of criticism allowed in the press, although there are limits to what the government will tolerate, and the line is not clearly defined.

The desks are bare, not a telephone, a filing cabinet, or a typewriter in sight. No paper anywhere. Even chairs are scarce. Only the heavy tables remain. This minimalism tells its own story about the lack of resources, shortage of funds, a shrinking readership. It is a sign of the conditions under which any newspaper in this country has to function. Freedom of the press is understood by the authorities in an abstract sense. It is impossible to predict which way they might jump, or what might draw their ire. The paper has been shut down countless times. They've had their print run seized and their editor-in-chief put in prison, but, still, people will tell you things are better than they used to be.

Whether it is scarce resources, or a pragmatic fear that the place might be closed down at any moment, nothing is left behind. The journalists bring everything they need with them – pens, paper, staplers – and take it all away again when they leave. There is one room with filing cabinets and a couple of computers that they share to write up their articles, and another computer for editing. The newspaper is one of those little unexplained miracles.

Al Ayyam was started in 1953, three years before independence. Two years later the army stepped in and for the next six the country found itself under military rule. The paper was closed for three of those years. This was to set a pattern in the years to come: the business of writing and publishing the news being obstructed by a succession of military rulers. Under Nimeiri in the 1970s the paper was nationalised for sixteen years. Their premises and machinery were seized and have still not been returned – forty years on. I can vaguely recall visiting the old offices in Khartoum North as a child. It made an impression. The wide editorial room thrumming with noise and movement, telephones ringing, the smell of ink and machine presses and the clickety-clack racket of heavy old typewriters and telex machines. It felt like an exciting place to be. Full of energy and plugged into a wider world than the narrow, domestic environment we inhabited.

The man who runs the paper is Mahgoub Mohammed Salih. I have no idea how old he is, but if he's roughly my father's age then he has to be in his eighties. You wouldn't think it to see the energy he has. He has been a journalist all his working life. Mahgoub was one of the kids who competed with my father for the chance to caddy for the British golfers. He lived on the wrong side of the road: 'The Shallali boys wouldn't let us through,' he laughs now. Despite this early rivalry, they remained friends. In the 1980s, during a brief lull when Sadig al-Mahdi was elected prime minister, Mahgoub and my father set up the *Sudan Times* along with a journalist from the South, Bona Malwal. This was a huge leap of faith for my father, who had spent his entire life being cautious, and doing what was expected of him. It only lasted three years but it gave him a new lease of life, something to believe in. He found himself facing the consequences of that choice in 1989, when the paper was closed down by the regime in its crackdown on the press. There was a very real possibility of imprisonment. Both of the paper's main editors, Mahgoub and Bona, were outspoken critics of the government. My father, more moderate by nature and not politically active, was guilty by association. In the end he decided it wasn't worth the risk and so, in early 1991, he and my mother joined the exodus of Sudanese who had fled to Cairo.

Journalists are still being arrested and in the offices of *Al Ayyam* there lingers a touch of the defiant spirit that prospered in the early years of independence. 'After thirty-five years things are no better than they were when I started,' Mahgoub declares wistfully. He has been arrested regularly over the years, usually on trivial, trumped-up charges. In January 2004, he was detained for allegedly not paying taxes equivalent to almost US $370,000, an impossible sum for a paper that had been suspended since 2003. They had no funds coming in.

He sits in his office wearing his traditional white gellabiya and imma, writing steadily with a cheap ballpoint pen on unlined paper. From time to time he sips tea from a flask, or turns to the screen next to him to consult the net. There are constant interruptions. Someone comes in needing a cheque authorised. As a rule there is no money available for anything. When any comes in it has to be kept quiet. So many people's salaries are in arrears that there would be a stampede if news got out. To be a journalist in this country today requires considerable faith.

That first generation of post-independence Sudanese is still talked about today in reverential terms. There was something about them that left its mark. They continue to inspire younger journalists to work under conditions that many would find intolerable. Mahgoub and his generation found themselves on the cusp of a new era. They had a belief in themselves and in the nation they were trying to build. Somewhere along the road, however, the path diverged and eventually snaked away to lose itself in the sand.

At nine o'clock in the morning the paper's offices are completely deserted. As I wander through, peering into empty rooms, a slim woman shuffles silently out of nowhere. Dressed in black, her face is hard and bony. It's too early, she says, shaking her head as she goes by. People work late into the night. They don't turn up for work until the afternoon. She is of indeterminate age – impossible to read from her face if she is closer to thirty or fifty. I am welcome to wait. I follow her the length of the corridor to step out onto a balcony. A narrow strip running around the building, cluttered with bits of discarded furniture stacked against the wall. During the day the journalists stand here to share a cigarette, exchange stories or the name of a

contact, the use of a telephone, or to borrow a biro, pens being
highly prized items. She slips past the obstructions to the corner
that turns out to be her little space. There is a square of coloured
nylon mat and half a chair. This, I realise, is where she lives. She
sits here and watches the world from on high. I am welcome
to stay, she repeats absently, already forgetting me, letting me
drift from her mind as she returns to whatever rhythm is running in her head. She is not from here, not from the city, but
from a place far beyond. Darfur or Kordofan maybe, but this
is where she is now, occupying this strange little eyrie beneath
electric cables and telephone wires, amid a jumble of broken furniture. There is something disturbing about her, as if wrapped
inside that shrouded silhouette are hundreds of untold stories
that never make it to the city. This is her life now. She waits for
others to appear, for people to come, for the day to begin, for
life to happen around her. And, for a time, I wait, too. At first
I take a few photographs, but I can't get the light right. After a
time I give up and just stand there, and so we wait, the two of
us, in silence.

From where we are standing you could easily toss a stone over
the narrow side street and it would land on the second house
down. Through the maze of walls and rooms that have sprung
up over the intervening years you can still catch a glimpse of the
garden where we used to play as children. The newspaper wasn't
here in those days. They still had their offices on the other side
of the river. This was the first house we lived in when we moved
back here.

I say moved back because in a way my father never really left this country. He never intended to settle in Britain. Everything that happened there was simply a prelude to the day the family would return here. When he was working for the Sudan Gezira Board, which is to say ever since I was born, we used to come back every year for three months' vacation. I remember a succession of houses, warm summer days spent playing in the gardens, and people who welcomed us.

This was our first real home here and there was an air of mystery about that house. To begin with it was overshadowed by the ghost of the previous occupant, who had managed to electrocute himself one evening while carrying a standing lamp out onto the damp lawn to read by. Something about it never felt right. To us children it was rich with ferocious possibility in the manner of the adventure books we devoured. A sloughed-off skin, desiccated and translucent, sitting on top of a stack of dusty packing cases told us the garage was inhabited by venomous snakes. A duck we kept in the garden died mysteriously overnight. One of our kittens staggered in one morning foaming at the mouth with rabies. Everything seemed to be infused with dangerous possibility.

It felt a far cry from Merseyside, where our early years had been spent. I am told that as a small child I spoke with a Scouse accent. The Gezira Board's office was there because of the harbour where the cotton was brought ashore. Liverpool's wealth was largely built on the slave trade in the seventeenth century. The façades of some of the buildings downtown are adorned with friezes displaying elephants and crocodiles, along with unnamed men and women whose enslavement built the city. Streets, including the celebrated Penny Lane, are named after slave traders. I can remember little. The windy shore, the enormous ships and the many Sudanese my father knew, many of the merchant seamen who had settled there. We went overnight from the dull monochrome skies of Liverpool to the heat and dust of a kaleidoscopic Kodachrome world.

Although we may not have appreciated just how fortunate we were, at the time we were living through a very brief age of optimism. Jaafar Nimeiri had come to power in May 1969 and the star

of socialism was in the ascendant. The enigma of who or what
Nimeiri really was remains unresolved. As a young colonel he was
inspired by Nasser. We would watch him on our old black and
white Hitachi television set, standing upright in an open car, riding
on the roof of a train, waving an ebony staff over his head, clasp-
ing his hands together in a symbolic gesture of fellowship. Young
and dynamic, a man in constant motion. North, south, east, west.
He was everywhere and nowhere at the same time. Women ulu-
lated, men sang and everyone cheered. He was forever inaugurat-
ing new development projects, leaping over bulls that were laid
down before him, their throats slit in sacrifice to spill their blood
into the sand. Factories, irrigation schemes, engineering colleges,
housing complexes, all appeared to come to life under his hand.

Nimeiri had come, he declared, to sweep away all that had gone
before. Like their Egyptian forerunners, the men of the Sudanese
Free Officers Movement were driven by discontent. In the South
they had found themselves fighting a war they could not win,
while in Khartoum the politicians quarrelled among themselves.
Revolutionary purity would, they believed, purge the system of
favouritism, immorality and corruption. Determined to break
the old sectarian grip on political power, Nimeiri introduced a
series of reforms to transform the political administration. A single party, the Sudan Socialist Union, was created to transcend
regional and ethnic divides. The old guard was replaced by new
thinkers: academics, technocrats. In this new age merit rather than
social standing was to count, a radical notion in a country where
family and patriarchal allegiance always trump ideology. Nimeiri
signified modernity and progress. His most celebrated achievement, the signing of the Addis Ababa Accord in 1972, brought
seventeen years of civil war to a close.

Not that we had really seen much of the war in the South. It
was a distant, low-key and diffuse conflict, more remote even
than the Palestinian struggle, which was ideologically more significant and certainly more present. This was the heyday of Arab
nationalism and we were subjected to daily propaganda messages,
stirring revolutionary songs over images of fedayeen fighters
jumping across trenches, crawling under barbed wire. Palestinian

women appeared in rags at our back gate asking for food. If we didn't eat up our lunch we would be shamed by reminders of children starving in refugee camps. The South, in contrast, was a world away, inhabited in an unlikely way by the lanky men we saw working on building sites around Khartoum. Wearing cut-off shorts slung over bony hips, they balanced jerrycans of orange sand on their heads as they climbed up flimsy wooden scaffolding. It hardly registered that these people might be at war with us, or why.

A handsome, burly figure of a man, the young Nimeiri bore a vague resemblance to the boxer Muhammed Ali, a hero at the time throughout Africa. Ali was soon to meet Joe Foreman in Kinshasa in 1974 for the famous 'Rumble in the Jungle'. Nimeiri was the champion of the people. He epitomised the dynamism of the nation. Through him we could believe we were destined for greatness.

It was a brief era that was eclipsed almost before it began and it marked the first – and perhaps last – time the nation was brought together. Racial and ethnic distinctions were discarded in favour of a Marxist belief in the proletariat. In poetry and art, too, there was a renaissance never seen before or since. A renewed sense of experimentation, exploring the unique cultural and geographic space the country occupied, rather than harking back to the divisive construct of an Arab heritage. There was an outpouring of artistic creativity that was dedicated to constructing a belief in who we actually were, rather than who we might have liked to think we were. It helped to stamp that period as one quite unique, something rendered all the more poignant by the fact that it is almost forgotten, erased by the passage of time. Subsequent events have swamped the triumphs of those years, eclipsing early achievements.

The Nimeiri era dominated my childhood. In civics class we learned about the nation's development, about ambitious five-year plans for this and that. We memorised how many tonnes of fish had been hauled from the Nile, how many hectares of wheat, dura and sugar cane had been grown. The photographs in the book revealed a country to be proud of: heaving fishing nets, fields of

bobbing white cotton, shiny new factories producing bottles of
oil, machine parts, shoes. We would feed the world, become the
breadbasket of Africa. We didn't need petroleum deposits. We
had water and land enough to grow food for the entire continent.

In the school yard we did Chinese calisthenics, raising our arms
and bending our legs in time to the commands barked at us by
a hard-faced military man with a microphone. The Presidential
Palace was renamed the People's Palace. When visiting heads of
state arrived we were herded out of class to stand by the roadside waving and cheering the presidential cortège. We were part
of the collective spirit that united north and south, Christian and
Muslim, east and west. In class we were given a choice between
physics and biology. The country had need of doctors and engineers. There was no time for history or geography, let alone the
humanities. As a result, with our eyes firmly fixed on the future,
we had no idea where we were, let alone who we were, or how we
had got here.

The modern Sudan crystallised out of the Ottoman Empire's
envoy Muhammed Ali and his ambitions of conquest, his quest
for gold and slaves, and by the Anglo-Egyptian condominium
that emerged out of that little adventure. The colonial age drew
towards the end of its natural life as the Second World War punctuated the old world order. European hegemony was no longer
a sustainable proposition, if only for pragmatic reasons. Early
nineteenth-century aspirations to mimic the Western model, culturally, politically and economically, had given way to a growing
awareness of a need to formulate a viable intellectual response to
the West. Elsewhere, in the Far East, this took the form of a series
of brutal conquests by Japan. For their own pragmatic reasons,
the Japanese tried to counter European imperialism by encouraging nationalist movements in Malaya, Burma, Java, Vietnam and
Manchuria. The influence of Japan's model of an Asian congress
appealed to many, who saw strength in unity, and this eventually
found expression at the Bandung Conference in 1955 when the
Non-Aligned Movement was founded. In the Muslim world, a
generation of thinkers and writers struggled to find a way to reconcile the need to modernise with the traditional demands of the

societies they hailed from. Chief among these was the Persian-
born Jamal al-Din al-Afghani, the man credited with raising
awareness in the 'dormant East'. Afghani lamented the decline of
the Islamic world, the ignorance of a people who allowed themselves to be subjugated by the West. Shrewdly, Afghani claimed
to know the Mahdi, famous at the time for his victories over the
Anglo-Egyptian forces. To a Muslim intellectual like Afghani,
the Mahdi was the living embodiment of Islam reasserting itself
in the modern spirit of nationalism and Pan-Islamism, which he
saw as the key to revolt against the West. In 1883, Jamal al-Din
al-Afghani had declared to a French newspaper: 'All Muslims
await the Mahdi.' One hundred years later Sudan appeared still
to be waiting. By then Nimeiri's time was coming to an end and
the country's experiment with socialism was all but over. We had
arrived at war, alienation, starvation, persecution, bitter recrimi-
nation, the politics of paranoia, along with cruelty, sectarianism
and superstition.

Formulating a reasonable synthesis of cultural and political
norms by which to rule a society that is fluent both with the modern world and with itself is not easy. And while socialism offered
a form of resistance against the Western Powers, religious belief
and praxis exercised an undeniable influence in Muslim societies.
Nasser empowered the people of Egypt with his call for socialist reform but was soon deeply mired in problems, notably from
the Muslim Brotherhood. Secularism provoked detractors such
as Sayyid Qutb, who, in his quest for an Islamic state, viewed
Nasser's socialist revolution as an attempt to ape Western atheism.
Nasser eventually hanged Qutb, but his accusations, and those
of other salafists, continued to resonate as Pan-Arabism suffered
one setback after another: the creation of the state of Israel, the
Arab defeat of 1948, the long-running war in Yemen and finally
the Six-Day War of 1967. A counter-movement began to grow,
this time with a longing for a return to tradition, and for a solution that was reconciled with Islam.

Communism emerged as a tool of the nationalist movement
back in the 1940s. Among the educated elite there was no distinction between communism and nationalism. What distinguished

Sudan from Egypt and Syria, say, where the experiments with Pan-Arab Nationalism and socialism that inspired Nimeiri and the Free Officers began, was that Sudan already had one of the strongest trade unionist movements in the region. There were close links between the Sudanese Communist Party and the Free Officers Movement. Despite opposing the use of force, the CP had considerable influence among the working class, trade unions, tenant unions, professionals, women's groups and students. They counterbalanced the influence of the elite, who had been groomed into their leadership role, not only by the British, but by their own upbringing that left them detached from the population at large.

But the idealism was unable to sustain itself. Almost immediately after they came to power in May 1969, Nimeiri's Revolutionary Command Council started to back down on their avowed aims. Their manifesto had stated that power would revert to 'the workers, peasants, soldiers, intellectuals and nationalist capitalists who are not associated with imperialism'. This was gradually whittled down, by petty disputes and corruption, encouraging their former partners, the increasingly disappointed communists, to mount their own coup just two years later.

This betrayal by the communists in July 1971 destabilised Nimeiri. The young Nimeiri symbolised the idea of belonging, of inclusiveness, of nationhood. He had led a charmed life. There is an apocryphal touch to the stories of him defying death: while leading a column of tanks in the war in the South he allegedly climbed down from the turret to go back to the next vehicle to beg a pinch of snuff. At that moment a shell landed on his tank and blew it to pieces. It had to be more than good luck.

Such stories of divine protection were to come back to haunt him. By the end of his term of rule, Nimeiri had begun to believe in his own myth. It is possible that he had always had a mystical streak. In any case, it now came to the fore. He ran amok, thinning out the country's political institutions to leave him the unchallenged master, the imam of all imams, until he reigned supreme, able to appoint and dismiss judges as he pleased. His closest advisers were now religious seers who believed they had the ability to transcend human experience, to communicate with the Prophet Mohammed. They assured him that it was his destiny to save the Islamic nation. They swore a *baya*, an allegiance that meant that to turn against him was to betray Allah.

By the late 1970s, the country was sinking into debt. A liberalisation policy enabled the selling off of liquid assets, shares, state land, petrol and gas, and this in turn encouraged corruption, which, by the end of the decade, had become endemic. The land, from which the breadbasket was to be replenished, was left fallow and unworked in favour of cash crops that could be exported for hard currency. Few development projects came to fruition and those that did arrived late, more expensive and less effective than intended. Projects were approved not because they were needed, but because they were accompanied by ready funding, or because the minister involved was assured of a kickback. There was no cohesive overview, no long-term plan. Rudderless, decisions were made impulsively. The grand plans dissolved in a spiralling confusion of high-level jinks – deals worth hundreds of millions of dollars borrowed at extortionate rates to fund projects that never came to fruition: refineries that were not built, cement factories that didn't materialise, helicopters delivered that no one had asked for.

In January 1983, after protests by students at the university, Nimeiri dissolved the Sudan Socialist Union – his own creation – dismissed his cabinet, and removed twenty-three senior military officers, including his vice president. In an open letter to academics, Nimeiri likened himself to Haroun al-Rashid, the eighth-century caliph of Abbasid Baghdad. He ordered the release of 13,000 inmates from the city's prisons. When he addressed them in Kober Prison, Nimeiri told them he had forgiven them, just as the Prophet Mohammed had forgiven the people of Mecca. In a country of saints and Sufis, the president had become disorientated, like some latter-day Lear. He seemed to believe in the sanctity of his own divine mission.

In January 1984, a year before he was ousted, *Time* magazine summed up the state of affairs in the country. President Nimeiri had begun the year, it said, by pouring a can of beer into the Nile, the first drop of five million dollars' worth of alcohol (later estimated at eleven million US dollars) destroyed to make the point that the country was now dry. Thousands lining the riverbank had cheered. Two weeks earlier, wrote the correspondent, a crowd of 500 had watched a thief have his right hand amputated. Meanwhile, only 10 per cent of the country's 200 million acres of arable land was under cultivation. The country was eight billion dollars in debt, crippled by shortages of goods, skilled workers, even electricity.

In February, the camp of the Compagnie de Construction Internationale at Sobat was attacked, bringing the construction of the Jonglei Canal to a halt. The canal was intended to channel the White Nile through the Sudd marshes. Half of the water that enters the area is lost through evaporation. Some 4.7 billion cubic metres of water would be saved. To John Garang the canal was another attempt to exploit the natural resources of the South, and that made it a target. Oil was the other obvious resource, and so the newly formed Sudan People's Liberation Army spearheaded armed resistance against Nimeiri's dictatorship, on behalf of the Sudanese nation (North and South), by attacking the Chevron base at Bentiu. The conflict would last twenty-one years.

By now Nimeiri's speeches included lengthy quotations from the Quran. He declared that anyone who joined the SPLA was an enemy of God. Socialist secularism was now a thing of the past. After seven years in prison, Hassan al-Turabi found himself not only released but instated as attorney general. It was at this point that Nimeiri attempted to redesign Islamic jurisprudence to suit his own purposes. What became known as the September Laws included legislation pertaining to 'intended adultery', which circumvented the traditional Sharia demand for four witnesses to the act. These *hudud*, or corporal punishments, were applied to hundreds of people, many of them non-Muslims, who were condemned to amputation of the right hand or cross-amputation – where the right hand and left foot are simultaneously removed – often for petty crimes such as stealing. The Sudanese Bar Association concluded that the September Laws were 'unconstitutional and not a true reflection of Islamic law'. It made little difference. By then a state of emergency had been declared and Nimeiri had only a few more months ahead of him in power.

In March 1985, Vice President George H. W. Bush paid a brief visit to Khartoum. Sudan was still an important regional ally. Nimeiri was advised to distance himself from the Muslim Brotherhood and to accept an IMF economic package. He was struggling to stay afloat. Realising the mistake he had made in the South, he engaged arms dealer Adnan Khashoggi and the businessman 'Tiny' Rowland to broker a deal with Garang. Nothing came of it. According to Rowland, Garang was 'an extremely difficult chap'. It was too late in any case. A month later, Nimeiri was flying back from America when news reached him of a popular uprising. Just in time, he managed to land in Cairo. Luck, or the divine hand? We shall probably never know, but the Nimeiri era remains one of the most beguiling yet contradictory in the country's history.

Many people trace the turning point in Nimeiri's politics to the failed *coup d'état* mounted by the communists in July 1971. Among those who perished in the aftermath was one of the most intriguing figures in the history of Sudanese politics: the general secretary of the Communist Party, Abdel-Khaliq Mahgoub. Abdel-Khaliq offered an original interpretation of Marxism as a way of bringing the Sudanese people together regardless of religion or ethnicity. He believed that a progressive culture could only be achieved by challenging the accepted norms. The key to this was to take an honest look at the country and ask what the problem was. Self-criticism is a cornerstone of Marxist thinking, and looking at the country today it's hard not to wonder if this isn't exactly what we need.

What Abdel-Khaliq advocated was nothing less than a synthesis of Islam and socialism. It might have been the key: a durable solution to the eternal conundrum; a viable political ideology that could empower the masses while respecting the role of traditional culture and religion. A creative response, in other words, to the dilemma of post-colonial national identity. The answer lay not in adopting Western or Eastern ideologies wholesale, but in finding an acceptable middle way that could be tailored to the needs of a particular nation.

Abdel-Khaliq and his fellow plotters were executed when the coup failed. The bond between the Sudanese Communist party and the Free Officers Movement was broken and this radically changed the direction Nimeiri's revolution took.

Looking back, it seems that what was almost within reach in the early 1970s was a workable alternative, a solution that might actually have allowed the country to come together. Abdel-Khaliq envisaged the coexistence of two contradictory streams of thought, bringing together his own version of Marxism with the needs of a traditional society. What he proposed was trying to achieve a progressive society through an analysis of social failings. The brilliance of this lies in the acceptance of the fact that no country with such a complex ethnic and cultural history could possibly achieve harmony and stability through the wholesale adoption of an existing political ideology. A degree of innovation is needed for any system to work. Socialism offered the opportunity of citizenship, of equality, the chance to participate in the construction of a nation, but it also threatened tradition, religious belief, and the ethnic hierarchies that had been handed down over centuries. From the British, through Egyptian Ottoman rule, to the transition to the elite effendis, authority had always been imposed from above. Here was a chance to change that.

Perhaps the country wasn't ready. No single political ideology has ever been successfully applied. Marxism, capitalism, even Wahhabi Islamism, none of them fitted the country's needs. Each has been hammered into place awkwardly and created its own

problems. To achieve the idea of a nation of equals requires, as
Abdel-Khaliq advocated, facing up to oneself, taking an honest
look at the contradictions and failings, embracing the diversity
of the country. What is needed is an unwavering examination of
what is holding society back, what needs to be changed. This is the
opposite of what has dominated politics here since independence.

It is surely significant that two of the most adventurous thinkers the country has ever produced, Mahmoud Mohammed Taha
and Abdel-Khaliq Mahgoub, were both executed. As if the very
idea of deviating from the norm could be met only by death. Why
did their ideas provoke such wrath? Were they such a threat to
what was acceptable? Are religious belief and cultural praxis so
insecure as to be unable to resist examination?

Nasser's socialism soon proved as dogmatic and authoritarian
as the monarchy he had overthrown. Critics such as Sayyid Qutb
were imprisoned and executed, although his ideas and accusations
continued to resonate long after his death. By the time Nasser
passed away in 1970, the revolutionary Arab defiance of the Suez
Crisis had begun to wither away. The oil boom had given rise to
images of decadent 'oil sheikhs' at play in the West. Confidence
was brought even lower by the defeats of 1967 and 1973, and a
wave of puritanism began to sweep through the region. In 1979,
the Iranian Revolution brought austere, political Islam to power
in the figure of the Ayatollah Khomeini. That same year, an apoca-
lyptic sect of radicals seized the Sacred Mosque in Mecca in a bid to
cleanse Islam. It triggered the rise of ultraconservative Wahhabite
Islam in a bid to redeem the religion, while in Egypt Nasser's
successor, Anwar Sadat, who had been busy undoing everything
his predecessor had done, was gunned down in October 1981 by
members of the Islamic Group, a radical faction guided by Sheikh
Omar Abdel-Rahman, the blind imam who was to pass through
Khartoum, only to surface later in New Jersey linked to the 1993
bomb attack on the World Trade Center. Further afield, the Soviet
Union invaded Afghanistan to find itself fighting the mujahideen.

The optimism of the early 1970s, the dream of a nation large
enough to encompass its own internal contradictions, one bounti-
ful enough to feed the continent, vanished in less than a decade.

A gap yawned between the aspirations of the middle classes and the opportunities available. Oil prices rose and trained labourers took their skills abroad, to the Gulf, where business was booming. Socialism was a poor memory.

Why has nationhood proved so elusive? It is possible that things might have been different if the 1971 coup had not failed? If Abdel-Khaliq had been given the chance to reinvent the country on a platform of equality? On the other hand, this might just be wishful thinking. There is no evidence that Adbel-Khaliq would have been able to turn his ideas into reality. But the fact remains that that period is one of the most remarkable in the country's modern history.

The old sectarian parties never offered a viable answer to modern politics. Ideologies twisted in the wind, trying to find a form that would endure and, in the face of the failure to find a lasting solution, politics became a game of personalities. And while some might dream of popular uprisings, in the past these never delivered a new order. In both October 1964 and April 1985, after a period of civilian rule, the military seized power. A pattern was emerging across the African continent. Attempts at finding an ideological alternative were invariably terminated by military intervention. In 1969 it was Nimeiri and his socialist revolution. In 1989 socialism was replaced by Islamism, an ideology that offers religion as the solution to all ills, social and economic. Like everything else, it was never more than a temporary illusion. In the end, it seems, ideals fade, to be replaced eventually by the ultimate admission of failure, the violent institution of repression.

My memories of the old house in Souk Two were placed in a
new light many years later when my father told me the story of
his connection to the July 1971 coup. That night he had apparently given shelter to a group of close friends, many of whom
were members of the Communist Party, many of whom were
involved in the plotting. While we were sleeping soundly in our
beds they had passed the hours in a nervous frenzy of smoking
and drinking, making tense phone calls, waiting. In the morning he drove them around town in the family car to assess the
situation. It didn't take long for them to realise that the coup had
failed. Within seventy-two hours Nimeiri managed to mount a
counter-coup. My father's friends disappeared. They fled abroad
or went into hiding – one remained underground in Khartoum
for fifteen years.

My father sensibly went home and explained to my mother
that he might be going away for a time. Then he sat down to sign
a series of blank cheques to allow her to draw money while he
was in prison. It seems such a fundamentally inadequate solution
as to suggest a man in panic. How long did he think he would
be away? Many of the plotters were immediately executed, along
with Abdel-Khaliq. I remember a darkness in the house at the
time. A sense of real dread as we watched the images of the plotters on television.

What inspired him to become so involved? Loyalty to his
friends, to the ideals they shared? Was he afraid to disappoint
them? Whatever it was, it was a reckless moment in the life of
a modest and cautious man. The episode must have scared him.
Soon after that he developed diabetes, a mysterious ailment
explained by my mother as being brought on by a shock. At the
time it made no sense. Barely aware of political events and their
consequences at the time, life for us went on, the daily routine
disrupted (coups became something of a regular occurrence) by
a few days off school. They never came for my father but, super-
stitious to the end, I believe he perceived his illness as a kind of
punishment, for audacity if for nothing else.

I no longer have any pictures of that house, or that time.
They were lost at some point, washed away in the tide of

displacement, along with many of our personal possessions. For as far back as I can remember my mother carried a camera with her everywhere she went, snapping everything and everyone in sight. When she died she left behind sackfuls, literally, of badly framed, often poorly focused snapshots of friends and relatives, many of whom I couldn't even name. In contrast, the early black and white ones that I recall were neatly arranged and stuck into large, cloth-covered albums. The serrated edges were held in place by adhesive corners that fixed them to the thick black pages. These were separated by thin leaves of translucent vellum. Each photograph was dated and annotated in neat, looping letters written in white ink. During my childhood those albums were a source of mystery. They occupied a shelf in the living room where I would sometimes go to leaf through the pages and wonder at the people in them. The old greyness that was Britain. The angled roofs of the houses and the rainswept streets. It was another world, one that I could hardly remember, yet it was a part of our story.

That simple villa with its veranda of dark red tiles and slim white pillars felt big and open. In retrospect, it can't have been all that big, but it never felt small or constricted. I have the impression that there were no closed doors, that it was possible to run through the house from one end to the other without meeting obstruction. My father's job with the Sudan Gezira Board had come to an end and now he managed a company importing building and agricultural equipment. The Sudanese Tractor Company Limited. We were part of the middle class. Not rich, but not poor either. Poverty was not as visible as it is today. On my mother's old Super 8 reels, the jerky images vibrate with unstable rainbow colours that rise and fall. In the background the streets appear deserted. A lone car slides by. A man leads a camel.

The past continues to exert a sense of unresolved mystery. We would go swimming at the university pool. It was open to the sky and rather neglected. High trees towered over the dark green wooden pergola that shaded the walls, giving it a somewhat gloomy feel. Large Nile monitor lizards would scuttle around the edges of the water. They lived in the culverts and drains. Mostly they left you alone, but would give you a leery glare if you startled them. In those days my mother was employed as a typist at the university. Every year they organised an excursion for the staff. One year I refused to go. Everything was arranged. We were in the backyard packing the last things into the cooler box. My mother was generally not one to stand for any nonsense, and I cannot explain why, but I threw a tantrum. It must have been a serious one because in the end we didn't go. Phone calls had to be made and apologies given. It was meant to be a big day out. The plan was to sail up the Nile on one of the old paddle steamers. There we would stop at a beach and go ashore. There would be a barbecue and swimming. Then we would come back in the evening. Late that night, as the steamer was returning downstream, it hit a sandbank and went down. Several people drowned.

Later, I would dream about being stuck in a cabin below deck. It was dark and completely submerged. Emily, a Coptic woman who shared an office with my mother, was one of those who drowned. A small, cheerful woman. In my dream it was she who was floating gently there in the flooded cabin. I'm not sure why she affected me so much. She seemed very peaceful, but I knew she was dead and somehow that meant that I, too, had drowned.

It must have been an intense period for my parents. They were in the midst of their lives. They were not the elderly people I knew later, when I was grown up enough to appreciate these things, but young and alive, still full of hopes and aspirations. My father with his dreams for the country, his intellectual friends and their revolutionary ideas. My mother had her own, private ambitions. In her spare hours at the university, she somehow found the time to write a novel. The typescript, pinned together between sheets of card, used to sit on the bookshelf at home, another source of mystery. I still have it today and rereading it I had the odd experience of realising that I was older than she had been when she wrote it.

As a work of fiction it is not entirely convincing, though it does provide a window into their life in that period. The story feels like a lightly veiled account of her own life. There are descriptions of that house that I recognise, and a rather loving portrayal of my grandmother, Haboba, as we called her. The climax of the novel is set at the moment of the 1971 coup, another reminder of how significant it was to my parents. Their lives could have changed forever, although in the novel this is largely glossed over.

I imagine her working away at this novel, typing when she had a spare moment in that office at the university, where the windows were open and the breeze blew in from the river. She was writing about her own life and for the most part it seems to suggest she was happy. If there was one thing that really bothered her it was the fact that in thirty-odd years of living in Sudan none of her family ever came out from Britain to visit her. Even now I find that strange. Her parents were old and travel was not as commonplace as it is today. It would have been a long, difficult and expensive trip to make, but she had a brother a couple of years younger than her.

In the novel, it is the narrator's brother who arrives from England and stays long enough to fall in love with one of the neighbour's daughters. I don't recognise the young man as my uncle, but perhaps that says more about how little I knew him. Nor do I recall a young woman living next door. There was a girl, rather pretty, who was slightly older than us, who would climb onto the high wall between our houses and chat to us in the quiet of the afternoon when our parents were sleeping. I don't think she could have been the one my mother had in mind, but I wonder who the bride of the story was based on. What drives the novel is the fulfilment of a deep-seated desire for closure; for her family to see how she was living, to witness the happiness she had found here. My mother wasn't the type to dwell on things, but she found a way, through writing, of dealing with something that in real life could not be resolved. As far as I know she never tried to have the novel published, and certainly never mentioned it. For years it sat on that bookshelf in our living room, gathering dust, waiting for me to find it.

Souk Two in those days was a tidier place than it is today. There was a big grocery store on one corner of the crossroads that was run by an old Greek couple. A dour woman, always dressed in black, used to sit by the door behind the cash register. I remember the dark wooden counters, the shelves piled high with boxes of soap and tins of olives. Oddly, she used to do a trade in pulp fiction of a cheap and tawdry kind. I can recall one particularly pornographic effort involving an undercover Navajo police agent, I think, about which I developed quite a fascination. Opposite this was a café whose refrigerator was stocked with glass pots of yoghurt. The pots were sealed only by a thick, dusty skin on the top. All that remains of this is a burned-out hole in the ground. There was a bookshop nearby, too, clean, air-conditioned and cool, run by a prim Coptic woman who never smiled.

My memory of those years is of a simple life. We lived and slept outdoors. The houses were open-sided and cooled by gentle fans rather than the sealed, air-conditioned units of today. Twice a week we were forced to assemble on the veranda for our Arabic lessons, which we hated. The teacher, Ustaz Hassan, would turn up in the afternoons in a grey Morris 1000, as immaculate as his spotless white gellabiya and imma, the turban perched like a floppy bird's nest on top of his head. We would run away. I think it was my idea to lead my brothers astray. This, at least, was generally my father's interpretation, since as the eldest he held me responsible for all his troubles with his sons. I convinced them that if we hid the teacher might simply give up and go away. I wasn't opposed to the language as such, and of course I am grateful now, but hated the tedious obligation of it. The looming hour, Tuesdays and Thursdays, that drew a dark cloud over the week. Most of the time we spoke English at home. The language of instruction at school was English. In the early years I attended Clergy House, a primary school situated in the grounds of the neo-Byzantine All Saints Cathedral, a relic of the British presence, where memorial services for Gordon were once held. We had a working knowledge of day-to-day Arabic picked up from my father and from conversation outside the classroom. It didn't seem an urgent priority to acquire more than that.

In contrast, the only book I can ever recall my father reading to me was in Arabic, a slim textbook involving a boy and a camel. There were vividly drawn illustrations evoking a desert setting and a sprinting camel. This was in Britain, and I was a young child. Studies apparently show that when fathers read to their children it has a greater impact (perhaps due to the rarity of meaningful interaction between fathers and children). It should have heralded a long and serious commitment to the language. All was eclipsed by that pompous man in his Morris 1000, bearing down the garden path in his flowing white cotton. My plan of hiding was pretty solid, I thought. My father and mother slept every afternoon, so in theory they wouldn't even have known whether we had had a class or not. If the teacher arrived to find no willing pupils he certainly wouldn't have bothered my parents. He would have got back into his car and gone home, and we would have gone on playing. In the end he complained and my father would stick around to make sure we were sitting on the veranda when Ustaz Hassan showed up.

Over the years other teachers would materialise, each more hopeless than the last, and many afternoons were spent toiling over grammar, dictation, struggling with pronunciation, with the letters and diacritics. Some lasted longer than others, but they never completely vanished from our lives. My Arabic is still worse than I care to admit, but that is mainly due to my own neglect, and the course my life has taken over the years. Now, there is no one to blame but myself and the lack of waking hours in the day.

The only real entertainment available in those days was the cinema, of which there were around a dozen altogether. My mother was an avid film buff and it was not uncommon for us to go with her several times a week. She would think nothing of setting off for some obscure and remote place on the far side of town to locate a dusty, forgotten cinema because they were showing something interesting. I can remember getting hopelessly lost in the dark, driving in circles through unfamiliar markets, along streets with no signs of life or even street lights. The cinema was always an experience in itself. The theatres were open-air in those days, the films projected onto a whitewashed wall. The men down in the cheap seats at the front would call out to the characters on screen, shine flashlights at the sky. Further back there were raised platforms with rows of boxes, fenced off by metal railings that sat four or five with a small table on which to balance your refreshments. Safragis wearing green cummerbunds would slip between the aisles bearing crates of ice-cold soft drinks on their shoulders.

The films were usually American or British. They were invariably several years old by the time they arrived, having done the rounds of the Middle East. The wear and tear showed as the celluloid snapped and stuttered through the gate, often causing delays and provoking uproar. With my mother we often went to the Blue Nile Cinema, originally built for the British soldiers stationed in Khartoum. We watched old Woody Allen and Jack Lemmon comedies, along with a slew of disaster movies starring Charlton Heston involving earthquakes and crashing airliners. It was an eclectic selection, and perhaps it was the age, but many of the films had a gloomy edge to them: Bob Rafelson's *Five Easy Pieces*, John Boorman's *Deliverance*, Sam Peckinpah's *Straw Dogs*, Nic Roeg's *Walkabout*. Then there were the conspiracy thrillers like *The Parallax View* or French *policiers* like *Sans motif apparent* with Jean-Louis Trintignant. All of them evoked a world full of terror and betrayal. Not the horror of monsters or violent dinosaurs; that was yet to come. The films of the 1970s were harshly critical of capitalist society. They often hinted at a darkness within human nature, of secret forces within the establishment who sought to impose their political agenda or an unsuspecting population. In retrospect, the cinema probably did me lasting damage.

When we were old enough to go to the cinema on our own we would find ourselves at the Coliseum, in among the common people watching films my mother wouldn't be dragged to screaming. Kung Fu films with the likes of David Chiang and Ti Lung, sleazy Italian action films like *Shanghai Joe* and *Heroes in Hell*. Klaus Kinski, with his magnetic psychopathic Nazi blond looks, appeared in an incredible number of truly awful movies. All were atrociously dubbed. For years I never saw anyone talk straight on screen. The films most popular among the crowds were the tame Egyptian melodramas and the Bollywood extravaganzas that offered song, dance and scantily clad women rolling about in the sea, all sealed into a scratchy, torn, frame-hopping kaleidoscope of meaningless hysteria.

And the highlight of a long, dull week at school was the unveiling of the poster for the coming Saturday's film in the wooden frame outside the warden's office. The school was founded by Daniele Comboni, an Italian missionary who believed his destiny was to breathe new life into Africa. It's not clear how he intended to achieve this through a steady diet of Giuliano Gemma and Terence Hill films, parodies of the spaghetti westerns that had been popular a decade or so earlier, but that's what we got.

The cinema was divided down the middle, with the girls from Sisters School on one side and us, the boys, who were more like rutting animals, on the left. The fathers and sisters would sit in a raised section at the back to keep vigil, and make sure there was no sneaking across in the dark. None of this protected you, of course, from the lecherous advances of older boys who, male sexuality being what it is, and females being unavailable, would furtively press their erections against you in the scrum that surrounded the refreshments counter.

Perhaps the strangest part of the school was the library. There were two days a week when it was open for half an hour during the morning break. It was run by a diminutive sister who seemed to view all little boys as suspect, perhaps with reason, but as a result barely uttered a word. All transactions were carried out in silence. The books were covered in brown paper, the same paper we used to cover our textbooks and exercise books. Underlying this exercise was some austere sense of egalitarianism. Some boys inherited textbooks from older brothers, or had acquired them from second-hand stalls. In their paper covering we were all equal. Every year we would spend an afternoon folding and cutting the paper, writing our names and the titles on the covers. In the library the same system was used to protect the books, but it meant that finding something to read involved moving very slowly along, reading the titles and authors' names written on the spines. We were not encouraged to browse. Every move you made would be scrutinised by the sister who stood behind a high counter next to the door. Visiting the library was not obligatory, and so there were normally very few people in there. Many of those who visited would walk around a bit and then leave, as if the presence of so many books made them uncomfortable. There was a wide range of fiction, mostly in English, though there were sections in Arabic, Italian and French. I often found myself unable to decide which book to take and would hesitate, caught between one title and another until the last minute. In the end I would hear the bell ringing, marking the end of break, and I would impulsively grab something and head for the door with little idea what I had taken. There was still the ritual of having the little card removed from the inside flap and then placed inside a small folder on which your name was printed and the class you were in. Finally, a date would be stamped inside the book and then you were free to go. I can remember the excitement of hurrying back up the stairs to my desk, knowing I had a treat in store. I would often read to get through tedious classes, the book concealed out of sight on my knees.

It was an odd school, I suppose, the way all schools are odd in their own fashion. During break every day they would play records by the Beatles. Only the Beatles. I'm not sure why. A school run by Italian priests in the middle of Africa. Why not? They played the same half-dozen records over and over, every day. In my head the soundtrack for that entire period was 'Penny Lane', 'Strawberry Fields Forever' and 'Eleanor Rigby'. It felt weird and yet, at the same time, quite personal because I felt a certain bond with the Beatles, for the simple reason that as a small child I had once lived in their hometown.

I used to sit next to a rather introverted boy named Amr. He would mumble to himself all day, lost in his own private world. At times he would stare out of the window and hold up his biro to estimate the size of a building across the street. Once I asked him what he was doing and he explained with a confident smile that if he knocked down the present structure he could construct a building with so and so many apartments. All of this he calculated in his head, right down to how much he would charge for each apartment. I would sit there reading my novels. Most of the books I read were adventure stories. So while I was dreaming of cattle drives to Abilene, or sailing the world's oceans, Amr would be imagining the city's future development. Somehow, looking around the city today, it's not hard to conclude whose vision won out over time. On a visit one day I discover that the library has been banished to a basement room. Nobody really uses it any longer. The books appear like preserved relics. A small, diminished version of the universe of infinite possibility that I recall.

Often it is to the abstractions of poetry that we turn for help in defining the complex swirl of identities that flow through a city, or, indeed, a country. Poets eulogise, they sigh with longing, they stand as beacons of virtue. We live in their spirit, in their ability to raise us above our simple mortality, putting hope and aspiration into words.

Muhammed Abdel-Hai might be one such poet. His own story begins with movement. Born in Ed-Damer, which lies on the bank of the Nile to the north, he migrated, first to the capital, then on to Leeds and Oxford before returning to teach at the English Department of Khartoum University. He died at the age of forty-five, leaving a legacy of engagement both theoretical and poetic.

One of his successors is a young woman, Fawzia (not her real name). On the wall of her office hangs a photograph of her post-graduate colleagues lined up on a lawn at Cambridge. She dresses demurely and speaks cautiously, but with passion and elegance.

The English Department is a gloomy place. Doors are locked. Halls deserted. It has never really recovered from the 1989 purge of all things Western. Nowadays, Fawzia's students can barely speak the language when they arrive here. The department was closed, textbooks replaced with anything in Arabic. It was a traumatic moment of release, as if the old colonial bond had held the country in slavery.

Standards have fallen so far that the diplomatic service has difficulty finding people fluent enough to be stationed abroad. The Arabisation of the university that was phased in from the early 1980s onwards, and that followed a similar change in secondary school education a decade earlier, has left a generation unable to read or write any other language than Arabic. Students can barely copy words correctly from their examination papers to their test sheets. Even the English exam paper for the Sudan School Certificate is riddled with errors. Only one in four will graduate. And since many textbooks are not available in Arabic the lack of English also affects other disciplines.

Two large black armchairs mushroom from the floor like padded thrones. A dining table takes up one half of the room. A plate of biscuits emerges from a glass vitrine. A bottle of water from a small refrigerator levered into the space between cupboard and wall. Fawzia tugs self-consciously at the sleeves of her blouse. Over the years she has learned to tread the line between what she would like to wear and what is acceptable. On the pavement outside the university street vendors sell long cotton gloves wrapped in cellophane packaging. Rows and rows of them are spread out on the ground. They come in a range of colours, from minty green through grey to dull variations of brown and black. Wearing gloves goes along with the headscarves and strict dress code observed by female students on campus. She stretches out her arms for me to judge the length of her sleeves. They look decent enough to me, but they extend only halfway down her forearms and for many they would be very risqué. Fawzia is in her thirties. Her hands are bare, her head is loosely covered only by a traditional scarf, a *tarha*; 'I can dress like this only if I have a car that brings me right up to the door of the department.' She doesn't seem the type to be easily intimidated, but to walk across the campus dressed like this would be asking for trouble.

Still, things are far better than they used to be. When she first started studying here other girls would shun her if she wore trousers or did not cover her hair properly. Part of that resentment was religious, but it was also class-driven. The family is not rich, but her father is a lawyer who was active in the early days of the nationalist movement, which provides a pedigree of sorts. Compared to many, her manners and tastes are those of a middle-class girl from an affluent home. Before university she attended Unity High School, a fifteen-minute walk away. A private institution, it was the first school for girls in the country, founded in 1902 with help from the Anglican bishop.

Fawzia's story is a reminder that the Revolution of National Salvation was as concerned with overturning the old social order as it was with Islamisation. Members of the People's Defence Force, *Al-Difaa al-Shaabi*, were assigned to monitor students. The simple fact that classes were mixed, that both sexes could move freely among one another, was new to first-year students. Fawzia and her friends tended to sit apart from the others. They were dubbed the *hanakish*, a slang term meaning something like 'fancy girls'. One day she arrived wearing white trousers, only to be confronted by another girl who accused her of going against tradition by not covering her hair and wearing provocative clothing. There were more than a hundred people in the class and not one of them stood up to defend her. Her accuser was an activist in the Students' Union. Like party membership, student activism, enforcing the regime's policies, offered an established career path towards lucrative high posts in government for many people (including the current vice president). By Fawzia's second year, in 1991, a strict dress code was enforced. Any woman could be stopped and asked for her identity card because the scarf she wore was too thin, or her skirt deemed too short, along with a number of other infringements. Although they found this humiliating, many women did not give way easily: 'There was a lot of negotiating. You didn't know how far you could go.'

There was also a morality police, the *Shurtat al-Adeeb*. These were civilians empowered to keep an eye on their fellow citizens, to ensure they behaved properly. Women were not allowed to move about alone. When in the company of a man they had to be able to produce a marriage certificate or proof they were related. The girls reacted like young women everywhere; they invented ways of getting around the restrictions. The campus had separate entrances for men and women. They would change their clothes once they had passed the checkpoint. The restrictive measures increased. To travel abroad you needed the permission of the senior male in the family, even if this was your younger brother, or your eighteen-year-old son. Whips were purchased from Iran to enforce public order on the spot. The degree of radicalisation imposed by the Bashir regime had never been seen before. Lecture halls and libraries were divided into gender-specific areas. The *Difaa al-Shaabi* were effectively a class of informers who collected information on students. Fawzia was warned that her behaviour had singled her out, and that this was jeopardising her chances of an academic career. Such an idea, that how she dressed could hinder her career, was anathema to someone who had grown up, thanks to her liberal father, with great respect for Khartoum University as an institution. It was a place of learning, a temple of free thinking. Walking through the gates she would recall that poets such as Mohammed Abdul-Hai had once passed through the same entrance.

Poetry played a leading role in the development of political consciousness in the years leading up to independence. The British set up the Gordon Memorial College at the turn of the century with the aim of preparing the Sudanese elite for administrative posts in the civil service. The first stirrings of a national consciousness began to flourish here in the 1920s. In the following decade, literary societies, or *Jamiyat al-Adabiyya*, played a key role, emerging as forums for discussing political and social issues. The first political parties crystallised out of these societies. Journals like *Al-Fajr* (The Dawn) and *Al-Nahda* (The Awakening) provided a space for the development of anti-colonial ideas. Alongside more overtly political material, the period saw the emergence of poetry, fiction and drama that reflected a growing confidence in the uniqueness and distinction of local culture. Early poetry praised the glory of Arabic civilisation and the golden age of Islam, but new terms defining a Sudanese character and culture began to circulate. The man who later became the country's first elected prime minister, Muhammed Ahmed al-Mahjub, writing in *Al Fajr* in 1935, called for a national literature, one that was written in Arabic but remained 'infused with the idiom of our own land, as this is what distinguishes one nation from another'.

The concept of idiom is crucial here, recognising the need to identify and develop a means of expressing what is unique to the country's history and culture. What the poets of the 1960s did, and it was not until then that this school of thought really came into its own, was to take pride in the 'African-ness' of Sudan. Like all such notions it is ultimately an abstraction, one that lends itself more readily to the writing of poetry than to policy-making. The assumption that it had to be an Arabic-derived idiom is not surprising, nor is it necessarily a disadvantage, so long as that Arabic is fluid enough to absorb other words and expressions.

Muhammed Abdel-Hai played a leading role in this development. His work was crucial in establishing the notion of a national identity. In his essay on cultural poetics, Abdel-Hai focuses on the nature of Northern Sudanese identity, spawning the notion of racial and cultural hybridity that came to expression in what became known as the school of 'The Forest and Desert'. The use of nature as metaphor to project a common national heritage dates back to Hamzah Tambal in the 1930s. Inspired by English Romantics such as Wordsworth, Tambal was the first to use a term referring to literature that was specifically Sudanese, *Al-Adab al-Sudani*. This search for common ground also touched on the matter of racial hybridity. Centuries of slaves and their traders, Arabs and Africans, left a legacy that is reflected in the diverse racial types of today, often with huge variations within in a single family.

The recognition of a diverse common heritage was the first step towards achieving the nation. The Forest and Desert school provided a chance to imagine a landscape in which contrasts were not competing or mutually exclusive. It recognised the existence of colour, and of discrimination. A poem by Muhammed Al-Makki Ibraheem alludes to the 'chains of slavery', to blackness and creolity. Along with the music of the time it was an expression of the search for a distinctive and inclusive Sudanese cultural identity.

The neglect of the old downtown area begins to look symptomatic of a deeper malaise, a lack of moral and intellectual rigour. The combination of oil wealth and piety has fostered a sense of privileged detachment, as if all the problems of the world will somehow take care of themselves. Nothing represents this void more clearly than the old Aboulela building. Now run-down and uncared for, once it was a symbol of the modernisation brought by the traders who settled here in the days of the *Turkiyya*, the period of Turco-Egyptian rule – Egyptians, Greeks, Syrians, Armenians, Copts and Jews. All brought with them a vital connection to the Mediterranean and beyond. They contributed a distinctly non-African element to the city. Today, they have almost all gone. Forty per cent of the Coptic population departed in the early years of the *Inqaz*, never to return. Far fewer remain of the other groups. Nowadays the covered sidewalks are inhabited by furtive men with darting eyes who loiter on the corners. They squat down in shuttered doorways or trail behind as you dodge mounds of pungent mud piled around jagged gashes in the ground. Gaping trenches flooded with putrid grey water that tell of some recurring plumbing disaster. In low whispers they offer to exchange any foreign currency you might have on you. There are many of them, and all are sensitive to the slightest flicker of interest as they move up and down restlessly, seeking out opportunity, competing with the banks across the street.

The entrance to the building, once grand, has grown grubby and unkempt, cluttered with discarded rubbish, strips of newspaper and cardboard. The cubicle where a concierge once sat is untended and dark. The floor is unswept and dirty; dirty, too, the beautifully carved groove of the handrail that spirals upwards in an elegant sweep to the upper floors. The white marble steps are like old teeth, chipped and broken, with sizeable chunks missing. There are almost no signs of life. The walls and hallways are deserted and bare. A conversation between two men standing on the first floor echoes up through the stairwell. The doors are unmarked and most appear to be unoccupied.

On the third floor a large and very fancy brass plaque announces that you have found the offices of Mohammed Ibrahim Khalil. The front door is open. Immediately to the right is a small kitchen in which a man sleeps, his head tilted back against the wall, eyes closed. It's mid-morning, but he is lost to the world and does not stir as I walk in. The secretary rises to her feet to offer her hand and a smile without knowing who I am. One has the sense that they do not get too many visitors.

What makes a man return home after decades in exile to set himself up in his old offices again? I am intrigued by the courage and determination of someone my father's age. They knew one another in London in the 1950s. They played tennis together. Mohammed Ibrahim Khalil still keeps up the style of those days. He dresses in sharp suits, striped shirts, cufflinks, and a colourful tie. I wonder what it takes to decide to abandon the safety of Washington, DC, now, at this stage in life, and start again.

The office itself is a picture of order. On the walls are framed certificates from various legal institutions in Britain and the United States. Behind the long desk is a high-backed chair. Facing this a low table for guests sits between two large leather armchairs. There is a bookcase and a computer screen and little more. The other half of the room holds a varnished dining table used for meetings. A sofa in the corner provides the only touch of colour against the otherwise monochrome tones of a legal document.

Mohammed Ibrahim Khalil has a long history of involvement in Sudan's politics and legal affairs. When Nimeiri was forced out of office by popular uprising in 1985, he was made speaker of parliament in the interim government. He had been instrumental in plans to create a National Charter that demanded a revival of the amended 1964 October Constitution. This would grant a degree of regional autonomy to the South. The draft Charter was key to uniting opposition forces and initiating talks with the SPLA, in preparation for when Nimeiri left power. It was meant to be a new beginning, which started promisingly, but ultimately failed to deliver. The new prime minister, Sadig al-Mahdi, proved ineffective, too tied to old-fashioned ideas, unable to correct the crippled economy or end the war in the South. In retrospect, he simply paved the way for what was to come.

Sadig dithered over revoking Nimeiri's ugly version of Sharia – the so-called September Laws – which were a major obstacle to ending the war. He tried introducing alternatives that, after three years in office, were revealed to be a recycling of the old laws. At this point Khalil, who been a loyal supporter and for years had represented the interests of Sadig's Umma party – one of the country's two traditional political parties – resigned as a matter of principle. Less than a year later what had been seeping slowly into the ether crystallised in the form of the Revolution of National Salvation. The *Inqaz* had arrived and Sadig was replaced by the wild card that was Brigadier Omar al-Bashir. Millions fled the country, including my parents and Khalil himself.

Two years ago he decided to come back and begin practising law again. A slim, fragile figure in his seventies, he seems focused in a manner that suggests he is keenly aware that time is short. As we sit and chat while tea is being prepared by the sleeping orderly in the kitchen, I sense his optimism. He is busy preparing a case to test the powers of the Constitutional Court.

In 1999, a former professor at the university lodged a formal complaint detailing the torture he had been subjected to in Kober Central Prison in Khartoum North. Farouk M. Ibrahim named names and demanded that those responsible be brought to justice. His complaint was ignored. The culprits were allowed to go free and torture continued. Ibrahim was held in 'Ghost House No. 1', formerly the offices of the election commission. In his detailed letter Farouk identified General Bakri Hassan Saleh, then minister of defence and Nafie Ali Nafie, the notorious director of National Security at the time, as being present. The professor alleged that he was beaten by Nafie, a former student and later colleague at the university.

Farouk attributes his release from the ghost house to the complaint he lodged with General Bakri, one of his torturers. Bakri responded by justifying the use of torture for a number of reasons, including the fact that Farouk had been teaching Darwin's theory of evolution in the Faculty of Science at Khartoum University. After Farouk was examined by a prison doctor a report was despatched to Amnesty International. An account of the torture was published in the *Financial Times*, written by a correspondent who was then himself briefly arrested.

In November 2000, in an open letter addressed to President Bashir, Farouk pleaded for the settlement of cases of torture. This was framed as a response to the president's call for members of the opposition to return home and participate in the political life of the nation. The current appeal argues that a South African-style Truth and Reconciliation Commission would be futile. Ibrahim's accusation offers the brutality of the treatment received by himself and others as proof of the irreconcilable nature of the crimes committed. He cites the example of an engineer who was whipped alongside him for hours and who later suffered a complete mental breakdown, subsequently murdering his wife and three other members of his family. The grace of those who have suffered, he argues, marks them as religiously and morally superior to their torturers. For this reason, he calls upon his torturers to confess publicly, to apologise for what they did. This would stand as an example for all who inflicted torture at one time or another. But he insists this must be a genuine and effective reconciliation, and dismisses the efforts of some to ask God's forgiveness. 'God does not change people unless they change what is in their souls,' he writes. If mutual reconciliation is unattainable, then he urges action in court. The aim of bringing this case is to challenge the immunity of the National Intelligence and Security Service officers.

For all his faith in the rule of law, Khalil is worried about the direction this country is taking. Public funds are vanishing into private pockets. Corruption is still relatively new. What is already established fact in places like Nigeria, Angola and Chad is now emerging here. And it goes all the way to the top. Everyone wants their cut. To tap into the spirit of free enterprise you need to be well connected. Politics is now simply a means to an end.

'Sheer dereliction of duty,' he declares in English, when speaking of the neglect of the public sector. Khalil is rightly appalled by the damage done to the education system. In 1990–91, Hassan al-Turabi – a former dean of the university's Faculty of Law – dismissed all the judiciary and legal council in the Ministry of Justice. The man Turabi placed as head of the Faculty of Law (Hafiz al-Shaykh) actually failed the LLB Bar Association exam and had to repeat a year. The faculty was converted to Arabic. Books on law written in English were simply given away, to wind up on flyblown pavement bookstalls in Omdurman market. Standards dropped so much that, invited to address a gathering of young lawyers, Khalil was dismayed to discover that two-thirds of the 150 lawyers present could not understand the terminology. The University of Cairo in Khartoum was taken over and renamed the Nilein University. That first generation of students under the *Inqaz* has now filtered up to the level of High Court judges. 'There are very few good people,' Khalil claims. It is not so much that their grasp of legal process is poor, but that their level of general knowledge is so low. Often they preside over cases they know nothing about, which means they are unable to comprehend the consequences of what they are ruling on.

The transformation of the education system during the 1990s is a prime example of Turabi's zeal outstripping his understanding. A total of twenty-five new universities were set up overnight. Some say that Turabi had some kind of personal grudge against the University of Khartoum, that somehow he was trying to destroy it. The aim was to give the world an impression of Sudan as an educated place. But to achieve it they made a

travesty of education. Today there are more than 240,000 unem-
ployed graduates looking for work, and they are still spitting
out more every year. The lesson has not been learned. The
Minister of Justice is now putting pressure on the universities to
increase their intake and lower standards, asking them to grant
more first-class honours. Already there are undergraduates who
can't even grasp the metric system, but can recite large chunks
of the Quran verbatim. The teaching of languages was drasti-
cally reduced. And it wasn't just English that suffered. Even
the level of Arabic among this generation is substandard. There
are already over 17,000 licensed advocates in the Sudan, 14,000
of whom are in Khartoum. By comparison, Washington, DC,
where Khalil used to live and work, has only about 4,000 registered attorneys.

The competition for work often leads to temptation, and
unlawful practices abound. In one of the more common schemes,
land is appropriated from its rightful owners. A land search is
conducted in someone else's name. Documents are then forged
and sold off to a third party without the original owner being
aware of it. One day they go along to take a look at their land
only to find someone has started building on it. New owners
and old owners then descend into a lengthy legal battle, while
the middleman has absconded with the profits. With land prices
around the capital shooting up in recent years this has become a
lucrative money-making scheme.

Despite all evidence to the contrary, Khalil's faith in the country remains strong: 'You cannot fundamentally change the character of a nation that easily,' he maintains. Beneath the corruption
and the newly developed appetite for greed, the lack of common
decency and manners, the character of the country, he believes,
remains intact. Wishful thinking perhaps, though, for the moment
at least, people remain generous and friendly. They are not
money-grabbing, or mean, which is still a pleasure to discover.
People still need one another to get anything done. It remains to
be seen, however, what the long-term effects of these changes will
be. Nothing can remain unsullied by the foul air it is breathing.
'The Sudanese people,' Khalil smiles, again switching to English,

'have never had the benefit of a government commensurate to the standards of the people in the street. You see my point?' He concedes that the current regime has presided over some of the worst the country has seen. If he is right, and it is the people who offer the country its best chance of redemption, there are signs that their patience is being sorely tried.

One ray of hope rests with the Constitutional Court. It was founded on the wave of euphoria that accompanied the signing of the Comprehensive Peace Agreement in 2005. The majority of the judges are independent and deal with cases of infringement of legal rights and property rights or appropriation. Farouk's case was not summarily dismissed, which is a hopeful sign. Despite the delaying tactics there remains due process of law. The Constitutional Court is not perfect. Some of the judges have close links to those in power, and it won't be possible to tell which way they will swing until the moment of truth.

Khalil belongs to a generation to whom self-sacrifice for the greater good was the norm. In a continent of juveniles and children, they have managed the extraordinary feat of growing old. Like Mahgoub at the newspaper *Al Ayyam*. In their youth they embodied the dreams of the newly born nation. Well-educated, intelligent, imaginative, they were given an impossible task: to construct a nation that did not exist out of a mosaic of peoples who barely knew of the existence of their fellow compatriots. The wonder is not that the dream was never achieved in their lifetime, but that they ever imagined it was possible.

There is something quaint and fatally flawed about this chivalrous man, whose code of ethics seems to hark back to a bygone age. Alerting the world to its moral failures, highlighting gaps in constitutional law. Who really cares? In a country that manages to twist the law to suit its own purposes, which persists in denying the complex diversity at the root of its problems, which sees solutions in short cuts and nepotism, which rests comfortably on a belief in its own superiority over other ethnic groups. The fine suit and tie, the expensive cufflinks, declare his allegiance to the West. It all adds up to a man labouring, struggling to stay afloat, fighting against the current.

One evening I find myself in the little room in my grandmother's house. Outside, the young men sit around in the dark and talk in low voices. In here, as always, a television is on. A grey-haired man sits and eats from a bowl, slowly and methodically cleaning it with his fingers and chunks of bread. He eats with the pace of a man who is too tired to notice what he is eating, and appears to derive no pleasure from the act of feeding himself. It is a duty that has to be performed. There are two single beds in the room, one against either wall. We sit opposite one another. He doesn't speak and he doesn't look up. I consider if perhaps I should leave the room while he is eating, though he doesn't seem to care. The intrusion of the television between us makes remaining like this possible, like a window on infinity. This is Hashim's brother Mustapha, whom I don't really know. When I was a child Hashim was the youngest in the house. He used to babysit us. There is a third person in the room, whom I also do not know. He is very thin, and he is not eating. I don't even know his name and he makes no effort to introduce himself. Instead, he sits crouched on a broken chair, all his attention focused on the television set, which he observes through a set of 1970s-style oval sunglasses. The glass on one side is missing. Through the empty gold ellipse his naked eye shines brightly, swivelling towards me from time to time before sliding, inevitably, back to the screen and the drama that is unfolding there. All attempts at conversation appear to fail; at best they elicit brief monosyllabic responses. Finally, I give in and turn to the television for respite.

The show is American, in English with Arabic subtitles. It takes time to work out what is going on. A man dressed as a priest appears to be trying to persuade a woman to betray her brother who is apparently up to no good. The actors exchange long, intense stares and make empty, exaggerated gestures. The priest turns out to be some kind of undercover law enforcement agent. It occurs to me that if we are subjected to a daily dose of action in which the hero is an American law enforcement agent, eventually we will start to feel sympathy for them, won't we? The thin man laughs once, harshly, like a cough. The others hang their heads and shrug. I am ruining their fun. I decide to shut up. The priest episode ends and is immediately replaced by a story about a murder. A girl has been found, naked and dead. The rapist apparently has a fondness for virgins. He rapes them and then his wife kills them to cover up his crimes. I am a little stunned at how explicit it is. It proves too much for the thin man, who leaves the room with a muttered farewell. He is replaced by Muataz, who is in his twenties and studying applied chemistry at the university. Various other young men come in from time to time to shake my hand and disappear. I can't keep track of all their names. In the old days this was my grandmother's sister Zeinab's room. Next door is the room where I used to sleep as a child.

The television drama comes courtesy of the *Waaliya*, the local municipality, which provides a cable service of about twenty-five channels. You pay forty Sudanese pounds a month (around twenty dollars) for access. Most of them are foreign stations broadcasting from around the Gulf. 'In the old days they used to censor the films,' Muataz explains brightly, 'cutting out the bits they didn't want us to see, but they don't bother with that any more.' I wonder if this means that the battle for National Salvation has been abandoned. Or are these shows being allowed to demonstrate how morally corrupt the West is? 'This is nothing,' says Hashim, as he finally wanders in, amused by my surprise. 'With digital you can see anything.' Anything covers a lot of ground but I don't doubt he knows what he is talking about. On the metal stand upon which the set rests is the ubiquitous copy of the Quran gathering dust. Rather than a functioning reference, a religious tool, it resembles a talisman to ward off evil. It is perhaps a flimsy veil, a moral assertion that whatever comes through this shimmering portal will not corrupt the souls of those in this house.

They watch the same programmes here as elsewhere on the planet, things like the hysterically right-wing, pro-torture *24*, or the long-running and highly convoluted *Lost*, which, Muataz tells me, is so popular among his friends at university that they even have their favourite seasons. The level of television suggests a kind of universal concordance, a common ground, a virtual landscape that connects viewers all around the world. East and West are really not as far apart as you might think. The fact that the service is provided by the local authority surprises me. I had somehow expected them to ban such things as being culturally incompatible – but I'm obviously out of touch. In this brave new world, technology cuts across all boundaries with no apparent friction. To some, of course, Western television is a plague, a demon let loose inside the Muslim world that threatens to destabilise the entire *umma*, the community of the faithful. But it is hard to see what you can do about it. Many of these channels are broadcast from inside the Middle East and the overwhelming majority of the films and shows are American products that are watched by millions of avid fans all over the region. It is not just the pampered middle class that is watching endless reruns of *Seinfeld* and *Friends*. There is even an Arabic version of *The Simpsons* in which beer and other offensive items are 'translated' into halal equivalents. Is this what cultural difference boils down to, substituting *basturma* for bacon? The most popular drink in town these days is a kind of malt liquor, non-alcoholic, but it looks like a foaming glass of beer with a good head on it. It is a strange fantasy projection of life on the other side. For many people this is their only insight into the West, how it thinks and lives. As such, it provides an odd kaleidoscope of fears, projected through the practised mannerisms and sexual habits of the protagonists. By turns, Westerners come across as obscene, narcissistic and obsessed with their own wellbeing and wealth. I find myself feeling ambiguous about my own situation. Having now spent most of my life in the West, I wonder how that makes me look.

Gradually, the endless succession starts to numb my mind and I long to go outside and sit in the yard under the stars, the way I remember it as a child, but the others all seem reluctant. This is the way they spend their evenings. In the sporadic bursts of conversation there lurks a submerged significance that I am reluctant to dispel, a hint of other things to come. Talk turns to a recent visitor from Cairo who came to give a lecture to the neighbourhood about Nubia. This awareness of Nubian heritage is new. Everyone seems excited about the prospect of reviving a language that none of them has ever spoken. My grandmother used to speak it with her sisters, but my father never really learned more than a few words. He was brought up with Arabic, as were all subsequent generations. 'The situation is much better in Egypt,' Hashim says. He means in Upper Egypt, around Aswan, which is where all the people of this quarter originally hail from. The Egyptians may be better organised but most of old Nubia lies on the Sudanese side of the border. There is optimism in their voices as they talk, as if this new eventuality holds great promise.

Migration lies at the root of this city's existence, even here. The people who settled in this neighbourhood a century ago belong originally to one of four main groups of Nubians – Mahas, Danagla, Halfaya and Kunuz – which is us. Kitchener allocated a large area on the north side of the river to Sheikh Hamad wad al-Mayroum. There is a mosque bearing his name, one of the chorus of *azzans* that fill the night-time air. My father's family come from the village of Shallal. The village itself no longer exists. It was flooded with the construction of the High Dam. In that sense, there is no way back. Despite this, there lingers a fond longing for the idea of a homeland, an emotion the nation is incapable of providing. As they talk, the men offer up potted fragments of their own history. Most of it is barely grasped rumour and has little grounding in scholarship. 'The Nubians once ruled all of Egypt,' says Hashim, in reference to the famous 25th Dynasty, but he is not sure when, or for how long. History becomes hearsay and at some stage, perhaps, hearsay becomes history.

As he warms to his subject, the television is forgotten. Hashim is eager to talk about the Egyptian visitor. Nubian culture and in particular the language have been dying away for centuries. Hardly anyone in the family speaks it. Now, Hashim says, they want to start introducing it in the schools. The Egyptian visitor was taken aback by what he found. 'He was surprised when he saw that we all spoke Arabic,' marvelled Hashim with a wry smile. 'He expected us to be speaking Nubian all the time. To him, Arabic was his second language.'

Everyone is keen to get into the discussion. Here, it seems, is a chance to restore pride and lost dignity. Here is the prospect of there being something that makes them distinct, unique even, as well as a heritage linking them to past glory. They are all eager to talk. As they do, they drift away from hard facts, slipping easily into vague generalisations that wash over the gaps in their knowledge. It strikes me that in some way all this talk of Nubian roots is also a reaction to the homogenising effect of what pours out of the television set into this room every evening, and to the monolithic notion of Islam as the common national pool of cultural origin. The contrast between the world on the screen and the room where we sit could not be greater. The dusty, unpaved streets, the faint lights, the barking of a dog in the distance. There is a sense that this longing, this desire to belong to something so completely removed from the here and now, is symptomatic of a broader, more deep-seated malaise: the fragmentation of the country from within, along with the breakdown of politics along sectarian lines. More rigorous assertions of regional identity are occurring in all corners of the country. From the south to the Beja in the east, to the Nuba Mountains and Darfur, these feelings find resonance even here, among displaced communities such as this one, which has never really been marginalised.

As the conversation dips into a lengthy lull we return inevitably, wearily, to the screen, where they are still in hot pursuit of the rapist and his murderous wife. It is hard to believe that we are sitting in a country still dealing with the fallout from one of the most severe Islamist purges the world has ever seen. People come and go. One of the men who wanders in and out talks about

Heglig, where he works. The Chinese are leaving their traces on the population, with mixed-race children becoming common-place in the area. Attacks on the Chinese-run oil extracting sites are increasing. The local Misseriya Arabs feel excluded from the deal as they are witnessing the environmental destruction of their land in exchange for very little benefit. The only way they can gain any direct benefit is by kidnapping workers or attacking convoys.

I find Muataz cheerful and more inclined to talk than the others. Perhaps it is because he is young enough to feel optimistic, but he still sees the future as being rich with possibility. It makes a change from the weary resignation of some of the other men, who have given up hoping and settle for mere existence. I ask him about his studies. All the textbooks he uses are facsimile photo-copies. You buy them directly from copy shops, which appear to serve now as centres of learning. Getting hold of textbooks is not as easy as getting your television connected to the global stream of entertainment. Muataz keeps all his possessions under lock and key in a wardrobe that takes up one side of the room: books, clothes, everything. There are few closed doors in the house, nothing to stop anyone walking in off the street. The front door is open most of the time. It is not that crime doesn't exist. As Ishraq told me, burglaries are becoming more common and are increas-ingly blamed on the city's new arrivals. But the notion of privacy is an unfamiliar one here. There are no secret places, nowhere you can go to be alone. When my mother first came to live here, she found this the most difficult aspect of life to adjust to. 'If you sat down to write a letter,' she used to say, 'people would be worried. They thought it strange that you wanted to be alone.' Even now, I know that if I say something to one person I am basically speak-ing to everyone in the family.

Inside that wardrobe Muataz stores all his ambitions, the hope that they will one day provide him with a way of escaping this room and going out into the world. It seems telling somehow that the screen projects its flickering glow onto the locked door; a window of light from the Hollywood fantasy world of glamor-ous women, fabulous cars, and melodrama that seems to accom-pany the trappings of wealth. It is an odd prism through which to view the world: the West, that distant Other that resonates here with the power of myth and legend. A surrogate that reinforces rather than challenges stereotypes. But perhaps it serves its purpose. Muataz has nothing to hold up against this pulsating screen. He has never been abroad, although he dreams of doing so. Everything seems to be against him. From the barely legible photocopies, written in a language he doesn't really understand, to the evenings spent in the company of his weary uncles and cousins. These tired men, home from work, barely able to summon the energy to eat, hold out the promise for his future. On screen, the West shines like a bright star of endless possibility. Of course he dreams of going there, of making it real, instead of being trapped like this, in dying conversations about ancient kingdoms and the lives of others. In the yard outside I watch as a young man prepares to pray. He lifts his feet one after the other to put them under the standing tap to wash them. It takes me a moment to realise that he is still wearing his socks.

For over a century Sudanese intellectuals have wrestled with the notion of national identity. In the 1930s, the earliest activists put aside their ethnic differences in favour of a perceived 'Sudanese' identity. To transcend differences they turned away from the notion of connecting to an Arab cultural strand and tried to identify themselves with black Africa. Writers connected to the literary journal *Al-Fajr*, such as Muhammed al-Mahdi al-Majdhub, identified themselves with a 'negro' heritage. 'My tradition,' he wrote, 'is beads and feathers and a palm tree I embrace while the forest is singing around us.' One of these poems, 'The Wedding

Procession', reflects the country's long historic process of cultural fusion that brings together the pagan and the Arab. Importantly, this movement stressed the use of a localised Sudanese Arabic, rather than apeing classical Arabic forms.

By the 1950s another generation of émigré poets found themselves living abroad, in Egypt where their contact with Arab and Mediterranean culture provoked an awareness of their distinctiveness from Egyptian culture. Writers like Ali M. Taha wrote of Africa in naive, naturalistic terms, as an innocent or a lost child. The most emblematic figure in this group was Muhammed al-Fayturi, whose background was itself very mixed, but whose identification with 'Black' Africa was largely a matter of choice: 'Their eyes follow me wherever I go. I have unsolved the riddle, the mystery of my tragedy: I am short, black and ugly.' In the 1960s this voice of Arab-African hybridity came into its own. Writers like Muhammed al-Mekki Ibrahim and Muhammed Abdel-Hai moved beyond the mythologising of Africa and the aspirations towards Arabia of previous generations. They found their strength in specificity. Harmony is a celebration of the racial and cultural intermarriage that distinguishes the country. Salah Ahmed Ibrahim put it like this: 'Liar is he who proclaims, I am the unsullied, the pure pedigree ...'

As Muhammed Abdel-Hai puts it in his seminal essay on the subject, 'In this poetry the Sudanese poet came to terms for the first time with himself, his landscape, his history and tradition. Arabic is accepted as an African language and its long history in Africa makes it the *prima materia* for poetic creation. [...] In the new poetry there are no more attempts to prove or to proclaim an identity; no groping for a home, but a concern with the essence of home where everything is near and familiar.'

Something of this connects back to Abdel-Khaliq Mahgoub and his bid to adapt Marxism to local tradition. His desire to 'turn dreams into lived experiences that embody bright futures and restore the rights to dignity and autonomy' sounds like an echo of what the poets in their own way were attempting. Abdel-Khaliq sought the liberation of the Sudanese people in 'the fullest sense of the term'. The nationalists and politicians had betrayed

their ideals. What drove him to Marxism was the quest for a political theory, an idea that would free people from the ignorance and
intellectual laziness that had turned them into mere objects, chess
pieces to be positioned and moved on a mere whim. Colonialism
was not an eternal, inevitable fate. It served to absorb and separate
nationals from their roots, to turn them into subjects of the new
authority. The nationalists were split between their yearning for
an idealised Arab past and their aspirations towards the European
way of life. Neither course was satisfactory. The past alone could
not provide solutions for the modern era. The European model
lacked critique. Those who objected to Marxism as an import
were busy drinking whisky, driving American cars and reading
The Times. Imported models turned people into puppets. Human
knowledge is the property of all humanity, Abdel-Khaliq wrote.
In Marxism he saw a model for national healing, an idea that could
'unite the Sudanese people irrespective of their religions and eth-
nicities', and he saw no conflict between this idea and Islam. His
was an enquiring mind that rejected not only the intransigence
of imagined traditions, but the unquestioned import of foreign
models, just as he refused to withdraw to an ivory tower of the
mind, seeing the paradoxes as a merely intellectual challenge.
Where would we be today if he had had a chance fully to develop
his ideas?

It is one of those days when nothing seems to work out. Half
a dozen people are not answering their phones, or perhaps they
are avoiding me, I'm not sure which. It happens. The novelty
of renewing old acquaintance wanes. Everyone has their own
problems. In some cases it sounds as though the line has been

disconnected. You get through finally only to be told that so and so is not available. 'He's not in his office,' they say, mildly surprised, as if people appear and disappear without explanation or warning. Where he might be or when he might reappear is not clear. These are things beyond anyone's control. Everything comes to nothing. This is the general inertia that you fight against on a daily basis in order to get anything done here. Visiting the human rights lawyer Amin Mekki after hearing he had been ill, I ask him what had brought on his heart attack. He studies me for a moment before replying, 'This country.'

In the end, despite all your efforts, it's not the heat and dust that overwhelm you, but the indifference. People live the way they do because this is the only way to get by. Try to change things and it just might end up killing you. I hear the same thing from Fahmy when I finally wind up in his office in the Merowe Bookshop. He looks out of place in the cluttered space under the low ceiling. It is an old person's room. Indeed, it was his father's office. There is an air of abandonment in the slumped sofa and ruptured chairs, the battered desk, the heaps of paper and books stacked everywhere. All of this came with the bookstore as part of his legacy. It looks impossible to make sense of any of it, but that, effectively, is what Fahmy tried to do. When his parents died tragically in a road accident on the very dangerous Medani road a couple of years ago, Fahmy decided to give up his life in England and come home to take over the business.

The Merowe Bookshop is a relic from the days when people would come downtown to spend the evening with their families, wandering the arcades, window-shopping. Now it is almost the only bookshop still functioning. I used to come here as a child. My mother's shop was around the corner. The air-conditioned interior was a cool sanctuary, a glimpse of sanity beyond the reeling madness of hot and dusty streets. As a teenager, this was an escape hatch, a little cave of wonders, filled with worlds waiting to be discovered. Now the books sit in tottering towers yellowing with age. There is still a loyal following. If it is closed for any length of time they come flocking back asking why. They wander in several times a week to feast their eyes on the books, in Arabic and English. They rarely buy anything. The women behind the counters keep a beady eye on browsers.

Fahmy's office is perched over the main shop like a treehouse that has been knocked together by a blind man. He's struggling to catch up. His father used to know where every book was, he says, glancing somewhat despairingly at the stacks that cover the floor. There was a painful period of adjustment, both to the loss of his parents and to the responsibility of taking on the family business. His family have owned the place for forty-two years. It is an institution. There was a lot to learn, such as not to go and negotiate with customs officials at the airport, but to send someone on your behalf. 'I was used to the way things work in the UK, where you have to do everything yourself.' Not here. Here, commanding respect hinges on being able to demonstrate that you wield power. The way to do that is by showing you have authority over others. There are people working for you. Doing everything yourself is a clear admission that you have no one under you. It undermines your position. Fahmy is a lively, quick-witted young man who is impatient to get things moving. He's not the type to stand still, or to leave things hanging, but he needs all of his wits about him to stay afloat in this game. The last years of his father's life were troubled by unscrupulous people who were trying to take advantage of him, he explains. Now he is trying to keep business lines as straight as possible, insisting on payment upfront for everything both ways. It is not easy, as this is not the way things are usually done. Again, his problems don't end there. Publishers in the UK are often slow to respond, unable to grasp the fact that speed is of the essence when you are already looking at being backed up further by containers waiting to be docked and processed through customs, which can take months. There are other hazards to running a bookshop. There have been times when every copy of a certain book has been purchased by a mysterious buyer. This is a standard form of censorship. Once the book is in the shop, they buy every copy available to make sure no one else reads it. And they burn them. Which is a crime by any standards, but, as Fahmy wryly admits, not bad for business, since it means their stock is sold out.

Fahmy's other great passion is salsa. He gives lessons once a week to an expanding group of devotees at an undisclosed location. To avoid trouble they have to keep a low profile, even in these relatively liberal days. 'Good clean healthy fun' is how he describes it. There are still incidents of the police stepping in to break up parties here or there, though usually these involve Southerners, to whom drinking and associating with the opposite sex are not taboo. The story is that even this kind of crackdown has acquired its own protocol. As long as the security forces are warned in advance, and paid something, they will look the other way.

One evening I turn up at the designated time and place to watch the class go through their paces. The event is announced beforehand via text messages to confirm where and when. By the pool of an embassy building somewhere in the centre of town a group of eager aspirants form two lines and let themselves be guided through the steps; '1, 2, 3 ... under ... paseo' and they all swing about face. Fahmy, in his northern English accent, calls out the changes. They swing their hips in an ungainly fashion, grind back and forth gamely, swivel and turn. It looks hellishly complicated and I make no attempt to follow them.

They are a mixed bunch, men and women, some of them foreigners, but with a good number of locals. They are clad in casual clothes, jeans and even pullovers as it is quite a chilly evening. A rather hefty girl is dressed in a thick heavy skirt and leather knee boots, an outfit that would seem more appropriate to a country and western line dance. Her partner is wearing a nylon anorak in red and black. But there is no doubting their enthusiasm. '1, 2, 3 ... casino!' the instructor calls and they all change partners. It could be a scene from a Fellini movie, if he had ever chanced to pass through. The dancers are entirely unselfconscious. Perhaps it is just me, but why would anyone risk life and liberty to take salsa classes? There is no flirtation or physical affection on display, but the enforcers of morality would no doubt take a dim view of men and women gyrating to Latin sounds. That would also be a fundamental misunderstanding of what is happening here. This is not about flirtation, it's about staving off boredom. They are here because it is something to do, something different. They all look very earnest and determined as they attempt to master a new set of skills, somehow to achieve the impossible, getting feet, hips, hands and shoulders all to work together.

You have to make your own entertainment here. There is nowhere to go, particularly for young people. The only really acceptable social pastime is eating. Food substitutes everything else you might otherwise devote your leisure time to. Mountains of kebab and falafel are washed down with bottle after bottle of fizzy drink. Learning salsa is just one of the more unusual expressions of the submerged life of this city. Alcohol, of course, is the most common form of escape. In the old days they used to brew Camel Beer here. Nowadays all drinking is underground. From bottles of Johnnie Walker you can buy under the counter around town, to the Veuve Clicquot that is served in the luxury villas, to bottles of *araki*, the often lethal date liquor that is distilled in mud-walled houses and sold in used plastic 7 Up bottles. An unhealthy tradition that, apart from the obvious health hazards, may lead to the miscreant being lashed and fined, even thrown in prison. Salsa is still probably a healthier vice, despite the moral perils involved.

I wake up wondering where I am. It sounds as if the end of the world has begun. Floodwaters are breaking over my head in great gouts, crashing onto the top of the old air cooler outside, which resounds like a metal drum. Rain, I think at first. I go over to the window and look up to see the Great Bear, or *Bier*, as it is in Arabic. It hangs low in the night sky but is perfectly visible. It's 3.30 in the morning and the water continues to gush down, making sleep impossible. I am forced to move and spend the rest of the night sleeping on the bed by the kitchen door, with the scratching of the mouse for company as he gnaws his way through whatever remains intact in there.

As soon as it is light I go down to see the landlord, Adil. His wife answers the door, only to slam it wordlessly in my face before I can open my mouth. After a moment or two it reopens as she finishes pulling a scarf over her head. Eventually Adil appears, rubbing sleep from his eyes. He's not overjoyed to see me, but reluctantly climbs the stairs to see what the trouble is. It's not serious, he explains. He forgot to switch off the water pump before he went to bed last night because the power was off. When the electricity returned the pump continued working all night until the tank overflowed. Now he places a sun-beaten plastic chair against the wall and clambers precariously up onto the flat roof. 'It's not too much water,' he calls down. Last night the whole terrace was flooded, but already the sun has dried most of it. He looks sceptical and seems to think that I am making a lot of fuss about nothing. The sun will dry it all out, he shrugs. The fact that the plaster is coming off the ceiling inside is not deemed a major problem. I begin to see why this flat is in such a raw, unfinished state. Once the walls are up and the doors can be locked there is very little incentive to do anything else. Half-heartedly, he sweeps the roof dry with a plastic scraper. 'It's not more than a *safina*,' he says referring to the old term for a jerrycan. 'Well, it sounded a lot more last night,' I insist. He seems unconcerned about the lost water and takes any remark on my part as a personal slight. I try to make it sound as if it is something we can solve together. 'All we need to do,' I suggest, 'is put a length of pipe there so that the water runs further out, if it ever overflows again. Then it doesn't fall on the air cooler.' Adil nods in agreement, but doesn't move. An arm lifts and then drops exhausted to his side. 'The other tank has a pipe like that,' he concedes. We both stare at the wall in silence, until it is clear that nothing further is going to happen.

On Fridays, the *mawlana* is to be found sitting in his salon upstairs where he receives guests before going to the mosque to pray. Before that prayers are broadcast on television from a mosque in Cairo. The screen shows rows of stern Egyptian men

in suits and ties. They look like public servants, ordered there
to fulfil the government's wish to make itself appear pious. The
recital is like a concert, with the imam pausing to lean into the
microphone like a bearded folksinger. His audience is attentive
to every syllable. Rapt. Some mouth the words silently with him,
humming along self-importantly, never letting their gaze stray
towards the camera. Every time I press my questions, the *mawlana* murmurs some reply and falls silent, his eyes resting on the
screen between us. This is his day of rest and I am disturbing his
weekly ritual. Eventually, he talks of the trouble he has seen. In his
job as a judge he sees many cases of people who have been caught
out by the sudden economic boom. Farmers in particular are having a hard time. The banks are all too keen to lend them money,
but they are unable to pay back the interest. Their produce now
has to compete with cheaply imported fruit and vegetables from
abroad. Heavily subsidised produce from South Africa and China
has flooded the market in recent years. There are wooden stalls
on every street corner piled high. On the pavement around them
scattered boxes display names like 'Golden Jasmine' or 'Snowy
Peak' printed in English and Mandarin characters. To add to the
farmers' difficulties there is a security problem. Armed bandits
roam the Blue Nile farm area. The farmers are afraid to go out to
work their land. As a result many default on their loans and wind
up in front of him in court.

The *mawlana*'s litany continues. Many parts of town, he
says, still lack essential services. Providing these is not a priority,
despite the huge growth in oil revenue. The sewage system dates
back to the days of the British in the 1930s. It cannot cope with
the increase in high-rise apartment buildings. It would cost an
estimated three billion dollars to replace it. There are about five
or six large housing projects around town and much of the money
is coming in from abroad, but no sewage system.

Many of the newly wealthy, the entrepreneurs who are importing Chinese fruit, are associated with the *jebha*, the front, as the
NIF is known. When Turabi was ousted, going off to form his
own party, the ruling party changed its name to the National
Congress Party. But just as with the street names and the currency,

everyone tends to ignore the new and carry on using the old terms as if nothing has changed. The same people still rule the country, and everyone still knows them as the *jebha*. Nothing can be done without their help. When it comes to business, a Lebanese entrepreneur told me, you have to forget about politics. The opposition seems to have understood this compromise, deserting their cause in droves to hop onto the NCP's bandwagon, which now occupies three-quarters of the parliament. To object to their policies is to risk being arrested or worse. Opposing them is now seen as a form of treason; it's un-Sudanese. 'They think what they are doing is religion,' he mutters.

As I leave a man wanders by. Possibly drunk, clearly destitute and deranged, his clothes hang off him in filthy shreds. In one hand he carries, for no apparent reason, a flattened plastic bottle. When he reaches the corner he stops and leans back to stare up at the sky. 'Look at that,' he says, to nobody in particular, pointing at a high-rise building in the distance. 'People live like that, up in the air. We live in the dust. We plant in the dust. We sit in the dust – while they live up there in the sky.' After a time he stops, waves to two men sitting under a tree further along the road. They ignore him. Then he walks in a circle. Stops. Looks up at the sky again. When his eyes come back down to earth he spies me, standing on the opposite corner, waiting. He breaks into laughter, shaking his head. 'These people are very clever. But they have no religion. They are together, but they have no god. They have no religion.' After a time he falls into a trance and stares in silence for a moment before moving on, still laughing to himself.

Late night at the paper. It is 9.30 and they are trying to put tomorrow's edition to bed. Kamal, the acting editor, sits at the computer, scanning the articles for mistakes. In one corner a television set has been tuned to Al Jazeera. People wander in and out. From time to time one of the stack of mobile phones scattered around the desk chirps into life. Kamal leaves the room to collect some printed sheets from next door. The main editorial room is on the other side of a partition wall that looks as though it is made of egg boxes. You could punch a hole through it without even trying. They shout to one another through the barrier.

A man I have never seen before walks into the room. He is smartly dressed in a clean, long-sleeved shirt and well-pressed trousers. *Salaam Aleikum* he greets us, shaking hands all round before sitting down opposite me in front of the desk. He produces a pen from his shirt pocket and begins to go through the A3 printout sheets that Kamal hands him. He works quietly, bending studiously over the pages before him. After a time he finishes and then looks up to ask if there is anything left for him to see. I can't work out who he is. An external editor of some kind, I guess. A senior journalist, perhaps, who works part-time on the final edit. Kamal hands over a typewritten sheet that has yet to be set. There are two articles on it. One is today's editorial. The man reads through these carefully. He underscores a couple of lines. 'These will have to go,' he says quietly, then, as he is getting to his feet, he changes his mind. 'All of this is out.' He tears the sheet in half and takes it with him as he heads for the door. Kamal gets up and follows him out of the room discreetly. I assume they have business of some kind that he doesn't want me to hear about. But when he comes back in he is smiling. He holds out his hand, rocking his head as we shake, as if we have just pulled off a trick together. I still have no idea what just happened.

'That was the *ruqab*,' he explains. The censor. Failure to comply can result in the seizure of the whole print run. They have officers at the printing press to check that nothing slips through that was not approved. Impounding a day's print run is devastating, especially to a paper that is barely keeping its head above water financially. They would have to shut down the paper. The loss of revenue is enough to ensure compliance, or closure.

'What about press freedom?'

'What freedom?' snorts Kamal impatiently.

The government's position on censorship is hard to follow. There is a history of one presidential decree after another, each being countered by the reinstatement of 'prior censorship', whereby print runs are seized before they hit the streets, damning the newspaper to financial disaster. Sometimes it is only a matter of weeks before the security forces step in to overrule the decree. This back and forth seems to suggest an internal conflict between the president's authority and the power wielded by the intelligence apparatus. How deep this rift goes is not clear, but censorship is a sensitive issue. There are, of course, journalists who are willing to play along. The Sudanese Union of Journalists is, like the official writers' union, loyal to the government, describing censorship in a statement as an 'exceptional measure'. All of this does not bode well for the state of freedom of the media in Sudan, and those journalists who dare to raise their heads still risk having them chopped off. Some turn to the internet to publish censored articles, though this effectively limits their local audience.

A tray of food arrives, fetched in from a restaurant across the street. Plump loaves of bread and a bowl of *ful*, mashed-up fava beans laced with cumin and olive oil, are set on a low table. People stop by to make themselves a sandwich before going back to work, glancing at the television screen to catch up on developments. Kamal is still trying to meet the deadline. He taps calls through the wall for the next article.

As I walk home I spy a police driver sitting idly on a corner revving the motor of his powerful pick-up. Again and again he presses the accelerator down. The car is humming as if about to explode. You sense that something bad is about to happen. You can feel it in the streets at night. There is too much hardware around. Too many armed men. Guns, cars, helicopters. It's all just waiting for an excuse to be used.

PART FIVE

PARTING THE WATERS
2012

'Their eyes follow me wherever I go.
I have unsolved the riddle, the mystery of my tragedy:
I am short, black and ugly.'

Muhammed al-Fayturi

'We have become irrevocably involved with,
and responsible for, each other.'

Marshall McLuhan

The old house has gone, fallen victim to the wave of reconstruction, a tiny consequence of the oil boom and the growth of the city. The neighbourhood now feels closer to the centre than the periphery. The place where I spent some of the happiest and most important years of my life is no longer. All that is left is a corner of rubble, broken bricks crushed into the dirt. On the far side a man is salvaging tiles from what remains of a bathroom wall. A metal sign hammered into the dirt proclaims that a Syrian company intends to build a block of flats in its place. People ask why we ever sold the place as it would have been worth a small fortune now. But when my parents passed away and it looked as if none of us would ever return to settle here, my brothers and I could agree on nothing, except that we didn't want anything tying us together. And the boom is really over. In the wake of secession, the capital is sinking once more into lethargy.

I stare at the empty wasteland and realise that it is strange this didn't happen earlier. I was surprised to find the place still standing the first time I came back. Changes had been made, but it was still basically the same house. Seeing it there was like going back in time to an age I thought had ceased to exist. Now, looking at the wasteland it used to occupy, it feels like the end of something, like a door swinging shut on the past. It is almost as if it had been waiting for my return, to see it one last time before it vanished from the world. This was the scene of my formative years, where my parents lived out the best years of their lives. The family is now, to all intents and purposes, gone, scattered, disconnected, dead. The absence of the house only underlines that fact.

This house, which now only exists in my memory and a handful of photographs, was important to me. It is the place I think of when I think of home. It was here that I learned about the world and the word. Hours spent in the living room, sprawled in those itchy chairs, working my way in a haphazard and inconsistent fashion through the books that I found there. I read recklessly, in too much of a hurry to get on, to consume as much as I could. I leapt from one author to another, urgently trying to grasp what they had to offer. I was very lucky to have parents who not only could afford books but who cared for them, kept them, crated them and carried them across the seas so that they could wind up there, ranged along those simple white shelves, waiting for me to find them.

Every evening, before he went out to drink with his friends, my father would insist we all sat around the big dining table with our school books. It didn't matter whether we had homework or not, we had to spend an hour studying. I would grow bored and my mind had a tendency to wander. I discovered that an easy way of getting the time to pass was to write. How old was I then? Probably around thirteen or so. I wasn't conscious that what I was doing was anything special. I just wrote down what popped up in my head. I described scenes that came to me. They were not constructed as stories. I was just feeling my way. It never occurred to me to show them to anyone. They were over as soon as I got up from the table. I would tear them out of my copy books and rip them up for fear of being discovered. I didn't consciously decide then to become a writer. That was well outside the scope of what was possible in the world around us. That would come later. What I learned in that house was that, through reading and writing, imagination can take you far beyond the circumstances you find yourself in.

It was in that house, too, that I began to develop a growing political awareness, a realisation that there were inequalities in the world I lived in. We were relatively well off compared to many of those in the country. We had a good home with running water and electricity. We had a car and both of my parents worked. My mother did the shopping and the cooking, but the cleaning, the washing and the ironing fell to Mubarak. In the afternoons, we would sometimes talk. He could not have been more than eighteen. He came originally from the Nuba Mountains and he had family there. He had a room of his own at the back of the house. During the day he had the ability to become invisible, especially when my parents were around. He swept and mopped the floors. He washed the clothes in a tub in the backyard. Some afternoons, when everyone was asleep, we would speak. I don't remember everything we talked about, but I still have the sense that those conversations taught me a lot about what was happening around us, about a world I couldn't really see. I don't remember much of the detail but I do know we covered politicians and racism and his frustration about the way the country was going. Mubarak had ambitions. He attended night school to learn English and he had a wife at home whom he went to visit every few months.

When I was about sixteen I went through a phase of distancing myself from my family. Teenage rebellion, I suppose you would call it. I wanted to connect with people in what I thought of as the real world: the city that lay outside the sphere of our immediate social circle. I felt an urgent need to create and inhabit my own world, to make the city mine in some way. It was difficult because there weren't clear avenues to follow. I tried. I stopped going to the American Club, where we used to go to swim and hang out with other Westernised kids. I began to volunteer at sports clubs to teach judo, about which I was fanatical at the time. I trained with the national team and then, as part of their programme, would travel all across town to obscure centres in distant corners of the city to coach people, spending hours sitting in the back of converted Toyota pick-ups that served as minibuses. I remember the excitement of the canvas awning flapping and the feel of the cool night air blowing into my face as I headed off to some part of town I had never been to before. This was me, I felt. This is who I really am.

In a more existential sense, too, I had begun to perceive the limits of my world. It was around this time that Ali Omer's father used to drive us out of town in his 4x4. He was bored, I think, with being cooped up in the city, in a house. He longed for the open spaces. Often he would just drive out into the flat emptiness that lay beyond the edge of the city. We didn't do anything. We just stood around soaking it in. The emptiness of it all. He would stand there smoking. Then he picked up a stone. The flat, hard ground was strewn with them. A simple pebble whose striations told of layers of sediment laid down in a riverbed millions of years ago. Another fragment was formed in a tropical sea. The stark landscape we were standing in seemed to tilt, to take on another aspect as he talked. It was possible to see enormous mountains that had since crumbled and fallen, oceans that had dried up. Every little stone contained its own story. It was a revelation that stayed with me, a moment of clarity; the sudden awareness of the scale of the physical world we inhabited and of our minuscule part in this vast wonder.

When I first left this city to go out into the world, I felt that this was my anchor; this house, these streets that we wandered in the sleepy twilight hours, the garden, the silence of the living room in the afternoons, broken only by the occasional passing car or ambulant trader calling out his wares as he went by on his donkey, asking for empty bottles or scrap metal. I knew it would always be there for me to come back to, which, of course, it wasn't.

I am wary of the use of the word exile, which is overused and romanticised. My parents were forced to abandon their home. They didn't make a big fuss about it, but that is what happened. My father was exiled in the sense that it was too dangerous for him to ever go home again, and he never did. It crushed his spirit, to find himself adrift at such a late stage in life. People do not leave home unless they have no choice. They made a life of sorts for themselves in Cairo, but it was never home, not really, just a temporary haven. Home was here, in this town, in that old house that has now been levelled to the ground.

I have always felt I had a choice. I was given an opportunity to study abroad, and other opportunities followed. I went out into the world voluntarily and it feels as if this journey, coming back to this place now, this corner, these crushed walls, marks the end of a period of my life. In some sense I never left. I took it with me. I wrote about it. I tried to understand, but also to explain, to describe this place to the world, to recreate this country through my imagination. This empty plot marks the end of that particular road.

Was that why I had come back, in the hope of finding some form of closure? There is a sense that somehow when I lived here, during that period I was complete. I knew my place in the world, I understood where I was and why I belonged there. From the moment I left, it seems to me, I have been explaining myself, one way or another. In speech or in books, explaining who I am and where I come from. Once you leave a place a part of you is left behind and from then on somehow you exist in fractions. You find temporary homes in people and places, but it feels incomplete. It occurs to me that it is meant to be like this, that displacement, not settlement, is our true state as human beings. I am keenly aware that I am mythologising my own life. It wasn't perfect and I wasn't completely content; if I had been, I would not have pursued the impulse to go out into the world.

In my notebooks, I find these words: 'This book should be not so much about me, my life, as about the evolution of the tragedy of a nation never achieved.' Have I done that? I'm not sure. It feels like trying to throw a rope around a cloud. No matter how hard you try so much slips out of your grasp. There is so much more to a country than can be summarised in accounts of the politics or history. Journalists, ethnographers, historians, experts of one ilk or another. All seem to cast a certain light on the facts but, like the elephant in the story, the reality eludes description.

And is it really possible to separate the personal from the subject in hand? I cannot write about this country without somehow reflecting on my own connection to it. Ostensibly, I may have returned out of some sense of responsibility, a desire to do something, to connect what was still happening in Darfur to the wider picture. At the end of the day, however, everything leads back to the greatest mystery of all: how we make sense of ourselves in the world.

Across the broken ground the shadows are lengthening and for a brief moment I have the sensation that I am looking the wrong way down a telescope, across time. My mind takes me back to when the trees were tall and lush, the rustle of leaves swaying in the breeze at dusk. When the walls were high and freshly painted and the world seemed rich with possibility. The future lay ahead of me, rich with opportunity. Then the moment passes, and I am staring at a wasteland littered with rubble.

It seems fortuitous, this clearing of space. Like the turning of a page, it brings a certain clarity of mind. Where once there were rooms and verandas, the cluttered, dusty shelves, the blue punch-bowl that was almost never used, my father's rack of novelty pipes (an American Indian in full headdress, a bearded sailor, a yellowed Meerschaum), the leatherbound volumes of the encyclopaedia, a fake boxed collection of volumes of Shakespeare's plays that contained a whisky decanter, never used, the folding escritoire, the potted fir that was decorated, absurdly, every Christmas, the gentle lime tree that towered over the house. Every day my mother would walk out and pick a handful to squeeze into a jug of lemonade, to the jangle of the thin gold bands that she had worn on her wrist since her marriage.

It was a ceremony that would mark the end of the afternoon, the siesta, the fall of night. Some days the sky would be tinged with red. In the distance, clouds of dust gathered and a hot wind would blow through, making the shutters rattle. In the *haboob* season you could shut all the windows and doors and listen to the terrible sound of a dust storm whipping by. The fine ochre grains would find their way into everything, pooling in little wavelets beneath the door, clogging up windowsills, so that everything you touched would leave an imprint, the colour staining your hands and clothes. It found its way into cupboards, forming tissue-thin layers between folded shirts and sheets, inside the pages of a book.

I begin to see that perhaps the real reason I came back here was to discover what this place still means to me. Nothing so grand as a country, nor so ambitious as a nation. Both concepts seem too vast to mesh with my memories of this house, these walls and rooms, the peace and security I felt here as a child.

When we write we make choices. Of the vast ocean of possible stories we choose which ones to make our own. I wrote about this country, trying to understand it, to unravel the mystery that was buried in its history, in its pain. I wrote about independence, about war, about corruption and torture. I wrote about hope and despair. But you cannot make a country out of a novel. You cannot construct a nation out of words set down on a page. Realising this makes me doubt everything I have ever written. What was the point of all of that? Are these questions the reason I really came back? Was it doubt that actually brought me here to find this place?

It dawns on me finally, staring at the empty waste ground where the old house used to be, that this is what brought me back here. To revisit what I worked on for all those years, over half a dozen books or more, whatever you want to call it. I see more clearly than ever, as I look out at that patch of broken ground, that this is why I came back. To find this.

A slight man comes along the road at a fast clip. He crosses over to the other side, stoops to pick up an empty bottle, spies another and collects that, too. And then he is off again at the same high pace, bottles safely tucked into his straw basket. Where his right foot should be there is a clumsy brace attached to a wooden block, painted white. The brace is made of metal rods that rise halfway up his shin, where his leg has been blown off by a shell or a landmine.

There are manufacturers who specialise in making lightweight 'anti-personnel' mines that contain just enough explosive to maim someone for life. It is cheaper and lighter than a device powerful enough to kill. Also, disabling someone is a more effective deterrent. The survivor will go on with his life. He doesn't just vanish. His disfigurement is a warning to anyone who might be considering going off to fight. A dead man who has been blown to pieces is soon forgotten. Nobody sees a dead person. A maimed man is a persistent warning, telling you not to bother going to war in the first place.

Early one morning I leave the house to walk across the bridge into town. Ahead of me two teenage boys walk briskly, chatting as they go. One of them carries a plastic bag out of which he produces a banana that he hands to the other. The bag is dropped without ceremony over the side of the bridge, followed by strips of peel as they carry on, talking and sharing the banana for breakfast. The remains of the old docks are still there on the bank at the foot of the bridge. A magnificent steamer, three floors high, sits in a floating dry dock. Nearby are other ferries that used to ply the river from here down to Kosti – the same route my grandfather worked as a cook. There are also a couple of the old landing craft used to ferry people across to Tuti Island, which now has its own bright new bridge, visible in the distance. As a child my father used to swim this strip of water to the island with his friends and eat watermelons from the fields that run down to the river.

Three pick-ups race by loaded with policemen in full riot gear, carrying batons and shields and wearing blue camouflage fatigues. The reason for the traffic congestion in town yesterday was a strike by soldiers and non-commissioned officers demanding to be paid. They haven't received any money for months so they decided to block the streets. Today they will be ready for them. In the old days the golden rule for any ruler wishing to avoid being displaced by military coup was to keep the army happy. This is no longer the case. The military has been slowly carved up. Real power is now in the hands of the myriad security forces, the complex web of intelligence agencies, with a combined force of somewhere between forty and fifty thousand operatives. The protests over pay suggest some form of brinkmanship is underway. The security forces are demonstrating they are not afraid of the army. With their network of informers it is they who rule the country.

A dark mood has settled over the city. People are uneasy. Basic commodities have risen by about 20–25 per cent; bread, kerosene, oil, etc. House prices and rent have gone down while luxury items have risen. Last year, buying a car would have cost around 18,000 Sudanese pounds. Today the same car costs 31,000. They no longer allow anything but brand new cars into the country. It is not uncommon for people to have two or three jobs. An office administrator earns around 800 pounds a month. An army officer might get as much as 1,000 pounds (US$500). He finishes work at 2 p.m., goes home, eats, sleeps, changes his clothes and then drives an *amjad* in the evening. He pays 500 a month in rent for his house, then there are school fees for his children, food, transport, etc. People can no longer afford to buy medicines. Instead they have begun to turn to local cures, medicine men. The papers carry adverts for 'habbat baraka oil from the holy lands'. In Islamic culture, *habbat baraka* (*Nigella sativa*) seeds are rumoured to be a common cure for every ailment known to man. Whether this particular oil contains any of the original ingredient is a matter of speculation. A few days later at my family's house in Hillet Hamed, I watch a small boy running about in his underpants, clearly in distress, his body bizarrely coated in some kind of yellow cream. This turns out to be a mixture of custard powder and yoghurt that they are hoping will cure a rash. None of the five doctors consulted was able to offer a better solution.

Everyone is eager to regale you with tales of medical mishaps. Malpractice has become commonplace, even at expensive private clinics. Cancer misdiagnosed as a stomach ulcer. A woman bleeding to death on the operating table while undergoing a Caesarean. The doctor who had been treating her was called away at the last minute and his son took over. There are cases in the newspapers that are coming to court. At the same time doctors in the public hospitals are striking over conditions, and the fact that they, too, are not being paid. The annual budget allocates 8 per cent to the Ministry of Health, 2 per cent to education, as opposed to some 80 per cent on military spending.

Yet still there is no sign of the public revolts seen elsewhere in the Middle East. The occasional protests are small and generally met with bemusement. After forty years of civil war and armed insurgency there is a genuine fear of instability. On the other hand, the old workers' collectives and trade unions no longer exist, and this in a country once reputed to have the most powerful unions on the continent. The first trade union was formed by workers on the old Sudan Railways back in the 1940s, largely as a means of organising against British colonial authority. Throughout the 1950s and 1960s, trade unionism remained an important political alternative to traditional sectarian allegiances. The 1964 popular uprising that dislodged the military government was viewed as a triumph for the labour movement. Successive governments since independence, however, found themselves challenged by the unions and the general tendency has been to combat and limit their power. Today they have little of their former influence.

This fact highlights the lack of any real political opposition. There is nothing, in short, around which to rally people, except perhaps Facebook. More than one newspaper carries the story that a rumoured one million people are connected to Facebook, which sounds wildly optimistic. A UNESCO survey estimates the number at a quarter of that, but others put the figure even lower; some say even 30,000 is considered high. But the government takes the threat seriously. Facebook is being monitored by the National Intelligence and Security Service. A number of journalists involved have been seized. Some are still missing. The media are rumoured to be deeply infiltrated by NISS.

Later in the day I find myself staring at a grubby white dog nodding back and forth on the dashboard of a taxi stuck in traffic. In the rear window there are two matching elephants. The driver seems to have a thing for acrylic furry animals. In this heat you would think they would catch fire by spontaneous combustion. But they don't. They just sit there nodding dumbly at the passengers. All that fur makes the cab feel suffocating. The driver fiddles with the radio until a news bulletin comes on and the subject of Darfur emerges again. 'The government doesn't want peace,' says the driver dismissively. A young, powerfully built man, he seems too big for the cramped little cab of this Korean microbus. 'That's the problem.' There is an air of pessimism over the way things are being handled. People are edgy, nervous and losing patience. They have given up on the notion that the government really wants to settle the matter peacefully. 'They are people too, human beings like us,' the driver says, meaning the people of Darfur. 'They have a right.' What happens, I wonder, when people reach the point where they no longer believe there is any end in sight?

The Lufthansa in-flight magazine carried a story on the German Aerospace Centre, founded in 1907 in Göttingen. The article explained that the centre had returned to 'humane' research in 1945, after what it termed 'a misguided excursion into rocket-driven aggression'. As an imaginative euphemism for Hitler's *Vergeltungswaffen*, or 'vengeance weapons' programme, designed to pay back the Allies for their bombing of German cities, it is impressive. However misguided that excursion was, it cannot be deemed irrelevant. The development of the V-1 and V-2 rockets at Peenemünde was supervised by Wernher von Braun and involved controversial experiments using slave labour at secret installations in the Harz Mountains. After 1945, the Americans offered von Braun a new life and he was quietly relocated to the United States where his skills were urgently required in the American space programme. The same V-2 rocket that was used to target London was now launched into space with chimpanzees as pilots. Those old flying bombs were the precursors of the Tomahawk cruise missiles used to deadly effect in Iraq, Afghanistan and, once, Sudan.

All this comes back to me as I listen to Mahgoub, who reclines on a bed in his front garden and points up at the night sky. This is where he lay one evening in 1998, talking to a group of young journalists, when he saw something odd flash by overhead. This turned out to be the cruise missiles of Operation Infinite Reach. Just prior to the strike, three vehicles with darkened windows had been seen drawing up close to the site of the Al-Shifa pharmaceutical plant a few streets away. They parked briefly before driving off at high speed. Ten minutes later the cruise missiles struck the factory, completely destroying it. A nightwatchman was killed. The case that chemical weapons were manufactured at the site was never convincing; no evidence has ever proven that anything other than essential vaccines and medicines were produced there. How did we get to this point, where the United States sees fit to launch cruise missiles at us?

Back in the days when Nimeiri was busy introducing his infamous September Laws, the world was not paying much attention. In the autumn of 1983, the largest country on the African continent was viewed as a vast, empty wasteland, poor in stability perhaps, but rich in water and fertile land. Beyond a low-key civil war that nobody cared about, little news of note emerged, apart from the occasional famine. A quiet backwater where nothing of any great significance ever happened. The 'Schleswig-Holstein of Africa', as one rather glib observer in the *Times Literary Supplement* dubbed it: 'If anyone knows what's going on there, they aren't telling.' If Darfur changed all that in 2003, it also transferred attention away from the main arena of conflict. However appalling the casualty figures might be in Darfur, they were a fraction of those in the South, where an estimated two million died and 4.5 million were displaced in a war that, all told, lasted nearly forty-two years. Nobody ever paid it much attention. It was a war that lay somewhere on the periphery of the known world, beyond the reach of most people's consciousness.

Imposing Sharia law might have been overlooked as an internal affair of little consequence, but when the president declared himself the country's imam, or spiritual leader, it ought to have set alarm bells ringing. It didn't. In 1983, Sudan was a trusted ally of the United States and the Americans were willing to overlook a few blemishes. Perhaps they were just grateful that we were still a long way from the far-off days of the 1970s when Nimeiri had declared that Khartoum would become the Havana of Africa. Still, even that should have given some hint that the needle of political stability was prone to wild, unpredictable swings.

Everything is relative, and by 1983 Sudan was playing a useful role in providing a potential jumping-off point if ever the US had reason to deploy militarily to the region, and the signs were that they might have to do just that. In April of that year a suicide bomber drove a truck full of explosives into the American embassy in Beirut, killing sixty-three, seventeen of them Americans. In October another attack in Beirut, this time on the Marine barracks, left 241 American servicemen dead along with fifty-eight French paratroopers. The United States needed all the help it could get. And then there was Israel. Sudan not only protected Egypt's southern flank – America's most valuable ally in the Middle East – it was also one of the few countries in the region to applaud the Camp David Peace Accords, signed by Menachem Begin and Anwar Sadat in 1978. Neighbouring states offered more hostile agendas: Ethiopia was ruled by Marxists, and Libya's leader, Muammar Gaddafi, was clearly trouble: aligned with the Soviets, and bearing his self-penned *Green Book*, he was busy spreading his own incendiary brand of revolutionary Islam across the Sahelian belt with the help of his Islamic Legion. Against all that, Sudan presented an inoffensive, more mild-mannered alternative, excusing to some extent Nimeiri's eccentric behaviour.

The attempted coup by the Communist Party in July 1971 had marked the beginning of the end of his relationship with the Eastern Bloc. By 1977, worried about the close proximity of the Mengistu regime in Ethiopia, a paranoid Nimeiri decided he wasn't happy having Soviet military advisers around and so expelled them all, setting up a new opening for the Americans.

A few amputations and floggings were not going to derail that, despite protests by human rights observers who declared the September Laws unconstitutional. At $400 million, Sudan was the largest recipient of US development aid in sub-Saharan Africa. In addition, the United States was providing an average of $100 million a year in military aid – effectively sponsoring the war in the South – with no apparent qualms about the death and devastation being perpetuated with their complicity. A month later, however, it was all over and Nimeiri was deposed.

Although the April 1985 uprising soon passed, like that of October 1964, into popular myth, in the end it achieved little. Sadig al-Mahdi, the newly elected prime minister, was a faint echo of his great-grandfather, the man who had ended the hated *Turkiyya* (Ottoman occupation) in the nineteenth century and expelled the foreign rulers. Army officers stationed in the South had grown tired of waging war on unfamiliar terrain and were demanding an end to it. There was a conviction that the war could not be won. A group of senior officers warned Sadig to make peace at all costs or suffer the consequences. A man known for his indecision, he chose not to act and the groundswell spilled into a military *coup d'état* that took the country further into religious obscurantism.

The state of emergency declared in June 1989 was to remain in place for almost a decade. The transitional constitution was abolished. All political parties were banned, as was the right to free association, along with trade unions, student organisations, youth clubs and federations. Newspapers were closed down, including the *Sudan Times*, and their owners arrested and tortured. Paramilitary training and religious indoctrination became compulsory for academics, civil servants, and students wanting to enter university, women as well as men. With the emergence of civilian bodies like the People's Defence Force and the National Islamic Front's Youth Militia accountability was waived and excessive force became commonplace.

Beneath Turabi's quirky take on Islam lay hardcore zealotry that imposed itself with a cruelty the North had not seen before.

Journalists, trade unionists, opposition leaders, human rights organisations and academics were targeted, arrested, tortured and kept in secret detention houses. Many fled abroad. Live ammunition was used in putting down demonstrations at the university, or clearing urban housing settlements around the capital. Dozens were killed and no one brought to trial. Twenty-eight army officers who mounted a counter-coup were executed. The *Inqaz*, or National Salvation, was a renaissance, Bashir rather grandly declared, a return to the true spirit of Sudanese independence. Those who died in the war in the South were to be known as *shuhada* – martyrs – and their death was to be celebrated as they flew up to join the *houria* brides that awaited them in heaven.

With godless socialism no longer a viable alternative, Islam became the new means of opposing an increasingly arrogant West and its ambition to impose a new world order. Turabi threw wide the doors, inviting in militants of every shade, assuring them they would be warmly welcomed. In 1992, a certain Osama bin Laden accepted the invitation and moved to Khartoum to set up shop. He agreed to build an airport in Port Sudan and a new road to get there from the capital.

Bin Laden, however, declared that his warring days were over – which must have been something of a blow to a regime that was trying to rebrand itself as the latest revolutionary Islamic state. Instead, Al Qaida became a building and farming enterprise. Its workers played football in the afternoons to stave off boredom. Some four hundred 'Afghanis' – Arab veterans of the war against the Soviets in Afghanistan – followed bin Laden. The government, debt-ridden and engaged in a protracted war, could pay for his services in the only commodity they had – land. He didn't mind. By all accounts the rather austere bin Laden found the Sudan trying, though he appears to have adjusted, at least in part, to its laid-back ways. Here people lived a simple life. In comparison to the corruption and decadence in his native Saudi Arabia, for which he blamed the Americans, he found Sudan unspoiled by oil money. That was yet to come. He saw consumerism as the great evil that destroyed all cultural values and replaced them with raw materialism.

It must have seemed idyllic, then, in its simplicity. He drove his tractors, bred his horses and tried to develop new strains of plants that would increase yields. He reportedly invested in gum arabic, of which Sudan produces 80 per cent of the world's supply. It appeared that he had decided to settle down.

When Mohammed Ibrahim Khalil was appointed to lead the commission to oversee the referendum process, it seems likely that it was precisely because of his known opposition to the regime; the government was hoping to demonstrate they had nothing to hide. At the same time, they did their best to sabotage his efforts, assuming they would be able to rig the results to suit their purposes, much as they had with the elections the previous year. To begin with they tried to get some of their people inside the commission. Khalil objected, particularly over one IT expert known to have been involved in the election results the previous year. His family bowed under pressure. His daughter was subsequently targeted in the press campaign against him. Khalil was approached by a government minister who suggested, gently, that perhaps he might like to resign. It was a difficult time. One of his closest assistants began to publish articles in the press clearly aimed at undermining the process they were engaged in overseeing, suggesting that the referendum was itself a direct road to secession and therefore against the national interest. Khalil, former speaker of parliament, has a long history of dealing with politicians. He informed the minister in no uncertain terms that while he might have considered resigning, the fact that they were trying to force him out made him change his mind; he was now determined to stay on and see it through.

Khalil does not dwell on the broader implications of the referendum. I imagine the split is too painful for him. He belongs to that generation of educated Northerners who were groomed to take over the reins of the country in 1956. Secession is the end of everything he worked for all his life. Still, pragmatic legal mind that he is, he sticks to the facts. The current regime has done nothing to prevent it happening. Secession had the support of the entire world and Khartoum now risks becoming isolated. The situation was closely monitored by the Americans with US ambassador to the UN, Susan Rice, and others making it clear that the referendum had to go ahead. Khalil had no choice but to persevere, trying to make sure everything was above board, knowing that his hands were, to some extent, tied. To resign would have been to concede defeat, to succumb to the inevitable, to abandon his belief in a united, inclusive Sudan.

Now the world is busy investing in the South; Kuwaitis, Qataris, Americans, Israelis, even the Egyptians have taken a keen interest after having been firmly opposed to the separation. There are farming developments, construction projects, etc. But the signs are that it would be a mistake to believe that secession is the solution to Sudan's particular affliction. Khartoum's problems do not end with the separation of the South. There is still Darfur, where the opposition groups have buried their differences and reunited. And more trouble is brewing in South Kordofan, in the Nuba Mountains, where brutal assimilation methods to force cultural Arabisation and Islamisation on the population have resulted in unrest. Abdel Aziz Adam al-Hillu, a former SPLA leader, currently contesting elections in the area, is to form a new party with remnants of the SPLM left on the north side of the new border. He wants to carry on Garang's idea of a New Sudan, applied to the North. Yasir Arman is also on board as secretary general along with another commander, Malik Akkan of the Blue Nile province, who has 18,000 ex-SPLA troops at his disposal. This regrouping defines a new bloc of opposition located in the North.

Events abroad are also having an impact. Sudan remains an exception to the uprisings across the region, from Tunisia, through Tripoli to Cairo and Syria. When Bashir visited Cairo recently the Ikhwan, or Muslim Brotherhood, was the only party that would meet him. People here are suffering. There is no work and what little there is remains in the hands of those close to the National Congress Party.

It seems optimistic to expect an Arab Spring type of uprising here. The country is subdued and wary. After so many years of war and division it is not surprising that people are cautious. Despite the existence of things like Girifna, a student protest movement that started a couple of years ago, the youth are generally not as well prepared, organised or educated as their counterparts in Cairo. In some ways, this may be due to the country's isolation. Many are ignorant of their own history. On a popular television game show contestants are asked the identity of Ismail al-Azhari (the country's first prime minister). One of them suggests he might be a footballer. This level of ignorance perhaps explains the distrust I encounter, which I can't remember having noticed before. It stems from decades of being unable to engage with the outside world. Foreign workers are largely assumed to be ignorant and inferior, in spite of the obvious fact that they bring badly needed skills with them. Young people have grown up learning the Quran by rote, not to understand it, or to think for themselves. Religion was deemed the only knowledge required. Islam pervades every aspect of education, sometimes to an almost absurd degree, such as the story someone told me about her sister recently having to explain the concept of *idda* (the amount of time a widow should remain at home mourning the death of her husband) to her eight-year-old son. The stress on conformity, on the importance of obeying the norms and not going against convention, does not encourage imaginative thinking. The need for public approval demands a rejection of any form of deviation from accepted practices, from scripture and the *sunna* model provided by the Prophet and his companions fourteen centuries ago. This outlook explains the humiliation of intellectuals, the denigration of the education system, the persecution of academics, and the disdain for non-religious learning.

Despite – or perhaps because of – all of this, secession came as a complete shock: 'I never realised how much they hate us,' one person who witnessed the split in Juba told me. She was crying. This bewilderment characterises the current mood here. A numb sense of disbelief. For years Northerners had convinced themselves that the Southerners would never dare to leave them. They subscribed to the old myth that enmity between different ethnic groups in the South meant they would rather stay bound to the North than be left under the domination of the two largest groups, the Dinka and Nuer. This proved to be wishful thinking. Still, just two months before the referendum, Vice President Ali Osman Taha, was reportedly convinced it would never happen. A resounding 98 per cent vote in favour of separation put paid to that particular myth, but Sudanese politics has always worked that way; wishful thinking is always more attractive than working for a resolution. The Southerners were tired of living with resentment. The lack of inclusiveness, the blatant racism, the ignorance, all told them that they had no other choice.

For the six years under the Comprehensive Peace Agreement no concerted effort was made to accommodate the Southerners, to integrate them into the notion of a united nation, in which all were equal, regardless of race or religion. The 2005 peace agreement stated that Khartoum was to become the capital of a Government of National Unity, that it should reflect the diversity of the population, and yet churches were constantly raided, 'parties' broken up, women wearing trousers persecuted, etc. Southerners were to be included in public service administration in proportion to the national population, i.e. 30 per cent, but they never got beyond 10 per cent. In the courts, out of 200 judges there were about ten Southerners. Of the 160 High Court judges, only three were Southerners. The interim constitution stated that all efforts should be made to make unity an 'attractive option' while in practice the opposite was the case.

The moment the results of the referendum were announced one minister declared that all Southerners should leave parliament immediately, whereas the law actually stated they should remain until after the new flag was raised in Juba. After the referendum, Southerners living in the North feared for their safety. The government did nothing to allay their fears. The minister of information, Kamal Obeid, announced that, should they vote for secession, Southerners living in the North would not enjoy citizenship rights, jobs or benefits. They would not be allowed to buy or sell in Khartoum market and would not be treated in the hospitals. 'Not even a [hypodermic] needle will we give them.'

It's hard to see secession as anything but an accident that was waiting to happen. No effort was really made to avoid it. It is hardly any wonder that even those who had known only the North all their lives were prepared to go south. When asked why they were going back to nothing, some of those waiting for transport in the makeshift camps and pick-up points around town allegedly said, 'When we came here we also came with nothing.'

There is something shameful about the lack of compassion shown by the North towards their Southern brethren. Some even went so far as to suggest separation was something to look forward to; that once unshackled of the South, the North would be able to truly achieve the kind of Islamic purity it had always sought. This pathetic notion is hardly borne out by the facts. If one thing should be patently clear it is that after a quarter of a century the idea of Islam providing a solution to the country's ailments is at best wishful thinking and at worse a dangerous delusion.

A senior officer in the NISS got carried away while talking live on Omdurman Radio when he stated, 'If the political parties agree to repeal the Sharia laws then Sharia should go.' The chief columnist of *Al-Intibaha*, one of the most reactionary and overtly racist papers in circulation, and very close to the regime, fiercely criticised the statement. The officer in question was declared an apostate, no less, and dismissed from his post. The vice president Ali Osman Taha responded by calling for a constitutional review to construct a Sharia state. While it is hard to understand such stubborn adherence to religious law, it explains the central role Sharia plays in the Arabised elite's desperate ambition to assert its version of ethnic nationalism.

The term 'Arab' in the Sudanese context is deceptive. Claims to Arab descendancy or genealogy are largely tentative and are more a reflection of aspiration rather than of any real connection. Most of those who might identify themselves as 'Arab' by culture refer more to the language they use and the religion they practise. Seventy per cent of the country is Muslim. The Arabisation and Islamisation of the country dates back to the fourteenth century, relatively late in the region's history. The first mosque on the African continent was built by the man who conquered Egypt in AD 640, Amr ibn al-'As (according to legend on the site where a bird laid an egg on his tent). The Arabic language and Islam brought with them an assimilationist element, and the belief that Arabic and Islam were superior to anything that existed locally beforehand. This tendency persists today, and has been a consistent hindrance to recognising the cultural diversity that exists in Sudan. The country contains fifty distinct ethnic groupings, which break down into 570 peoples. In the South alone there are more than a hundred languages.

The spurious, largely imagined, link to Arab history and genealogy explains to a large degree why Sudanese politics has been so obsessed with the question of origin. It is common to be asked the question, '*Jinsek shenu?*', which roughly translates as, 'What are you?' The word *jins* can, as we have seen, refer to race, gender or nationality, as well as your class, but in this context it means tribe; what group do you belong to? Identity is seen as being founded on one's 'authenticity', rather than the more general and realistic notion of where you were born and where your parents are from, or, to take it a step further, what nation you are part of.

The Northern 'Arab' elite sees any compromise of their Arab–Islamic identity as a threat to their link with Arab–Islamic civilisation, a hierarchical distinction that was reinforced under British rule. Since 1983, when Nimeiri reneged on the Addis Ababa Accord of 1972, the country has drifted further and further away from the possibility of achieving cohesive and lasting nationhood based on pluralism, lurching instead towards hard-line repression through the imposition of Islamist rule, a road that, as John

Garang pointed out in 1989, can only lead to disintegration and partition, which is precisely what we are seeing now.

The 1972 Addis Ababa Accord laid down for the first time in the country's history the foundations for an ethnically pluralist state that recognised the rights and individuality of the people of the South. Garang's vision of a New Sudan was founded on the principle that no single element should subjugate all others, that all should be equally respected.

Back in 1992, Bashir declared in an interview with the London-based Arabic-language newspaper *Al Hayat* that the Sudan was now being run according to 'God's will'. There was, and still is, a belief – embodied in Turabi's early years in power – that Islamisation and Arabisation hold the key to the country's problems. In this view, the interference by the British, who maintained a barrier between North and South (along the same line that now divides the two countries) during the half-century that they ruled the country, slowed the diffusion of these forces to the South. But the process continued almost immediately after independence. General Abboud, who seized power in 1958, two years into independence, set about Arabising the bureaucracy and education in the South. Subsequent governments continued the process on and off during the interim periods when the two parts of the country were not at war.

Garang's death marked the end of any hope for unity. Many of those who came after him, such as Pagan Amum and Riek Machar, were secessionists to begin with. It was Garang who, in his own forceful way, persuaded them to go along with his plans to rule a united 'New Sudan'. After his death, even his widow, Rebeka, claimed she was against the idea. Luka Deng, who served as minister of cabinet affairs in the interim Government of National Unity, says Dr John's dream died with him and with it went the united Sudan. Even had he lived, Deng suspects that Garang would have found himself marginalised, or even got rid of in some way. He doesn't buy into the notion of Ali Osman Taha, Garang's opposite number in the CPA negotiations, as a peacemaker. He was at best a pragmatist. At the time of the agreement, the government's military options had run out, both sides had arrived at a stalemate. The North needed peace more than they might have wanted it. The army was tired of fighting and the war was costing an estimated one million US dollars a day.

In that sense, the six-year hiatus of peace under the Government of National Unity was really nothing more than a false dawn. Independence for the South had been a goal as far back as the earliest armed rebellion in 1955, when the country was still ruled jointly as the Anglo-Egyptian Sudan. The Anyanya fighters, who were poorly equipped and trained, fought a low-level bush war for nearly twenty years, which was brought to an end by the 1972 Addis Ababa Accord. The collapse of that agreement was also the outcome of distrust. The North was keen to exploit the South's natural resources, namely water and the newly discovered oil reserves, and it was this that led to the outbreak of hostilities again in 1983.

According to Luka Deng, an uprising such as we have seen in Egypt and elsewhere is unlikely to happen here. Bashir is surprisingly popular, he says. Coming from a Southerner in opposition, this is a surprise. According to Luka, Bashir 'is a nice guy'. He is shrewd and tells jokes and has the ability to put people at their ease. Like Salva Kiir, Bashir seems to be able to bring people together, to occupy the middle ground. Kiir is rumoured to have the ability to recall the details of everyone he meets. He can store facts, make people feel they have been noticed and remembered. If Bashir is under pressure these days it is not out of a fear of the International Criminal Court. There is a lot of division within the NCP and Bashir is said to be paying much attention to the party youth. An intifada-type uprising will not happen here, his supporters argue, because Islamist rule – the final outcome that appears to be emerging in Egypt and beyond – is already here.

Secession has produced a general malaise, a lack of vision, both North and South, a kind of reluctant acceptance of one's fate that pervades everything. Five days in a row I go to the exchange shop, but in these nervous times people are holding on to whatever hard currency they have; the system is locked down. A woman sits in the far corner, behind the glass screen, leaning her head against the wall as if suffering from some terrible ailment. On the first day she manages to stir herself to sit up, listen attentively and then explain that the system is down. After that I only get a brief shake of the head and by the fifth day she can barely bring herself to lift her eyes to look at me.

There is something wrong about the colour of the car. Even at a distance I can see that the shade of yellow is slightly off. It is more watery, lighter, less intense than normal. The driver, a man in his sixties, pulls over all the same and the car judders to a halt in front of me, clearly on its last legs. A couple of bare wires protrude from the ignition like insect feelers. When it goes out, he touches them together to get the engine started. There is no handle on the passenger side, so I wait for him to come round and poke a couple of fingers through a hole in the door. He wiggles them around until it creaks open. Once I am seated he turns his attention to roping in other potential customers along the roadside and spends the next five minutes leaning over me trying to persuade two teenage girls standing nearby to join us. They are in no hurry and want to haggle over the price. Both are dressed in black from head to toe. They clutch each other's hands while trying to reach an agreement. My impatience is shunted aside by my fascination as I observe all of this. It makes me aware of just how complex and fraught with peril something as simple as getting from one place to another can be. The girls drive too hard a bargain, refusing to accept more than half of what he is asking, and so the old man is forced to concede defeat. 'I'm trying to do them a favour,' he says, shaking his head as we shudder away.

'For that price they would have to put petrol in the car as well.' He is clearly an optimist by nature and doesn't let the setback affect his mood. I soon realise that there aren't many things capable of doing that. In high spirits and eager to talk, we have gone barely two blocks before he has embarked on his entire life story: 'Twenty-six years in the military. I don't need the money. I get a pension, but this gives me a little extra.' He doesn't like to sit still, he says. It's not good for you to be idle. I begin to suspect that this is not a real taxi at all, and that the off shade of yellow is the outcome of some kind of DIY experiment. It doesn't take long before he comes clean: 'I painted it this colour because I like it that way.' As a retired soldier he is still entitled to live on an army base. 'When I drive into the militarised zone, I just slip the sign off the roof and that's it. I can't complain. You see people who are crawling on all fours like animals. So what do I have to complain about?' As if on cue, a boy with crooked legs hobbles up to the car at the traffic lights extending a twisted arm to ask for spare change.

The car has worn itself down around the old man's body. There is a grubby halo above him where his head has rubbed a hole in the padding, taking his hair with it. The lining has gone, leaving a dirty brown circle that perfectly mirrors his bald spot. He thanks Allah that his children are all doing well. A daughter graduated as a geological engineer and one son is a mechanic while another is in the army. He is the singular most optimistic person I have met so far. No talk of politics or corruption, simply happy with what life has given him. 'If the Lord gives us something then who are we to complain? We should make the most of it, right?' There is nothing about him to suggest he is a particularly pious man. No beard. No hanging suras, no muttered invocations as we set off. He is not even wearing traditional clothes, just trousers and a long-sleeved shirt. He is a survivor. When he gets out again to fix the door I notice the little inflatable rubber ring on his seat. It, too, has collapsed out of fatigue and age. Without him, the car seems incomplete, as though the two, man and machine, have knitted themselves together into one organic entity.

Khartoum in the early 1990s became a modern-day equivalent of the movie *Casablanca*. The capital was flooded with intelligence operatives and militants of every shade. The city was teeming with figures from every organisation on the CIA's list of radical organisations: Abu Nidal, the PFLP, Algerian FIS, Hamas, Hezbollah, Islamic Jihad, the Islamic Group, they were all flitting around the dusty, broken streets.

There were a few celebrities, such as Osama bin Laden and Carlos the Jackal, who rode around town with a gun on his hip. There were also some more contemporary threats about. In February 1993, a man named Ramzi Youssef tried to bring down the World Trade Center in New York with a massive bomb inside a van left in the underground car park. Youssef had frequented a mosque in Jersey City where Sheikh Omar Abdel-Rahman preached. The Egyptian sheikh had entered the US on a visa issued, unwittingly or not, by a CIA operative employed in the visa section of the embassy in Khartoum. This would appear to have been a failure of intelligence, since his name was clearly listed as a suspected terrorist on the Automated Visa Lookout System. In Egypt, the blind sheikh was wanted for the murder of a policeman and attempting to overthrow the government. The oversight was explained differently by the sheikh's son. According to him the visa was issued because the Americans thought Sheikh Omar would eventually succeed in overthrowing President Mubarak. In other words, they believed that Egypt might go the same way as Iran in 1979, with Sheikh Omar standing in for Ayatollah Khomeini. In American, perhaps, they could keep an eye on him.

It was not until the 1993 attack that the CIA began to realise they had a 'blowback' problem, with former 'Afghani' mujahideen turning their sights on the US. From then on Osama bin Laden began to appear on lists of possible suspects. He was still not considered a serious threat to the United States even though his name kept cropping up. It is almost as if both sides needed one another. In October 1993, eighteen Americans soldiers died in Somalia while trying to apprehend Farah Aideed. Bin Laden claimed it as a 'victory', but only much later, long after the fact and long after he had been expelled from Sudan and was safely ensconced back in Afghanistan.

President Clinton placed Sudan on the list of states that sponsored terrorism and the decision was taken, against the advice of the ambassador, Timothy Carney, to vacate the US embassy in Khartoum. In an open letter, Carney, along with Mansoor Ijaz, a businessman who acted as a go-between connecting Sudanese intelligence with Washington, accused the Clinton administration of getting their facts wrong. When Major General Erwa, Sudan's state defence minister, met CIA operatives at a hotel in Virginia, he demanded to know what they could do to get Sudan taken off the list of terror sponsors. Carney suggested they would be doing the US a favour by sending Osama bin Laden back to Saudi Arabia. To the major general this was asking a bit much; bin Laden had been a friend to Sudan and, besides, he had not actually done anything to qualify him as a serious threat. They were, however, willing to hand him over. The problem was what the Americans did not have enough to indict bin Laden in the United States. Rather than embarrass themselves, they urged the Sudanese to expel him. Major Erwa argued that it was better to keep him where he was, under surveillance, but the Americans were adamant; send him anywhere but Somalia, they said.

Carney and Ijaz argued that this bad intelligence, or the bad use of good intelligence, was the result of a refusal, on the part of the Americans, to engage with what was really happening in the Muslim world. By focusing on combating terror, the Americans had lost sight of the broader political picture of how things were evolving in the region. Authoritarian regimes such as Egypt, which were facing serious internal threats from Islamic militants of their own, were keen to brand all Islamist groups as potential threats. By following this line the United States lost any chance of steering a clear path through the complex transformations that were taking place. Unwittingly, they had empowered the Muslim radicals, making them almost exclusive agents of political dissent.

There is a degree of theatricality to much of Osama bin Laden's behaviour. He emerges as something of a dreamer, a fantasist who dubbed Afghanistan *Khorasan* after the name given to the eighth-century Arab warriors who rode back from the east to restore order to the Islamic caliphate, laying the foundations of the Abbasid dynasty in Iraq. His followers took the names of the Prophet's first companions. He longed to hide in a cave, concealed behind a spider's web curtain, just as the Prophet once had. His wealth and record in Afghanistan drew people to him, but also his strangeness, his alienation – the esoteric wilderness he seemed to inhabit.

By 1996, after two attempts on his life, ostensibly by Afghan Arabs with a personal grudge and Saudi backing, bin Laden had grown weary of Khartoum. He was worried that the Sudanese might hand him over, just as they had Carlos. In May of that year he left, travelling in a chartered and rather ancient Tupolev plane on a Sudanese passport that would admit him to few places in the world, and carrying only a fraction of what he had invested in the country, which was estimated at between $20 and $30 million. His assets were confiscated by the government. Turabi's party, he concluded finally, was a blend of religion and organised crime. It was an inglorious departure.

In November 1997, President Clinton issued an Executive Order imposing economic trade sanctions on Sudan, with the notable exception of gum arabic, an essential ingredient in soft drinks (which begs the question of whether consuming such beverages is lending support to terrorism). Clinton believed that there was enough evidence (never revealed) to support the theory that the Sudanese state was providing support for international terrorism and trying to destabilise neighbouring governments. It constituted an 'unusual and extraordinary' threat to the national security and foreign policy of the United States according to Clinton, who envisaged their use of chemical, biological or nuclear weapons. The CIA claimed to have information tying bin Laden to the Al Shifa pharmaceutical plant, implying that weapons of mass destruction were being produced there. A massive suicide attack had taken place two weeks earlier on the American embassy in Nairobi killing 245 people, most of them local bystanders, along with twelve Americans. A smaller bomb went off simultaneously in Dar Es-Salaam in neighbouring Tanzania, killing eleven people.

And then there was the business of Monica Lewinsky, over whom Clinton was facing possible impeachment. Whatever his real motive, on the evening of 20 August 1998 as Mahgoub lay in his front garden gazing up at the night sky, President Clinton decided to launch thirteen Tomahawk cruise missiles, at a cost of around three-quarters of a million dollars each, at the Al Shifa pharmaceutical plant. Three reasons were given: 1) the plant was a military facility, 2) it was owned by Osama bin Laden, and 3) it was involved in the production of chemical weapons, in particular a VX nerve agent. The plant was owned by millionaire businessman Salah Idris, a man known less for his links to the regime than to the opposition. No evidence was ever provided of chemical or biological weapons being produced there. The German ambassador at the time, Werner Daum, denounced the attack, estimating the number of casualties as a consequence of the shortage of drugs for malaria, tuberculosis and diarrhoea at 'several tens of thousands'.

The episode is perhaps best understood as an illustration of how, by the early 1990s, an irrational logic applied to the Muslim world in general and to the Middle East in particular. The Al Shifa attack emerges as a precursor to the 2003 invasion of Iraq, which relied on fabricated evidence to prove the existence of WMDs and a connection between Saddam Hussein and Al Qaida. Nobody understood the consequences. Nobody really understood anything. By 2005, when the slogan 'Out of Iraq and into Darfur' came into vogue, as if the separate parts were somehow interchangeable, the Middle East had become a kind of Neverland in the American imagination.

The dream that began on 1 January 1956 hinged on the collective imagination, the belief that the continent could somehow emancipate itself from history, from the fetters of colonialism and the racism and discrimination that followed. Here was a chance to end that, to demonstrate to the world that Africans were capable of taking charge of their own destiny. In the decades that followed, imperialism was succeeded by neo-colonialism, by socialism and eventually by Islamism, all punctuated by episodes of military intervention. Sudan, like most newly-minted African nations, found itself buffeted by external forces. It oscillated between east and west, descending gradually from the idealism of the 1970s to a cynicism brought on as a substitute for a lack of ideas. When you have lost your belief in an inclusive society, all that remains is the urge to create an exclusive one. All across the continent the old frameworks inherited from the colonial era are showing signs of cracking. Somehow, Africa has to step out of its old shell.

From the outside, the perception of Africa is invariably one of inexplicable cruelty and irredeemable disaster. Stripped of all historical–political context it stands only as an object of pity. An area of opportunity, primarily for the exploitation of natural resources, and, on the other hand, to demonstrate the civilised generosity of spirit that epitomises how the West likes to see itself. Old Christian values of faith, hope and charity reborn in the guise of trendy pop initiatives, such as Bob Geldof's Band Aid – a movement defined as much by its naivety as by its good intentions; Ethiopia was exporting more tonnes of food (fava beans for Europe's cattle) than it ever received in aid. Charity, it is now generally accepted, creates dependency. Aid works as a buffer, maintaining people at subsistence level, dissipating resistance, allowing dictators to ignore the needs of their people and assigning Africans the role of victims. Of course, the alternative is to leave people to die, which would be inhumane. But often charity seems like an easy solution. Nothing is really resolved. The symptoms are alleviated. And we all sit back and wait for the next disaster to, inexplicably of course, hit us.

Beyond that we rarely speak of the international deals made for the dumping of toxic waste, or the massive industrialised fishing fleets that deplete stocks and destroy incomes, of the IMF that enforces agricultural policies that favour debt repayment over feeding the people, or of the race for resources such as diamonds or coltan that fuels war, rape and social disintegration in places like the Congo or Sierra Leone. We are horrified by the barbarity of Islamic State, or Boko Haram in Nigeria, yet their actions are perhaps best explained as a perversion of the desperation that ensues when socio-economic breakdown follows unbridled greed and corrupt global capitalism. Africa, in short, cannot depend on the West to provide the ideas and moral guidance it needs.

As the ideals of nationhood have given way to a politics of sectarianism, tribalism and personal wealth; few ideas seem to be coming from within Africa itself. There is even a prize, created by telecoms entrepreneur Mo Ibrahim, that pays a lifetime stipend of millions of dollars a year to African statesmen who do not succumb to the temptations of corruption, as if corruption was the default condition. It seems oddly cynical, rewarding people for what should come naturally to them as part of their responsibility to public office. Rather than investing in something positive, this prize feels like a declaration of despair, as if trying to appeal to Africans' sense of moral values is pointless, since they are incapable of understanding anything other than money.

And, besides, perhaps it is not the country that is at fault, but the concept of the nation itself. It is not only in Africa that

the model of the nation state finds itself challenged. In the face of
the globalised economy modern industrialised nations in the West
today find themselves having to deal with an increasingly fractured social fabric. The nation is largely an emotional concept. We
feel we belong. A nation was never defined simply as those people
who lived within a geographical space, but as those who identified themselves as part of a greater whole. When migrants arrived
from the Caribbean to rebuild Britain after the Second World War
there was no doubt in their minds that they were travelling to the
'Motherland'.

Sudan was defined in the nineteenth century as a geographic
entity squeezed out between the territorial ambitions of the various European powers. All across Africa it was a one-size-fits-all
concept that worked better in some cases than in others. It was
the largest country on the continent. How do you create the idea
of a nation from the outside?

The answer is, you can't. Yet, with so much hope invested, so
much sacrifice made and so much pain suffered over the years, it
seems tragic to think that it was founded on a fundamental misconception. Where were the mutual values, common language,
culture, shared history upon which a nation could be founded?
In Sudan's case lines of race, religion, language and culture dissect the country into a million kaleidoscopic fragments. The
independence movement provided a common belief around
which people could unite; this was the nation defined by what
it was not.

There have been imaginative attempts at this along the way.
The talk of federalism, the artists and poets with their Forest
and Desert School in the 1960s, although this hardly reached the
population at large, and so on. Socialism flared briefly to offer a
temporary solution in the 1970s. By the 1980s and 1990s Islam
surfaced as a last resort, when all other ideologies had failed, an
attempt to create a common identity based on the principle of
exclusion: either you are with us, or you are out.

The old cliché of the country being a microcosm of Africa is
probably truer today than ever before. It seems to resonate with
new significance. With global migration, expanding mega-cities

and multiculti metropoles, we all have, to one extent or another, multiple identity traits. The word nation derives from *naissance*, the French word for birth. But being born somewhere is no longer a prerequisite for nationality, just as the possession of a passport no longer implies belonging. We must find new ways to define the nation. In this sense Sudan stands as a case study for the world to come.

It is almost as if the old idea of post-colonial development has been reversed; it is not so much that the Third World, as it used to be known, is becoming more like the First, but that the First has come increasingly to resemble the Third. There are parts of London, Paris and Barcelona that are unrepentant re-creations of Asia or Africa. The West finds its moral authority reduced to how well it can defend its borders. Civilisation can only truly be measured by the way in which we deal with others, with strangers, with those who do not look like us, think like us, or believe in the same things we do. This is such a fundamental challenge that even the advanced social democracies in Scandinavia find themselves at something of a loss.

In Africa, Asia and the Middle East we see rapid steps towards more divided, stratified societies. It is not just the West Bank, the Mexican border, or Fortress Europe; as frontiers grow more porous there is a tendency to try to draw them more sharply. Rather than address the issues causing mass migration, it is easier to put up fences. Gated communities, separation walls, razor wire and all the rest of it are expressions of the breakdown of the internal glue that binds a society together.

If proof were needed that separation is not the answer one has only to look at the South. Rather than solving a national problem, secession has split it into two parts. The root issues have not been addressed, either North or South, and so there are already conflicts in South Kordofan, the North's 'new South', while in the South itself tension between Dinka and Nuer is increasing.[*] Take away the Arab/Muslim element and you lay bare other conflicts that date back centuries; ancient founding myths that have never

---

[*] War between the government and the opposition would not break out until December 2013.

been challenged but put to one side in the name of the struggle against Khartoum. There are leadership issues, representation issues, questions of land rights, water rights, oil revenue. Despite the oil boom and the Comprehensive Peace Agreement there are no roads and hospitals built. Millions of petrodollars have already disappeared and countless more will undoubtedly vanish. Extortionate fees demanded by Khartoum for transport of oil to the Red Sea for export (oil accounts for 97 per cent of the land-locked South's GDP) have led to a shutdown of the pipeline. It is, as one observer put it, a potentially suicidal move. Just reopening the pipeline after such a closure is a complicated procedure that can cost millions.

I've never understood the idea of national pride. The notion of being proud of the place one happened, by chance, to have been born requires fetishising the complete randomness of the fact. Allegiance is one thing, but believing that one's national habits, the food you eat, the clothes you wear, the language you speak, and so-forth are somehow self-determined is plainly absurd. Yet we cling to the notion of our unique difference as if it were a personal virtue. That every country, every region takes pride in its customs and language is not surprising. When everything else is stripped away, this is all that is left and national pride starts to border on the edge of delusion. Here, no matter how bad things are, pride is the answer to everything, eclipsing all the country's shortcomings. There is so much left to be done. The oil revenue literally went south with secession. The wild days of the oil boom are over and there are no real initiatives to restart the economy, very little production of any kind. People clutch at dreams, driven by rumour; the latest has it that vast deposits of gold, uranium and undiscovered oil will vouchsafe the country's future. It reminds me of when I was at school and we used to joke that the Saudi oil reserves were slowly draining in our direction and one day we would all be rich.

In concordance with this Klondike spirit; gold prospecting has taken off in a big way. There is a thriving trade in gold detectors and up north in Abadia there are rows of crude assaying machines. They drive bellows with bicycle wheels to extract the gold that is dissolved in mercury first and then strained, by hand, through a scrap of cloth. Nobody wants to think too hard about the health consequences of this. What matters is that a family's fortunes can turn on a single, solid nugget. People are even making metal detectors of their own since the price is prohibitive.

Desperate measures for desperate times. Still, everyone tells you that the problem with this country is that nobody wants to work, that people are lazy, that all they dream about is making a bit of money and retiring, or, rather, opening (yet another) grocery shop. Such all-purpose stores are to be found on every corner, selling everything from washing powder to chewing gum, usually with a couple of men lounging about outside, their wealth piled up around them in stacks of bottled water, soft drinks and sugar by the sack. Their ambition extends no further than being able to sit back, relax and watch the money roll in. Even when the economy was booming this laid-back attitude left gaps to be filled by enterprising outsiders. Comments about laziness usually veer into complaints about too many foreign workers flooding the country.

There is no denying that this is true. In the fluid world of migrant workers there are Turks and Eastern Europeans in the building sector, Indian and Bangladeshi cleaners, Filipina maids, and the Chinese, of course, who come as specialists to set up oil refineries, drilling sites and huge infrastructure projects such as the controversial dam at Meroë, where they

numbered some 10,000 and built their own housing and even
a brand new hospital, which now lies empty. They also come
individually. Some are ex-convicts who were given a choice
of remaining incarcerated or heading for the Wild West that
Africa has become.

Mr Tang and Miss Liu work on a small farm where they are
employed to take care of a piece of land by the river. They are
clearly good at what they do. They endure hardships that few
would accept. They seem to be gifted with a certain flexibility,
an ability to adapt, which other foreign workers generally do
not possess. They are also hard workers. The owner of the land,
a friend, says the vegetable plots look better than they have in
thirty years of being tended by Sudanese. Mr Tang and his wife
were sent to prison for having a third child. They were given the
choice of staying there or coming here to work. It's not clear
where Mrs Tang is, or what long and tangled story lies behind
the relationship between Mr Tang and Miss Liu. They live in a
metal shipping container with an air conditioner tacked onto the
side. They keep to themselves and toil over the earth under the
African sun. They speak no English and only a few words of
Arabic.

There are those who argue that China's engagement in Africa
goes beyond the mere pursuit of raw materials to feed its industrial and economic growth. Africa is the new frontier for the
Chinese, and not just in the sense of expanding the economy.
This is their pioneer country. Coming generations will no doubt
be regaled with tall tales of their exploits here, in Angola, or
Kinshasa. Reforms introduced by Deng Xiaoping twenty years
ago brought an end to four decades of isolation. Beginning with
the petroleum industry, Beijing began to demand efficiency and
profit from its state organisations, rather than just obedience.
Industries were split into a national parent company and a free-
wheeling international subsidiary registered on the world's stock
markets. The aim of these semi-multinationals is to raise hard currency. They are geared towards competing around the globe. This
official *zou chuqu*, or 'going out policy', began in 2001. It encouraged the best of these companies, offering tax benefits, improved

financial assistance and political support. Africa gives China an edge that it doesn't have in other markets. Its lack of involvement in domestic politics and the skilled labour it can provide at very competitive rates mean that it is perfectly aligned with Africa's development needs.

There is nothing new about this combination of political and economic interests. European involvement in Africa has always tangled up politics with economic interests. French involvement in Chad or South African interest in the Democratic Republic of Congo are two recent examples. Still, there is something old-fashioned about China's involvement that makes it feel like a throwback to the 1970s and the days of the Cold War, when the Eastern Bloc was busy building dams and roads, hotels and conference centres across the continent to increase its influence. Even the photographs by the side of the road showing Bashir and premier Wen Jiabao seem reminiscent of that bygone age. Perhaps an alliance with a country that is emerging from state-controlled socialism to a free-market economy is more suited to Africa's current needs than the top-down imposition of capitalism the continent has been grappling with, mostly unsuccessfully, for the last half-century.

Yet there is something new here as well, something that goes beyond the mammoth construction projects, the refineries and the dams. The Chinese presence here also includes the everyday consumer goods being hawked at intersections in the capital. Small entrepreneurs have flooded the market with boxes stuffed with all manner of objects: electrical goods, bicycles, toys, shoes, clothing, not to mention fruit and vegetables. These are affordable not just to a small elite, but to a good portion of the population. The people here have become global consumers. Affordability marks a significant departure from trade ties with the West; this is not about catering to the wealthy elite. There may be other factors to support their success: the fact that the Chinese find it easier to deal with living conditions in Africa compared to Westerners. Like Mr Tang and Miss Liu, happily living in their air-conditioned shipping container by the river, they settle here with a minimum of fuss, bringing with them technical expertise and business contacts. This is a postmodern version of colonialism. The per capita GDP in China is below that of some African countries. In the new global economy the impact is not always positive. In South Africa, textile factories are closing down thanks to cheap Chinese imports resulting in thousands of jobs lost. Here, farmers cannot compete with the stacks of fruit and vegetables being shipped in. Even garlic is being imported, which is about as absurd as it gets.

People say they don't integrate, but in places like Heglig, as I heard in my grandmother's house, evidence of a substantial Chinese presence for over twenty years can be seen in the mixed Afro-Chinese features of passers-by on the street. This, in itself, seems to be an expression of what drives this pact between such apparently discordant partners – mutual desire.

Dealings with the Chinese are free of the parochialism that underlies all dealings with Europe. With its low industrial development and abundant natural resources, Africa provides the raw materials for Chinese industry and, in return, a huge market for the tide of manufactured goods that it produces. China's refusal to interfere in the internal affairs of African countries is convenient for those who want the benefits of trade without having to reform. One might argue that China is offering Africa the chance to transform itself. African countries make up one third of the United Nations, yet their influence remains paltry, and often it is seen as simply a pool of purchasable votes for other players.

Visiting Chinese officials often cite 'Chinese' Gordon as an example of the historical bonds that exist between the two countries. Professor He Winpeng, a specialist in China–Africa relations, suggests that China has actually played a role in trying to solve the Darfur crisis; that Sudan's decision to allow a joint UN–AU peacekeeping force into the country in August 2007 was in part due to Chinese pressure, in particular the visits of President Hu Jintao and China's first special representative for African Affairs, Liu Guijin. China has donated eleven million dollars in humanitarian aid and a further 1.8 billion to the AU peacekeeping force. And while the relationship is obviously one of mutual benefit and non-interference, China clearly has influence.

China stepped in at just the right moment. In 1994, five years after Bashir seized power, the country had managed to isolate itself from the world. Khartoum was blacklisted as a sponsor of terrorism. An arms embargo was imposed by the European Union. Three years later, in 1997, the US Congress passed a law imposing trade sanctions. The Chinese remained unswayed by this. They bought a substantial interest in the oil fields under exploration, none of which looked particularly promising at the time. They now own 40 per cent of the Greater Nile Operating Petroleum Company along with a 40 per cent stake in the Petrodar Operating Company and 35 per cent of the Red Sea Petroleum Operating Company. They built a 1,600-kilometre pipeline and a refinery in Khartoum that can deal with 100,000 barrels a day. Sixty per cent of Sudan's oil goes to China.

The boom really began in 1999. Over the next two years the country's oil revenue increased by nearly 900 per cent, a staggering 80 per cent of which was spent on arms. China is busy arming the continent – from Chad to Zimbabwe, passing by way of Ethiopia, Nigeria, Sierra Leone, Uganda and others. Another former staple of Western investment in the continent gone East. In the 1990s, helicopters, fighter planes and bombers with Chinese-trained pilots, along with howitzers, mines, tanks, etc., were all in use in the war in the South. The Chinese also helped to set up three factories that would make Sudan self-sufficient in certain areas. The GIAD military-industrial complex produces armoured vehicles, tanks, rocket-propelled grenades and anti-tank weapons. The new tanks are dubbed (what else?) *Bashir I* and *Digna* (after one of the Mahdi's commanders, Osman Digna). Even Zubayr, Gordon's nemesis, has one named after him. UN Comtrade data show that from 2003 to 2005 China's arms trade with Sudan increased from one million to twenty-three million US dollars.

By the end of the decade, it was evident that Islam had failed to iron out social inequalities. The country's finances were now in the hands of Islamic banks, and the old order had been replaced

by a new, more acceptable breed of opportunists. But essentially
nothing had changed. By 1999 the yawning gap between Turabi
and Omar al-Bashir had grown too wide. Zealotry was getting
in the way of profits and so Bashir cut Turabi loose, to be swept
aside by the oil boom. When you have money, ideology can take
a back seat.

The most audacious expression of the yawning abyss between the
hazy mirage of oil-fuelled ambition and everyday lethargy is taking place out on the emblematic point where the two great rivers
meld into one, the Mogran. There is a park there that I remember
as a magical place when we came here as children. Narrow paths
led through the lush gardens. Strings of coloured lights looped
through the trees like darkly charged rainbows.

The site of the Al Sunut Development lies immediately to the
south, in the forest on the other side of the approach road to the
bridge. This is almost the exact spot where the Mahdi's forces
breached the city's defences in January 1885, on the night General
Gordon was killed. The forest of *sunt* trees (*Acacia nilotica*) was
popular for excursions. Now it is fated to become an example
of what Rem Koolhaas has dubbed 'The Generic City', having
more in common with other such places around the world than
with anything in its immediate vicinity. Airports, shopping malls,
places that are complete unto themselves and to one another.
Hermetically sealed. Elsewhere there is already at least one example of a commercial centre, the rather seedy Afra Mall, which has

proved popular despite being an architectural and structural disaster. Needless to say, this will be in quite a different class. Plans to develop the area around the Mogran date back to the days of the British.

So far only a couple of towers have been built, but if; the Al Sunut Development ever fully materialises it will be a surreal vision rising from the riverbank. The original plan was for it to be fully functioning in about seven years, but the government is stalling and holding up progress. The developers claim to have filled most of the tenders put out. When complete it will comprise conference centres, shopping malls, marinas, hotels and apartment blocks, along with the ubiquitous golf course. 'A complete city' is how the promotional video describes it, 'a city within a city'. The science fiction analogy seems even more relevant when you consider what the lives of future residents might be like: a new Sudanese society, self-contained in the manner of gated communities around the world, cut off to all intents and purposes from their surroundings. A floating island of air-conditioned luxury in the midst of a country that is going up in flames.

Whichever way you look at it, pursuing this 'Dubai on the Nile' model in such unpredictable times seems wildly optimistic. Regional insurgency has already proved able to touch the capital. In March 2008, a column of some two hundred vehicles of the Justice and Equality Movement in Darfur managed to reach the outskirts of the city. They took the security forces by surprise and the fighting lasted several days. Some of the worst of it actually took place on the very same bridge that looks down over the southern end of the Al Sunut site. Many of the fighters were young men, boys high on the amphetamines they had swallowed to keep them awake for the six days it took to cross the desert. They were so disoriented they had to ask directions to the Presidential Palace. When they looked down from the bridge and glimpsed the first completed buildings rising out of the ground they must have thought they were hallucinating.

Standing at this curious intersection of past and future, I find myself caught in the strands of my own web. Half of the forest has been stripped away. As I watch the motor graders and earth-moving machines running back and forth across the dusty trench I am taken back to my childhood, to the days when my father worked for the local Caterpillar agent, the Sudanese Tractor Company.

On our way to school every morning we would stop off at the company workshop, a nondescript compound of simple brick walls and a high gate of corrugated-iron sheets. We would sit in the car impatiently as my father walked around checking with Musa, the manager, about what they had planned for that day. He often talked with pride of the work they did in that yard. With only very basic tools and a challenging shortage of spare parts, they inventively managed to keep a fleet of bulldozers, motor graders and so forth in running order. The machines themselves were fascinating to see up close, brightly coloured leviathans hidden in the deep shadows of dark sheds. Musa and his men could take them apart and then put them back together in ways that would have astonished the original manufacturers. Around the yard stood the skeletal remains of vehicles that had been stripped and scavenged of whatever could be turned to better use.

These were the same vehicles now grinding their way down into the dust of the old forest. The Sudanese Tractor Company has since grown into the DAL Group, which is behind the Al Sunut Development. It's a long way from the ball bearings, fire extinguishers and tractors my father dealt with. Today they are the third largest company in the country, behind the Kenana Sugar factory and Sudan Telecom. The DAL Group are currently agents for about thirty big international firms, including Rolls-Royce, Mitsubishi and Mercedes-Benz. They seem not only incredibly ambitious but also wildly optimistic, and while the Al Sunut project seems to epitomise that ambition the truth is that their strength lies in grand agricultural projects, equally audacious if less striking visually.

In his 'researches', as he calls them, Herodotus of Halicarnassus describes how Cambyses, the 'furious' son of the Persian King Cyrus, had contracted spies from among the 'Fish Eaters' of Elephantine and sent them south. Cambyses' army had torn through Egypt, desecrating the royal tombs and burning the corpses of the former kings. When he looked around for new conquests only one objective stood out: the land known in Greek as *Aethiopia*. More specifically, what drew him to it was a legend.

The story of the Table of the Sun describes a lush meadow upon which a lavish feast was laid out. Anyone could eat there during the day and each night the food was mysteriously replenished. Locals believed that the food was a gift from the earth, and that it materialised spontaneously. Archaeologists later identified the Temple of the Sun at Meroë in Nubia as being the likely source of Cambyses' quest. What is curious about this legend is how it fits with the persistent idea of this part of the world being a rich source of food, a notion that was still around in the 1970s when I was in civics class at school, learning about how we were to become the 'breadbasket of Africa'. Somehow the idea has persisted into the present, finding form in the DAL Group's impressive plans.

Alaifoun farm lies some thirty kilometres south of Khartoum. It may not look like much now, but eventually it will be the site for what is claimed will be the largest herd of cattle in Africa. The Capo Dairy is part of the DAL Group's agricultural division. An expansion of the existing dairy operation is underway. More milking stalls are being built. Friesian cattle are being imported, brought in on trucks from the Red Sea coast and beyond, from Australia and Canada (because of the ban on European imports due to Creutzfeldt-Jakob, or 'mad cow', disease). At present they have 800 head, but in the next couple of years that number will grow to about double that. The herd will be increased after that in phases until it reaches the designated target of 10,000. Partly they will come from imports, but the plan is to make the dairy self-sufficient and for that they need the skills of the chief veterinarian.

Doctor Mohammed trained in Japan. He did his research on cloning. For the time being he concerns himself with improving the herd, enhancing production by extracting the eggs from the best producers, fertilising them and then placing them in up to fifteen host cows. This is how the herd will grow, by increasing the quality of the cattle and raising the milk yield. They currently get 8,000 litres a year per cow. In Saudi Arabia, they have a larger cow that produces around 13,000 litres, but Dr Mohammed assures me the quality here is better.

He is a curious character. While attending the University of Hokkaido he would visit abattoirs to collect ovaries and wombs from slaughtered animals to dissect, extracting eggs and fertilising them. He managed to achieve a 40 per cent growth rate. The work he did in Japan paved the way for the current project, which, he assures me, is unique in Africa. While working on the Capo herd he had to put his cloning work to one side, though he hopes to be able to get back to it at some point in the future. While in Japan he developed a keen interest in the local culture. He taught himself around a thousand characters, which is enough to get by on. You need at least three thousand to be able to read a newspaper easily.

Neither Doctor Mohammed nor his assistant, Doctor Wasfa, can hide their enthusiasm for their work. It is symptomatic of everyone you talk to at Alaifoun. If there is a key to the success of the DAL Group then this is it. The workers seem deeply committed to their work. It is hard to overstress the significance of this in a country notorious for its lackadaisical, laissez-faire, *bukra-inshallah* attitude (the Arabic version of *mañana*). The comparison with government, with the public sector, with just about anything, is astonishing.

To feed the cattle they are increasing the production of alfalfa. There are currently a thousand *feddans* (one *feddan* is approximately one acre) under cultivation. To expand this, they are busy installing irrigation pivots, each of which measures some 400 metres across. Motorised wheels under each of the seven spans keep them turning in wide circles. Each pivot waters an area of fifty hectares, turning it into a lush green disc of alfalfa on the desiccated brown earth. At Alaifoun, the water is fed in from the Nile at 1.8 cubic metres per minute via a canal that was dredged by DAL's engineering division. The plentiful supply of water and the intense sunlight means it grows faster. It takes twenty-one days, which means they get twelve harvests or 'cuts' a year, which is high compared to five or six in most places. They produce thirty tonnes per acre per annum. The man in charge of installing the pivots is Duncan, an enthusiastic white Kenyan who strides around the place in shorts and big boots. He has worked on similar projects in other parts of Africa but never anything as big as this. Every couple of weeks he flies in from Kenya to check on how things are progressing. His enthusiasm is contagious and his beaming smile tells you that he enjoys his work. Despite the size of it, this project is dwarfed by what is to come.

From the roof of the milking plant, which is not quite finished, the circles of green alfalfa dotting the brown land can be glimpsed stretching away into the distance. The pivots resemble strange, plodding insects, giant locusts with arched ribs and wavy antennae. They turn slowly, taking a full day to complete a cycle. From the electric motors on the wheels to the amount of water released, all is controlled by computer via a WiFi connection. You could monitor it from anywhere in the world. The alfalfa is harvested and packed in twenty-four hours. It is dried in the sun, which I am told is better than the ultraviolet method they use in places like Spain. Then it is double-packed for volume and shipped across the Red Sea to Saudi Arabia and the Arab Emirates where they have herds of 15–20,000 head, camels as well as cattle, but no water. The price of alfalfa is rising, which makes this a lucrative business right now.

Alaifoun is more than just a dairy farm. In the greenhouses they are producing high-quality vegetables – tomatoes, peppers and cucumbers – which are sold to hotels and restaurants. 'We could produce a hundred times this and they would still all be sold,' says Duncan. Still, at four dollars a kilo, the prices are comparable to those in Europe. They produced 100,000 trees for the nine-hole golf course that is being built down the road and a similar number will be needed for the Al Sunut development. At any given time the greenhouses contain some 30,000 plants along with 40,000 trees and flowers. There are ponds where tilapia fish are being farmed. Another of their projects is to grow dura, or sorghum, a staple part of the diet in this country. Until now nobody has found a way of storing it once it is ground into flour, as it goes off easily. The Swiss appear to have discovered a method that will save people hours every day in preparing their meals. As we wander round, Duncan beams proudly. 'Nothing like this anywhere else in Africa.' And he has travelled all over the continent, putting in irrigation systems and running agricultural projects.

The workforce is mixed. There are Nepalis, Malays and Thais working alongside Sudanese. It is hoped that the work ethic of the more motivated foreign workers will rub off. Changing people's mentality is not easy, but Duncan has seen it happen. Apart from the two white managers they also have black Kenyan supervisors, who are learning Arabic. 'It won't work with white staff,' he says, but the work ethic of the more experienced Kenyans is having an effect: 'You can see the Sudanese workers trying harder. The mentality here is that once you have an education, you get to sit back in an office and relax. But they see our guys working alongside them, harder than they do, and so they have to keep up.' The Sudanese are now working better than the Nepalis. This goes against everything that people tell you; that Sudanese are lazy, that they don't like to work. All they need, it seems, is the right motivation.

What is fascinating about the DAL venture is that, even while it is a commercial exercise, it is somehow an extension of the political aspirations of the previous generation. The initials DAL stand for the founder, my father's old friend, the man he worked for in the days when it was still the rather more humble Sudanese Tractor Company. Daoud Abd al-Latif was born in 1914 in the village of Degheim near Wadi Halfa. His father was a shopkeeper. By all accounts he was quite a character, even as a young man. His habit of speaking his mind got him into trouble more than once. At the Gordon Memorial College his independent spirit and forthright manner earmarked him early on as a rebel, and eventually led to his being expelled. He was banished to Wadi Halfa in the North, where he worked as a bookkeeper in the District Commissioner's office.

Early on Daoud developed a loathing for the British, although later this was to change; over time he grew to admire the tenacity and dedication of the District Officers, living alone in remote parts of the country for months on end. The Sudan Political Service was quite distinct from other branches of the British Colonial Civil Service. They were regarded as the most highly qualified. According to Daoud, interviewed on the living history of that period, 'They had a tremendous sense of mission, most of them, a real sense of mission, and were really idealistic. These DCs came from Oxford and Cambridge just after their schooling with all the idealism of young people, and lived amongst a people who respected them and, many times, loved them – and whom they loved.'

One day he took the District Commissioner to task over his having insulted an old man. To his credit, the DC apologised and, impressed by his conviction, offered Daoud the chance to apply to become a Sub-Mamur (Assistant Governor). It was a sign of the times; the relationship between the British administrators and their subjects had begun to change in the run-up to independence. In time, he began to see that one could achieve more through cooperation than through hostility. For their part, the British began to understand that when one of their Sudanese subordinates said, 'No, sir,' it was not necessarily a negative thing.

In 1948, Daoud became one of the first Sudanese District Commissioners. By 1952 there were still only nine Sudanese DCs out of a total of fifty-seven. After independence he served as governor in two provinces in the South, Bahr al-Ghazal and Equatoria. His problems continued under the country's new rulers. Interestingly, he was eventually recalled for being too supportive of Southern issues.

In 1960, Daoud was forced to retire from government service following his support for the case of the 50,000 Nubians who were forcibly resettled due to the flooding caused by the Aswan High Dam. It was at that point that he went into business for himself, using many of the contacts he had made to become director of several British concerns. One of these, the engineering company Sayer & Colley, provided the foundations for what has mushroomed into the enterprise now bearing his initials.

If the DAL Group represents an alternative to the general sense of malaise in the country it also has to face the same fundamental problem as most companies – the lack of trained and motivated staff, and not just at the managerial level. Plumbers, bricklayers, carpenters, even unskilled labourers, are in short supply – hence the Bangladeshi cleaners. The DAL Group have a choice – to begin investing in educating people from scratch, with the implied twenty-year wait, or simply to carry on bringing in people from abroad. Today's university graduates lack basic skills, as well as initiative, another consequence of the narrow bandwidth of their education; reciting religious verses all day teaches passivity, not resourcefulness.

The company is already taking up the slack left by ineffective governance. Major pillars of state industry such as Sudan Railways, or the Gezira Board cotton scheme, have long since foundered or been dismantled. To ensure the regular transport of materials from the coast, they run their own train from Port Sudan to Khartoum. The rise of the DAL Group over the last decade has coincided

with the entry of a degree of pragmatism into Bashir's rule, which
goes some way to explaining why they have survived in such difficult times. The state is so weakened that it would never be able
to attempt an undertaking as comprehensive as that which the
DAL Group is engaged in, although the danger of nationalisation,
which Daoud suffered in the 1970s, always remains present.

The DAL Group aspires more towards a Brazilian model of
development than a Western one. The Brazilians get down to
work, I am told; they don't stand on formality. Their CEOs and
directors dress down – short-sleeved shirts and slacks or jeans.
They drive their own cars. This bears comparison to the attitude
here, where company directors and managers generally expect
perks, and being able to swan around in Armani suits on per diems
that are five times what DAL representatives get. They want to
fly everywhere first class, etc. The last thing they worry about
is efficient management. This self-serving attitude applies across
the board. University graduates want air-conditioned offices and
menials to jump to their command.

Down the road at the Al-Waha site they are busy installing a
total of 130 irrigation pivots, eventually covering an area of 22,000
acres. Even this pales in comparison to the scheme they are planning further north in Halfa on the Egyptian border, which will
turn an area of one million *feddans*, just over a million acres, or
roughly twice the size of Lebanon, into fertile agricultural land.
The water will come from aquifers some eighty metres deep that
are replenished by underground streams flowing down from the
highlands of the Great Lakes area. This water is not affected by
the Nile Waters Agreement with Egypt, which regulates how
much water Sudan can take from the river. Desert sand will be
mixed with soil and nutrients will be added. It will cost around
$3,000 per acre to do all this, but, once it is done, they are con-
fident that they will be able to grow enough wheat to stop them
being dependent on imported grain. And there are other projects.
It is hard to keep track. But the overall impression is one of an
innovative approach that is striking for its boldness in very difficult times. From a lowly tractor company the DAL Group has

grown into one of the biggest and most diverse enterprises in Sudan today.

At the Coca-Cola plant I discover that they employ deaf people in quality control, because of the level of noise and because their visual skills are much sharper. They observe every bottle passing a light box, checking for flaws in the glass and the level of liquid. The young woman showing me around tells me that head office apparently thinks this is the best plant outside the USA. How do they get around the trade sanctions? I ask. She smiles. They buy the concentrate they need from Egypt. The same applies to the Caterpillar division of DAL, which nowadays deals exclusively with the Geneva office. So much for embargoes.

The man who set up the Coca-Cola plant in 2001 is Ronnie Shaoul. He is also responsible for the Sayga Flour Mills and is currently in charge of the expansion of the dairy operation at the Capo Dairy. A large, ebullient man, Ronnie is of Jewish-Armenian origin. He grew up in Khartoum North, a stone's throw from my grandmother's house. With the Arabisation of the education system back in the 1990s Ronnie lost his job teaching in the Agriculture Department at Gezira University. He is now general manager of the Food Section of the DAL Group. He talks with great enthusiasm of their latest plans. First of all there is the expansion of dairy production, which currently falls far short of the country's needs. Taking the minimum daily requirement as 100 millilitres of milk per person per day, a city of seven million would require around 700 tonnes, which is a hundred times what Capo is currently producing. Milk production in this country still takes place on a traditional small scale; this is one of the last countries in the world to allow the sale of untreated milk. There is no legislation, nothing to govern the quality of milk products. In the absence of the government's willingness to act, DAL has taken it upon itself to ensure the quality and hygiene required for this project. All of this makes me wonder if there is such a thing as responsible capitalism, and if this is perhaps the only workable approach to development in this day and age.

To Ronnie, it all comes down to the courage of his boss: 'He could just sit back and say that's it, I can manage with what I've got, but he doesn't do that. Osama is a model for the country. The difficulty here is instilling professionalism. Sudanese find it hard to be rigid. If someone comes late to work, they say, *maal-ish* [never mind].' Loyalty percolates through the entire company, from factory line to top management. I heard a similar story from Duncan at the Alaifoun farm: 'Mr Osama likes to see things grow. He loves it. Watching it grow. People like working for Mr Osama, they tell you, because he cares. If you work hard you will be rewarded. If not, you're out.'

Mr Osama is Osama Daoud, the DAL Group's current director and the eldest son of the founder. He is the man who spearheaded the company's remarkable expansion over the last two decades and has somehow managed to stay clear of the regime. He appears to have done this by not giving way, by not compromising, but also by making himself irreplaceable. The fact that he has delivered one of the country's great success stories, that he is known and respected both here and abroad, makes him a valuable asset. He doesn't subscribe to their version of Islamic piety, and he makes no secret of this, but there is clearly respect for him, despite the obvious ideological differences. In meetings with government officials, he refuses to go out and pray along with the rest of them. Instead, he remains seated, waiting patiently for them to return and the meeting to go on. It is a difficult balance to strike. The DAL Group's growth owes much to the oil boom of the last decade in which they have played a major role.

When Osama took over the reins of the company in the 1980s he was keen to make his mark. The obstacle in his path was the company's somewhat old-fashioned general manager, who just happened to be my father. It was, by all accounts, a turbulent relationship. My father had his own ways and Osama was the son of the company's owner, one of his oldest and dearest friends. He was a cautious man who was not fond of taking risks, quite the opposite of Osama, who was then barely into his thirties and impatient for change.

Hearing all this over dinner one day makes me think about my father and his part in my reasons for coming back. I wonder if I came here out of some feeling of filial duty. My father had a strong sense of responsibility, to his family, to the society he was a part of, to his friends, and to the country, and he instilled these values in his sons. He believed in this country, in its potential to succeed, and it pained him to see it being driven into the ground by short-sighted men who offered simplistic solutions, defending prejudice in the name of religion. These were not the great men he had known and respected all his life. But my father's generation had failed to implement a vision that was sustainable, that would allow the country to find stability and a place in the world. If he had lived long enough he would have been saddened to see the secession of the South, for he believed the key to the nation lay in embracing its diversity.

I was brought up to believe that this was my country and that I had a role to play. The sense of facing up to your responsibilities was drummed into me as a child. As the eldest of three sons I was expected to set an example for my brothers: to do well at school, to work hard and, in the long term, to help this country achieve itself. As it happened, I did none of those things. I wasn't particularly good at school. I preferred reading novels to studying. Higher education was mainly an exercise in fulfilling obligations. Against his will, I left to study abroad when an opportunity presented itself in the form of a scholarship. I wanted to see the world, to travel, to write. We argued a lot in those years. He didn't understand my decision to move away. Nobody made a living from writing books. I was squandering my talent, throwing away the best opportunity I would ever have, one that neither he nor my mother had had.

No matter how far away I went, I still felt that sense of duty pulling me back. I applied for film school, tried acting, but somehow I knew I would never be free until I had a university education, something he prized greatly, partly because it had never been available to him. As a result, I became probably the worst geology student Sheffield University had ever seen. I wasn't particularly happy in England. I found life there cold and unwelcoming. It was a shock to realise that where I came from still qualified as one of Conrad's blank spaces on the map. Nobody knew anything about Sudan, despite the historical links. I came from a forgotten place. Not much seemed to have changed since the days when my father had travelled up and down the country sorting out digs for young Sudanese students, although I never saw signs saying, 'No Blacks or Irish' as he had, which was perhaps something.

I drifted from one odd job to another, trying to support my writing. As for building the nation, it was probably the furthest thing from my mind. There were, I was sure, plenty of people far better qualified than I was. I did, however, believe that writing offered some form of redemption. Yet what was it, I ask myself now, that I was constructing? An imaginary homeland? A fictional version of the utopia my father and his generation envisaged and devoted their lives to, or the failed state it had become? Those early novels are all concerned with exploring the nature of this country, what it means to be Sudanese. I wrote about the civil war in the 1980s, about the rise of the Mahdi in the nineteenth century, and about the experience of my father's generation. What was I doing, if not trying to construct the nation?

At the same time, and in some strange parallel, my father decided, after a lifetime of conformity, to take an unconventional change of direction. Realising that with Osama's arrival his influence in the company was diminishing, he decided to take early retirement and threw himself into a collective project with two friends to start a newspaper – the *Sudan Times*. The move was completely out of character, although later it became clear that this was really what he had waited his whole life to do.

It was a decision that was to have serious and long-lasting consequences for himself and my mother. They went from a steady, organised existence in Khartoum to a peripatetic life of exile and displacement. They settled in Cairo, but it was never home; there was always the sense that one day things would change and they would be able to return. They never did.

From the moment he had first crossed the river, as a young man in his twenties, to work in what was later to become the British Council library, he had been in full-time employment, always following someone else's orders. He often boasted of never having had to ask for a job in his life; people had need of his services. But this was different. The *Sudan Times* was intended as a forum for writers from North and South to come together as equals. It went against the cultural norm by being printed in English and it lasted for little over three years. When the *Inqaz* arrived in June 1989, all the papers were closed down. Public criticism was not part of the new agenda.

The *Sudan Times* was probably the proudest achievement of his life and the last job he was to have. When they shut down his two partners went their separate ways, Mahgoub to prison and Bona Malwal to exile in Britain. Still, in those few years he finally found a way to play a personal part in the construction of the nation that was so close to his heart. I imagine it brought him back, towards the end of his working life, to the young man who had spent his nights churning out pro-independence flyers on the stencil machine at the library where he worked. Nothing gave him more pleasure than composing an editorial piece about the failings of government or the prime minister, Sadig al-Mahdi. The people he most admired throughout his life were those intellectuals, writers, journalists, professors, men and women who were able to formulate ideas, to argue, to stir the mind and the heart with their use of words, to formulate the dreams they all shared in words and ideas. I like to think that, towards the end, he felt he had achieved something he had never dared to dream. Finally, he was a part of that world. It is always difficult to claim that we can ever really know what our parents experienced, what they felt, what drove them, but it feels as though somehow this book is a meeting of those two separate trajectories; the closing chapter of his desire to contribute, and mine. In that sense, it feels like a reconciliation of sorts.

In his 1863 novel *Five Weeks in a Balloon*, Jules Verne describes at length a vision of world history in which Africa rises to take the lead. With the climate purified by cultivation and irrigation the country over which our intrepid adventurers are floating would become rich and fertile, a 'grand realm where more astonishing discoveries than steam and electricity will be brought to light'.

If I feel a sense of déjà vu when looking at Alaifoun farm it is because it resembles the old dream they tried to sell us at school, about our being able to feed the world. We believed it was happening, even as we sat there scribbling gibberish messages to one another, surreptitiously reading cowboy novels, or covertly eating a sandwich under the desk. We didn't have to worry. The future was set and soon we would be able to feed the continent by a magical combination of progress, the abundance of natural resources, good fertile soil and plenty of water. This was what made us so perfectly suited to the task. It was a nice dream, but it wasn't sustained.

In retrospect so much of that euphoria was founded on illusion. Castles in the air. By 1975 the country had borrowed some $300 million to revitalise the road and railway systems, to renovate the telecommunications network, even to build a satellite relay station. There were private initiatives, to build the Jonglei Canal across the Sudd marshes and to construct the world's largest sugar plantation at Kenana. The plan for the 'breadbasket' envisaged $6,000 million invested in a hundred projects, of which less than ten actually saw the light of day. The sponsors made their own demands. The West imposed strict economic constraints while Arab finance brought its own political influence. By 1978 the dream had hit a brick wall. The IMF stepped in to play a role in steering the country's economic and agricultural planning. For the next seven years Nimeiri toed the line they drew in the sand in the vain hope that it would bring about his salvation. It didn't.

It was a critical moment in the country's evolution. In line with what they were doing elsewhere in the developing world, trying to transform emerging economies into burgeoning capitalist hives, the IMF insisted the government introduce drastic measures to force the transformation from a state-run economy to a free market. Subsidies on basic commodities were cut, taxes were raised and the currency devalued. The markets were liberalised and the banks denationalised. This process of liberalisation was to have a marked polarising effect on society. The Americans were keen on the country remaining stable and prosperous, sandwiched as it was between Marxist Ethiopia on the one side and Gaddafi's personal brand of radical socialism on the other.

By now the signs were that Nimeiri was losing it. Alcohol only added to his problems. He passed out on television a couple of times in front of the nation. Increasingly isolated within a cabal of palace aides and soothsayers, he saw conspiracy everywhere, subscribing to such far-fetched notions as the Libyans dumping toothpaste in the Nile to create unrest. What happened to the bouncy, pugilistic young officer who had started out a socialist? Perhaps there was never any real conviction in his beliefs. Men of conviction tended to wind up in prison, in exile, or dead, like Abdel-Khaliq Mahgoub. After that it was simply a matter of holding on to power. He slid across the political scale while trying desperately to cling on by his fingertips. In the end he ran out of ideas. The country was so far in debt that it would have taken a miracle to pull it out of the downward spiral. And so, ailing and paranoid, he took the final, fateful step, towards religion.

Islam had, after all, come to countries' aid before in times of need, guiding the Mahdi to victory. Like the Mahdi, there was an element of reason in Nimeiri's madness. While it may have provided some spiritual comfort, religion had the added benefit of allowing him to outflank his political rivals. Islam was fast becoming a significant presence in Sudanese politics, as it was in the Middle East generally. Perhaps it was facing the economic hardships of the 1980s and, more importantly, the inability of either East or West to provide a solution to the country's problems that gave him the incentive to turn back to traditional ways.

By 1983, five years into the IMF programme, the country's foreign debt had risen from three to eight billion dollars. In March 1985, crowds took to the streets, driven to desperation by soaring prices and chronic shortages. There was a lack of staple commodities such as sugar. Prices shot up. Bread by 75 per cent, petrol by 65 per cent. 'Down with Nimeiri,' they chanted. 'Down with the IMF.' On 1 April there were calls for a general strike. The trade unions were still able to unite workers, lawyers, doctors and teachers. After five days of unrest the army stepped in as usual to restore order, bringing an end to the Nimeiri era.

The country's financial problems continued. In February 1986 the country declared itself bankrupt. The war in the South, which was costing over a million dollars a day, only added to the downward spiral. The four years that bridge the gap between Nimeiri's demise and the arrival of Brigadier Omar al-Bashir in June 1989 witnessed a deepening of the country's problems.

In this setting, the DAL Group project stands out as an anomaly. The ambition, the work ethic and the sense of social responsibility seem out of place, a throwback to more optimistic times and the spirit of nation building. To the new wave of entrepreneurs produced by the oil boom wealth is an end in itself. They do not see beyond immediate material benefits. They want bigger cars and first-class travel, properties in the Gulf paradises. And one company, no matter how big and successful, is not enough to bring about the needed change. It seems all the more astonishing to witness the courage that drives newspapermen like Mahgoub Mohammed Salih, the dignity and moral righteousness of human rights lawyers like Amin Mekki, or Mohammed Ibrahim Khalil; all display qualities that seem inherently lacking in the political class.

Tempting though it might be to consider the rise of large-scale agricultural projects such as Alaifoun as a way forward, there are no indications that the newly wealthy classes cruising the capital in their SUVs have any understanding of, or interest in, the plight of their less fortunate brethren, of the sacrifices that would be called for in order to ensure stability and long-term growth. Without that awareness the country appears to be set on a perilous course.

From the start, the country has lacked the political vision to achieve its potential. A vision that is muscular, creative and inclusive; one that could inspire people to overcome their ethnic, religious and racial differences, and provide a framework in which it was possible to see beyond the here and now of their discontent towards the prosperity of a shared future. Back in 1990, former minister Mansour Khalid advocated a Keynesian approach to social liberalism. A transformation that would end the grip of the urban elite on the country's power and economy. In his book *The Government They Deserve*, he outlines three basic prerequisites for a reversal of the country's economic plight: first, the end of the civil war; second, addressing the debt issue; and third, the country would have to undergo what he described as a 'socio-economic self-transformation' by democratic means.

The recent building frenzy around the capital has created an air-conditioned bubble of luxury, a shelter from reality. Rather than economic self-transformation, this looks more like a magnified reprisal of past inequalities. But the gap seems wider now, the contrasts more stark. Cut off from the rest of the country in order to safeguard its own luxurious lifestyle, it's not hard to see that the main priority of this new urban elite is to protect itself. This strategy is already in place. The staying power of the Bashir regime derives from its investment in internal security forces, present in the capital, to the detriment of the national army. The message is clear: the enemy is within, not without. Wars and low-level conflicts will continue, at a distance, on a manageable scale, but force will always be needed to put down insurgency and control natural resources. We seem to have slipped backwards in time to a new age of feudalism.

The West has largely lost its role, both as long-term investor and as a moral mentor. For centuries it has exploited the continent for its own benefit, aiding and abetting corruption wherever necessary and contributing to the pollution and depletion of natural resources. What it did not provide was an ideology that could be moulded to the country's needs, an idea strong enough to nurture long-term stability. In more recent times, whether it is buying blood diamonds or fishing rights, purchasing coltan for PlayStations, dumping toxic waste, turning a blind eye to the environmental disaster of the Niger Delta or selling arms, the West has been complicit in the steady degradation of the continent. An industry of aid workers and charity organisations has grown on the back of that. Governments often rely on international NGOs to do their dirty work. It relieves them of having to be concerned about the poorest and most destitute levels of society.

Time and again Western governments have failed important moral challenges, leaving them open to accusations of double standards. Events since September 2001 have only accelerated this tendency. The International Criminal Court is widely seen as being unfairly biased towards prosecuting African leaders at the expense of others, such as George W. Bush and Tony Blair. The perception that the West is effectively waging a war against Islam plays into the narrative of anti-Western resentment. What is desperately needed in this new, post-ideology age of capitalism is the realisation that new global solutions are needed to some very old problems.

From the balcony, I spy a man moving slowly along the road, carefully sweeping up the fallen leaves. The trees are sparse along this stretch and he follows a line of kerbstones that are relatively new, collecting the bright yellow leaves into a little pile that he then scoops into a black plastic bag before moving on his way. The leaves fall regardless of the distinction made between road and kerb. The slim, serrated neem leaves are scattered haphazardly all over, covering both dusty sides of the street. But the man takes care to concentrate his attention only on those leaves that have crossed the magic line and fallen into the road. As he walks away a leaf tumbles down in his wake. He doesn't look back.

Despite the glut of oil money that has flowed through the country in recent years, there is little to show for it in terms of improving the infrastructure of the capital. Even in the relatively affluent New Extension where we used to live the drains lie uncovered and uncared for, choked by a dirty grey sludge that is a fertile breeding ground for malaria-carrying mosquitoes. Nearby is the Ibn Khaldun eye hospital, a nod to one of the great names of Arab scholarship. In a country that pleads its Islamic credentials the contrast could not be more damning. From the Golden Age to blocked drains. Perhaps this neglect is symptomatic of the country's problems in a more general sense, the lethargy and disinterest shown towards distant conflicts, regional complaints. It is easier to ignore what is happening rather than work to find real, lasting solutions.

People are tired of being abused, another irate taxi driver tells me one day. It will soon all end in violence. The police stop you from crossing the new bridge, not because it is illegal, but because they are running their own taxis and want to keep the business for themselves. They impose on-the-spot fines. And there are no political solutions to the malaise. The opposition is corrupt. 'What's the point of elections? Look what that thief in Egypt did. He won the elections every time. You think they can't do the same here?' The reference to Mubarak leaves him dismayed and he falls silent. 'When it comes,' he says, finally, the violence, he means, 'it will come with force. People will die. It has to happen. There is no other way with these people.'

On the street outside my grandmother's house a man is busy chopping down a large neem tree. With great energy he climbs up the thick branches and hacks away furiously with an axe. I can't recall his name, but he knows me. He stops his work to come over and shake my hand. There are flecks of fresh white wood chips in his greying hair and stuck to his skin with sweat. 'Why are you chopping it down?' In this intense heat every scrap of shade seems worth worshipping, let alone preserving. 'The wind,' he says, pausing in his work to scratch his head. 'When the wind blows the noise is too much.' He surveys his handiwork and a look of sadness crosses his face, as if he had been unaware until that moment of the consequences of his actions. The fine tree has been reduced to a pile of broken branches, the rich green foliage lies trampled in the dust. 'It's a shame,' I say. He laughs at this, unsure how to respond, before taking up his axe and beginning to swing it again.

There are few trees around. Outside some houses plants are arranged along the walls in large jerrycans and split oil barrels. Any touch of green in this landscape is a relief to the eye. The small trees are protected by a little circle of bricks half buried in the ground. Every day they are sprinkled with water. That's all it takes, but it makes all the difference. It's a fine line between desolation and verdant luxuriance.

The young men who gather in my grandmother's old house every evening are all educated. They are biologists and chemists and goodness knows what, but the idea of taking care of the street in which they live does not occur to them. Most of them spend their spare time and money on cable television, not on watering trees. Everyone has at least one mobile telephone and several relatives abroad, in Europe, North America, Australia, yet these streets have not really improved in over a century since their great-grandparents moved here. As I stumble along the uneven, unmetalled street a woman steps out of a doorway and hurls a bucketful of dirty water into the air. It hits the dry earth with a hiss, leaving a blue stain on the muddy ground.

'Jamal, where are you going?'

I turn to see a man I do not know. He gives me a suspicious stare as he walks past, joining a boy of about thirteen who is further

along the road. Both of them cast a look over their shoulders as
they walk away. I pause to survey the street. The scruffy white
goats chew mournfully on plastic bags, their jaws gyrating in little
bony circles. The plastic bags are scattered everywhere, trampled
into the ground, orange and black, stuck to wire fences like weird
foliage, their colours faded by the sun. Bottles are flattened into
grey oval slates that I trample underfoot. They are dotted everywhere on the ground, like strange fossils. A milkman goes by on
his donkey, the silver churns strapped into the saddle under his
legs, clicking his tongue to get the skinny beast to move. He is
talking into his mobile telephone as he goes by. It is like watching
two centuries slowly colliding.

I find that I am at my most content when wandering the streets
alone, pacing from one available scrap of shade to the next, the
sound of the trees stirring restlessly, the heaving air infused with
hot white peppery dust. In part this stems from the sheer physical
experience of space. The crazy jigsaw geometry of decay, the broken pavements, the slabs of concrete that seesaw over the drains,
the fallen neem leaves that lie like glowing embers in the dust.

It doesn't take long, walking in the midday heat, to realise that
just managing to stay upright is quite a task. Anything beyond
that is impossible to contemplate. People wander by in a daze,
mumbling to themselves, lifting their hands in half-gestures and
then letting them fall like unfinished sentences.

There is an element of self-indulgence, escapism, to this aimless walking that takes me back about thirty years to the time when I was a teenager. Coming home from school. Travelling in ever-widening circles away from the locus of my parents. That growing sense of consciousness, trying to connect with a side of the country I felt I wasn't really a part of. Now I wonder, not for the first time, what would have become of me if I had stayed. What would become of me now if I were to decide to stay here. What niche could I occupy as an adult?

There is a circle of fashionable socialites who move in a shadowy demi-monde, tolerated by the intolerant authorities because of their wealth and influence. Life takes on a slightly surreal slant in such company. It's a Greeneland of diplomats and consuls, local representatives of obscure European states who can't be bothered to maintain their own embassies here. They mingle with businessmen, charity representatives, aid workers, United Nations staff and a smattering of entrepreneurs, both sides seeking reassurance or, failing that, salient information. Everybody is looking for a soothsayer, a fortune teller, someone who will be able to predict what is coming, which of course nobody can.

In among this crowd are the dwindling representatives of the old Levantines, Greeks, Copts, the last remnants of the country's Syrian community. Almost all of them have similar tales to tell. Their grandparents travelled up the Nile with Kitchener in the nineteenth century. For the next half a century they invested in the country and built up an impressive range of companies. Gum arabic, soap production, cigarettes. The women resemble settlers from a decaying empire. The men are paunchy with liver spots and thinning white hair. They have a nostalgic feeling for this country, where most of them grew up and many of them were born. In the old days this whole set lived a wild life, having affairs with one another. There were, I am told, plenty of scandals, suicides, etc. When Nimeiri came to power their businesses were nationalised. This country doesn't really want them. Despite having made lots of money they live modestly, in simple houses rather than the more modern mansions of the recent generation of petro-rich upstarts. They have nowhere else to go. They have invested their money abroad, setting up their children there and could easily go themselves, but in London, Paris, or Geneva they are just people with money. Here, they have a status. They are something.

At one, rather grand, soirée, drinks are served by a waiter in a white gellabiya, his head bound in a cotton imma. Around his waist a rather quaint green cummerbund seems perfectly matched to the surrealism of the setting. The last days of the Raj, or the deck of the *Titanic* spring to mind, but none of the images quite fits. There is something quite modern about it all, in a way. The women are dressed in figure-hugging, generally rather glamorous outfits, while the men range from formal shirtsleeves to Hawaiian prints that would not be out of place in *Miami Vice*. Less Greeneland, then, than Carl Hiaasen or Elmore Leonard.

There is nothing more surreal than spending an evening sitting in a garden listening to an account of the benefits of milk-based food supplement over a peanut-based formula. Experts are divided, apparently, but it all seems rather academic – the plight of the starving in the refugee camps, the slum dwellers of Nairobi – when set against the smoked salmon and the champagne, all of it laid out by Filipina maids. The conversation turns to insurrection in Egypt. The Ikhwan will banish tourism. The people are not ready for democracy.

At the end of the evening I speak briefly to the British ambassador, who is as slim and jittery as a greyhound, lean, whiskered and eager to be off. Two cars wait for him in the street, engines and air con running the entire time he is inside. Around the car stand bodyguards, young men, mostly of mixed race, in neat shirts and slacks. They carry trim little bags dangling over their shoulders, presumably containing weaponry of some sort. The threat is no doubt real. Four years ago a serious attack on the embassy was apparently foiled by local agents of the National Intelligence and Security Service.

The ambassador is shrewd and looks well prepared for trouble. Part diplomat, part man of action, he has served in Afghanistan and the Congo. We don't share the same politics. That much is clear. He was in Madrid at the time of the Atocha bombings, where, he tells me, they enjoyed 'excellent' relations with the Aznar government. No sense of irony there. Aznar lost the elections because he tried covering up inconvenient evidence that clearly indicated the attack had been carried out by Islamists. Islamist terrorism provoked by Aznar's vain and rather foolish participation in the invasion of Iraq alongside Bush and Blair would have been unfortunate since public opinion was very much against the war. Instead he wanted to point the finger at ETA. The fumbling turned the election around in a matter of days, handing Zapatero and the socialists a landslide victory.

Aznar could have used a crystal ball to decide what strategy to employ, and the same is true here, where nobody seems to have a clue what will come next. There could be a *coup d'état* tomorrow, or tonight even, or perhaps never. But even if it were to happen tomorrow, the real question is what would come next? Who would replace Bashir? Who would want to take over, considering the problems the country is facing? If he knows what is going on here, the ambassador is keeping it to himself. There are, he hints, voices of reason within the NCP. Then he leaps into his car and races off into the empty streets, poised for ambush.

One of the best jobs I ever had was running a library. I can't call myself a librarian because it's a profession that requires a formal degree of qualification. I had no training or experience and no real ambition to acquire it, but the opportunity presented itself and I was immediately drawn to the idea. It was a small, self-service library that largely ran itself. To borrow a book you filled out a form and dropped part of it into a cardboard box, which it was my job to process.

The library was part of the Institute of Social Anthropology in the Danish town of Aarhus. The buildings belonged to an old estate located out in the forest at Moesgaard. In the modest little museum next door lay the bronzed figure of the Grauballe Man, murdered in the third century, preserved in a peat bog and immortalised – 'hung in the scales with beauty and atrocity' – by Seamus Heaney.

I had a desk and a telephone, access to a coffee machine and a small IBM word processor. There weren't many visitors. My boss was a curious, reclusive figure who never left his office. He sat there all day staring out of the window at the trees. His wife had died and he seemed to carry an intense sadness within him. When he finally retired the grey metal filing cupboards in his office were revealed to be stacked from top to bottom with neatly folded Tetra Briks that had been drained of every last drop of the cheap wine they once contained. He rarely ventured into the library, and when he did it was usually because he had taken a wrong turn, or needed to remind himself that it was still there. And so for the most part I was left to work undisturbed. I had certain duties, such as collecting the mail and delivering newspapers to the staff common room every morning. I was expected to oversee the general running of the library, process lending forms, replace returned books in their proper place and chase up others that were long overdue or had been requested by somebody else. Most of the time I sat there staring into space, but even this was lent a degree of gravitas by the mere presence of the silent stacks of books surrounding me. Somehow, the sheer physical mass of hundreds of bound volumes containing pages and words seemed to add weight to the simplest of thoughts. I was in good company, or so it felt. It wasn't that I did nothing else with my time. I did manage to write a novel, but I have never, before or since, found myself so much at home in gainful employment.

In spare moments I had time to explore the library's contents. I wandered the stacks and dipped into Lévi-Strauss and Bronisław Malinowski along with Michel Foucault, although his books happened to be in demand, which made reading them awkward. I learned about the Inuits and about Melanesian cargo cults, of life among the Bedouins of Yemen, or the Yanomami of Brazil. When the day was over I would lock up and cycle home through the woods. It was about as idyllic as it gets. There was something familiar and comforting about that space that for a long time I couldn't explain, until one day I realised that everything about it, including the grey Dexion shelves, reminded me of another library, one that I had seen only once, years before, as a child.

It was one of the few occasions I can recall when my father and I did something together, just the two of us. I must have been ten or eleven at the time. Friday was his day off; which meant he would abandon the short-sleeved safari suits he usually wore to the office and instead don the traditional gellabiya and imma; this last entailed the laborious process of winding the strip of white cotton, twisting and binding it tightly around the head. Traditionally it was meant to be long enough to cover your body as a shroud if and when you died (being always prepared for your own death might seem fatalistic, but also reassuring in its light, portable simplicity). Then, in a move that was a lot less easy than it looked, the whole construction was lifted and tilted, to be set loosely, so that it crumpled a little and sat like a wobbly crown, or a poorly fed python, on the top of the head.

I was aware that the actual purpose of the day was to instil in me, the first-born son, the obligations of familial duty. We were on our way to visit my grandmother across the river in Khartoum North. This was his usual Friday routine. For some reason that I can no longer recall, we stopped off along the way. I don't really remember much about what else we did that day. What does remain, however, engraved in my memory, is the library.

My most enduring impression was of a very long room. It was set apart from the main house, alongside but completely separate from it. I can recall standing in the doorway and seeing rows of bookshelves stretching away from me down both sides. It seemed a long way to the far end, almost as if it had grown, or I, by some Alice in Wonderland-type magic potion, had shrunk. There were no windows on either side as I recall. The only light entered through a window high up on the wall at the far end. It illuminated the man who sat behind the wide desk. His head was framed by a wild shock of white hair that stood on end. He was bowed over the desk and writing in longhand on a sheet of paper. This was Jamal Mohammed Ahmed, the man I was named after, one of my father's dearest friends. We didn't have much contact. His children were older than us and if we did visit the family it would be with my mother and then to the women's side of the house. I had the sense of this being a privilege, being admitted to an exclusive society of men. Houses were often traditionally divided into a men's area and a family area where the women lived, but this was slightly different.

I have no idea what he might have been writing. A letter to a friend, a shopping list? He might have been writing a poem, or copying out a quotation. The books along the walls were in English and Arabic. There were piles of dusty manuscripts, type-written sheets and curling photostats. Until that moment I don't think I had formed any real sense of him as a writer, or even of what a writer was. He was simply a familiar face, an old friend of my father's. I never, as far as I can recall, ever returned to visit that room again.

Nothing like this existed in our home. We had books, mostly my mother's, as she was the one who read regularly, almost religiously, every day, but nothing on this scale. Although my father liked to think of himself as a well-read man his interests tended to veer in the direction of trashy thrillers by people like Harold Robbins, well-thumbed paperbacks that we later skimmed for the racy bits. Ours was not a house with any great intellectual aspirations. Neither of my parents was university-educated. They were down-to-earth, humble people who believed that hard work and honesty would see you through life. My father maintained a firm admiration for education and although many of his friends could be defined as intellectuals, he was never under any illusion that such a path lay before him, or his children. On the contrary, he saw it as his duty to nudge us in the most sensible direction possible, to find a solid, reliable profession that would see us through life.

My discussions with my father about my future had left me in no doubt that we were not a family of philosophers, or even writers for that matter. These were things for extraordinary people, which we clearly were not. I had always assumed that education was about expanding the mind, not about finding a job. The idea of learning was to grow inwardly, to seek the profound in our experience as human beings with a finite amount of time on this earth. We should follow our instincts, our passions, no matter where they led. I had not really considered what a career teaching Heidegger and Wittgenstein might entail. My notion of philosophy was a far more meditative, personal one. It was unconsciously linked in my mind with the idea of being a writer, a point that my father had inadvertently put his finger on. This notion was still unformed in the abstract ether of my mind, but it was encapsulated in that instant of standing in the doorway to Jamal's room, seeing him sitting behind his desk surrounded by books.

There were other libraries, such as the one at school, a strange, austere chamber, narrow and high-walled, the books trapped inside glass cases like Catholic relics, each volume bound in plain brown paper with the title and author's name handwritten on the spine. Finding a book that you wanted to read in there was like digging through a haystack looking for an interesting piece of straw. Then there was the British Council library, where my father had worked for a time as a young man. It was set in a grand villa by the university, surrounded by a lush garden where students would lounge in the evenings to talk. There were louvred shutters on the windows and long aisles of shelves over which fans turned lazily (all of this is now sadly long gone, rationalised away, books and building alike). All were important and played a part in my life, but the one that I recalled in Denmark, twenty-odd years later, was that room of Jamal's. The garden was now a pine forest and the writer behind the desk was me.

In idle moments I would read about Oceania and the islanders of the Pacific. How, in the years following the Second World War, the inhabitants of Vanuatu and other Melanesian islands began building mock airfields, runways and control towers on which they would march and assemble with wooden rifles, just as they had seen American soldiers doing during the war. They sat in bamboo huts with earphones made of wood on their heads. They believed these rituals would bring back the airdrops; that tinned food, clothing, even jeeps would come tumbling from the sky. There were days, sitting in that library struggling with my novel, when I wondered if I had somehow created my own little cargo cult of wishful thinking.

Over the years I assembled my own meagre library. It expanded and contracted in time according to means, availability, interests and trends. Books were purchased, borrowed, inherited, received as gifts in an uneven, inconsistent way. Above all, books were lost or displaced, left behind or abandoned along the way. Books lent out and never returned, sacrificed in break-ups and divorce, stolen, flooded in unreliable storage spaces. I look at the shelves in the room where I sit now and can identify where one author's work once stood, like gaps in the fossil record. They still exert a powerful emotional tug. The desire to revisit a book I once used to own, to turn the pages and recall where and when I first read it.

The riddle of the library in Borges' famous story *The Library of Babel* is 'the formless and chaotic nature of all books'. Trying to find sense in books is a vain and supercilious habit,' he writes, akin to finding meaning in dreams or in the lines in the palm of the hand. But there is something about the physical presence of books that has always brought comfort. Perhaps it is the sense of the infinite worlds contained within the finite space of an object that can be carried in the hand. The lined pages of a book like stepping stones leading outward from the self into the vast realm of the unknown. Not only to the edge of the known universe, but beyond, into the depths of the earth, back through the history of mankind, across millions of years of evolution, space, light, time, geology, palaeontology and the extinction of myriad life forms.

Eventually, the opportunity arose to revisit Jamal's library. Various institutions had asked to house the collection, but the family had so far insisted that it remain where it has always been. One day I go there to visit his son, Atif. Naturally, like everything else in my memory, it had shrunk. It was much smaller than I remembered. Perhaps this is only to be expected. I had the sensation that this was a mere fraction of the room I had glimpsed as a child. In my memory I had preserved the image of a vault of infinite possibility, an endless tunnel through wisdom, history, philosophy, politics, science and literature. I could see that what I recalled was a myth of my own making. Over the years that room had come to symbolise a kind of idealised existence. As a child, I had instinctively known that this was the space I wanted to inhabit. This was the life I wanted. To be the man in the room, writing. This magical place filled with books, set in a place that was green and rich, bright with sunlight. And here it was, the lush garden, dominated by a huge palm tree, itself a symbol of rootedness, continuity, of the date fields that line the Nile in the far north, a token of that timeless sense of the eternal.

The long, seemingly endless library had been truncated by time. The desk itself had sunk into the ground. The bookshelves, too, appeared to have shrunk, the number of volumes a fraction of those I have carried in my memory over the years. Of course, all of this is easily explained by the fact that I was just a little boy at the time. Everything, including this room, would have seemed bigger. But it had grown in my imagination into a library of the infinite. For years I had lived with the illusion of this room as a shrine of sorts, which is what it had now become, for others, too. In place of the great man behind the desk there was a framed photograph of him hanging on one of the walls of books.

There is a sense of calm in that room and for a time I lose myself in exploring the shelves. In Arabic there are sets of Tabari's history of literature, along with religious studies, classical poetry, a whole wall of learning. Each leather-bound volume is embossed with the author's name down the spine in gold lettering. More unexpected is a set of vinyl recordings of Sir John Gielgud reading Shakespeare's monologues. Elsewhere Graham Greene, handsome hardbacks by Faulkner and Hemingway as well as books on Africa, the Middle East, Egypt. Surprises, such as Mishima's *Spring Snow*, in which I find annotations in Arabic marking out dreams, underlining passages and analyses of the author's intentions. In a Penguin edition of *One Hundred Years of Solitude*, a dedication signed by the writer Tayeb Salih, dated November 1973, is addressed to 'My brother Jamal – This book that I wish I had written'.

Rereading the story by Borges, I am struck by the length to which he goes to describe the physical aspects of the library. The detailed description of a labyrinth of bookshelves and staircases. The hexagonal units. Books on four sides, shelves that only come up to the height of the librarian. There are air shafts and staircases that vertically link the units. Little vestibules between the units contain two tiny compartments, one for sleeping, the other for satisfying one's physical necessities. It's all so complete that it feels as though he is describing the comforts of a cocoon.

There is something humbling about the thought that perhaps we cannot deal with the notion of an unlimited, open-ended universe, the cold infinity of the void. Instinctively, we long for the rigid parameters of a house with four walls and a roof to keep the sky at bay. The structure that the edges of a page or a shelf of books provides. The other way lies madness. The lunatic on the grass, howling at the moon.

So many of my memories of this city are associated with the river. Water provides a singular line of reason, heralding life where the encroaching dust brings only chaos and decay. I grew up with a healthy respect for the river, partly as a result of that disastrous university outing that had brought death so close. I had only ventured into the water on rare occasions, my head filled with warnings of dangerous undercurrents and electric fish that could paralyse you and cause you to drown. The river seemed best admired from a distance, through the swiftly passing spars of the old railway bridge, between the stout trunks of banyan trees along the road.

The majestic, cool flow was always a source of comfort and reassurance. Venturing out into it seemed foolhardy at best. Swimmers were respected, as were ferry pilots and fishermen. There were apocryphal tales of taxi drivers wading in to wash their cars only to be snatched away by scaly jaws, although the truth was that crocodiles were an increasingly rare phenomenon, held at bay by dams upstream and insurmountable cataracts further down.

To my surprise I discover that the *Melik* is still there, the gunboat that brought Kitchener to Khartoum in 1898. It is smaller than I remember, naturally, and no longer afloat. Long since dragged ashore, it has become absorbed into the riverbank so that now it appears almost as if it is emerging from the earth. The hull is half buried in the earth and the vessel is shrouded in neem trees and banyans. Lilac bougainvillea flowers bloom from every corner, bobbing in the sunlight like something out of a magical realist novel.

This used to be the sailing club. We weren't that kind of a family, which made it all the more absurd when my father decided to buy half a motor launch along with Mahgoub Osman, a hardline communist friend of his. Where the idea came from, I have no clue. His interest in the river was inspired, I believe, by some notion of connecting with the spirit of his grandfather, Bilal Abd al-Tawab, who, as we had heard countless times, had once sailed a big, two-masted *dahabiya* boat in the far north.

We were very small at the time and it became one of those excursions, like having our hair cut at the Sudan Hotel, where the barber was a friend of my father's and we would sit patiently in the lobby feeling rather grand as we waited our turn. Likewise, visiting the boatyard became a ritual. We would all get into the car and drive down to the riverside. Invariably, we would find that the launch had been hoisted out of the water and was standing on trestles, the engine uncovered and various wires and cables protruding. It seemed to be in a permanent state of deconstruction. What exactly was wrong with it was hard to understand, but my father would stand and listen as the old man who ran the yard muttered his excuses. Eventually the mechanic would wander over, his hands covered in oil. There was something of the mystic about him, as if the workings of a diesel engine were connected to some deep mystery at the heart of the universe. He would explain the problem in terms nobody seemed to comprehend but my father would nod his understanding. Then the man would disappear, his shoulders bowed under the weight of responsibility so that your impatience was turned into sympathy for his difficult plight.

After the obligatory inspection came our reward and we would walk up the gangway to the deck of the *Melik* and climb the steep and narrow stairs to the upper floor, which had been converted into a club room. It was lined with dark wood and there was a bar that served Sudan Railway lemonade and ginger beer in their characteristic rounded bottles – no longer in existence, alas. This was the real treat. This was what it was all about for us, to sit up there and survey the river from on high. I had no idea who Kitchener was, or what this gunboat was doing here. It was just one of those incongruities of life.

The one occasion when we did actually venture out onto the water turned out to be an unmitigated disaster. I can recall there was a lot of excitement, dampened only by my mother who, not being able to swim, had her own reasons for being wary of trusting her life to my father's, as yet unproven, nautical skills. We piled down to the yard to find the boat no longer high and dry but, for the first time any of us could remember, actually floating out there on the water. All of the waiting seemed to have paid off. The taciturn old man, his back bent like a bow by age, ferried us out in a small rowing boat. It may have been my imagination, but he seemed to look upon us with contempt. Perhaps, having spent his life on the river, he felt a certain disdain for people like us: day trippers, coming around making demands on his time, even if we were paying him. The slow, regular strokes of the oars instilled a sense of confidence, certainly more so than my father's skittish joviality and, on the other side, my mother's tight-lipped anxiety.

We reached the mooring and managed to make the transfer of children and cooler box from one vessel to the other safely, without losing anything or anyone. There was something theatrical, even faintly absurd about the whole exercise. We never went out together as a family, or very, very rarely. My father was always busy with one thing or another, and that meant that most of our extra-curricular activities – going to the cinema, to the swimming pool, visiting friends, etc., were done almost exclusively with my mother alone. This added a certain novelty to the excursion, lending it greater significance. After some discussion my parents agreed that my mother should stand, or, rather, sit, on the bow so as to peer into the water and spot sandbanks before we hit them. Nobody had warned us about sandbanks. I had imagined the usual things, drowning, crocodiles, snakes, etc., but nothing as benign as sandbanks. We were in safe hands, though. She was equipped with a pair of Polaroid sunglasses – highly modern at the time – which in our eyes gave her the equivalent of Superman's X-ray vision, allowing her to see though the water and spot any danger before we hit it.

Confident that we were now prepared for any eventuality, we set off upstream. Over the stern I watched the sanctuary of the sailing club and the majestic *Melik* slipping further and further away. From time to time my mother would yell commands frantically that my father invariably misinterpreted, spinning the wheel back and forth while instructing her to please calm down. It all seemed to take forever, but we really can't have gone that far before we suddenly and without explanation came to a complete halt. The engine puttered into silence. We were under the old steel archway of the railway bridge built by the British. My father duly fiddled with the controls, pushing the levers back and forth. There was some frothing around the stern but nothing really happened. We weren't moving. The engine refused to start again. The bow drifted back and forth with my mother poised on top calling back for an explanation while my father frowned at the dashboard.

I found the underneath of the bridge interesting. We had driven over the top so many times, it seemed to me, yet never given a thought as to what lay below. It was a narrow bridge, comforting in its own way, because of the light blue colour of the steel girders perhaps, and the rounded shape of the arches and the thickness of the iron and the bolts. It was a solid piece of work, designed and built by a British engineer named Cooper. A man who had long since passed away yet here his bridge stood. Broad pillars stretched away to the riverbank on either side of us. It was dark and cool under there. The sunlight was just out of our reach. Then an overwhelming stench of dead fish came over us. A harsh smell that made us all nauseous. It added the finishing touch to our idyllic outing.

Eventually somebody noticed that we were not moving and the old man came out to rescue us, still rowing in that slow, deliberate fashion of his, as if he had all the time in the world. With a look of disdain, he reached down into the water and freed the propeller, which was tangled up in the fishing nets that were strung between the pillars. We puttered slowly back to shore in silence, our great day on the river over. We never tried to go out in the boat again. Sooner or later it was sold and we never talked about it again. How long we were out there I am not sure, but there was something about the episode that has stayed with me all these years. Perhaps it is the enduring sense of us together as a family, held by the forces of nature, floating on the flowing river yet going nowhere. A brief moment of eternity encapsulated in one tiny vessel.

Acknowledgements

A long list of people to whom I owe a debt of thanks has, of course, accumulated over the ten years or so I have been working on this book. I thank them all for their contribution. I have tried to include all of them here, but I am aware there is a strong possibility some have eluded me, and for this I offer my sincere apologies. There are also those whom I feel it would be unsafe to mention, whose names I have changed, or whose influence is unquantifiable, even though it is ever-present for me. To all of these I also my sincere thanks.

In more tangible terms the Netherlands Institute of Advanced Studies provided me with the time and the resources to conduct my final research and to undertake a big chunk of the writing, and in the process change the course of my life. My thanks to them. Many people have helped me during the course of writing this book, either through reading sections or in conversation. A lot of this help is again hard to define. Sometimes a conversation sits with you for months before it makes sense. I can only hope that I have already made my gratitude plain to them.

This book really could not have happened without the assistance of many people, in Khartoum and elsewhere. Some of them may recognise themselves within these pages, others may not. There was not room for everything. People have provided me with help in the form of support and information, introductions, or even a simple phrase that resonated and made its way into the text. Other pearls of wisdom were lost in the shuffle. I would hate to leave anyone out and so this book is dedicated to everyone I have spoken to over the years, on or off the subject in hand. All have contributed to the journey this book became. It goes without saying that ultimately the only person who bears full responsibility for what lies here is the author.

Parts of the text have appeared in various publications and on websites; my thanks to Ndone Edjabe and all at Chimurenga; Michael Archer and Guernicamag.com; Warscapes magazine; Fleur van Koppen and all at Letterenfonds in Amsterdam. A version of the section on Leni Riefenstahl first appeared in *Transition* magazine and was later included in *Best American Essays 2008* (ed. Adam Gopnik).

Furthermore, my thanks go to:

Suad Abdelrahman; Atif Jamal Mohammed Ahmed; Ellah Alfrey; Hayder Ibrahim Ali; Manzoul Assal; Faisal El Baghir; Fadil Banyouti; The Blue Nile Brewery Company; Chris Calhoun; Samia and Osama Daoūd; Durham University Sudan Archive; Taghred ElSanhouri; Mamoun Eltlib; Stella Gaytano; David Godwin; Anis Hajjar; Samia Hassan; Lieve Joris; Amira Khair; Jannah Loontjens; Mansour Khalid; Netherlands Institute of Advanced Studies; Tigani El-Karib; Mohammed Ibrahim Khalil and Sawsan; Simona Opitz and staff at IOM; OXFAM; Palestine Festival of Literature; Rosa Mercader i Verdés; Faisal Mohammed Saleh; The family of Ustaz M.M. Taha; Osman Shinger; SOAS library; Mahjoub Mohammed Saleh and everyone at Al Ayyam newspaper, especially Nadir Mahjoub; Amin Mekki Medani; Scott Moyers; Ronnie Shaoul, Fathi Osman and everyone at DAL corporation; Ahdaf Soueif; Sudan National Archives; Nada Hussein Wanni; Alex de Waal.

A debt is also owed to Alexandra Pringle and everyone at Bloomsbury who has supported my work over the years. More immediately in the editing of this book, Michael Fishwick, Sarah Ruddick and all those who have come and gone. Thanks also go to Euan Thorneycroft and everyone at A.M. Heath & Co.

Credits

PICTURE CREDITS

Photographs are from the author's personal collection unless credited otherwise.

p. 42 General Charles Gordon and Muhammad Ahmad al-Mahdi. Wikimedia Commons.

p. 71 Pupils at Gordon College, photographed by George Naaman Morhig. Courtesy of the Sudan Archive at Durham, University of Durham. R.G. Dingwall collection (SAD.16/6/6).

p. 102 John Garang, photographed by Simon Maina in 2001. Courtesy Simom Maina/Stringer/Getty Images.

p. 107 Wikimedia Commons.

p. 150 Zubayr Pasha, photographed by Somers Elderton. Courtesy of the Sudan Archive at Durham, University of Durham. Rowland Percy Somerset/Somers Elderton collection (SAD.1/22/71).

p. 157 AF archive/Alamy Stock Photo.

p. 207 Hassan al-Turabi, photographed by Karim Jaafar in 2003. Courtesy Karim Jaafar/Stringer/Getty Images.

p. 254 Gaafar El Nimeiri, photographed by Patrick Jarnoux/Paris Match via Getty Images.

TEXT CREDITS

p. 95 Both extracts from Mansour Khalid, *The Government They Deserve* (Kegan Paul International, 1990).

Index

A Note on the Author

Jamal Mahjoub was born in London and grew up in Khartoum, Sudan. Since then he has settled in a number of other cities, including London, Cairo, Aarhus, Barcelona and, more recently, Amsterdam.

He is the author of seven novels, and his work – fiction and non-fiction – has been critically acclaimed and widely translated. He has published crime novels under the pen name Parker Bilal.

A Note on the Type

The text of this book is set in Linotype Stempel Garamond, a version of Garamond adapted and first used by the Stempel foundry in 1924. It is one of several versions of Garamond based on the designs of Claude Garamond. It is thought that Garamond based his font on Bembo, cut in 1495 by Francesco Griffo in collaboration with the Italian printer Aldus Manutius. Garamond types were first used in books printed in Paris around 1532. Many of the present-day versions of this type are based on the *Typi Academiae* of Jean Jannon cut in Sedan in 1615.

Claude Garamond was born in Paris in 1480. He learned how to cut type from his father and by the age of fifteen he was able to fashion steel punches the size of a pica with great precision. At the age of sixty he was commissioned by King Francis I to design a Greek alphabet, and for this he was given the honourable title of royal type founder. He died in 1561.